# UK GAAP for Business and Practice

Paul Gee

*Technical Director, Solomon Hare,*
*Member of the Smith & Williamson Group*

AMSTERDAM • BOSTON • HEIDELBERG • LONDON
NEW YORK • OXFORD • PARIS • SAN DIEGO
SAN FRANCISCO • SINGAPORE • SYDNEY • TOKYO

CIMA Publishing is an imprint of Elsevier

ELSEVIER

CIMA
PUBLISHING

CIMA Publishing is an imprint of Elsevier
Linacre House, Jordan Hill, Oxford OX2 8DP, UK
30 Corporate Drive, Suite 400, Burlington, MA 01803, USA

First edition 2006
Reprinted 2007

**British Library Cataloguing in Publication Data**
A catalogue record for this book is available from the British Library

**Library of Congress Cataloging-in-Publication Data**
A catalog record for this book is available from the Library of Congress

ISBN: 978-0-7506-6873-6

For information on all CIMA publications
visit our website at www.cimapublishing.com

Printed and bound in *Great Britain*

07 08 09 10   10 9 8 7 6 5 4 3 2

Working together to grow
libraries in developing countries

www.elsevier.com | www.bookaid.org | www.sabre.org

ELSEVIER    BOOK AID
International    Sabre Foundation

To Helen, Mark and Simon

# Acknowledgements

Extracts from exposure drafts, accounting standards and statements of recommended practice are reproduced by kind permission of the Accounting Standards Board.

Extracts from the annual reports and accounts of the following companies are reproduced:

AIM Group plc
Boots Group plc
Bovis Homes Group plc
Cable and Wireless plc
Charteris plc
CJ plc
Computacenter plc
Dixon Motors plc
Durlacher Corporation plc
ebookers plc
Focus Solutions Group plc
Fundamental-e-Investments plc
Hays plc
Honeycombe Leisure plc
IDS Group plc

Ideal Shopping Direct plc
KBC Advanced Technologies plc
Lastminute.com plc
Lincat Group plc
Reliance Security Group plc
Ryanair Holdings plc
Somerfield plc
The Sage Group plc
Three Valleys Water plc
Uniq plc
Universal Salvage plc
W S Atkins plc
Winchester Entertainment plc
Wm Morrison Supermarkets plc
Wyevale Garden Centres plc

# Contents

# Executive Summary 2005

**This chapter covers:**
* UK GAAP or IFRS?
* Regulatory developments
* Recently-issued Financial Reporting Standards, UITF Abstracts and Exposure Drafts
* The Financial Reporting Standard for Smaller Entities (effective January 2005)
* Company law changes affecting disclosure
* Financial Reporting Review Panel activity

## 1.1   UK GAAP or IFRS?

Prior to 2005, all UK companies were required by the Companies Act 1985 (CA 85) to adopt UK GAAP (Generally Accepted Accounting Practice).

Following changes in EU Regulations, *fully listed groups* are required to adopt International Financial Reporting Standards (IFRS) in their *consolidated* accounts for accounts periods commencing on or after 1 January 2005. The European Regulation is mandatory for the *consolidated* accounts only. The Companies Act 1985 offers a number of options for the individual accounts of the members of a group (see 7.3).

Companies listed on the Alternative Investment Market (AIM) are outside the scope of the EU's so-called IAS Regulation, but are required by the London Stock Exchange to adopt IFRS for accounts periods commencing on or after 1 January 2007 (AIM companies may adopt earlier if they so choose).

All other categories of UK companies are permitted (*but not required*) to adopt IFRS for accounts periods commencing on or after 1 January 2005, but CA 85 prohibits earlier adoption.

The terms "International Financial Reporting Standards" (IFRS) and "International Accounting Standards" (IAS) are effectively interchangeable. The Companies Act 1985 and the relevant tax legislation refer to "IAS". However, the more widely used (and more modern) term IFRS is used in this book.

This book deals mainly with the application of UK GAAP, although Chapter 7 refer to IFRS and convergence issues, and IFRS is referred to at the end of each chapter. In addition, Chapter 23 gives a brief overview of listed company issues.

## 1.2    Recent Developments

The Accounting Standards Board (ASB) has issued a number of Financial Reporting Standards (FRSs) and Financial Reporting Exposure Drafts (FREDs) as part of its programme for converging UK GAAP with IFRS. The FRSs are:

- FRS 21, Events after the balance sheet date;
- FRS 22, Earnings per share;
- FRS 23, The effects of foreign exchange rates;
- FRS 24, Financial reporting in hyperinflationary economies;
- FRS 25, Financial instruments: Disclosure and presentation;
- FRS 26, Financial instruments: Measurement;
- FRS 27, Life Assurance.
- FRS 28, Corresponding amounts;
- FRS 29, Financial instruments: Disclosures.

No further reference is made to FRS 27 in view of its specialized application. FREDs are referred to in 1.4 below.
Chapter 29 deals with ASB's future plans for converging UK GAAP with IFRS. Other key pronouncements from ASB include:

- An updated version of the Financial Reporting Standard for Smaller Entities (FRSSE) – referred to as the "effective January 2005" version – see below and also Chapter 22;
- Reporting Standard 1 (RS 1) dealing with the Operating and Financial Review, superseded in January 2006 by best practice statement with non-mandatory status but with similar content and wording.

The Urgent Issues Task Force (UITF) has issued a number of Abstracts, in draft or final form. Of these, the most important is Abstract 40 dealing with Revenue recognition and service contracts. In essence, this requires that revenue on service contracts should be accrued as contract activity takes place (the "stage of completion" method).
Company law changes include:

- Companies Act 1985 (International Accounting Standards and Other Accounting Amendments) Regulations 2004 [Statutory Instrument 2947];
- Companies (Audit, Investigations and Community Enterprise) Act 2004;
- Companies Act 1985 (Operating and Financial Review and Directors' Report etc.) Regulations 2005 [as amended 2006];
- Companies Act 1985 (Investment Companies and Accounting and Audit Amendments) Regulations 2005 [Statutory Instrument 2280].

These are available on the Office of Public Sector Information website (*www.opsi.gov.uk*).

# 1.3   Recent Financial Reporting Standards

## (a) Events after the Balance Sheet Date (FRS 21)

This standard is identical to IAS 10 and is one of many bringing UK GAAP closer to IFRS. The standard mirrors changes to the Companies Act 1985 and supersedes SSAP 17 for accounts periods beginning on or after 1 January 2005 (for legal reasons, earlier adoption is not permitted).

With one important exception, the standard is broadly similar in effect to SSAP 17. The exception is the treatment of proposed *equity* dividends. Dividends declared after the balance sheet date should not be reported as liabilities. Declared dividends will be reported in a memorandum note in the accounts of the current year, and entered in the accounting records in the following year when the payment is actually made (see Chapter 20).

## (b) Earnings per Share (FRS 22)

FRS 22, based on International Accounting Standard 33 (IAS 33), is to be applied to entities whose ordinary shares or potential ordinary shares (for example, convertible loan stock) are publicly traded, and by entities that are in the process of issuing ordinary shares or potential ordinary shares in public markets.

This standard will not be relevant for fully listed companies which head up a group as the consolidated accounts should follow IFRS. However some companies whose shares are publicly traded, for example AIM companies, may not be required to adopt IFRS immediately in which case FRS 22 will be relevant.

FRS 22 supersedes FRS 14, Earnings per share and is mandatory for accounts periods beginning on or after 1 January 2005.

## (c) The Effects of Foreign Exchange Rates (FRS 23)

This standard is based on IAS 21 and over a period of time will supersede SSAP 20. FRS 23 cannot be adopted earlier than FRS 26, but once FRS 26 has been adopted, then FRS 23 must be adopted at the same time.

FRS 23 is broadly similar in effect to SSAP 20 although there are some important differences of detail (see Chapter 28).

## (d) Financial Reporting in Hyperinflationary Economies (FRS 24)

In a hyperinflationary economy, reporting of operating results and financial position in the local currency, without any restatement, does not provide useful information in view of the rate at which money is losing purchasing power.

The aim of FRS 24 is to provide a mechanism for restating historical amounts that will enhance comparability of results and financial position.

## (e) Financial Instruments: Disclosure and Presentation (FRS 25)

The objective of FRS 25 is to

> "enhance financial statement users' understanding of the significance of financial instruments to an entity's financial position, performance and cash flows".

The *presentation* requirements of the standard deal with a number of issues including:

- Classification of a company's financial instruments into liabilities and equity – for example, whether preference shares should be presented in the balance sheet as debt or equity;
- Classification of related interest, dividends, losses and gains – whether they should be presented in the profit and loss account as finance items, or whether they should be taken direct to equity and presented as a movement on profit and loss reserves;
- The circumstances in which financial assets and financial liabilities should be offset.

The extensive *disclosure* requirements of FRS 25 deal with risk management policies and hedging activities.

The *presentation* aspects of the standard are mandatory for all types of companies for accounts periods beginning on or after 1 January 2005. The *disclosure* parts of the standard come into effect as soon as an entity adopts or is required to adopt FRS 26.

## (f) Financial Instruments: Measurement (FRS 26)

The objective of FRS 26 is to establish principles for recognizing and measuring financial assets and liabilities. The standard sets out detailed rules as to the basis on which particular categories of assets and liabilities should be measured. The standard is based on the measurement parts of IAS 39—this standard is sometimes referred to as a mixed measurement model (effectively a mix of historical cost measurement rules and fair value rules).

FRS 26 applies to all types of financial instruments including cash, accounts receivable, accounts payable, loans, debt, equity securities held as assets, and derivatives. There are a number of exemptions from aspects of the standard, particularly in specialized areas.

The standard is mandatory for listed entities (for example, where the *individual* accounts of the listed parent are prepared in accordance with UK GAAP as opposed to IFRS or where the listed parent does not prepare consolidated accounts) as well as for any other entity that prepares its accounts in accordance with the fair value rules in the Companies Act 1985. Other entities may adopt it voluntarily in which case they must also adopt FRS 23, FRS 24 and the disclosure parts of FRS 25. The transitional provisions are complex—they are referred to in Chapter 17.

## 1.4    Recent Financial Reporting Exposure Drafts

ASB has issued the following exposure drafts:
- FRED 36, Business combinations;
- FRED 37, Intangibles;
- FRED 38, Impairment of assets;
- FRED 39, Amendments to FRS 12 and FRS 17.

These are referred to, where applicable, within the relevant chapter.

## 1.5    Earlier Financial Reporting Standards

### (a) FRS 17, Retirement Benefits

FRS 17 is mandatory in full for accounts periods beginning on or after 1 January 2005. Companies with defined benefit schemes who have not already adopted FRS 17 will need to change their accounting policy from SSAP 24 to FRS 17, making a prior period adjustment and restating comparative figures. Companies should already have the information necessary to put the adjustments through, in view of the memorandum disclosures provided over the long transitional period before FRS 17 became fully mandatory.

### (b) FRS 20, Share-Based Payment

FRS 20 is mandatory for fully listed entities (i.e. those that have not adopted IFRS) for accounts periods beginning on or after 1 January 2005. The relevant date for AIM companies who have not voluntarily adopted IFRS prior to 2007, and unlisted entities, is 2006.

The standard is complex and sets out a new approach for assessing the appropriate charge to the profit and loss account. The standard supersedes Abstract 17 on Employee share schemes. The transitional provisions are complex and are referred to in Chapter 10.

## 1.6    The Financial Reporting Standard for Smaller Entities (FRSSE)

Following consultation during 2004, ASB published an exposure draft in November 2004, incorporating its earlier "One-stop shop" proposals, followed by the final version of the FRSSE in April 2005. This version is referred to as the Financial Reporting Standard for Smaller Entities (effective January 2005).

The latest version of the FRSSE extends the existing content in the June 2002 version to incorporate the accounting requirements of companies legislation applicable to smaller companies (as amended by Statutory Instrument 2947).

The content has also been updated to reflect various changes in accounting standards and Abstracts since the publication of the June 2002 version, including UITF Abstract 40 on Revenue recognition and service contracts.

The revised FRSSE is effective for *accounting periods beginning on or after 1 January 2005*.

For legal reasons, earlier adoption is not permitted (see Chapter 22).

## 1.7  Urgent Issues Task Force Developments

UITF has issued two further Abstracts:

- Abstract 39 – Members' Shares in Co-operative Entities and Similar Instruments;
- Abstract 40 – Revenue recognition and service contracts.

The latter was issued in response to requests for clarification of FRS 5, Application Note G, as regards contracts for the provision of services. Abstract 40 is mandatory for accounts periods ending on or after 22 June 2005. The main thrust of the Abstract is that revenue should be recognized as contract activity progresses. The Abstract is likely to result in accounting policy changes for a significant number of entities, including sole traders, partnerships as well as companies (see Chapter 8).

Apart from Abstract 40, much of the UITF's recent activity derives from the work of the IASB's International Financial Reporting Interpretations Committee (IFRIC)—see 7.8.

Details of current activity can be found on the UITF part of the Financial Reporting Council website.

## 1.8  Company Law Changes

*(a) Companies Act 1985 (International Accounting Standards and Other Accounting Amendments) Regulations 2004 [Statutory Instrument 2947]*

The main changes here are:

- CA 85 will explicitly require transactions to be reported in accordance with their substance as opposed to their legal form, for example preference shares in future will have to be classed as either equity or liability (see Chapter 18). The concept of reporting substance is well established in UK GAAP (see FRS 5, Reporting the substance of transactions, Chapter 6);
- Companies will no longer be allowed to accrue proposed equity dividends (this links in with FRS 21, Events after the balance sheet date);
- Companies will be allowed, but not required, to use fair value accounting to adopt IFRS instead of UK GAAP (apart from fully listed groups for whom the change will be mandatory);
- Companies will be allowed to use fair value accounting – but the extent to which this may be used by non-IFRS companies will effectively be determined by the Accounting Standards Board (i.e. as a result of issuing FRSs which

converge UK GAAP with the relevant IASs/IFRSs. In the short-term, the fair value rules are unlikely to be widely used under UK GAAP.

## (b) Companies (Audit, Investigations and Community Enterprise) Act 2004

This legislation deals with a diverse range of issues including audit issues; accounts and reports; directors' liabilities; investigations; Community Interest Companies.

A new disclosure requirement is inserted in the Directors' report for 31 March 2006 year-end onwards: a statement confirming that as far as each director is aware, there is no relevant audit information of which the company's auditors are unaware and that directors individually have taken all steps to make themselves aware of all information needed by the auditors in connection with their report (see 2.7).

## (c) Companies Act 1985 (Operating and Financial Review and Directors' Report etc.) Regulations 2005

This legislation brings in a number of changes:

Quoted companies were originally required to prepare an Operating and Financial Review (OFR), for financial years commencing on or after 1 April 2005. Hitherto an OFR has been recommended best practice but has not been mandatory. The Regulations specify statutory disclosure requirements for the OFR and require it to comply with ASB's Reporting Standard 1.

The Government subsequently decided that it would no longer require quoted companies to produce an Operating and Financial Review, and that regulations to repeal this requirement would come into effect on 12 January 2006.

All companies, except for small companies, must include a Business Review within the Directors' Report. The Business Review should contain an analysis relating to key performance indicators (KPIs). Concessions are available for medium-sized companies (see 2.8).

## (d) Companies Act 1985 (Investment Companies and Accounting and Audit Amendments) Regulations 2005 [Statutory Instrument 2280]

The Statutory Instrument brings in three changes:

- Changes regarding comparative figures – effectively deleting existing CA 85 requirements for replacement with equivalent rules in a new Financial Reporting Standard (FRS 28);
- Small company exemption for disclosure of particulars of staff – a technical adjustment which effectively restores the previous statutory requirements;
- Audit exemption for certain small financial services companies who had not hitherto been exempt (see Chapter 2).

## 1.9    Listed Company Reporting

New requirements relevant to listed companies are referred to briefly, above.

This book does not deal in detail with listed company reporting issues. However, Chapter 23 provides a brief overview of the principal requirements, including the recent developments mentioned above.

## 1.10    Financial Reporting Review Panel (FRRP)

The Panel has published a number of important Press Notices, including:

- Announcement of Risk-based Proactive Programme (FRRP PN 81, December 2004);
- Publication of First Report on Pro-activity (PN 88, August 2005).

Chapter 2 includes a summary of Recent Panel activity.

## 1.11    Statements of Recommended Practice (SORPs)

In March 2005, the Charity Commission issued "Accounting and Reporting by Charities: Statement of Recommended Practice which must be applied to accounting years commencing on or after 1 April 2005, although charities *may* choose to adopt earlier if they wish". (See 2.6 for details of SORP activity.) The Consultative Committee of Accountancy Bodies (CCAB) published an exposure draft of a SORP on Limited Liability Partnerships on 30 September 2005 (see Tech 56/05 on www.icaew.org.uk).

## 1.12    International Financial Reporting Standards

Chapter 7 deals with progress to date on convergence of UK GAAP with IFRS, whilst Chapter 29 deals with the ASB's convergence workplan. IFRS comparisons and issues are referred to at the end of each chapter.

**Frequently Asked Questions**

1 When will unlisted companies have to comply with IFRS?
   No date has been set by DTI—consultation will precede introduction of new legislation. IFRS is unlikely to be mandatory prior to 2009.

2 Can any company with a 30 September 2005 year-end adopt IFRS?
   No, because the accounting period does not commence on or after 1 January 2005.

3 Do the Schedule 4/8 format rules still apply to a company which adopts IFRS on a voluntary basis?
   No—DTI guidance states that in broad terms, the provisions in the 1985 Act relating to the form and content of accounts (in particular, the accounts formats in Schedules 4 & 8) will no longer apply to companies using IFRS. Effectively, this means that form and content requirements will be determined by IAS 1 and other related standards.

**Useful Website Addresses**

**www.frc.org.uk**
Information regarding: Financial Reporting Council; Accounting Standards Board; Urgent Issues Task Force; Financial Reporting Review Panel; SORPs; useful Press Notices.

**www.dti.gov.uk**
Information regarding: Company Law "Hot Topics"; consultative documents; white papers; draft Bills; guides to recent legislation; useful contact details.

**www.opsi.gov.uk**
Statutory Instruments; new Acts etc.

**www.iasb.org**
A wealth of information including summaries of key points in new standards; progress on current projects.

# The UK Regulatory Framework

**This chapter covers:**
* Financial statements and annual reports
* Companies Act 1985
* FRS 28, Corresponding amounts
* The UK standard-setting structure
* UK Accounting standards
* Urgent Issues Task Force Abstracts
* Statements of Recommended Practice (SORPs)
* Statement of principles
* Key legislative changes
* Legal Opinion on Role of Accounting Standards and True and Fair
* True and fair override
* Directors' reports
* Revision of defective accounts
* Financial Reporting Review Panel
* International Financial Reporting Standards

## 2.1 Companies Act 1985 Requirements

### (a) Requirement to Produce Accounts

The Companies Act 1985 uses the term "accounts", whilst standard-setters use the term "financial statements" (see 2.2 below).

For single companies, Section 226 (as amended by Statutory Instrument 2947, see below) requires the directors to prepare accounts, referred to as the company's "individual accounts". Under the revised requirements of the Companies Act 1985 which come into effect for accounts periods commencing on or after 1 January 2005, (see below), the individual accounts may be prepared either:

(a) In accordance with Section 226A: these are referred to in the Act as "Companies Act individual accounts" and effectively constitute UK GAAP; or

(b) In accordance with International Accounting Standards: these are referred to in the Act as "IAS individual accounts" and must be based on IFRS requirements (see Chapter 7).

Section 227 (as amended) has equivalent requirements for group accounts.

## (b) Content Requirements

Section 226A specifies that "Companies Act individual accounts" must comprise a balance sheet and a profit and loss account.

The accounts of an individual company prepared and presented on the basis of UK GAAP should comply with the provisions of Schedule 4 of the Companies Act 1985 (as amended by SI 2947) as regard form and content (small companies may use Schedule 8, as amended by SI 2947—see Chapter 22).

Schedule 4 also contains requirements on accounting rules.

Group accounts should comply with Schedule 4A.

Under UK GAAP, the term "financial statements" refers to the four primary statements:

- Profit and loss account (required by CA 85 and FRS 3, Reporting financial performance);
- Statement of total recognized gains and losses (FRS 3);
- Balance sheet (CA 85) (see Chapter 4);
- Cash flow statement (required by FRS 1) (see Chapter 5).

## (c) Approval, Signing and Dating

CA 85 requires the balance sheet to be approved by the board of directors and signed on behalf of the board by at least one director (in practice, except for very small companies, it is common for two directors to sign). CA 85 also requires the directors' report to be approved by the directors and signed on behalf of the board either by a director or by the company secretary.

For accounting periods which commenced *before* 1 January 2005, SSAP 17, Post balance sheet events, requires the financial statements to disclose the date on which they are approved by the directors.

For accounting periods commencing on or after 1 January 2005, FRS 21, Events after the balance sheet date, requires an entity to disclose the date when the financial statements are authorized for issue and who gave that authorization.

## (d) Comparatives

CA 85, Schedule 4, paragraph 58(2) has hitherto required comparative figures to be provided for all items in the accounts (including the notes) except for:

- Movements on fixed assets;
- Details of substantial investments;
- Movements on provisions;

- Movements on reserves;
- Disclosure of transactions involving directors (except to the extent that such transactions fall within the scope of FRS 8, in which case comparatives would automatically be required);
- Details of accounting treatment of acquisitions.

Where the corresponding amount is not comparable, CA 85 has required that it be adjusted and particulars of the adjustment and the reasons for it be given.

A recent Statutory Instrument, 2280, has removed the requirement to present the above comparatives, and also the requirement to adjust. SI 2280 is effective for accounts periods commencing on or after 1 January 2005. FRS 28, Corresponding amounts, effectively reinstates the equivalent requirements – the broad effect of the standard is to restore the status quo. The key requirements of the FRS are:

- Corresponding amounts shall be shown for every item in the primary financial statements;

> This includes the profit and loss account, the statement of total recognized gains and losses, the balance sheet and the cash flow statement.
>
> The movement in shareholders funds is also included, whether this is presented as a primary financial statement or as part of the notes to the financial statements.

- Where there is no amount to be shown for the current period but there was a corresponding amount in the previous period, that corresponding amount shall be shown;
- Where corresponding amounts are not directly comparable with the amount to be shown in respect of the current financial year, they should be adjusted;

> Disclose in a note particulars of the adjustment and the reasons for it

- Corresponding amounts should be shown for items all items in the notes to the financial statements, except for the following:

> Details of additions, disposals, revaluations, transfers and cumulative depreciation of fixed assets;
>
> Transfers to or from reserves and provisions and the source and application of any transfers;
>
> Accounting treatment of acquisitions;
>
> Details of shareholdings in subsidiary undertakings held by a company or, where group accounts are prepared, held by the parent company and by the group;
>
> Significant holdings in undertakings other than subsidiary undertakings where group accounts are not prepared, details of the identity of each class of share in the undertaking held by the company, and the proportion of the nominal value of the shares of that class represented by those shares;

> The proportion of the capital of the joint venture held by undertakings included in the consolidation;
>
> Details of shareholdings of associated undertakings held by the parent company and group;
>
> Details of other significant shareholdings of the parent company or the group.

The only significant difference compared with the previous legal requirements is that FRS 28 does not provide an exemption for comparatives relating to loans and other dealings in favour of directors and others. This would include disclosures relating to director's overdrawn current accounts. However, many director's disclosures would in any event fall also within the scope of FRS8 on Related party disclosures.

## (e) True and Fair View Requirement

As regards "Companies Act individual accounts" (= UK GAAP), the balance sheet should give a true and fair view of the state of affairs of the company as at the end of the financial year, and the profit and loss account must give a true and fair view of the profit or loss of the company for the financial year. The ASB's Legal Opinion on the Role of Accounting Standards and True and Fair, is referred to in 2.10 below.

AS regards "IAS Individual Accounts", CA 85 does not expressly contain a true and fair requirement. Section 226B requires the note to the accounts to state that the accounts have been prepared in accordance with International Accounting Standards. The Auditing Practices Board has suggested a standard wording to apply to audit reports (see www.frc.org.uk). However, the Financial Reporting Review Panel has published a legal opinion on the effect of the IAS Regulation on the requirement for accounts to give a true and fair view (Press Notice 85, June 2005).

## (f) Relationship with Accounting Standards

As regards UK GAAP, Schedule 4, paragraph 36A requires the accounts to state whether they have been prepared in accordance with applicable accounting standards and to give particulars of, and reasons for, any material departures.

Financial Reporting Review Panel Press Notice 85 comments that "Companies that continue to prepare accounts in accordance with UK national standards remain subject to the overriding requirement of the Act that accounts give a true and fair view, which in all but highly exceptional cases, requires compliance with UK accounting standards".

## (g) True and Fair Override

CA 85 provides that where compliance with the accounting and disclosure requirements of the Act would not be sufficient to give a true and fair view, the necessary additional information should be given either in the accounts or in the notes to the accounts.

If, in special circumstances, compliance with any of the Act's accounting provisions conflicts with the requirement to give a true and fair view, the directors are required to depart from that provision to the extent necessary to give a true and fair view (Sections 226(5) and 227(6)).

This requirement should be used with great caution and not used as a mechanism to bypass "inconvenient" requirements in either the Act or in particular accounting standards. The following examples relate to situations expressly permitted in particular accounting standards:

- Investment properties – SSAP 19 requires that such properties should not be depreciated, contrary to the general rules in CA 85 (Part 4 of the Standard expressly comments on the acceptability of the true and fair override in this situation);
- Goodwill – FRS 10 permits non-amortization of goodwill subject to specific requirements, contrary to the requirements of the Act (this is referred to in paragraphs 18, 59 and 60 of FRS 10).

The Act requires the following disclosures in cases where the true and fair override is invoked:

- Particulars of the departure;
- Reasons for the departure;
- The effect of the departure.

(See also the extended and more detailed disclosure requirements in FRS 18 (see 3.7(b).)

## (h) The Companies Act 1985 (International Accounting Standards and Other Accounting Amendments) Regulations 2004 [SI 2947]

### 1 Overview
The Regulations deal with implementation of EU Directives and the implementation of International Accounting Standards and come into effect for financial years beginning on or after 1 January 2005. They may not be adopted in advance of this date.

The Regulations are published on www.opsi.gov.uk and DTI guidance (Guidance for British companies on changes to the reporting and accounting provisions of the Companies Act 1985) on the DTI website (www.dti.gov.uk/cld).

### 2 Change in treatment of proposed equity dividends
Revised paragraph 2 to Schedule 4 removes the requirement to show proposed equity dividends in the profit and loss account. This, taken together with FRS 21, Events after the balance sheet date, means that for accounts periods beginning on or after 1 January 2005, UK companies will *not* be permitted to

accrue proposed equity dividends as a current liability (but this change in accounting policy may not be adopted before that date).

### 3  Reporting the substance of transactions

New paragraph 5A to Schedule 4 [i.e. as part of UK GAAP] states:

> "The directors of a company must, in determining how amounts are presented within items in the profit and loss account and balance sheet, have regard to the substance of the reported transaction or arrangement, in accordance with generally accepted accounting principles or practice".

An example of a practical implication is the classification of preference shares—see Chapter 17.

### 4  International financial reporting standards

For companies and groups adopting IFRS in 2005, new provisions in the Companies Act 1985 take effect in respect of companies' financial years which begin on or after 1 January 2005 (but not sooner).

The legislation gives individual companies and groups, a choice between preparing accounts under UK GAAP and preparing under IFRS.

Parent companies whose shares are fully listed *and who prepare consolidated accounts must* adopt IFRS in their *consolidated* accounts for 2005, and AIM-listed companies for 2007 (see 7.3 for the options available to members of a group).

*IFRS is likely to continue to be optional for unlisted companies for the foreseeable future.*

### 5  The fair value option

CA 85 allows specified categories of financial instruments to be included in the balance sheet at fair value provided that their fair value can be determined reliably. These include derivatives (whether assets or liabilities), held for trading investments and available for sale investments.

However, those UK companies considering adopting the fair value option should proceed carefully and note the following comment in paragraph 6.7 of the DTI's guidance statement:

> "A new Section D has been inserted into Schedule 4 to the 1985 Act. This allows companies to choose to value some of their financial instruments, investment property and living animals and plants at fair value. There is no requirement in the legislation to use fair value; it is an optional accounting treatment.
>
> However, the ASB's accounting standards may in practice determine the circumstances in which fair value measurement is applied…".

For example, unlisted companies *may* adopt FRS 26, "Financial instruments—measurement" with effect from accounts periods beginning on or after 1 January 2005. This would allow such companies to apply the fair value rules to their financial instruments.

However, by voluntarily adopting FRS 26 these companies would then immediately have to adopt the new foreign currency standards (FRS 23 and 24) as well as the extensive disclosure (as opposed to presentation) requirements of FRS 25. Had the company not adopted FRS 26, it would not have needed (nor would it have been able) to adopt the above standards at this stage.

*6 Risk management objectives and policies*
The directors' report must give an indication of the financial risk management objectives and policies of the company and the exposure of the company to various categories of risk (CA 85, Schedule 7, paragraph 5A). For companies not involved in overseas transactions and complex financing, the main area to look out for might be the risk arising from fluctuations in future interest rates on variable rate borrowings.

Small companies who claim exemption under Section 246 and consequently adopt CA 85 Schedule 8, are exempt from the above disclosure requirements.

*7 Fair value disclosures*
Companies with derivatives (e.g. interest rate swaps or forward exchange contracts) that have *not* been fair valued in the accounts are required to disclose in the notes to the accounts, by category of derivatives, the fair value of the derivatives and the extent and nature of the derivatives.

Small companies who claim exemption under Section 246 and consequently adopt CA 85 Schedule 8, are exempt from the above disclosure requirements.

## 2.2    Financial Reporting Council (FRC)

### (a) Functions

FRC is the UK's independent regulator for corporate reporting and governance. It has a wide range of functions including:

- Setting, monitoring and enforcing accounting and auditing standards;
- Statutory oversight and regulation of auditors;
- Operating an independent investigation and discipline scheme for public interest cases;
- Overseeing the regulatory activities of the professional accountancy bodies; promoting high standards of corporate governance.

### (b) Structure

The structure of the FRC is set out in the diagram below:

[www.frc.org.uk]

The Accounting Standards Board (ASB), Urgent Issues Task Force (UITF) and the Financial Reporting Review Panel (FRRP) are referred to below.

## (c) The Professional Oversight Board for Accountancy (POBA)

POBA has three main roles:

- Independent oversight of the regulation of the auditing profession by the recognized supervisory and qualifying bodies (i.e. bodies offering a recognized professional qualification);
- Establishing and overseeing an independent Audit Inspection Unit to monitor the audit of major listed companies and other public interest entities, including both the audit process and the decisions taken by auditors;
- Overseeing the regulatory activities of the individual professional accountancy bodies, including education and training, standards, professional conduct and discipline.

## (d) The Auditing Practices Board (APB)

APB's long-standing (and continuing) role is the development of auditing and assurance services standards and their effective application.

Its responsibilities have been extended to the development of ethical standards relating to the independence, objectivity and integrity of auditors.

## (e) The Accountancy Investigation and Discipline Board (AIDB)

The FRC's Regulatory Strategy, December 2004, states:

> AIDB "contributes to confidence in corporate reporting and governance by providing an independent body to investigate the conduct of members or member firms of the professional accountancy bodies and to take disciplinary action in public interest cases— matters which raise or appear to raise important issues affecting the public interest".

Accountancy Investigation and Discipline Board (AIDB) has published two recent Press Notices relating to investigations into accountancy firms in relation to MG Rover Group (Press Notice, 17 August 2005) and The Mayflower Corporation PLC (Press Notice 14 September 2005).

# 2.3   Accounting Standards Board (ASB)

ASB develops and issues Financial Reporting Standards (FRSs). On its formation, ASB adopted all Statements of Standard Accounting Practice (SSAPs) which were issued by its predecessor body, the former Accounting Standards Committee (ASC).

Current standards are listed in Appendix 2 and convergence issues are referred to in Chapter 7.

## 2.4    Urgent Issues Task Force (UITF)

### (a) Main Role of UITF

UITF is effectively a sub-committee of ASB and assists it where unsatisfactory or conflicting interpretations have developed (or seem likely to develop) about a requirement of an accounting standard (SSAP or FRS) or the Companies Act 1985.

UITF seeks to arrive at a consensus on the accounting treatment that should be adopted. These consensuses are published in the form of UITF Abstracts, and compliance is necessary in accounts that claim to give a true and fair view.

A recent example in an area that has proved to be controversial is Abstract 40 dealing with revenue recognition and service contracts [see Chapter 8].

A list of current Abstracts is provided in Appendix 2.4.

### (b) Impact of IFRIC Developments

UITF has published a number of draft Abstracts which are derived from draft Interpretations issued by the IASB's International Financial Reporting Interpretations Committee—these are referred to in 7.8.

The ASB section of the Financial Reporting Council website includes the text of all Abstracts. UITF Information Sheets give useful background on recent developments and what is in the pipeline (this may include the draft text of proposed Abstracts on which comment is invited).

## 2.5    Statements of Recommended Practice (SORPs)

### (a) Introduction

SORPs are recommendations on accounting practices for specialized industries or sectors, for example Banking, Charities, Higher education institutions and Investment trusts (see (b) below for a list of recognized SORP-making bodies).

The purpose of SORPs is to supplement general and other legal and regulatory requirements in the light of special factors relating to the industry and sector.

SORPs are not issued by the Accounting Standards Board but by specified industry or sector bodies recognized by ASB.

### (b) Recognized SORP-making Bodies

Currently these are:

- Association of British Insurers;
- Association of Investment Trust Companies;
- The Investment Management Association;
- Universities UK;
- British Bankers' Association;
- Charity Commission for England and Wales;

- Finance and Leasing Association;
- Consultative Committee of Accountancy Bodies;
- The Chartered Institute of Public Finance and Accountancy;
- Oil Industry Accounting Committee;
- Pensions Research Accountants' Group;
- National Housing Federation.

Contact details for each of the above can be obtained from the ASB section of the Financial Reporting Council website.

### (c)  Current SORPs and Recent Developments

In March 2005, the Charity Commission issued "Accounting and Reporting by Charities: Statement of Recommended Practice". SORP 2005 applies to accounting years commencing on or after 1 April 2005, although charities *may* choose to adopt earlier if they wish.

The new SORP can be accessed at the Charity Commission's website (www.charitycommission.gov.uk). The website also includes a version of the new SORP which indicates the changes which have been made to SORP 2000.

ASB published a SORPs update in July 2005, as part of its publication Inside Track number 44 (Financial Reporting Council website). Apart from the Charities SORP referred to above, this refers to the following:

- Update of SORP used by the social housing sector;
- Exposure draft of SORP on Insurance Business;
- Exposure draft of SORP on Financial Statements of Investment Trust Companies;
- Exposure draft of SORP on Financial Statements of Authorized Funds;
- Code of Practice on Local Authority Accounting in the UK.
- Exposure draft of SORP on Limited Liability Partnerships.

A list of current SORPs is set out in Appendix 2.

## 2.6   Statement of Principles

The Statement of Principles (SOP) sets out the conceptual background which underpins the Financial Reporting Standards issued by the Accounting Standards Board.

SOP is divided into eight chapters:

- The objective of financial statements;
- The reporting entity;
- The qualitative characteristics of financial information;
- The elements of financial statements;
- Recognition in financial statements;
- Measurement in financial statements;
- Presentation of financial information;
- Accounting for interests in other entities.

SOP is *not* an accounting standard, and does not contain requirements on how financial statements should be prepared or presented. Nevertheless, SOP has until comparatively recently played a pivotal role in the development of UK GAAP. In practical terms the future role of SOP is less clear, as new UK standards reflect International Financial Reporting Standards (which itself has a "Framework", the equivalent of SOP).

## 2.7 Companies (Audit, Investigations and Community Enterprise) Act 2004

### (a) Overview

The Act deals with two main areas:

- Auditors, Accounts and Reports, Directors' Liabilities and Investigations;
- Community Interest Companies.

"Accounts and Reports" deals with: Auditors right to information; Statement in directors' report as to disclosure of information to auditors (see (b) below); Defective accounts; various regulatory issues.

### (b) Statement in Directors' Report as to Disclosure of Information to Auditors

The Act inserts a new Section 234ZA into the Companies Act 1985 and applies to Directors' reports of companies other than those who have claimed exemption from audit under either Section 249A(1) or Section 249AA(1).

This new section does not apply to any directors' report relating to a financial year *beginning* before 1 April 2005, nor to a financial year *ending* before 6 April 2006. So for companies whose financial years cover a 12 month period, the first year for which the new disclosures apply will be the year to 31 March 2006.

The commentary accompanying the Act states that the aim of the new Section is:

> "to ensure that each director will have to think hard about whether there is any information that he knows about or could ascertain which is needed by the auditors in connection with preparing their report".

Section 234ZA(2) requires that the Directors' report must contain a statement to the effect that, in the case of each of the persons who are directors at the time when the report is approved, the following applies:

- so far as the director is aware, there is no relevant audit information of which the company's auditors are unaware, and
- the director has taken all the steps that he ought to have taken as a director in order to make himself aware of any relevant audit information and to establish that the company's auditors are aware of that information.

"Relevant audit information" means information needed by the company's auditors in connection with their report (Section 234ZA(3)).

## (c) Community Interest Companies

The Explanatory Notes to the Act state that Part 2 [of the Act] makes provision for the establishment of a new corporate vehicle, the "community interest company", intended to make it simpler and more convenient to establish a business whose profits and assets are to be used for the benefit of the community.

The website (www.cicregulator.gov.uk) contains valuable information, including a list of Registered Community Interest Companies, and detailed guidance notes covering a wide range of topics.

The overview on the website's home page states:

'CICs are a new type of limited company designed specifically for those wishing to operate for the benefit of the community rather than for the benefits of the owner of the company. This means that a CIC cannot be formed or used solely for the personal gain of a particular person or group of people.

The Regulator comments:

'...... A CIC is first and foremost a limited company carrying on a social activity and must be viable as such. A CIC carrying on a business will need to generate surpluses to support its activities, maintain its assets, make its contribution to the community and in some cases make a limited return to its investors. Other CICs may well depend on grants or donations to achieve these ends.

The phrase 'not for profit' is frequently used in this area. This can be misleading and should only be used in the context of the company not having as its primary purpose the generation of profits for its owners. If a CIC fails to make profits from its activities (or in some way generate sufficient income to cover its running costs) it will eventually fail altogether. Therefore rather than thinking in terms of CICs being non-profit making they should be thought of a making profits for their community purposes ......'

## 2.8 The Companies Act 1985 (Operating and Financial Review and Directors' Report etc.) Regulations 2005

### (a) Overview

The aim of these Regulations was to introduce a new requirement for directors of quoted companies to present an Operating and Financial Review, and to implement EU Directive requirements relating to directors' reports of companies apart from those regarded as "small".

The Goverment subsequently decided that it would no longer require quoted companies to produce an Operating and Financial Review, and that regulations to repeal this requirement would come into effect on 12 January 2006.

The regulations as amended (including the requirement to present a Business Review, see below) are effective for financial years commencing on or after 1 April 2005. The DTI website contains a "Hot Topics" page and a very useful statement entitled "Guidance on the changes to the Directors' Report requirements in the Companies Act 1985, April and Decmber 2005" (www.dti.gov.uk/cld).

*The Regulations include important exemptions for small companies and medium-sized companies.*

## (b) Directors' Report: Business Review

Revised Section 234 requires the directors of a company to prepare a business review, as specified in Section 234ZZB (*apart from small and companies which are exempt from all of this requirement, and medium-sized companies which are exempt from part—see below*).

The directors' report must contain a fair review of the business of the company (referred to below as a "business review"), and a description of the principal risks and uncertainties facing the company.

The business review should be a balanced and comprehensive analysis (consistent with the size and complexity of the business) of the development and performance of the business of the company during the financial year, and the position of the company at the end of that year.

The review should include analysis relating to *financial* "key performance indicators" (KPIs), to the extent necessary for an understanding of the development, performance or position of the business.

Analysis relating to other KPIs, such as those relating to environmental and employee matters, should be provided "where appropriate".

*KPI means "factors by reference to which the development, performance or position of the business of the company can be measured effectively".*

*Small companies* are exempt from the requirement to include a business review within the directors' report.

*Medium-sized companies* are required to include a business review, but this review need not refer to KPIs "so far as they relate to *non-financial* information".

---

Examples of KPIs – financial

- Gross profit/trading margin
- Return on capital employed
- Comparable sales growth
- Comparable trading profit growth
- Interest cover
- Effective tax rate.

Examples of KPIs – non-financial

- Market share
- Number of subscribers
- Sales per square foot
- Environmental spillage
- $CO_2$ emissions
- Employee health and safety.

## 2.9 Companies Act 1985 (Investment Companies and Accounting and Audit Amendments)

Regulations 2005 [Statutory Instrument 2280].
The SI deals with the following three areas:

### (a) Changes Regarding Comparative Figures

*Disclosures in the notes to the accounts*
CA 85 removes the requirement to disclose certain comparatives for all companies, including those claiming small company exemptions (see 2.1(d) above for disclosures affected).

Note that FRS 28, Corresponding amounts, effectively restore these disclosure requirements.

### (b) Small Company Exemption for Disclosure of Particulars of Staff

Section 231A requires details of staff numbers and costs to be disclosed (previously contained in Schedule 4 paragraph 56). Small companies are exempt from this disclosure (Section 246 as amended).

This change has effect for financial years commencing on or after 1 January 2005 and which end on or after 1 October 2005.

### (c) Audit Exemption for Certain Small Financial Services Companies

Institute of Charted Accountants in England and Wales (ICAEW) in a Press Notice had pointed out that an unintended consequence of the recent expansion of the regulated sector to cover mortgage and general insurance intermediaries was that a number of small intermediaries lost their right to audit exemption.

SI 2280 ensures that small and medium-sized companies which carry out certain activities for which permission *is required under Part 4 of the Financial Services and Markets Act 2000 "do not cease to be able to take advantage of special accounting and audit exemptions by reason only of carrying on those activities" (Explanatory Note to SI).*

The legislation is not straightforward to interpret and care should be taken in applying it.

These changes apply to accounts which are delivered to the registrar of companies on or after 5 September 2005.

## 2.10    Legal Opinion on Role of Accounting Standards and True and Fair

### (a) Introduction

The statutory requirement for accounts to give a true and fair view was referred to above. In April 1999, the Accounting Standards Board obtained legal opinion to consider the relationship between accounting standards and the statutory true and fair requirement. The comments below refer to some of the main points in the Opinion. The full text of the Opinion is contained in the ASB's Foreword to Accounting Standards.

### (b) The Role of the Courts

Whether particular accounts satisfy the true and fair requirement is a question of law to be decided by the Court. The Court cannot make a decision without obtaining evidence regarding the practices and views of accountants. It is likely that the Court will hold that compliance with accounting standards is necessary to meet the true and fair requirement.

### (c) The Status of Accounting Standards

Since the early 1980s, responsibility for setting accounting standards has rested with ASB. The Foreword to Accounting Standards states:

- Accounting standards are authoritative statements of how particular types of transactions and other events should be reflected in financial statements and accordingly compliance with accounting standards will normally be necessary for financial statements to give a true and fair view (paragraph 16);
- In applying accounting standards it is important to be guided by the spirit and reasoning behind them, as set out in the individual standards and based on the Statement of Principles for Financial Reporting (paragraph 18).

### (d) UITF Abstracts

The Opinion considers that compliance with Abstracts is also necessary to meet the true and fair requirement.

### (e) Impact of Ongoing Accounting Developments

The Opinion considers that "true and fair" is a dynamic concept and what is required to show a true and fair view is subject to "continuous rebirth" as new standards and Abstracts are developed and issued.

# 2.11    Directors' Report

## (a)  General Requirements

The following is a summary of the main matters which the Act requires to be disclosed in the directors' report—it does not deal with matters specifically relating to listed companies:

- Principal activities of the company and any significant changes.
- A fair review of the development of the business of the company during the financial year and of its position at the end of it.
- Risk management objectives and policies.
- Statement of disclosure of information to auditors.
- Names of persons who were directors at any time during the year.
- The difference, as precisely as is practicable, between the market value and the book value of land and buildings, where such difference is substantial.
- Directors' interest in shares or debentures of this company or any other group company both at the beginning of the financial year (or date of appointment as director, if later) and at the end of the year.
- Particulars of any important events which have occurred since the balance sheet date.
- An indication of likely future developments in the business of the company.
- An indication of the activities (if any) of the company in the field of research and development.
- Amount recommended to be paid by way of dividend.
- Charitable and political donations:
  - if combined amount exceeds £200, the split between charitable and political;
  - details of any individual amount for political purposes where amount exceeds £200; name of recipient and amount given.
- Disabled persons – statement describing policies for:
  - employment;
  - training;
  - career development;
  - promotion.
  (Not applicable to companies which employ fewer than 250 persons within the United Kingdom).
- Particulars of acquisitions of company's own shares.
- Policy for payment of creditors: number of days purchases represented in year-end creditors.

## (b)  Directors' Shareholdings

### 1  Introduction – private companies and unlisted plcs

Directors' shareholdings should normally be disclosed in the Directors' Report (alternatively, they may be given in the notes to the accounts).

The main requirements of Schedule 7 are referred to below and relate to holdings in both shares and debentures. The rules also apply to shareholdings of shadow directors.

Disclosures should disclose shares held by each director at the beginning of the year (or date of appointment) and at the end of the year. Additional disclosures apply to listed companies (see Chapter 29).

Some disclosure issues can cause problems in practice—these are referred to below.

### 2 Disclosures in accounts of wholly owned subsidiaries

Directors' shareholdings disclosed should relate to the company and any other company in the same group (i.e. holding company, subsidiary or fellow subsidiary). Where the company is a wholly owned subsidiary, details of holdings in other group companies need not be given, provided that the individual company accounts make some reference to disclosure of their shareholdings in the parent's accounts.

### 3 Shares held by members of the director's family

The total shareholdings attributed to a director should include shares held by the following:

- the director,
- director's spouse – unless he or she is also a director,
- infant children, including step-children.

### 4 Trust-related holdings

The following should be included:

- a beneficial shareholding where a director or spouse has a life interest in a trust which holds shares in the company;
- trustee shareholdings in all cases where the trustee has powers of decision or management – this includes non-beneficial shareholdings where the trustee does not benefit from the income or capital of the trust.

The following should be excluded:

- a bare trustee (nominee shareholding) who has no interest or duty except to act in accordance with the instructions of the beneficial interest;
- a reversionary interest in trust property, provided that the life interest subsists during the year;
- interest of a person as a trustee or beneficiary of an approved superannuation fund or retirement benefit scheme.

### 5 Shares held through other companies

The total of shares attributed to a director should include certain shareholdings held through a body corporate.

This point is complex, but essentially a person is taken to be interested in shares or debentures if a body corporate is interested in them and either:

- that body corporate or its directors are accustomed to act in accordance with the person's directions or instructions, or,
- the person is entitled to exercise or control the exercise of one-third or more of the voting power at general meetings of that body corporate.

*Illustration*

A Ltd holds 6,000 ordinary shares in B Ltd (it does not matter whether the 6,000 shares represents 1% or 60% of the total capital of B Ltd).

John is a director of B Ltd and owns 3,000 shares in the company. John also owns 14,000 shares representing 35% of the ordinary share capital of A Ltd.

The shareholding to be disclosed in respect of John in the directors' report of B Ltd is 3,000 + 6,000 = 9,000 shares.

### 6 Share options in private companies

CA 1985 does not require disclosure of the existence of options to subscribe for shares or debentures. However, disclosure is required of options granted to or exercised during the tear by a director or his immediate family.

## (c) Financial Risk Management Objectives

The directors' report must give an indication of the company's financial risk management objectives and policies, and the exposure of the company to various categories of risk. Small companies are exempt from this disclosure requirement (Section 2.1(h).6). This applies to accounting periods commencing on or after 1 April 2005.

## (d) Business Review

The directors' report must contain a business review, comprising a balanced and comprehensive analysis of the development and performance of the business of the company during the financial year and the position of the company at the end of the year. This applies to accounting periods commencing on or after 1 January 2005.

Exemptions from these requirements are referred to above (see 2.9).

## (e) Statement as to Disclosure of Information to Auditors

The Act inserts a new Section 234ZA into the Companies Act 1985 and applies to Directors' reports of companies other than those who have claimed exemption from audit under either Section 249A(1) or Section 249AA(1).

This new section does not apply to any directors report relating to a financial year *beginning* before 1 April 2005, nor to a financial year *ending* before 6 April 2006. So for companies whose financial years cover a 12 month period, the first year for which the new disclosures apply will be the year to 31 March 2006.

Section 234ZA(2) requires that the Directors' report must contain a statement to the effect that, in the case of each of the persons who are directors at the time when the report is approved, so far as the director is aware, there is no relevant audit information of which the company's auditors are unaware, and the director has taken all the steps that he ought to have taken as a director in order to make himself aware of any relevant audit information and to establish that the company's auditors are aware of that information (see 2.7 above).

## 2.12   Revision of Defective Accounts

### (a)  Overview

The Companies Act 1985 provisions relating to revision of defective accounts are: Section 245—dealing with voluntary revision and Section 245B dealing with compulsory revision.

The aspects of the accounts deemed to be defective may result from non-compliance with the Companies Act 1985, accounting standards or UITF Abstracts. The issues concerned may affect previously reported profits or assets. Alternatively, they may relate solely to disclosure issues such as directors' remuneration.

The revision should reflect the position as at the date of preparation and approval of the original accounts. It should be restricted to correction of matters where the original accounts failed to comply with the relevant regulations.

The revision is not intended as an updating of the accounts and should not take account of assets, liabilities, income or expenditure arising after the above date.

### (b)  Voluntary Revision

Section 245 offers a number of options—it is up to the directors to decide what action, if any, to take. The course of action will depend upon the nature of the defect, the time which has elapsed since the defective accounts or directors' report were issued, and whether the company's shares are held privately or publicly listed.

The two *statutory* options are:

- A revision of the accounts and/ or directors' report by the replacement of the original set with a corrected set (referred to as "replacement accounts" or "replacement directors' report"), or
- The issue of a supplementary note indicating the corrections to be made to the original accounts and/or directors report ("revision by supplementary note").

Alternatively, the directors may decide to incorporate the corrections in the following year's accounts, using the mechanism in FRS 3, Reporting Financial Performance. This involves a prior period adjustment with restatement of comparative figures.

### (c)  Compulsory Revision

Section 245B involves a detailed and costly procedure (which to date has not been used) whereby the Secretary of State for Trade and Industry obtains a court order requiring the revision of defective accounts.

## 2.13    Financial Reporting Review Panel

### (a) Panel's Role

The role of the Panel is to examine the annual accounts of public and large private companies to see whether they comply with the requirements of the Companies Act 1985 and with applicable accounting standards. The latter may refer to either compliance with UK Financial Reporting Standards (UK GAAP) or with International Financial Reporting Standards (IFRS).

### (b) Scope of Coverage

Whilst large private companies are within the Panel's remit, the Panel intends to focus its resources on the larger listed companies.

Press Notice 88 has commented that the Panel "will pay particular attention to interim reports with a view to identifying companies whose year-end accounts are expected to be subject to significant changes following the adoption of international accounting standards from 1 January 2005". The aim is to highlight any difficulties that need to be addressed prior to publication of the full year's results.

### (c) Correction of Defective Accounts

On discovery of breaches, the Panel seeks to take corrective action that is "proportionate to the nature and effects of the defects, taking account of market and user needs".

Where a company's accounts are defective in a material respect the Panel will, wherever possible, try to secure their revision by voluntary means (see 2.12 above).

If the "voluntary approach" fails, the Panel is empowered to make an application to the court for an order for revision under Section 245B of the Companies Act 1985. As at the beginning of July 2005, no court applications have been made (although earlier Press Notices have commented that "in some instances, the necessary steps have been at an advanced stage") (see also 2.12 above).

### (d) Revised Operating Procedures

Until comparatively recently, the Panel's approach was reactive, taking account of complaints received or Press coverage. In Press Notice 88, the Panel noted that it had "developed a more systematic approach to accounts selection based on business sectors, accounting themes and company-specific factors" (Press Notice 88). In December 2004, the Panel had announced the 2005 Risk-based Proactive Programme, which referred to monitoring activity focusing on five industry sectors: Automobile; Pharmaceutical; Retail; Transport; Utilities.

The first report on the results of the Panel's pro-active approach was published in August 2005 (Press Notice 88).

Revised operating procedures were published for public comment in February 2005 (see FRC website).

## (e) Review Panel Findings

Recently published Review Panel Findings relating to the accounts of named companies are summarized in the table immediately following. Earlier Press Notices can be printed off the FRRP section of the FRC website.

| Press Notice No | Date | Company (PLC unless otherwise stated) and accounts year (* = audit report qualified) | Issues | Follow-up by the company concerned |
|---|---|---|---|---|
| 78 | 5/04 | Thorn Group (2002) | Non-depreciation of hire stock (FRS 15) Treatment of reorganization costs (FRS 3) | Accounting policy change reflected in 2003 accounts |
| 79 | 6/04 | McKechnie Holdings (UK) Limited (2002)* | Omission of cash flow statement (FRS 1) Failure to produce group accounts (CA 85, FRS 2) | Correct treatment reflected in 2003 accounts, with restated comparatives to include omitted information |
| 80 | 12/04 | Alertblind Limited (2000, 2001)/ AMSAP Limited (2002)* | Failure to produce group accounts (CA 85, FRS 2) | Correct treatment reflected in 2004 accounts, with restated comparatives to include omitted information |
| 84 | 6/05 | Royal Bank of Scotland (2004) | Majority owned company treated as subsidiary but should have been accounted for as a joint venture (FRS 9) | Announcement on 8/6/05 gave relevant information |
| 87 | 7/05 | Seymour Pierce Group (now Investment Management Holdings) (2001, 2002) | Basis used to value assets acquired on acquisition of a subsidiary (FRS 7) Omission of disclosures about certain financial commitments (CA 85) | No further action in view of time that has elapsed and fact that company has now largely ceased to trade |

In addition, a number of Press Notices of a "generic" nature, relating to specific technical areas, have also been published. A recent example is Press Notice 77 issued in May 2004 dealt with the inadequacy of disclosures where goodwill and intangible assets were either not amortized or were amortized over periods in excess of 20 years.

### (f) Other Press Notices

In addition to the Press Notices referred to above, FRRP has recently published the following:

- FRRP to gain increased powers and to co-operate with the Financial Services Authority and the Inland Revenue (PN 83, April 2005);
- Legal opinion on the effect of the IAS Regulation on the requirement for accounts to give a True and Fair View (PN 85, June 2005);
- Memorandum of Understanding with HM Revenue and Customs (PN 86, June 2005).

## 2.14 International Financial Reporting Standards

The option to adopt IFRS is referred to in 2.1(h) above and in Chapter 7.

The general implications of adopting IFRS are outlined in the DTI Guidance for British Companies on Changes to the Reporting and Accounting Provisions of the Companies Act 1985.

Paragraph 4.18 comments:

> "Companies that are required to use IAS or choose to use IAS will need to prepare their accounts in accordance with the requirements of IAS rather than the 1985 Act. IAS deals with the form and content of accounts. Therefore, in broad terms, the provisions in the 1985 Act relating to the form and content of accounts (in particular the accounts formats in Schedules 4, 4A, 8, 9 and 9A) will no longer apply to companies using IAS. For example, instead of the profit and loss account and balance sheet required by the 1985 Act, companies will need to prepare the primary financial statements and supporting notes required under IAS".

Paragraph 4.21 of the DTI guidance contains a [long] list of sections of CA 85 that will continue to apply to companies preparing accounts under IAS.

**Frequently Asked Questions**

1  Will the fair value option be available to any company which continues to adopt UK GAAP?

   In theory the fair value option should be available to all UK companies, whether or not they adopt IAS.

   However, the DTI's guidance on the changes to the Companies Act 1985 states that "...ASB's accounting standards may in practice determine the circumstances in which fair value measurement is applied...".

2  Will all companies—whether they adopt UK GAAP or IAS—have to disclose information about the fair value of derivatives in the directors' report?

   No—small companies are exempt from that requirement.

**Website Addresses**

**www.frc.org.uk**
Information regarding: Financial Reporting Council; Accounting Standards Board; Urgent Issues Task Force; Financial Reporting Review Panel; SORPs; useful Press Notices.

**www.dti.gov.uk/cld**
Information regarding: Company Law "Hot Topics"; consultative documents; white papers; draft Bills; guides to recent legislation; useful contact details.

**www.opsi.gov.uk**
Statutory Instruments; new Acts etc.

**www.iasb.org**
A wealth of information including: summaries of key points in new standards; progress on current projects.

**www.charitycommission.gov.uk**

**www.cicregulatory.gov.uk**
Community Interest Companies

# Accounting Policies and Estimation Techniques

This chapter covers:
* Scope and objectives of FRS 18
* Accounting policies and estimation techniques
* Disclosure requirements
* International Financial Reporting Standards

## 3.1 Objectives of FRS 18

An entity should:

- Adopt accounting policies most appropriate to its particular circumstances for the purpose of giving a true and fair view;
- Review accounting policies regularly to ensure they remain appropriate;
- Change accounting policies when a new policy becomes more appropriate to its particular circumstances;
- Disclose sufficient information in the financial statements to enable users to understand the accounting policies adopted and how they have been implemented, as well as disclosure of details of estimation techniques.

The standard also seeks to clarify the distinction between a change of accounting policy and a change in estimation technique.

## 3.2 Concepts

FRS 18 regards the concepts of going concern and accruals as crucial in the selection of accounting policies. An entity should:

- Prepare financial statements on a going concern basis except where an entity is being liquidated or has ceased trading, or where the directors have no realistic alternative but to liquidate the entity or to cease trading;

- Prepare financial statements, except for cash flow information, on the accruals basis of accounting;
- Adopt accounting policies that enable the financial statements to give a true and fair view.

Accounting policies should be consistent with the requirements of accounting standards (FRSs and SSAPs), Urgent Issues Task Force Abstracts and companies legislation.

In exceptional circumstances, where compliance with Standards or Abstracts is inconsistent with requirements to give a true and fair view, an entity should depart from those requirements to the extent necessary to give a true and fair view.

In such circumstances (i.e. where "true and fair override" is adopted) an entity should give the disclosures required by FRS 18 (see 3.7, below).

# 3.3   Definitions

## (a) Accounting Policies

These are defined as those principles, bases, conventions and rules and practices applied by an entity that specify how the effects of transactions and other events are to be reflected in its financial statements through:

- Recognizing assets, liabilities, gains, losses and changes to shareholders' funds;
- Selecting measurement bases for assets, liabilities, gains, losses and changes to shareholders' funds and
- Presenting assets, liabilities, gains, losses and changes to shareholders' funds.

Accounting policies do not include estimation techniques. Accounting policies define the process, whereby transactions and other events are reflected in financial statements.

An accounting policy for a particular type of expenditure, for example, may specify:

- Whether an asset or a loss is to be recognized;
- The basis on which it is to be measured;
- Where in the profit and loss account or balance sheet it is to be presented.

## (b) Estimation Techniques

These are defined as the methods adopted by an entity to arrive at estimated monetary amounts, corresponding to the measurement bases selected, for assets, liabilities, gains, losses and changes to shareholders' funds.

Estimation techniques implement the measurement aspects of accounting policies. An accounting policy will specify the basis on which an item is to be measured; where there is uncertainty over the monetary amount corresponding to that basis, the amount will be arrived at by using an estimation technique. Estimation techniques include for example:

- Methods of depreciation, such as straight line and reducing balance, applied in the context of a particular measurement basis, used to estimate the proportion of the economic benefits of a tangible fixed asset consumed in a period;
- Different methods used to estimate the proportion of trade debts that will not be recovered, particularly where such methods consider a population as a whole rather than individual balances.

## 3.4   Examples

### (a)  Accounting Policies Examples

| Recognition | • Capitalization of interest costs<br>• Capitalization of development costs<br>• Expensing of start-up costs<br>• Recognition of revenue |
|---|---|
| Selection of measurement base | • Fixed assets at revalued amount<br>• Stocks at FIFO<br>• Discounting of deferred tax liability<br>• Foreign subsidiary's profit and loss account translated at average rate |
| Presentation | • Dividend income shown net<br>• Costs reclassified from administrative to cost of sales<br>• Website costs reclassified from intangible to tangible |

### (b)  Estimation Techniques Examples

- Determining net realizable value of stocks either by reference to the entity's own experience or by reference to prices quoted in advertisements;
- Depreciation of motor vehicles previously provided on reducing balance method at 40% per annum; proposes to depreciate over 5 years using straight line basis.

### (c)  Accounting Changes which Involve Both a Change of Presentation and a Change of Estimation Technique

Suppose an entity proposes change from reducing balance to straight line basis; also has previously recorded depreciation charge within costs of sales but now proposes to include within administrative expenses.

This accounting change involves both a change to presentation (reclassification of depreciation charge) and a change of estimation technique (change to straight line basis).

The two changes must be accounted for separately.

## 3.5   Concepts and Objectives – Further Comments

### (a) Summary

The appropriateness of accounting policies should be judged against the four objectives of: Relevance; Reliability; Comparability; Understandability.

These four objectives should be considered together in assessing appropriateness of policies.

### (b) Relevance

The objective of financial statements is to provide information about an entity's financial performance and financial position that is useful for assessing stewardship of management and for making economic decisions. Financial information is relevant if it has the ability to influence the economic decisions of users and is provided in time to influence those decisions.

### (c) Reliability

Financial information is reliable if:

- It reflects the substance of the transaction and other events that have taken place;
- It is free from deliberate or systematic bias ( i.e. is neutral);
- It is free from material error;
- It is complete within the bounds of materiality;
- Under conditions of uncertainty, it has been prudently prepared;

Prudence is still relevant under FRS 18. Prudently prepared means that a degree of caution has been applied in exercising judgement and making the necessary estimates.

However, the application of prudence is restricted to situations *where uncertainty is present*, for example as regards existence of assets, liabilities, gains and losses, or at amounts at which they should be recognized.

- Accounting policies should take account of uncertainty in recognizing and measuring items;
- Conditions of uncertainty will require more confirmatory evidence;
- Prudence should *not* be exercised where there is no uncertainty;
- Prudence should not be used as a reason for creating hidden reserves, making excessive provisions, deliberately understating assets or gains, or deliberately overstating liabilities or losses.

### (d) Comparability

FRS 18, following the Statement of Principles, regards comparability as a more fundamental objective than consistency. *However, it notes that comparability can be achieved through a combination of consistency and disclosure.*

An entity, when judging whether new policy is more appropriate, should give due weight to impact on comparability.

## (e) Understandability

FRS 18 states:

> "...Information provided by financial statements needs to be capable of being understood by users having a reasonable knowledge of business and economic activities and accounting and a willingness to study with reasonable diligence the information provided..."

# 3.6  Changes in Accounting Policies

An entity should review its accounting policies regularly to ensure they remain the most appropriate to its particular circumstances, and give due weight to impact on comparability in judging whether a new policy is more appropriate.

An entity may need to implement a new accounting policy or change an existing one as a result of a recently issued Financial Reporting Standard. However, there is no *requirement* in FRS 18 to implement early as the effective date of a new FRS allows time to consider any implementation issues.

An entity may take account of a recently issued Financial Reporting Exposure Draft (FRED) in judging which policies are most appropriate. However, it may not adopt an accounting policy based on a FRED unless that policy is consistent with existing Standards and Abstracts. Also, there may be significant changes before a FRED becomes a definitive FRS.

An entity should account for a material adjustment applicable to prior periods arising from a change in accounting policy as a prior period adjustment in accordance with FRS 3. The only exception to this is where other Standards, Abstracts or companies legislation requires otherwise.

FRS 18.49 cautions against frequent changes to accounting policies but concludes that "...consistency is not an end in itself and therefore does not impede the introduction of improved accounting practices that result in an overall benefit to users..."

# 3.7  Estimation Techniques

Where estimation techniques are required to enable the accounting policies adopted to be applied, an entity should select estimation techniques that enable its financial statements to give a true and fair view and are consistent with the requirements of Standards, Abstracts and companies legislation.

Where it is necessary to choose between estimation techniques that satisfy the requirement above, an entity should select whichever of those estimation techniques is judged to be most appropriate to its circumstances for the purpose of giving a true and fair view.

An entity should not account for a change to an estimation technique as a prior period adjustment unless:

- It represents the correction of a fundamental error, or
- Another Standard, Abstract or companies legislation requires the change to be accounted for as a prior period adjustment.

## 3.8 Disclosures

### (a) General Disclosures (FRS 18.55)

- Description of each of the accounting policies that is material in the context of the entity's financial statements;
- Description of those estimation techniques adopted that are significant;
- Details of any changes to accounting policies followed in previous period, including a brief explanation of why each new accounting policy is thought more appropriate;
- Where practicable, the effect of change on results for preceding period should be given, and an indication of change in policy on results for current period;
- Where it is not practicable to disclose the effect on the current or the preceding period, the notes should state the fact and the reasons;
- Details of effect of a change to estimation technique where material.

### (b) True and Fair Override

The requirements relate to disclosure of particulars of departure, reasons for it, and its effect and require all of the following disclosures:

- A clear and unambiguous statement that there has been a departure from the requirements of an accounting standard, a UITF Abstract or companies legislation;
- That departure is necessary to give a true and fair view;
- A statement of the treatment that the standard, Abstract or companies legislation would normally require;
- A description of the treatment actually adopted;
- A statement of why the treatment prescribed would not give a true and fair view;
- A description of how the position shown in the financial statements is different as a result of the departure with quantification except where quantification is already evident in the financial statements themselves, or the effect cannot reasonably be quantified, when directors should explain the circumstances.

# 3.9    Illustration

Extract from annual report and accounts of Boots Group PLC, year ended 31 March 2005

**Accounting policies**

The following accounting policies have been applied consistently in dealing with items which are considered material in relation to the group and company financial statements except as noted below.

**Implementation of FRS20 – Share-based payment**

During the year, the company has adopted FRS20, issued by the Accounting Standards Board in April 2004, and has restated comparatives accordingly. The directors believe that the fair value approach underlying FRS20 gives a more appropriate view of the impact of share-based payment transactions than the previous amortisation treatment, and so the standard has been adopted early. The effects of the implementation are shown in note 21.

**Implementation of UITF38 – Accounting for ESOP trusts**

During the year, the company has adopted UITF38, issued by the Accounting Standards Board and requiring adoption for accounting periods ending on or after 22 June 2004. Comparatives have been restated accordingly. The effects of implementation are shown in note 21.

**Basis of accounting**

The financial statements have been prepared in accordance with applicable accounting standards and under the historical cost convention, modified to include the revaluation of certain land and buildings.

A separate profit and loss account for the company has not been presented as permitted by section 230 (4) of the Companies Act 1985.

**Consolidation**

The group financial statements combine the results of the company and all its subsidiaries and joint ventures, to the extent of group ownership and after eliminating intra-group transactions.

Unless otherwise stated, the acquisition method of accounting has been adopted. Under this method, the results of subsidiary undertakings acquired or disposed of in the year are included in the consolidated profit and loss account from the date of acquisition or up to the date of disposal.

Joint ventures are those undertakings, not recognised as subsidiaries, in which the group has a participating interest and are jointly controlled. The group's share of the results of joint ventures, which are accounted for under the gross equity method, are included in the profit and loss account and its share of their net assets is included in investments in the group balance sheet.

In the company balance sheet, investments in subsidiaries and joint ventures are stated at cost (being the par value of shares issued where merger relief applies) less impairments.

### Foreign currencies

The results and cash flows of overseas subsidiaries and the results of joint ventures are translated into sterling on an average exchange rate basis, weighted by the actual results of each month. Assets and liabilities including currency swaps are translated into sterling at the rates of exchange ruling at the balance sheet date.

Exchange differences arising from the translation of the results and net assets of overseas subsidiaries, less offsetting exchange differences on foreign currency borrowings and currency swaps hedging those assets (net of any related tax effects), are dealt with through reserves.

Where foreign currency hedges are taken out for committed future foreign currency purchases, the fair value of those hedges are not included in the profit and loss account and balance sheet. All other exchange differences are dealt with in the profit and loss account.

The cost of the company investment in shares in overseas subsidiaries is stated at the rate of exchange in force at the date each investment was made, except where hedge accounting applies in which case the year end rate is used.

### Goodwill and intangible assets

Goodwill on acquisitions comprises the excess of the fair value of the consideration plus any associated costs for investments in subsidiary undertakings and joint ventures over the fair value of net assets acquired. Fair values are attributed to the identifiable assets and liabilities that existed at the date of acquisition, reflecting their condition at that date. Adjustments are also made to bring the accounting policies of acquired businesses into alignment with those of the group. The costs of integrating and reorganising acquired businesses are charged to the post-acquisition profit and loss account.

Goodwill arising on acquisitions prior to 1st April 1998 has been set off against reserves. On disposal of such businesses, any goodwill previously set off against reserves is charged in the calculation of the profit or loss on disposal. For subsequent acquisitions goodwill is recognised within fixed assets in the year in which it arises and amortised on a straight-line basis over its useful economic life, not exceeding 20 years.

The cost of intangible assets acquired (which are capitalised only if separately identifiable) is not amortised except where the end of the useful economic lives of the acquired intangible asset can be reasonably foreseen. Similar assets created within the business are not capitalised and expenditure is charged against profits in the year in which it is incurred. The carrying value of intangible assets (including in particular those being amortised over periods greater than 20 years) is reviewed annually and any impairment in value charged to the profit and loss account.

### Tangible fixed assets and depreciation

Depreciation of tangible fixed assets is provided to write off the cost or valuation, less residual value, by equal instalments over their expected useful economic lives as follows:

- Freehold land, assets in the course of construction – not depreciated
- Freehold and long leasehold buildings, depreciated to their estimated residual values over their useful economic lives of not more than 50 years
- Short leasehold properties – remaining period of lease when less than 50 years
- Computer equipment including software – 3 to 8 years
- Motor cars – 4 or 5 years
- Other motor vehicles – 3 to 10 years
- Fixtures and plant – 3 to 20 years.

Any impairment in the value of fixed assets is recognised immediately.

The group adopted the transitional provisions of FRS15 'Tangible Fixed Assets' to retain the book value of land and buildings many of which were last revalued in 1993 and has not adopted a policy of annual revaluations for the future.

Profits and losses arising from the disposal of properties which have previously been revalued are calculated by reference to their carrying value.

### Share-based payment transactions

Shares in the company which have been purchased for the benefit of employees under various incentive schemes, are held in three employees share ownership trusts:

- The qualifying employee share ownership trust (QUEST) provides for the all employee SAYE scheme
- Shares owned by the ESOP trusts form part of the Boots Long Term Bonus Scheme for executive directors and senior employees
- Shares owned by all the employee share ownership plan (AESOP) are conditionally gifted to all employees employed at a qualifying date and then held in trust for a qualifying service period of not less than three years.

Shares are held at original cost in the own shares reserve which forms part of the overall profit and loss reserve.

### Expense arising from share based payments

The fair value of the shares/options granted is recognised as an employee expense with a corresponding increase in equity. The fair value is measured at the grant date and spread over the period during which the employees become unconditionally entitled to the shares/options. The fair value is based on market value. The amount recognised as an expense reflects the estimated number of shares/options that are expected to vest except where forfeiture is only due to 'total share holder return' targets not being achieved.

In accordance with the transitional provisions of FRS20, no expense is recorded in respect of grants made under the above schemes prior to 7th November 2002.

### Cash and liquid resources

Cash, for the purpose of the cash flow statement, comprises cash in hand and deposits repayable on demand, less overdrafts payable on demand.

Liquid resources are current asset investments which are disposable without curtailing or disrupting the business and are either readily convertible into known amounts of cash at or close to their carrying values or traded in an active market. Liquid resources comprise term deposits of less than one year (other than cash).

### Derivative financial instruments

The derivative financial instruments used by the group to manage its interest rate and currency risks are interest rate swaps, currency swaps and forward rate contracts. Interest receipts and payments arising on interest rate swaps are recognised within net interest payable over the period of the contract. Termination payments made or received are amortised over the life of the underlying exposure in cases where the exposure continues to exist, and taken to the profit and loss account immediately where the underlying exposure ceases to exist. Interest receipts and payments arising on currency swaps are recognised gross within interest payable and interest receivable over the period of the contract. Gains and losses arising on forward currency contracts entered into hedged trading transactions are recognised in the profit and loss account in the same period as the underlying exposure. Forward contracts hedging cash and borrowings are valued at closing rates of exchange at each period end, with gains and losses offset against the related cash and borrowings. The interest differential on these instruments is recognised against net interest payable.

**Turnover**

Turnover comprises sales to external customers (excluding VAT and other sales taxes) and rental income. Consideration received from customers is only recorded as turnover when the group has completed full performance in respect of that consideration.

**Stocks**

Stocks are valued at the lower of cost and net realisable value. Cost comprises purchase cost of goods, direct labour and those overheads related to manufacture and distribution based on normal activity levels.

**Pensions**

Pension costs are recognised in the financial statements in accordance with the requirements of SSAP24 'Accounting for Pension Costs'.

The company and its UK subsidiaries operate pension schemes under which contributions by employees and by the companies are held in trust funds separated from the companies' finances. Actuarial valuations of the schemes are conducted at three year intervals and include a review of contributions.

The cost of providing pensions is spread over the employees' working lives with the companies. The cost charged to the profit and loss account in any year may not always equal the employer contributions to the pension schemes.

The group continues to follow the transitional provisions as permitted by FRS17 'Retirement Benefits' at 31$^{st}$ March 2005 which are disclosed in Note 27.

**Leases**

The rental costs of properties and other assets held under operating leases are charged to the profit and loss account on a straight line basis. Benefits received as an incentive to sign a lease, whatever form they may take, are credited to the profit and loss account on a straight line basis over the lease term, or, if shorter than the full lease term, over the period to the review date on which the rent is first expected to be adjusted to the prevailing market rate.

The cost of assets held under finance leases (being leases which give rights to the group approximating to ownership) is included under tangible fixed assets and depreciation is provided in accordance with the policy for the class of asset concerned. The corresponding obligations under these leases are shown as creditors. The finance charge element of rentals is charged to the profit and loss account to produce, or approximate to, a constant periodic rate of charge on the remaining balance of the outstanding obligations.

**Deferred taxation**

Deferred tax is provided in respect of all timing differences that have originated, but not reversed, by the balance sheet date except as required by FRS19 'Deferred Tax'. Deferred tax is measured on a non-discounted basis at the tax rates that are expected to apply in the periods in which timing differences reverse, based on tax rates and laws substantively enacted at the balance sheet date.

No provision is made for taxation liabilities which would arise on the distribution of profits retained by overseas subsidiaries and joint ventures as there is no commitment to remit these profits. It is not anticipated that any significant taxation will become payable on the revaluation surplus or sale of properties, as taxation on gains on properties used for the purpose of the group's trade is expected to be deferred indefinitely or eliminated by capital losses.

# 3.10 International Financial Reporting Standards

IAS 8, Accounting policies, changes in accounting estimates and errors, sets out:

- The criteria for selecting and changing accounting policies;
- The accounting treatment and disclosure of changes in accounting policies, changes in accounting estimates and corrections of prior period errors.

As regards accounting policies and accounting estimates, IAS 8 and FRS 18 are similar in terms of their practical effects.

IAS 8 requires *material* prior period errors to be corrected by retrospective restatement, i.e. by correcting previous period's financial statements as though the error had never occurred. The standard deals with situations where such restatement would be impracticable. FRS 3 deals with correction of *fundamental* errors.

---

**Frequently Asked Questions**

1 How should errors which are material but not fundamental be dealt with under UK GAAP?
FRS 3 requires fundamental errors to be corrected by retrospective restatement and prior year adjustment. Material errors should be dealt with as current year items only, with appropriate disclosure.

2 What types of accounting policy changes do not require a PYA?
A PYA is not required where the effect of the change is considered to be immaterial.
Secondly, a PYA is not required for accounting policy changes which relate solely to presentation changes, for example reclassifications of assets and expense items which do not affect shareholders' funds. However, comparatives must be restated as for all accounting policy changes.
Thirdly, a PYA is not required where a new FRS requires a change of accounting policy but the standard contains special transitional provisions which give exemption from the usual principle of retrospective restatement.

3 Is it necessary to provide disclosures relating to accounting estimates?

Yes. Disclosure is required of:

- Description of those estimation techniques adopted that are significant;
- Details of effect of a change to estimation technique where material.

---

# Profit and Loss Account, Statement of Total Recognized Gains and Losses (STRGL) and Balance Sheet

**4**

---

**This chapter covers:**
* Compliance with CA 1985 format rules
* Disclosure of effects of acquisitions and discontinued operations
* Identifying the two categories of exceptional items
* Disclosure of operations in the process of being discontinued
* Additional statements required by FRS 3
* Prior period adjustments – accounting policy changes and fundamental errors
* International Financial Reporting Standards

---

## 4.1 Introduction

### (a) Companies Act 1985 form and Content Requirements

These are set out in Schedule 4 to the Companies Act 1985 (for small companies: Schedules 8 and 8A).

Regarding the balance sheet, UK companies, mostly adopt Format 1, which shows subtotals for net current assets (liabilities) and total assets less current liabilities. Many European companies outside the UK adopt Format 2 where the top part of the balance sheet shows "Assets" and the bottom part shows "Liabilities" and "Equity".

Most UK companies adopt profit and loss Format 1, which analyses expenses by function:

* costs of sales;
* distribution costs;
* administrative expenses.

A minority of UK companies adopt Format 2 which analyses expenses by type:

- changes in stocks of finished goods and work in progress;
- raw materials and consumables;
- other external charges;
- staff costs;
- depreciation;
- other operating charges.

Illustrations are given below. The Act specifies terminology and permitted modifications, as well as the minimum which must be shown on the face of the balance sheet and profit and loss account rather than relegated to accompanying notes.

1. Extract from annual report and accounts of KBC Advanced Technologies PLC, year ended 31 December 2004.

| | Notes | 2004 £000 | 2004 £000 | Restated (note1) 2003 £000 | Restated (note1) 2003 £000 |
|---|---|---|---|---|---|
| **Fixed assets** | | | | | |
| Intangible assets | 9 | | 4,094 | | 4,770 |
| Tangible assets | 10 | | 1,809 | | 1,999 |
| Investments | 11 | | 2 | | 302 |
| | | | 5,905 | | 7,071 |
| **Current assets** | | | | | |
| Debtors | 13 | 13,215 | | 12,664 | |
| Investments | 11 | 300 | | 300 | |
| Cash and short-term deposits | 14 | 1,696 | | 4,275 | |
| | | 15,211 | | 17,239 | |
| **Creditors**: amounts falling due within one year | 15a | (4,120) | | (4,932) | |
| **Net current assets** | | | 11,091 | | 12,307 |
| **Total assets less current liabilities** | | | 16,996 | | 19,378 |
| **Creditors**: amounts falling due after one year | 15b | | – | | (300) |
| **Provision for liabilities and charges** | 22 | | (390) | | (1,180) |
| | | | 16,606 | | 17,898 |
| **Capital and reserves** | | | | | |
| Called-up share capital | 17 | | 1,202 | | 1,202 |
| Share premium account | 18 | | 6,038 | | 6,038 |
| Capital redemption reserve | 18 | | 79 | | 79 |
| Merger reserve | 18 | | 147 | | 147 |
| Reserve for own shares | 18 | | (2,136) | | (2,136) |
| Profit and loss account | 18 | | 11,276 | | 12,568 |
| **Shareholders' funds:** equity interests | | | 16,606 | | 17,898 |

2. Extract from annual report and accounts of Honeycomb Leisure PLC, Consolidated Profit and Loss Account, for the 53 weeks ended 2 May 2004.

|  | Note | 53 weeks ended 2 May 2004 £'000 | 52 weeks ended 27 April 2003 £'000 |
|---|---|---|---|
| **Turnover** | 2 | **33,649** | 32,971 |
| Cost of sales |  | **(19,665)** | (20,034) |
| **Gross profit** |  | **13,984** | 12,937 |
| Distribution costs |  | **(417)** | (419) |
| Administrative expenses |  |  |  |
| – exceptional | 4 | **(283)** | (610) |
| – amortisation goodwill |  | **(432)** | (432) |
| – normal |  | **(9,690)** | (7,945) |
| Administrative expenses |  | **10,405** | (8,987) |
| **Operating profit** |  | **3,162** | 3,531 |
| Profit on sale of fixed assets |  | **186** | 1,858 |
| **Profit on ordinary activities before interest** | 3 | **3,348** | 5,389 |
| Interest payable and similar charges |  |  |  |
| – exceptional | 4 | **(980)** | – |
| – normal | 6 | **(2,077)** | (2,811) |
| Interest payable and similar charges |  | **(3,057)** | (2,811) |
| **Profit on ordinary activities before taxation** | 3 | **291** | 2,578 |
| Taxation on profit on ordinary activities | 7 | **(377)** | (642) |
| **(Loss)/profit on ordinary activities after taxation** |  | **(86)** | 1,936 |
| **Dividends** | 8 | **(1,020)** | (938) |
| **Retained (loss)/profit for the period** |  | **(1,106)** | 998 |
| **Earnings per Share – Basic** | 9 | **(0.3p)** | 6.6p |
| **– Diluted** | 9 | **(0.3p)** | 6.6p |
| **Adjusted Earnings per Share\* – Basic** | 9 | **3.9p** | 3.8p |
| **– Diluted** | 9 | **3.9p** | 3.8p |

All amounts relate to continuing operations.

There were no other recognised gains and losses during the period other than those shown above.

\*Adjusted Earnings Per Share is calculated after adding back amortisation of goodwill, profit on sale of fixed assets and exceptional costs.

3. Extract from annual report and accounts of KBC Advanced Technologies PLC, year ended 31 December 2004.

## GROUP PROFIT AND LOSS ACCOUNT

| | Notes | Before Exceptional income/ (charges) and goodwill amortisation £000 | Exceptional income/ (charges) £000 | Goodwill amortisation £000 | Total 2004 £000 | Total 2003 £000 |
|---|---|---|---|---|---|---|
| Turnover | 2 | 29,252 | – | – | 29,252 | 32,274 |
| Other operating income | 3 | – | 2,083 | – | 2,083 | – |
| Staff costs | 4 | (15,746) | – | – | (15,746) | (17,491) |
| Depreciation and amortisation | | (806) | – | (491) | (1,297) | (1,437) |
| Other operating charges | 3 | (13,775) | (1,111) | – | (14,886) | (15,529) |
| Operating loss | 3 | (1,075) | 972 | (491) | (594) | (2,183) |
| Interest receivable | | 46 | – | – | 46 | 200 |
| Loss on ordinary activities before taxation | | (1,029) | 972 | (491) | (548) | (1,983) |
| Taxation on loss on ordinary activities | 5 | 62 | (330) | – | (268) | 499 |
| Loss on ordinary activities after taxation | | (967) | 642 | (491) | (816) | (1,484) |
| Dividends – equity interests | 7 | | | | (93) | (1,906) |
| Retained loss for the period | | | | | (909) | (3,390) |
| Loss per share (pence) – basic | 8 | | | | (1.76) | (3.19) |
| Basic (loss)/earnings per share (pence) before exceptional items and goodwill amortisation | 8 | | | | (2.08) | 1.37 |

**GROUP STATEMENT OF TOTAL RECOGNISED GAINS AND LOSSES**

for the year ended 31 December 2004

| | Notes | 2004 £000 | 2003 £000 |
|---|---|---|---|
| Loss attributable to shareholders of the Group | | (816) | (1,484) |
| Exchange difference on retranslation of net assets of subsidiary undertakings | 18 | (383) | (594) |
| Total recognised losses for the year | | (1,199) | (2,078) |
| Prior year adjustment | 1 | 1,451 | – |
| | | 252 | (2,078) |

The cumulative impact of implementing UITF 38 is to reduce shareholders' funds by £685,000 as at 1 January 2003.

## (b) FRS 3 – Reporting Financial Performance

The main areas covered by FAS 3 are:

- The presentation of the profit and loss account, distinguishing between continuing operations and discontinued operations.
- The presentation of exceptional items.
- The virtual extinction for practical purposes of extraordinary items.
- Additional statements and notes:
  - statement of total recognized gains and losses (STRGL),
  - note of historical cost profits and losses,
  - reconciliation of movements in shareholders' funds.
- Definition of discontinued operations, together with reporting implications.
- Presentation and measure of profits and losses on disposal of fixed assets.
- When comparative figures have to be restated.

# 4.2    FRS 3 – The Profit and Loss Account

## (a) Companies Act 1985

CA 1985 offers a choice of profit and loss formats. Note that paragraph 46 of FRS 3 requires that "operating" exceptional items should *not* be aggregated on the face of the profit and loss account under one heading of exceptional items. Instead, each exceptional item should be included within its natural statutory format heading. This is an area where some companies have been caught by the Financial Reporting Review Panel (see 4.3).

Illustrations of alternative formats were shown above. Further illustrations dealing with FRS 3 issues are referred to below.

*Format 1*

Main expense categories are:

– cost of sales,
– distribution costs,
– administrative expenses.

*Format 2*

Main categories are:

– change in stocks of finished goods and work in progress,
– raw materials and consumables,
– other external charges,
– staff costs,
– depreciation,
– exceptional amounts written off current assets,
– other operating charges.

   Following the FRS 3, para 46 rule, above, "operating" exceptional items should be allocated to one of the sub-headings above.

## (b) Analysis of Revenue Items

FRS 3 requires the aggregate results of each of the following to be disclosed separately:

• Continuing operations – ongoing operations;
• Continuing operations – acquisitions;
• Discontinued operations.

   The key disclosures are set out in FRS 3, para 14:

"... The minimum disclosure required down to the operating profit level on the face of the profit and loss account in respect of continuing operations, acquisitions and discontinued operations is the analysis of turnover and operating profit...

   ... The analysis between continuing operations, acquisitions (as a component of continuing operations) and discontinued operations of each of the other statutory profit and loss account format items between turnover and operating profit should be given by way of note where not shown on the face of the profit and loss account...".

(See 4.5 regarding discontinued operations.)

*Illustration 1*

Extract from annual report and accounts of Boots Group plc, year ended 31 March 2003.

**Note 3 – Exceptional items**

| | Continuing Operations 2003 £m | Discontinued operation 2003 £m | Total 2003 £m | Continuing Operations 2002 £m | Discontinued operation 2002 £m | Total 2002 £m |
|---|---|---|---|---|---|---|
| **Profit/(loss) on disposal of fixed assets** | 5.1 | – | 5.1 | (12.2) | 6.2 | (6.0) |
| **Loss on disposal or closure of operations** | | | | | | |
| Provision for loss on closure of operations | (34.5) | – | (34.5) | – | – | – |
| Loss on disposal of business (see note 4) | – | (123.2) | (123.2) | (12.6) | (2.3) | (14.9) |
| Share of joint venture loss on closure of business | – | – | – | (5.6) | – | (5.6) |
| **Total exceptional items before taxation** | (29.4) | (123.2) | (152.6) | (30.4) | 3.9 | (26.5) |
| **Attributable tax credit (see note 6)** | 9.4 | 1.7 | 11.1 | 1.6 | 0.4 | 2.0 |
| | (20.0) | (121.5) | (141.5) | (28.8) | 4.3 | (24.5) |

Provision for loss on closure of operations relates to the withdrawal from certain wellbeing services.

As detailed in notes 5, an exceptional interest credit of £92.1m arose in the year to 31st March 2003, the tax on which is £27.6m.

In addition, in 2002 the following items included in continuing operating profit were regarded as exceptional:

– £10.4m charge relating to the withdrawal of the on-line photographic services of bootsphoto.com; and
– £6.0m additional costs incurred within Boots The Chemists on the cost reduction programme and leisure exit.

The attributable tax credit was £4.9m.

## (c) Acquisitions

The aggregate results of acquisitions should be disclosed separately, down to operating profit level. For groups using CA 1985, format 1, this will require separate disclosure of turnover, cost of sales, distribution costs and administrative expenses.

This may be achieved by showing the impact on turnover and operating profit on the face of the consolidated profit and loss account, as indicated in the pro forma below. The required information for costs of sales, distribution costs and administrative expenses would be shown by way of note.

PRO FORMA CONSOLIDATED PROFIT AND LOSS ACCOUNT
for the year ended 31 December 19X8 (extract)

|  | £ | £ |
|---|---|---|
| **Turnover** | | |
| Continuing operations | | X |
| Acquisitions | | X |
| | | X |
| | | (X) |
| Cost of sales | | |
| Gross profit | | X |
| Net operating expenses | | (X) |
| Operating profit | | |
| Continuing operations | X | |
| Acquisitions | X | X |
| Loss on sale of business | | (X) |
| Profit on disposal of fixed assets | | X |
| | | X |
| Profit on ordinary activities before interest | | (X) |
| Interest payable | | X . |
| Profit on ordinary activities before taxation | | X |

Additional disclosure issues are referred to in FRS 3:

- "In respect of acquisitions, the requirement is to disclose their post-acquisition results for the period in which the acquisition occurs. In some circumstances it may also be useful to users for the results of acquisitions for the first full financial year for which they are a part of the reporting entity to be disclosed in the notes" (para 38).
- "If an indication of the contribution of an acquisition to the results of the period cannot be given, this fact and the reasons should be explained" (para 16).

# 4.3   Exceptional Items

## (a) "Operating" Exceptional Items

Apart from three specified categories referred to below, all exceptional items should be included under the relevant statutory format heading and taken into account in arriving at profit on ordinary activities before taxation. As an example, an abnormal loss on a long-term contract would (for companies using format 1) be included under cost of sales.

## (b) "Non-operating" Exceptional Items

The three special cases where exceptional items should be shown immediately below operating profit as separate line items, but before interest payable and receivable are:

- Profits or losses on the sale or termination of an operation, for example the profit or loss on the sale of a business.
- Costs of a fundamental reorganization or restructuring which have a material effect on the nature and focus of the reporting entity's operations. This is a complex area of FRS 3 and one that will apply mainly to larger companies and groups.
- Profits or losses on the disposal of fixed assets. This would include, for example, profits on the sale of freehold property but not profits and losses which are little more than marginal adjustments to depreciation previously charged.

The profit or loss on disposal of a fixed asset should be recognized in the accounts of the period in which the disposal takes place. The profit or loss should be calculated by comparing the net sales proceeds, and the net carrying amount.

*Illustration 2*

Extract from annual report and accounts of lastminute.com plc, year ended 30 September 2003.

**Note 4**

**Exceptional items**

**Operating exceptional items**

|  | *Year ended* *30 September* *2003* *£'000* | *Year ended* *30 September* *2002* *£'000* |
| --- | --- | --- |
| Exceptional costs of integration of holiday autos | 2,822 | – |
| Exceptional costs of reorganisation of the cost base | 2,256 | – |
|  | 5,078 | – |

The exceptional costs of integration of holiday autos relate to the implementation of the synergies relating to the acquisition. These primarily consist of a reduction in head-count, consolidation of properties and termination of certain contracts.

During 2003 we also incurred exceptional costs in order to improve the flexibility of our cost base by moving more costs from fixed to variable. These exceptional costs principally relate to redundancy costs following the outsourcing of various non-core functions.

The tax effect of the exceptional items was £nil.

## Non-operating exceptional items

|  | Year ended 30 September 2003 £'000 | Year ended 30 September 2002 £'000 |
|---|---|---|
| Exceptional costs of a fundamental reorganisation | – | 3,094 |

Following the acquisition of the Travelprice.com Group in 2002, the nature and focus of our combined operations in France and Italy were fundamentally restructured, including moving to a single technology platform, the introduction of a more efficient management structure and restructuring our call centre and operating locations. The costs related principally to redundancy and surplus property costs.

The tax effect of the exceptional items was £nil.

## *Illustration 3*

Extract from annual report and accounts of Ideal Shopping Direct plc, year ended 31 December 2002.

### Consolidated profit and loss account (extract)

...

| | Note | 2002 £'000 | 2002 £'000 | 2001 £'000 | 2001 £'000 |
|---|---|---|---|---|---|
| **Turnover** | 1 | | 32,634 | | 17,651 |
| Cost of sales | | | (19,128) | | (12,030) |
| Gross profit | | | 13,506 | | 5,621 |
| Distribution costs | | | (1,498) | | (1,145) |
| Administrative expenses | | (10,611) | | (10,598) | |
| Business interruption claim income | | 2,213 | | 3,433 | |
| Irrecoverable fire costs | | (170) | | (555) | |
| Total net administrative expenses | | | (8,568) | | (7,720) |
| Net operating expenses | | | (10,066) | | (8,865) |
| Operating profit/(loss) | 23 | | 3,440 | | (3,244) |
| Net interest | 2 | | (202) | | (340) |
| **Profit/(loss) on ordinary activities before taxation** | 1 | | 3,238 | | (3,584) |

...

### Principal Accounting Policies (extract)

...

### Insurance

The treatment of insurance claims and proceeds in the financial statements is as follows:

(i) Amounts received (or receivable) in respect of shortfall of profits for the year are disclosed as other operating income. To the extent that these amounts had been claimed but not received by the previous year end, they were included in debtors. All amounts have been received by 31 December 2002;

(ii) Amounts received (or receivable) in respect of additional working costs have been matched against relevant expenditure. To the extent that these amounts had been claimed but not received by the previous year end, they were also included in debtors. All amounts have been received by 31 December 2002;

(iii) Amounts in respect of stocks were received in full in the previous year;

(iv) Amounts estimated as being due from the insurers for payments in respect of replacement of owned fixed assets lost in the fire were included within debtors in the previous year;

(v) In respect of leased fixed assets lost in the fire, the insurers settled the due amounts directly with the lessor. The lessor has replaced all of the assets during the period after the fire. In the previous year, debtors included an amount representing the remainder of the assets to be supplied to the Company by the lessor.

The fixed assets lost in the fire have been written off to the profit and loss account, but there has been no profit or loss arising because there is no significant difference between the carrying amount and the insurance proceeds.

## (c) Pitfall to Avoid – Classification and Presentation of Exceptional Items

An early Review Panel press notice (PN 29) commented:

"...The Panel acknowledged and took full note of the fact that the nature of the exceptional items had been disclosed in a note to the accounts but felt that this did not fulfil the requirement of the standard that these items should be shown on the profit and loss account under the statutory format headings to which they relate.

In reaching its conclusion the Panel noted that the treatment of exceptional items by inclusion under the statutory format headings to which they relate, and disclosed separately under those headings on the face of the profit and loss account or by way of note, was an integral part of the standard...".

*Note:* as referred to in 4.2 above, the captions under which exceptional items are classified will vary according to which of the Companies Act 1985 profit and loss formats the company adopts.

# 4.4    Extraordinary Items

FRS 3 defines extraordinary items as:

"Material items possessing a high degree of abnormality which arise from events or transactions that fall outside the ordinary activities of the reporting entity and which are not expected to recur. They do not include exceptional items nor do they include prior period items merely because they relate to a prior period".

Paragraph 48 of the explanation section to FRS 3 makes the following comment: "... in view of the extreme rarity of such items no examples are provided...".

For practical purposes, extraordinary items can be ignored.

## 4.5    Discontinued Operations and Provisions

### (a) Definition

Discontinued operations are defined in para 4 of FRS 3 as operations of the reporting entity that are sold and terminated and that satisfy all of the following conditions:

- The sale or termination is completed either in the period or before the earlier of three months after the commencement of the subsequent period and the date on which the financial statements are approved.
- If a termination, the former activities have ceased permanently.
- The sale or termination has a material effect on the nature and focus of the reporting entity's operations and represents a material reduction in its operating facilities resulting from either its withdrawal from a particular market (whether class of business or geographical) or from a material reduction in turnover in the reporting entity's continuing markets.
- The assets, liabilities, results of operations and activities are clearly distinguishable, physically, operationally and for financial reporting purposes.

FRS 3 specifies that operations which do not satisfy all of these conditions must be classed as continuing. The Standard provides guidance as how the above should be interpreted (see Explanation section, paras 42 to 44).

### (b) Provisions in Respect of Discontinued Operations

#### (i) Key requirement

Para 18 of FRS 3 deals with "the consequences of a decision to sell or terminate an operation". Para 18 has been amended by para 100 of FRS 12 on provisions, contingent liabilities and contingent assets.

The key points of this complex paragraph are:

- Where a decision has been made to sell or terminate an operation, any provision arising from this should reflect the extent to which obligations have been incurred that are not expected to be covered by the future profits of the operation.
- The reporting entity should be demonstrably committed to the sale or termination:
  - in the case of a sale, this should be evidenced by a binding sale agreement,
  - in the case of a termination, this should be evidenced by a detailed formal plan for termination from which the reporting entity cannot realistically withdraw.
- The provision should be restricted to:
  - the direct costs of the sale or termination
  - any operating losses of the operation up to the date of sale or termination.

In both of these cases, the provision should be arrived at after taking account of the aggregate profit to be recognized in the profit and loss account from the future profits of the operation.

*(ii) Further considerations*

In many cases, the provision set up will relate to an operation which qualifies for classification in the period as discontinued. However, para 18 refers also to situations where a provision is permitted but where the operations do not fall to be classed as discontinued until the following accounting period. FRS 3 specifies disclosure requirements in such situations and provides an illustrative example (Profit and loss account example 1).

Para 45, Explanation section, provides further guidance on the application of the principles in para 18. For example,

> "... Evidence of the commitment might be the public announcement of specific plans, the commencement of implementation, or other circumstances effectively obliging the reporting entity to complete the sale or termination. A binding contract entered into after the balance sheet date may provide additional evidence ... of commitments at the balance sheet date ...".

(Note the discussion in subsequently issued FRS 12 relating to constructive obligations.)

## 4.6   Operations in the Process of Being Discontinued

Business operations which at the year end are in the process of being disposed of or run down may not qualify under FRS 3 as discontinued activities. In such cases, attributable turnover and profits/losses must be classified as a part of continuing operations.

Paragraph 41 of FRS 3 states:

> "... In some cases it may be appropriate to disclose separately in a note to the profit and loss account the results of operations which although not discontinued are in the process of discontinuing, but they should not be classed as discontinued ...".

## 4.7   Profit or Loss on Disposal of Fixed Assets

The profit or loss on disposal of a fixed asset should be recognized in the accounts of the period in which the disposal takes place. The profit or loss should be calculated by comparing:

- the net sales proceeds, and
- the net carrying amount.

The net carrying amount will be based on either:

- historical cost, less any provision, less depreciation (historical cost accounting rules) or
- valuation less depreciation (alternative accounting rules).

*Illustration 4*

A company acquired an asset in 19X2 at a cost of £120,000. The asset was revalued in 19X6 at £250,000 the surplus of £130,000 being transferred to revaluation reserve.

The asset was sold m 19X8 for proceeds of £400,000. Ignore depreciation.

Under FRS 3 the profit on sale included in the profit and loss account is £150,000 (£400,000 – £250,000). Any amount previously held in revaluation reserve (£130,000) now becomes realized and is accounted for by making a transfer within reserves of £130,000. The £130,000 has no effect on the reported profit for the year but does form part of the cumulative realized profit in the balance sheet and is thus available as distributable profit.

## 4.8 FRS 3 – The Statement of Total Recognized Gains and Losses (STRGL)

FRS 3 requires a statement of total gains and losses to be included as a primary statement. The statement should be given the same prominence as the balance sheet, the profit and loss account and the cash flow statement.

*Illustration 5*

The surplus on revaluation during 19X6 amounted to £130,000. This would be included in the statement of total recognized gains and losses. Assuming the profit and loss account showed profit for the financial years of £253,427 and £313,562 respectively, the statement would appear as follows:

**Statement of total recognized gains and losses**

|  | 19X6 £ | 19X5 £ |
|---|---|---|
| Profit the financial year | 253,427 | 313,562 |
| Unrealized surplus on revaluation of property | 130,000 | – |
| Total gains and losses relating to the year | 383,427 | 313,562 |

Several companies adopt historical cost accounting without incorporating fixed asset revaluations into their accounts, have no foreign currency translation differences and will thus have no recognized gains or losses other than the profit or loss for the year. FRS 3 permits such companies simply to include an appropriate statement at the foot of the profit and loss account, e.g. "All recognized gains and losses are included in the profit and loss account". For such companies a STRGL will be required wherever there is a change in accounting policy.

The main point to watch out for is where a prior year adjustment arises—this should be included within the STRGL.

## 4.9 FRS 3 – Other Statements

### (a) Historical Cost Profits Note

This note, required by FRS 3 provides a reconciliation between:

- reported profit before tax (where, say, depreciation charges are based on revalued amounts); and
- profits measured on the basis of unmodified (i.e. pure) historical cost.

The note is effectively an abbreviated restatement of the profit and loss account on the basis that no asset revaluation has been made. Its aim is to put companies that have revalued assets on a more comparable basis with those who have not.

A key consideration here is the impact of incorporating fixed asset revaluations into the accounts. This practice, sometimes referred to as modified historical cost, can have two important effects:

- On disposal of a revalued asset – considered above.
- On the depreciation charge – where revaluations are incorporated into the accounts, FRS 15 requires the depreciation charge to be based upon the revalued amount (see 12.5(e)).

The note required by FRS 3 should include two pieces of information:

- a reconciliation of the reported profit on ordinary activities before tax to the equivalent historical cost amount; and
- the retained profit for the financial year reported on a historical costs basis.

*Illustration 6*

Note of historical costs profits and losses

|  | 19X8 | 19X7 |
|---|---|---|
|  | £ | £ |
| Reported profit on ordinary activities before taxation | 454,217 | 396,543 |
| Realization of property revaluation gains of previous years | 130,000 | – |
| Difference between a historical cost depreciation charge and the actual depreciation charge of the year calculated on the revalued amount | 2,000 | – |
| Historical cost profit on ordinary activities before taxation | 586,217 | 396,543 |
| Historical cost profit for the year retained after taxation, minority interests and dividends | 196,250 | 177,130 |

This note is not required if the difference between the two profit before tax figures is not material.

## (b) Movement in Shareholders Funds

A note is required reconciling the opening and closing totals of shareholders' funds, using the figures in section 4.8:

*Illustration 7*

Reconciliation of movements in shareholders' funds

|  | 19X6 | 19X5 |
|---|---|---|
|  | £ | £ |
| Profit for the financial year | 253,427 | 313,562 |
| Dividends | (90,000) | (80,000) |
|  | 163,427 | 233,562 |
| Other recognized gains and losses | 130,000 | – |
| Purchase of shares during the year | (50,000) | |
| Net addition to shareholders' funds | 243,427 | 233,562 |
| Shareholders' funds at 1 January | 860,763 | 627,201 |
| Shareholders' funds at 31 December | 1,104,190 | 860,763 |

In straightforward cases, e.g. where the only movement on shareholders' funds related to retained profit (loss), a separate statement may not be necessary.

## (c) Reserve Movements

FRS 3 states that

> "…Gains and losses may be excluded from the profit and loss account only if they are specifically permitted or required to be taken directly to reserves by this or other accounting standards, or, in the absence of a relevant accounting standard, by law".

Examples that would fall within the above statement include:

- FRS 3:
  - surplus and deficits on fixed assets revaluations; or
  - realization of property revaluation gains of previous years;
  - the difference between historical cost depreciation charge and the actual depreciation charge of the year calculated on the revalued amount.
- SSAP 20 – certain exchange differences required to be taken direct to reserves.
- SSAP 19 – changes in value of investment properties.
- Amounts required by law to be charged direct to share premium account:
  - preliminary expenses;
  - commission on issue of shares or debentures and discount on issue of debentures;
  - premium on redemption of shares or debentures (if permitted by the Companies Act 1985);
  - purchase by company of own shares (other than out of proceeds of a new issue of shares).

## (d) Reserves Note

This is not an additional requirement of FRS 3—it is the statutory note which shows the movement on each category of reserves.

*Illustration 8*

| **Reserves note** | Share premium account £ | Revaluation reserve £ | Profit & loss account £ | Total £ |
|---|---|---|---|---|
| At 1 July 19X3 | 150,000 | 296,000 | 532,000 | 978,000 |
| Transfer from profit and loss Account | – | – | 297,550 | 297,550 |
| Transfer of realized profits | | | | |
| – disposal of assets | – | (80,000) | 80,000 | – |
| – depreciation | – | (2,000) | 2,000 | – |
| Surplus on property revaluations | – | 115,000 | – | 115,000 |
| At 30 June 19X4 | 150,000 | 329,000 | 911,550 | 1,390,550 |

Explanatory notes:

(1) The £80,000 relates to a revaluation surplus, first created several years ago, and realized in the current year on the sale of the asset. The £80,000 now forms part of the company's distributable profits.

(2) The £115,000 relates to a revaluation surplus created this year. The amount would also appear in this year's statement of total recognized gains and losses.

(3) The depreciation adjustment of £2,000 represents the difference between the depreciation charges based on revaluation and historical cost respectively.

# 4.10    Prior Period Adjustments

## (a) Definition

FRS 3 defines these as "Material adjustments applicable to prior periods arising from changes in accounting policies or from the correction of fundamental errors. They do not include normal recurring adjustments or corrections of accounting estimates made in prior periods".

FRS 3 requires prior period adjustments to be accounted for by:

- Restating the comparative figures for the preceding period in the primary statements, i.e. balance sheet, profit and loss account, statement of total recognized gains and losses.
- Adjusting the opening balance of reserves for the cumulative effect.

The cumulative effect of the adjustments should also be noted at the foot of the statement of total recognized gains and losses of the current period. Where practicable, the effect of prior year adjustments on the results for the preceding period should also be disclosed.

## (b) Prior period adjustment – change of accounting policy

The example below relates to a change in the accounting treatment of development expenditure. In previous years such expenditure was capitalized and amortized over ten years. The new policy is to write off such expenditure as it is incurred. This policy is to be first adopted in the accounts for the year ended 30 June 19X5.

The calculations and relevant disclosures are set out below—please note that for simplicity, taxation has been ignored.

*Illustration 9*

**(i) Relevant Information**
The movement on intangible fixed assets under the old policy was as follows:

|  | £ |
|---|---|
| 1 July 19X3 b/f | 22,000 |
| Expenditure | 13,000 |
| Charge to p/I | (8,600) |
| 1 July 19X4 | 26,400 |

Expenditure for the year ended 30 June 19X5 amounted to £15,000. Had the old policy been continued in 19X5, the charge to p/I would have amounted to £7,200 compared with a charge under the new policy of £15,000 i.e. an increase of £7,800.

Assume that the previously reported shareholders funds at 30 June 19X4 were made up as follows:

|  | £ |
|---|---|
| Ordinary share capital | 50,000 |
| Profit and loss reserves | 120,400 |
|  | 170,400 |

### (ii) Prior year adjustment

Had the new policy been in operation last year, the intangible fixed assets shown at £26,400 at 30 June 19X4 would not have been capitalized.

The prior year adjustment at 1 July 19X4 is therefore £26,400.

The effect of adopting the new policy is to reduce shareholders funds at 1 July 19X4 by £26,400 i.e. to £144,000.

### (iii) Relevant disclosures

The relevant disclosures required, so far as information permits, are as follows:

*Statement of recognized gains and losses*

|  | 19X5 £ | Restated 19X4 £ |
|---|---|---|
| Profit for the financial year | X | X |
| Total recognized gains and losses relating to the year | X | X |
| Prior year adjustment | (26,400) | |
| Total gains and losses recognized since last annual report | XX | |

*Reconciliation of movements in shareholders' funds*

|  | 19X5 £ | Restated 19X4 £ |
|---|---|---|
| Profit for the financial year | X | X |
| Dividends | (X) | (X) |
| Net addition to shareholders' funds | X | X |
| Opening shareholders' funds (originally £170,400 before deducting prior year adjustment of £26,400) | 144,000 | X |
| Closing shareholders' funds | XX | XX |

*Reserves note*

|  | Profit and loss account £ |
|---|---|
| At 1 July 19X4 | |
| − as previously reported | 120,400 |
| Prior year adjustment | 26,400 |
| − as restated | 94,000 |
| Retained profit for the year | X |
| At 30 June l9X5 | XX |

Accounting policy note (extract)

Change of accounting policy

In prior years, the Group has capitalised expenditure on major software and development projects where it believed that a sustainable value had been created. However, in line with current prevailing accounting practice it is now felt that a more appropriate policy is to write off all such expenditure as incurred. Prior years' figures have been restated to bring them into line with this policy. The effect is to reduce shareholders' funds as at 30 June 19X4 by £26,400 and to reduce operating and pro-tax profits for 19X5 by £7,800 (19X4, £4,400).

## Illustration 10

Extract from annual report and accounts of Lincat Group plc, year ended 30 June 2003.

**Accounting policies (extract)**

...

**a) Change of accounting policy**
Given the significance of Warranty provisions in recent years, the directors consider it appropriate that these should be disclosed separately under 'Provisions for liabilities and charges' and an accounting policy included. The warranty provision has historically been included within 'Other creditors'. Note 23 sets out the impact of this change on current and prior year financial statements.

**Note 23, Prior year adjustment**

The prior year adjustment relates to the reclassification of product warranties of £462,000 within provisions for liabilities and other charges. These were previously included in other creditors.
    The change in accounting policies had the following effect on the Group's financial statements:

|  | 2003 £'000 | 2002 £'000 |
|---|---|---|
| **Balance sheet** | | |
| Reduction in other creditors | (489) | (462) |
| Increase in provisions | 489 | 462 |
| Change in shareholders' funds | – | – |
| **Cash flow** | | |
| Change in creditors | (27) | (190) |
| Change in provisions | 27 | 190 |
| Change in net cash inflow from operating activities | – | – |

**Profit and loss account**
    The prior year adjustment has had no effect on current or prior year profits.

# (c) Prior Period Adjustment – Correction of Fundamental Error

## (i) Examples
    Examples of fundamental errors could include:

- The discovery that last year's stock figure was wrong because of the omission of an important section of stock.

- A fraud carried out over a number of years by a senior employee involving fictitious invoices which had been paid to a separate company.
- A systems breakdown which had not been detected at the time but which came to light in the following year.

## (ii) Requirements

The key issue is whether fundamental errors should be corrected within the figures for the current period or as prior year adjustments through reserves and comparatives.

The key reference is paragraph 63 of FRS 3, in the standard's Explanation section.

> "In exceptional circumstances it may be found that financial statements of prior periods have been issued containing errors which are of such significance as to destroy the true and fair view and hence the validity of those financial statements.
>
> The corrections of such fundamental errors and the cumulative adjustments applicable to prior periods have no bearing on the results of the current period and are therefore not included in arriving at the profit or loss for the current period. They are accounted for by restating prior periods with the result that the opening balance of retained profits will be adjusted accordingly, and highlighted in the reconciliation of movements in shareholders' funds...".

In practical terms, two possible situations may arise.

(1) Where the financial effects of the error(s) can be reliably allocated between accounting periods – a "proper" FRS 3 prior year adjustment should be accounted for.
(2) This procedure should be followed in "normal" cases where reliable information is available.

## Illustration 11

Extract from annual report and accounts of Reliance Security Group plc, year ended 25 April 2003.

**Financial Review (extract)**
**Prior year adjustments and exceptional items**

In October last year, we announced the correction of accounting errors in Reliance High-Tech Limited, our electronic systems specialist, and the write-off of goodwill relating to its acquisition. In accordance with account requirements, the resulting charges of £5.3 million have been treated as prior year adjustments and prior year comparatives have been restated accordingly. There is no impact on the Group's profits for the year ended 25 April 2003.

The £6.6 million write-down in the carrying value of the Group's investments in Chesterton International plc and Command Security Corporation is explained fully in the Chairman's Statement.

...

**Group statement of total recognised gains and losses**

for the year ended 25 April 2003

| | Note | 2003 £'000 | *Restated* 2002 £'000 |
|---|---|---|---|
| **Profit for the financial year** | | | |
| Group | | **3,742** | 3,424 |
| Associates | | **(1,646)** | 1,531 |
| | | **2,096** | 4,955 |
| Loss on foreign currency translation | | **(74)** | – |
| **Total recognised gains relating to the year** | | **2,022** | 4,955 |
| Cumulative effect of prior year adjustments | 9 | **(5,256)** | |
| **Total gains and losses recognised since last financial statements** | | **(3,234)** | |

## Illustration 12

Extract from annual report and accounts of Honeycombe Leisure plc, year ended 30 April 2003.

### Note 1 – Prior period adjustments

Following a review, the Directors now consider that it was inappropriate to recognise certain income in the accounts for the period ended 28 April 2002. Bad and doubtful debt provisions against trade debtors and insurance claims should have been made. In addition, a number of other individually small items were identified relating to asset write offs and unaccrued liabilities. These errors have been corrected by making a prior period adjustment of £563,502 (net of tax) for the period to 28 April 2002 and £259,307 (net of tax) for prior periods.

The effect of these changes is as follows:

| | 2002 £ |
|---|---|
| **Profit and loss account** | |
| Cost of sales | (61,370) |
| Administrative expenses | (626,907) |
| Tax – deferred tax | 124,775 |
| Decrease in profit for the financial period | (563,502) |
| Decrease in profit and loss account brought forward | (259,307) |
| | (822,809) |
| **Balance sheet** | |
| Decrease in stock | (61,370) |
| Decrease in debtors | (819,479) |
| Increase in accruals | (190,350) |
| Decrease in provision for liabilities and charges – deferred tax | 248,390 |
| Decrease in net assets | (822,809) |

## Illustration 13

Extract from annual report and accounts of Honeycombe Leisure plc, year ended 27 April 2003.

**Note 4 – exceptional items**

The exceptional items relate to the following items:

|  | 2003 | 2002 |
|---|---|---|
| Cost of sales: |  |  |
| Discounts foregone due to renegotiation of trading agreements | – | 66,000 |
|  |  |  |
| Administrative expenses: |  |  |
| Additional costs following the acquisition of Devonshire Pub Company Ltd | – | 436,709 |
| Impairment of non-trading asset | 300,000 | – |
| Professional fees in connection with an aborted warranty claim | 112,827 | – |
| Costs associated with the management agreement with Nectar Taverns Plc | 34,060 | 50,350 |
| Sundry asset write offs | 163,170 | – |
|  | 610,057 | 487,059 |

## Illustration 14

Extract from annual report and accounts of Honeycombe Leisure plc, year ended 27 April 2003.

**Consolidated profit and loss account, year ended 27 April 2003 (extract)**

|  | Note | 2003 £ | 2003 £ | 2002 Restated £ | 2002 Restated £ |
|---|---|---|---|---|---|
| **Turnover** | 2 | 32,971,147 |  | 32,451,688 |  |
|  |  |  | 32,971,147 |  | 32,451,688 |
| **Cost of sales** |  |  |  |  |  |
| – exceptional | 4 | – |  | (66,000) |  |
| – other |  | (20,034,012) |  | (19,636,680) |  |
|  |  |  | (20,034,012) |  | (19,702,680) |
| **Gross profit** |  |  | 12,937,135 |  | 12,749,008 |
| Distribution costs |  |  | 418,649 |  | 327,552 |
| Administrative expenses |  |  |  |  |  |
| – exceptional | 4 | 610,057 |  | 487,059 |  |
| – other |  | 8,376,904 |  | 8,421,293 |  |
|  |  |  | 8,986,961 |  | 8,908,352 |
| **Operating Profit** | 3 |  | 3,531,525 |  | 3,513,104 |

...

# 4.11   Comparative Figures

An aspect of FRS 3 that has attracted little comment is the issue of comparative figures for companies whose operations fall to be classified as between continuing and discontinued.

Paragraph 64 of FRS concludes by stating:

> "... Similarly, the comparative figures for discontinued operations will include both amounts relating to operations discontinued in the previous period and amounts relating to operations discontinued in the period under review, which in the previous period would have been included as part of continuing operations...".

# 4.12   International Financial Reporting Standards

IAS 1, Presentation of financial statements, sets out overall requirements for presentation of financial statements, guidelines for their structure, and minimum requirements for their content. A complete set of financial statements should comprise: Balance sheet; Income statement; Equity statement; Cash flow statement.

## Balance sheet

The standard offers two main balance sheet formats:

*Format 1*

This format is equivalent to the "Net assets" format used currently by almost all UK companies.

*Format 2*

This format presents total assets (split between non-current and current) in the top part of the balance sheet, with total equity and liabilities (split between non-current and current) in the bottom part.

## Income statement

As regards the Income statement, the choice is between:

*Format 1*

This format analyses expenses by function (for example, cost of sales; distribution; administrative), and is the option currently preferred by the majority of UK companies.

*Format 2*

This format analyses expense by nature or type of expense (for example, raw materials; employee benefits; depreciation, etc), and is used mainly by a minority of larger UK companies.

## Equity statement

IAS 1 offers a choice of alternative Equity statement formats:

Format 1 – a columnar format that reconciles opening and closing balances for each element within equity; or

Format 2 – to present a Statement of recognized income and expense. This is identical to the Statement of total recognized gains and losses (STRGL).

## Exceptional items

IAS 1 does not refer to exceptional items as such, but requires separate disclosure of the nature and amount of material items of income and expenditure such as:

- Inventory and plant write-downs (and reversals of such write-downs);
- Restructuring costs;
- Disposals of items of property, plant and equipment;
- Discontinued operations;
- Litigation settlements.

IAS 1 does not make a distinction between "operating" and "non-operating" exceptional items.

In addition, IAS 1 does not mandate a separate line item for operating profit, although it does require additional line items and subtotals to be presented on the face of the income statement where this is relevant to an understanding of the entity's financial performance.

IAS 1 prohibits the use of extraordinary items.

---

**Frequently Asked Questions**

1  Does CA 85 give any options as regards where the balance sheet totals should be drawn under Schedule 4/8?

   CA 85 allows the balance sheet total to be drawn at any point provided the balance sheet follows the strict sequence of items under Schedule 4/8 and presents any mandatory caption headings or subtotals shown in the formats in Schedule 4/8.

2  Does FRS 3 allow operating exceptional items to be shown as separate line items (assuming CA 85 format 1 is followed).

   No—exceptional items which are required to be taken into account in determining operating profit must be allocated to format headings (for example, cost of sales, distribution costs and administrative expenses).

3  When is a Statement of total recognized gains and losses (STRGL) *not* required?

   STRGL is not required if all gains and losses arising during the year have been included in the profit and loss account.

   STRGL is required where accounting policy change this year gives rise to prior period adjustment, but not if the policy change took place last year (i.e. a STRGL not required simply because prior period adjustment arose last year).

# Cash Flow Statements

**This chapter covers:**
* Scope
* Exemptions
* Form and content – single companies
* The direct method and the indirect method
* Operating activities' cash flows
* Returns on investments and servicing of finance
* Taxation
* Investing activities
* Financing
* Cash
* Additional notes
* Problem areas
* Group cash flow statements
* How cash flow statements are presented in practice
* Using cash flow statements
* International Financial Reporting Standards

## 5.1 Background and Scope

FRS 1, Cash flow statements applies to all financial statements intended to give a true and fair view of financial position and profit or loss but is not mandatory for the following entities:

(a) Certain subsidiaries which are included in consolidated accounts—provided specific conditions are satisfied:
  • 90% or more of the voting rights must be controlled within the group;
  • the consolidated accounts must be "publicly available";
  • "publicly available", a term used also in FRS 8 on Related party disclosures, is not defined. However, it seems reasonable to assume that the consolidated accounts must be filed in a public registry. Additionally, it may be advisable to state in the subsidiary's accounts where the consolidated accounts may be obtained.

(b) Mutual life assurance companies.

(c) Pension funds.

(d) Certain open-ended investment funds – as defined in FRS 1.

(e) Building societies.

(f) Small companies entitled under the Companies Act 1985 to file abbreviated accounts.

(g) Entities that would have qualified as small companies as per (f) above had they been companies incorporated under Companies Act 1985 – e.g. accounts of small unincorporated entities intended to present a true and fair view.

### Not exempt

The implications of the above are that the following are not exempt from publishing cash flow statements (unless they fall within (a) above):

- PLCs – big and small;
- Financial services companies (authorized persons under the Financial Services Act 1986);
- Medium-sized companies;
- Medium-sized groups:
  - if group accounts are prepared, the cash flow statement will relate to the group;
  - if the exemption from the preparation of group accounts is claimed, the cash flow statement will be that of the parent company.

## 5.2 Format and Content – Single Companies

### (a) Basic Elements of the Statement

Individual cash flows should be classified under certain standard headings according to the activities that gave rise to them.

The standard headings required by FRS 1 are:

- operating activities;
- returns on investments and servicing of finance;
- taxation;
- capital expenditure and financial investment;
- acquisitions and disposals;
- equity dividends paid;
- management of liquid resources;
- financing.

The cash flow statement then concludes with changes in cash.

### (b) Operating Activities – Methods of Computation

The net cash inflow from operating activities can be calculated and presented in two alternative ways – the direct method and the indirect method.

Both methods are referred to in this chapter although in practice almost all UK companies use the indirect method.

*(i) Direct method*
The inflows and outflows relating to operating activities are derived directly from the company's records and summarized as follows:

|  | £ |
|---|---|
| Cash received from customers | X |
| Cash payments to suppliers | (X) |
| Cash paid to and on behalf of employees | (X) |
| Other cash payments | (X) |
| Net cash inflow from operating activities | X |

Where the direct method is used, the above information should appear on the face of the cash flow statement. In practice, the use of this method is rare.

*(ii) Indirect method*
Under this method the net cash inflow (outflow) from operating activities is derived directly from operating profit.
Calculation of net cash inflow from operating activities:

|  | £ |
|---|---|
| Operating profit | X |
| Depreciation charges | X |
| Increase in stocks | (X) |
| Increase in debtors | (X) |
| Increase in creditors | X |
| Net cash inflow from operating activities | X |

Operating profit is determined on an accruals basis i.e. after adjusting for opening and closing stocks, debtors and creditors and after charging depreciation. The above calculation thus converts accruals-based profit to net cash inflow.

*Illustration 1*

The balance sheets of Bamford Ltd at 31.12.X3 and 31.12.X2 were as follows:

|  | 31.12.X3 £ | 31.12.X2 £ |
|---|---|---|
| Tangible fixed assets – freehold property | 301,000 | 391,000 |
| Tangible fixed assets – plant and machinery | 225,600 | 160,200 |
| Stock | 520,000 | 440,000 |
| Debtors | 83,100 | 53,100 |
| Cash | 70,300 | 1,700 |
| Investment in Upton Ltd | 200,000 | – |
|  | 1,400,000 | 1,046,000 |

|  | 31.12.X3 | 31.12.X2 |
|---|---:|---:|
|  | £ | £ |
| Called-up share capital (£1 shares) | 150,000 | 100,000 |
| Profit and loss account | 615,000 | 405,000 |
| Share premium account | 100,000 | – |
| Long-term loans | – | 170,000 |
| Creditors | 65,000 | 51,000 |
| Corporation tax | 350,000 | 230,000 |
| Proposed dividends | 120,000 | 90,000 |
|  | 1,400,000 | 1,046,000 |

**Additional information**

(1) *Extracts from profit and loss account for year ended 31 December 19X3*

|  | £ | £ |
|---|---:|---:|
| Operating profit |  | 760,000 |
| Corporation tax |  | 350,000 |
| Profit on ordinary activities after tax |  | 410,000 |
| Dividends on ordinary shares |  |  |
| Interim (paid) | 80,000 |  |
| Final (proposed) | 120,000 | 200,000 |
| Retained profit |  | 210,000 |
| Balance at 1.1.X3 |  | 405,000 |
| Balance at 31.12.X3 |  | 615,000 |

(2) During the year, depreciation charged on plant and machinery amounted £16,400. There were no disposals of plant and machinery.

(3) Freehold property with a net book value at sale of £90,000 was sold for net book value.

(4) The investment in Upton Ltd is held as a fixed asset investment. No dividends were received during the year.

(5) A further 50,000 £1 shares were issued during the year for cash.

Net cash inflow is calculated as follows:

|  | £ |
|---|---:|
| Operating profit | 760,000 |
| Depreciation | 16,400 |
| Increase in stocks | 80,000 |
| Increase in debtors | 30,000 |
| Increase in creditors | 14,000 |
| Net cash inflow from operating activities | 680,400 |

This reconciliation should not appear on the face of the cash flow statement but should be included by way of note.

The cash flow statement may be completed as follows:

|  | £ | £ |
|---|---:|---:|
| Net cash inflow from operating activities |  | 680,400 |
| Returns on investment and servicing of finance |  |  |
| Tax paid |  | (230,000) |
| Capital expenditure and financial investment |  |  |
| Payments to acquire fixed assets | (81,800) |  |
| Sale of fixed assets | 90,000 |  |
| Purchase of investments | (200,000) |  |

| | £ | £ |
|---|---:|---:|
| | | (191,800) |
| Equity dividends paid | | (170,000) |
| Cash inflow before financing | | 88,600 |
| Financing | | |
| Issue of shares | 150,000 | |
| Repayment of loans | (170,000) | |
| | | (20,000) |
| Increase in cash in the period | | 68,600 |

**Workings:**

| (1) Purchase of plant | |
|---|---:|
| NBV b/f | 160,200 |
| Additions (balancing figure) | 81,800 |
| Depreciation | (16,400) |
| NBV c/f | 225,600 |

| (2) Equity dividends paid | |
|---|---:|
| Proposed 19X2 | 90,000 |
| Interim 19X3 | 80,000 |
| | 170,000 |

## (c) Operating Activities – Further Considerations

Cash flows from operating activities are essentially the cash effects of transactions and other events relating to operating or trading activities.

The reconciliation between operating profit and net cash flow from operating activities should be given as a note to the accounts. It may alternatively be included above the cash flow statement, provided it is not described as forming part of the statement.

The reconciliation should disclose separately:

(1) movements in stock, debtors and creditors;
(2) other differences between cash flows and profits.

### (1) Movements in debtors and creditors
These two items are likely to include the following elements:

- trade debtors and trade creditors;
- accruals and prepayments;
- VAT debtors and creditors;
- creditors and PAYE and NI.

The following should not be included:

- other creditors – e.g. movement on creditors for fixed assets would be used to calculate the cash flow for fixed asset purchases disclosed under investing activities;
- dividend creditors – dividends paid are disclosed under "returns on investments and servicing of finance";
- corporation tax debtors and creditors – these are used to calculate the taxation cash flows in the taxation section of the cash flow statement.

*(2)  Other differences between cash flows and operating profits*
These will normally include:

- depreciation on owned assets and on assets subject to finance leases;
- provisions relating to "operating profit items" – for example, provisions for:
  - warranty costs for goods sold,
  - vacant leasehold property,
  - redundancy and reorganization costs classified as exceptional items in the profit and loss account,
- profits and losses on sale of fixed assets.

## (d)  Returns on Investments and Servicing of Finance

*(1)  Cash inflows*
These include:

- interest received (including any related tax recovered);
- dividends received.

*(2)  Cash outflows*
These include:

- interest paid including any tax deducted and paid over. This will include all interest paid irrespective of whether it is charged in the profit and loss account or capitalized in the balance sheet (e.g. under development properties);
- non-equity dividends paid;
- interest (or finance charge) element of finance lease rental payments.

## (e)  Taxation

In the majority of cases this part will simply include payments of corporation tax. It will not include payments of PAYE and NI—these are part of the cash flows from operating activities.

VAT receipts and payments will usually be dealt with under operating activities cash flow. However, in cases where VAT is irrecoverable, the related tax should be dealt with under the appropriate heading in the cash flow statement.

## (f)  Capital Expenditure and Financial Investment

*(1)  General considerations*
This part of the cash flow statement should include cash flows related to the acquisition or disposal of any asset held, other than those required to be classified under "acquisitions and disposals".

*(2)  Cash inflows*

- receipts from sales or disposals of fixed assets;
- receipts from sale of investments in entities other than subsidiaries and associates;

- receipts from repayment of loans made to other entities by the reporting entity.

*(3) Cash outflows*
These include:

- payments to acquire fixed assets;
- payments to acquire fixed assets investments (other than subsidiaries and associates);
- payments to acquire investments in other entities;
- loans made by the reporting entity (other than cash equivalents).

## (g) Acquisitions and Disposals

This should include cash flows related to the acquisition or disposal of any trade or business, associate, joint venture or subsidiary undertaking.

## (h) Equity Dividends Paid

Cash outflows include dividends paid on the reporting entity's equity shares.

## (i) Management of Liquid Resources

This includes cash flows in respect of liquid resources such as short-term deposits, government securities and quoted shares.

## (j) Financing

*(1) General considerations*
This part of the cash flow statement should include receipts from or repayments to external providers of finance of amounts relating to principal amounts of finance.

*(2) Cash inflows*
These include:

- receipts from issuing shares or other equity instruments;
- receipts from issuing:
  - debentures,
  - loans,
  - notes,
  - bonds,
  - other long and short-term borrowings (other than those included within cash equivalents).

*(3) Cash outflows*
These include:

- repayments of amounts borrowed (other than those included within cash equivalents);

- the capital element of finance lease rental payments;
- payments to re-acquire or redeem the entity's shares;
- expenses or commissions paid in relation to any issue of shares, debentures, loans, notes, bonds or other financing.

## (k)  Cash

Cash is essentially cash in hand and deposits repayable on demand with any qualifying financial institution, less overdrafts from any qualifying financial institution repayable on demand. Cash includes cash in hand and deposits denominated in foreign currencies.

## (l)  Additional Notes

(1) Net cash flow from operating activities: the cash flow statement should include a reconciliation between operating profit and net cash flow from operating activities (comparitives are required).
(2) Reconciliation to net debt: the aim of this new reconciliation is to link together cash changes with changes in net debt. This reconciliation, together with that of operating profit to operating cash flow, should ensure a close link between the information in the cash flow statement with that in the profit and loss account and the balance sheet (comparitives are required).

The reconciliation may be positioned adjoining the cash flow statement (clearly labelled and kept separate) or alternatively in a separate note.

Changes in net debt should be analysed down from opening to closing and showing separately (comparitives are *not* required):

- cash flows of the entity,
- acquisition or disposal of subsidiary undertakings,
- other non-cash changes,
- recognition of changes in market value and exchange rate movements.

# 5.3    Worked Example – A Single Company Using the Indirect Method

## (a)  Basic Information

*Illustration 2*

The summarized balance sheets of Waddev plc are as follows:

|  | 31.12.X8 | 31.12.X7 |
| --- | --- | --- |
|  | £'000 | £'000 |
| Freehold property | 1,096 | 1,100 |
| Plant and machinery (cost less aggregate depreciation) | 726 | 732 |
| Stock | 537 | 365 |
| Trade debtors | 413 | 236 |

|  | 31.12.X8 £'000 | 31.12. X7 £'000 |
|---|---|---|
| Prepayments | 19 | 22 |
| Cash at bank | 212 | 35 |
|  | 3,003 | 2,490 |
| £1 ordinary shares | 1,000 | 800 |
| Revenue reserves | 929 | 619 |
| Share premium account | 400 | 300 |
| Bank loan | – | 250 |
| Trade creditors | 184 | 158 |
| Other creditors | – | 50 |
| Accrued expenses | 35 | 25 |
| Corporation tax | 395 | 243 |
| Proposed dividend | 60 | 45 |
|  | 3,003 | 2,490 |

## PROFIT AND LOSS ACCOUNT

### for the year ended 31 December 19X8

|  | £'000 | £'000 |
|---|---|---|
| Turnover |  | 2,960 |
| Opening stock | 365 |  |
| Purchases | 2,073 |  |
|  | 2,438 |  |
| Less closing stock | 537 |  |
| Cost of sales |  | 1,901 |
| Gross profit |  | 1,059 |
| Distribution costs and administrative expenses |  | 197 |
| Depreciation – buildings | 4 |  |
| – plant | 65 |  |
| – over provision on disposals of plant | (7) | 62 |
| Profit before tax |  | 800 |
| Corporation tax |  | 395 |
| Profit after tax |  | 405 |
| Dividends – paid | 35 |  |
| – proposed | 60 | 95 |
| Retained profit added to reserves |  | 310 |

## (b) Basic Approach

Under the indirect method, cash flow statement items are essentially derived from: a comparison of opening and closing balance sheets; a profit and loss account and additional information. The method illustrated below makes use of a simple work sheet which readily lends itself to a computer spreadsheet.

It is important to bear in mind that the effect of non-cash items is excluded from the cash flow statement. For example, suppose a company issues debenture stock as consideration for the acquisition of a property. Neither the increase in debentures nor the increase in the property will appear in the cash flow statement.

WORKSHEET – CASH FLOW STATEMENT OF WADDEV PLC

for the year ended 19X8 (£'000)

| | Balance sheet | | | Cash flow statement headings | | | | | | |
| Item | 31.12.X8 B/S A | 31.12.X7 B/S B | Change C (B – A) | Operating activities D | Returns E | Tax F | Capital expenditure G | Equity dividends paid H | Financing I | Cash J |
|---|---|---|---|---|---|---|---|---|---|---|
| Land & buildings | 1,096 | 1,100 | 4 | 4 | | | | | | |
| Plant & machinery | 726 | 732 | 6 | 58 | | | 128 (180) | | | |
| Stocks | 537 | 365 | (172) | (172) | | | | | | |
| Debtors | 413 | 236 | (177) | (177) | | | | | | |
| Prepayments | 19 | 22 | 3 | 3 | | | | | | |
| Cash | 212 | 35 | (177) | | | | | | | (177) |
| Trade creditors | (184) | (158) | 26 | 26 | | | | | | |
| Other creditors | – | (50) | (50) | | | | (50) | | | |
| Accrued expenses | (35) | (25) | 10 | 10 | | | | | | |
| Tax | (395) | (243) | 152 | | | 152 | | | | |
| Dividends | (60) | (45) | 15 | | | | | 15 | | |
| Loan | – | (250) | (250) | | | | | | (250) | |
| OSC | (1,000) | (800) | 200 | | | | | | 300 | |
| S. Prem | (400) | (300) | 100 | | | | | | | |
| P/L B/F | (619) | (619) | – | | | | | | | |
| Profit before tax | (800) | – | 800 | 800 | | | | | | |
| Tax | 395 | – | (395) | | | (395) | | | | |
| Dividends | 95 | – | (95) | | | | | (95) | | |
| Total | 0 | 0 | 0 | 552 | – | (243) | (102) | (80) | 50 | (177) |

## (c) How the Work Sheet Should be Completed

The key items in the cash flow statement may be derived by completing the following steps:

(1) Enter the closing and opening balance sheets in columns A and B respectively. The closing profit and loss reserves is split between balance B/F; operating profit; tax; dividends.

(2) Calculate the difference between each respective item in columns A and B. Enter the result in column C, taking care over brackets! Column C should total to zero.

(3) The changes in the stock, debtors and creditors items affecting operating profit should be extended into column D. Other creditors relates to fixed assets and so the change (i.e. decrease) of £50,000 is extended into column G. The total depreciation charges of £4,000 for building and £58,000 for plant should also be entered in column D. The items in column D represent the components of the operating profit/cash inflow reconciliation.
The total of column D, £552,000, represents the net cash inflow.

(4) The change in dividend creditors is extended into column H. The total of column H represents equity dividends paid.

(5) The change in tax creditors is extended into column F. The total of column F represents tax paid.

(6) For land and buildings/plant, the combined effect of columns C and D is extended into column G and analysed between acquisitions and disposals. When these are combined with the "other creditors" change and totalled, the figures of £128,000 and £230,000 represent the receipts and payments in respect of fixed asset transactions.

(7) In this example columns I and J are straightforward.

**Solution**

## (d) Waddev plc – Cash Flow Statement

For the year ended 31 December 19X8 using the indirect method.

|  | £'000 | £'000 |
|---|---|---|
| Net cash inflow from operating activities |  | 552 |
| Taxation – corporation tax paid |  | (243) |
| Capital expenditure |  |  |
| Purchase of tangible fixed assets | 230 |  |
| Sale of tangible fixed assets | (128) |  |
|  |  | (102) |
| Equity dividends paid |  | (80) |
| Net cash inflow before financing |  | 127 |
| Financing |  |  |
| Issue of share capital | 300 |  |
| Bank loan repaid | (250) |  |
|  |  | 50 |
| Increase in cash during the period |  | 177 |

*Note 1: Reconciliation of operating profit to net cash in flow from operating activities.*

|  | £,000 |
|---|---|
| Operating profit | 800 |
| Depreciation charges | 62 |
| Increase in stocks | (172) |
| Increase in debtors | (177) |
| Decrease in prepayments | 3 |
| Increase in trade creditors | 26 |
| Increase in accured expenses | 10 |
| Net cash inflow from operating activities | 522 |

*Note 2: Reconciliation of net cash flow to movement in net debt*

|  | £'000 |
|---|---|
| Increase in cash during the period | 177 |
| Cash used to repay bank loan | 250 |
| Change in net debt | 427 |
| Net debt at 1.1.X8 | (215) |
| Net funds at 31.12.X8 | 212 |

*Note 3: Analysis of changes in net debt*

|  | At 1.1 19X8 £'000 | Cash Flows £'000 | At 31.12.19X8 £'000 |
|---|---|---|---|
| Cash in hand and at bank | 35 | 177 | 212 |
| Bank loan | (250) | 250 | – |
| Net debt (funds) | (215) | 427 | 212 |

# 5.4    Problem Areas – Single Companies

## (a) Finance Leases

Finance lease payments are split between the finance charge element (returns on investments and servicing of finance) and the capital element (financing).

Where significant finance lease commitments have been entered into during the year, these may need to be reported by way of note to the accounts under the heading "major non-cash transactions".

## (b) Non-Cash Transactions

The basic principle is that transactions which do not result in cash flows of the reporting entity should not be reported in the cash flow statement.

However, para 48 of FRS 1 states:

"Material transactions not resulting in movements of cash of the reporting entity should be disclosed in the notes to the cash flow statement if disclosure is necessary for an understanding of the underlying transactions".

Although FRS 1 refers to the notes to the cash flow statement, these may be integrated with other notes to the accounts.

Possible examples include:

- significant finance lease commitments entered into shortly before the end of the year;
- convertible loan stock converted during the year into equity shares;
- property assets exchanged for equity in another entity;
- transactions with both cash and non-cash elements, e.g. purchase of shares in a subsidiary undertaking by a combination of cash and shares consideration.

## 5.5  Group Accounts Considerations

### (a) General Approach

A group cash flow statement should deal only with flows of cash and cash equivalents external to the group.

In practice, many subsidiary undertakings are likely to be wholly owned and therefore exempt from preparing cash flow statements under the exemption referred to earlier. In addition, a large number of groups (if not the majority) are likely to opt for the indirect method.

Whenever possible therefore, the group cash flow statements will be derived directly from the consolidated accounts. This approach will be simpler as the effect of inter-company transactions will already have been eliminated on consolidation.

### (b) Dividends Paid to Minority Shareholders

These should be disclosed separately under the heading returns on investments and servicing of finance, whether they relate to equity or non-equity shares.

### (c) Associated Undertakings

Care should be taken over the cash flows of any entity such as an associated undertaking, which is equity-accounted in the consolidated accounts. The group cash flow statement should only include the entity's cash flows to the extent that they result in actual cash flows between the group and the entity concerned.

Examples of such cash flows could include:

- dividends received – required by FRS 9 to be separately disclosed before returns on investments, etc (returns on investment and servicing of finance);
- shares in associated undertakings (investing);
- loans from associated undertaking (financing).

### (d) Acquisitions and Disposals of Subsidiary Undertakings

Amounts of cash and cash equivalents paid or received in respect of acquisitions and disposals of subsidiary undertakings will be included under the "acquisitions and disposals" heading. FRS 1 effectively requires a one-line approach.

Note that the amounts should be net of any cash balances transferred as part of the purchase or sale of the subsidiary undertaking.

The group cash flow statement should include a note giving a summary of the effects of acquisitions and disposals indicating:

(1) how much of the consideration comprised cash and cash equivalents; and
(2) the amounts of cash transferred as a result of the acquisitions and disposals.

The group cash flow statement should include the cash flows of the subsidiary undertaking for the same period as that for which the subsidiary undertakings results are included in the profit and loss account.

Paragraph 45 states:

'... Material effects on amounts reported under each of the standard headings reflecting the cash flows of a subsidiary undertaking acquired or disposed of in the period should be disclosed, as far as practicable. This information could be given by dividing cash flows between continuing and discontinued operations and acquisitions'.

## (e) Foreign Subsidiaries

Cash flows of foreign subsidiaries should be included in the group cash flow statement on the same basis as that used for translating the results of the subsidiaries for consolidated profit and loss account purposes.

The effect of exchange rate changes should be dealt with in the balance sheet reconciliation note. This is dealt with in paragraph 44 of FRS 1 and for some groups will be a particularly complex area.

## (f) Non-cash Transactions

An example relevant to groups is the acquisition of a subsidiary undertaking partly by the issue of shares, partly by the payment of cash (see below).

(Illustrations of presentations for groups are included in the appendix to FRS, 1, illustrative example 2 (not reproduced), see below.)

# 5.6 Worked Example – A Group

## (a) Basic Information

The consolidated balance sheets of Southdale plc at 31.12.X3 and 31.12.X2 were as follows:

|  | 31.12.X3 £ | 31.12.X2 £ |
|---|---|---|
| Tangible fixed assets | 1,068,900 | 640,600 |
| Goodwill on consolidation | 320,000 | 250,000 |
| Shares in associated undertakings | 245,000 | 206,000 |
| Stock | 586,000 | 492,000 |
| Debtors | 307,000 | 164,000 |
| Cash | 71,100 | 32,100 |
|  | 2,598,000 | 1,784,700 |

|                                                 | 31.12.X3  | 31.12.X2  |
|-------------------------------------------------|-----------|-----------|
|                                                 | £         | £         |
| Called-up share capital                         | 210,000   | 50,000    |
| Profit and loss account                         | 701,000   | 580,000   |
| Revaluation reserve                             | 320,000   | 100,000   |
| Share premium account                           | 160,000   | –         |
| Minority interest:                              |           |           |
|   Ordinary share capital and reserves | 325,000   | 295,000   |
|   Dividends payable                   | 16,000    | 13,700    |
| Corporation tax                                 | 380,000   | 360,000   |
| Proposed dividends                              | 190,000   | 165,000   |
| Creditors                                       | 296,000   | 221,000   |
|                                                 | 2,598,000 | 1,784,700 |

*Additional information*

(1) Extracts from consolidated profit and loss account for year ended 31 December 19X3

|                                          | £       | £       |
|------------------------------------------|---------|---------|
| Operating profit                         |         | 850,000 |
| Profit of associated undertaking         |         | 120,000 |
| Profit on ordinary activities before tax |         | 970,000 |
| Corporation tax                          |         |         |
|   Group                        | 380,000 |         |
|   Associated undertaking       | 50,000  | 430,000 |
| Profit on ordinary activities after tax  |         | 540,000 |
| Minority interest                        |         | 69,000  |
|                                          |         | 471,000 |
| Dividends on ordinary shares             |         |         |
|   Interim (paid)               | 160,000 |         |
|   Final (proposed)             | 190,000 | 350,000 |
| Retained profit                          |         | 121,000 |
| Balance at 1.1.X3                        |         | 580,000 |
| Balance at 31.12.X3                      |         | 701,000 |

(2) During the year, the group acquired a wholly owned subsidiary, Dunster Ltd. The details of the acquisition were:

|                                               | £        |
|-----------------------------------------------|----------|
| Purchase consideration:                       |          |
|   160,000 £1 ordinary shares issued at £2 | 320,000 |
|   Cash                              | 20,000   |
|                                               | 340,000  |
| Tangible fixed assets                         | 140,000  |
| Goodwill on consolidation                     | 70,000   |
| Stock                                         | 70,000   |
| Debtors                                       | 85,000   |
| Cash                                          | 5,000    |
| Creditors                                     | (30,000) |
|                                               | 340,000  |

(3) Details of tangible fixed assets:

|  | Freehold Property £ | Machinery and vehicles £ | Total £ |
|---|---|---|---|
| NBV at 1.1.X3 | 410,000 | 230,600 | 640,600 |
| Additions | 55,000 | 195,000 | 250,000 |
| Revaluation | 220,000 | – | 220,000 |
| Depreciation | (10,000) | (31,700) | (41,700) |
|  | 675,000 | 393,900 | 1,068,900 |

(Comparative figures are required in published accounts but are ignored in this example.)

## (b) Workings

### (1) Associated undertaking
The relevant information may be summarized as follows:

|  | £ | £ |
|---|---|---|
| Investment (shares) |  |  |
| 31.12.X3 |  | 245,000 |
| 31.12.X2 |  | 206,000 |
| Increase (= retained profit) |  | 39,000 |
| Share of profits | 120,000 |  |
| Share of tax | 50,000 | 70,000 |
| ∴ Dividends received |  | 31,000 |

### (2) Dividends paid to parent company shareholders

|  | £ |
|---|---|
| Last year proposed final | 165,000 |
| This year interim paid | 160,000 |
|  | 325,000 |

### (3) Minority interest
To the extent that a partly owned subsidiary pays dividends to its minority shareholders, there is an outflow of cash from the group.

Dividends paid to minority shareholders may be calculated in the above example as a balancing item by reconstructing a minority interest account as follows:

MINORITY INTEREST ACCOUNT

|  | £ |  | £ |
|---|---|---|---|
| Cash paid (balancing figure) | 36,700 | Balances at 1.1.X3 |  |
| Balances at 31.12.X3 |  | OSC + reserves b/d | 295,000 |
| OSC + reserves c/d | 325,000 | Dividends b/d | 13,700 |
| Dividends c/d | 16,000 | P/L | 69,000 |
|  | 377,700 |  | 377,700 |

*(4) Taxation paid (parent company and subsidiaries)*

|  | £ |
|---|---|
| Last year tax liability | 360,000 |

## *(c) Using a Worksheet*

The worksheet below extends the approach developed in section 35.3 above. The following additional points are relevant:

(1) Acquisition details should be entered in column D so that purchase of a subsidiary may be calculated as a one-line item, net of cash balances transferred (i.e. £20,000 − £5,000 = £15,000).

(2) Dividends paid are dealt with in two columns:
  - column L – dividend paid to parent company shareholders (£325,000);
  - minority shareholders (£36,700) – see also alternative "T" account working above ((b)(3)) – column H.

(3) Dividends received from associated undertaking (£31,000) was explained above (b(1)).

(4) In column J, the contra-adjustment of £220,000 is to eliminate the effect of the non-cash item (revaluation £220,000).

(5) The shares issued do not appear in the financing section (column M) as they were not issued for cash consideration. They are adjusted for in column D.

| Item £ | Consolidated balance sheets 31/12/X3 A | 31/12/X2 B | Change (A–B) C | Acqn Details New Sub D | Change (C–D) E | Operating activities F | Returns (assoc) G | MI Div H | Tax I | Capital expenditure J | Acquisitions K | Equity div paid L | Financing M | Cash N |
|---|---|---|---|---|---|---|---|---|---|---|---|---|---|---|
| Fixed assets | 1,068,900 | 640,600 | (428,300) | 140,000 | (288,300) | 41,700 | | | | (110,000) | | | | |
| Goodwill | 320,000 | 250,000 | (70,000) | 70,000 | – | | | | | (220,000) | c | | | |
| Associate | 245,000 | 206,000 | (39,000) | – | (39,000) | | (39,000) | | | | | | | |
| Stocks | 586,000 | 492,000 | (94,000) | 70,000 | (24,000) | (24,000) | | | | | | | | |
| Debtors | 307,000 | 164,000 | (143,000) | 85,000 | (58,000) | (58,000) | | | | | | | | |
| Cash | 71,100 | 32,100 | (39,000) | 5,000 | (34,000) | | | | | | 5,000 | | | (39,000) |
| Investment in subsidiary | – | – | – | (20,000) | (20,000) | | | | | | (20,000) | | | |
| Ordinary S.C | (210,000) | (50,000) | 160,000 | (160,000) | – | – | | | | | | | | |
| Share premium | (160,000) | – | 160,000 | (160,000) | – | | | | | | | | | |
| Revaluation reserve | (320,000) | (100,000) | 220,000 | – | 220,000 | – | | | | 220,000 | c | | | |
| P/L B/F | (580,000) | (580,000) | – | | – | | | | | | | | | |
| Operating profit | (850,000) | – | 850,000 | – | 850,000 | 850,000 | | | | | | | | |
| Associate | (120,000) | – | 120,000 | | 120,000 | | 120,000 | | | | | | | |
| Tax – group | 380,000 | – | (380,000) | | (380,000) | | | | (380,000) | | | | | |
| – assoc | 50,000 | – | (50,000) | | (50,000) | | (50,000) | | | | | | | |
| MI (P/L) | 69,000 | – | (69,000) | | (69,000) | | | (69,000) | | | | | | |
| Dividends (P/L) | 350,000 | – | (350,000) | | (350,000) | | | | | | | (350,000) | | |
| MI: non c | (325,000) | (295,000) | 30,000 | | 30,000 | | | 30,000 | | | | | | |
| MI: current | (16,000) | (13,700) | 2,300 | | 2,300 | | | 2,300 | | | | | | |
| Tax (B/S) | (380,000) | (360,000) | 20,000 | | 20,000 | | | | 20,000 | | | | | |
| Dividends (B/S) | (190,000) | (165,000) | 25,000 | | 25,000 | | | | | | | 25,000 | | |
| Creditors | (296,000) | (221,000) | 75,000 | (30,000) | 45,000 | 45,000 | | | | | | | | |
| Total | 0 | 0 | 0 | 0 | 0 | 854,700 | 31,000 | (36,700) | (360,000) | (110,000) | (15,000) | (325,000) | – | (39,000) |

## SOUTHDALE PLC CASH FLOW STATEMENT

### for the year ended 31.12.19X3

|  | £ | £ |
|---|---|---|
| Net cash inflow from operating activities |  | 854,700 |
| Dividends received from associated undertaking |  | 31,000 |
| Returns on investments and servicing of finance |  |  |
| Dividends paid to minority shareholders |  | (36,700) |
| Taxation |  |  |
|   UK corporation tax paid |  | (360,000) |
| Capital expenditure |  |  |
|   Purchase of tangible fixed assets |  | (110,000) |
| Acquisitions |  |  |
|   Purchase of subsidiary undertaking | (20,000) |  |
|   Cash acquired with subsidiary | 5,000 | (15,000) |
| Equity dividends paid |  |  |
|   Dividends paid to parent company shareholders |  | (325,000) |
| Net cash outflow before financing |  | 39,000 |
| Financing |  | – |
| Increase in cash during the period |  |  |
|  |  | 39,000 |

# 5.7    Illustrations from Published Accounts

## Illustration 3

Extract from annual report and accounts of the Boots Company plc, year ended 31 March 2003.

**Group cash flow Information**

| **Group cash flow statement** | Notes | **2003** **£m** | *2002* *£m* |
|---|---|---|---|
| For the year ended 31 March 2003 |  |  |  |
| **Cash inflow from operating activities** | 23 | **582.3** | 722.4 |
| **Returns on investment and servicing of finance** |  |  |  |
| Interest paid |  | **(16.1)** | (58.6) |
| Interest received* |  | **91.9** | 99.5 |
| Dividends paid by subsidiaries to minority interests |  | **(0.8)** | (0.2) |
|  |  | **75.0** | 40.7 |
| **Taxation** |  | **(196.7)** | (139.2) |
| **Capital expenditure and financial investment** |  |  |  |
| Purchase of fixed assets |  | **(145.8)** | (172.1) |
| Disposal of fixed assets |  | **118.6** | 62.2 |
| Disposal of own shares |  | **3.1** | 7.7 |
|  |  | **(24.1)** | (102.2) |
| **Acquisitions and disposals** | 4 | **358.1** | 3.9 |
| **Equity dividends paid** |  | **(238.3)** | (234.5) |
| **Cash inflow before use of liquid resources** **and financing** |  | **556.3** | 291.1 |
| **Management of liquid resources** |  |  |  |
| Decrease/(increase) in short term deposits |  | **15.8** | (234.3) |

|  | 2003 £m | 2002 £m |
|---|---|---|
| **Financing** | | |
| Capital element of finance lease rental agreements | **(8.1)** | (7.9) |
| Decrease in other borrowings | **(37.9)** | (12.1) |
| Cash outflow from change in borrowings and lease financing | **(46.0)** | (20.0) |
| Issue of ordinary share capital (net of expenses) | **(0.3)** | 0.7 |
| Repurchase of shares | **(465.5)** | (35.9) |
| | **(511.8)** | (55.2) |
| **Increase in cash in the year** | **60.3** | 1.6 |

Cash is defined as cash in hand and deposits repayable on demand, less overdrafts repayable on demand.

*Including exceptional interest received of £53.8m. In addition £46.8m was received in 2002 in relation to this item.

| **Reconciliation of net cash flow to movement in net debt** | Notes | 2003 £m | 2002 £m |
|---|---|---|---|
| For the year ended 31st March 2003 | | | |
| **Increase in cash in the year** | | **60.3** | 1.6 |
| Cash (inflow)/outflow from change in liquid resources | 24 | **(15.8)** | 234.3 |
| Cash outflow from change in borrowings and lease financing | 24 | **46.0** | 20.0 |
| **Movement in net debt resulting from cash flows** | | **90.5** | 255.9 |
| Finance lease additions | | **(1.8)** | (11.6) |
| Increase in value of investment in 10.125% bond 2017 | | **5.8** | 21.9 |
| Currency and other non-cash adjustments | | **0.3** | (2.3) |
| **Movement in net debt during the year** | | **94.8** | 263.9 |
| Opening net debt | | **(146.3)** | (410.2) |
| **Closing net debt** | 24 | **(51.5)** | (146.3) |

Net debt comprises cash, liquid resources, financial leases and all other borrowings.

| **23 Reconciliation of operating profit to cash flows** | 2003 £m | 2002 £m |
|---|---|---|
| Group operating profit | **557.3** | 630.0 |
| Operating exceptional items | **–** | 16.4 |
| Group operating profit before exceptional items | **557.3** | 646.4 |
| Depreciation, amortisation and impairments of fixed assets | **162.8** | 163.4. |
| Loss on disposal of fixed assets | **5.5** | 5.6 |
| Increase in stocks | **(77.1)** | (3.3) |
| Increase in debtors, including pension prepayments | **(27.0)** | (126.1) |
| (Decrease)/increase in creditors | **(28.7)** | 65.5 |

| | 2003 £m | 2002 £m |
|---|---|---|
| Other non-cash movements | **(2.4)** | (0.2) |
| Net cash inflow before expenditure relating to exceptional items | **590.4** | 751.7 |
| Exceptional operating cash flows (see below) | **(8.1)** | (29.3) |
| **Cash inflow from operating activities** | **582.3** | 722.4 |
| **Exceptional operating cash flows:** | | |
| Restructuring and integration Costs paid | **(8.1)** | (29.3) |

| 24 Analysis of net debt | As at 1 April 2002 £m | Cash flow £m | Other non-cash Changes £m | Currency £m | As at 31 March 2003 £m |
|---|---|---|---|---|---|
| Cash at bank and in hand | 100.4 | 98.6 | – | 4.4 | 203.4 |
| Bank loans and overdrafts repayable on demand | (111.2) | (38.3) | – | (0.2) | (149.7) |
| Net (overdraft)/cash | (10.8) | 60.3 | – | 4.2 | 53.7 |
| Liquid resources | 308.7 | (15.8) | – | 0.2 | 293.1 |
| Obligations under finance leases | (18.1) | 8.1 | (1.8) | – | (11.8) |
| Other borrowings (including currency swaps) | (426.1) | 37.9 | 1.7 | – | (386.5) |
| Total | (146.3) | 90.5 | (0.1) | 4.4 | (51.5) |

Liquid resources comprise listed investments and short-term deposits.

## 5.8    Using Cash Flow Statements

### (a) The Usefulness of Cash Flow Statements

The previous version of FRS 1 stated that

> "historical cash flow information may assist users of financial statements in making judgements on the amount, timing and degree of certainty of future cash flows".

The section also stated

> "Accordingly, cash flow statements should normally be used in conjunction with profit and loss accounts and balance sheets when making an assessment of future cash flows".

However, given the frequent volatility of cash flows between one year and another, a comparison of two years figures is likely to be of only limited help. Cash flow statements may well be of greater assistance if several years statements are available.

### (b) Additional Information Provided by Cash Flow Statements

Some of the disclosures required by FRS 1 will provide information beyond that available from the balance sheet, profit and loss account and notes. In addition, some companies produce information in excess of that required by FRS 1. The following are examples of areas where additional information may be available:

(i) for companies using the direct method, information relating to cash received from customers and cash paid to suppliers;
(ii) memorandum information relating to non-cash transactions e.g. finance lease arrangements entered into during the year;
(iii) cash information e.g. cash payment for fixed assets, which might otherwise be difficult to calculate from accruals-based accounts;
(iv) for groups, cash flow information relating to acquisitions and disposal of subsidiaries;
(v) the impact of foreign exchange differences;
(vi) for some groups, additional information regarding investing activities.

# 5.9  International Financial Reporting Standards

## Comparison with UK GAAP

IAS 7 is the equivalent of UK GAAP FRS 1 with the same title. IAS 7 does not exempt *any* entities from presenting a cash flow statement.

FRS 1 reports changes in cash, whereas IAS 7 reports changes in cash and cash equivalents (Short-term highly liquid investments that are readily convertible to known amounts of cash and which are subject to an insignificant risk of changes in value).

The main differences between the two standards relate to format and disclosures issues.

FRS 1 requires cash flows to be analysed and grouped under up to nine separate sub-headings, whereas IAS 7 requires cash flows to be grouped under only three sub-headings:

- *Operating activities*
  This includes "operating activities" as under FRS 1; tax paid; interest paid; dividends paid (alternative position is under "investing activities").
- *Investing activities*
  This includes "capital expenditure and financial investment" as under FRS1; "acquisitions and disposals" as under FRS 1; interest received; dividends received.
- *Financing activities*
  This includes "financing" as under FRS 1; dividends paid (alternative position is under "operating activities".

IAS 7 requires disclosure of the components of cash and cash equivalents, as well as a reconciliation of the amounts in its cash flow statement with the equivalent items reported in the balance sheet.

There is no requirement in IAS 7 equivalent to the net debt disclosures specified in FRS 1.

The reconciliation between net profit and net cash from operating activities, including the reconciling items, may be shown on the face of the cash flow statement or in the notes.

---

**Frequently Asked Questions**

1  How are cash deposits treated under UK GAAP?
   Deposits may be treated as "cash" provided repayable on demand or at no more than 24 hours notice. Otherwise deposits should be excluded from cash and dealt with under "Management of liquid resources".

2  Are UK subsidiaries owned by overseas parent companies exempt from publishing a cash flow statement?
   Yes—provided the exemption conditions in FRS 1 must be met. In particular the subsidiary must be at least 90% owned and it must be included within consolidated accounts which are publicly available.

3  What comparatives are required as regards the notes to the cash flow statement?
   Comparatives are required for everything except the net debt analysis (FRS 1, paragraph 48).

# Reporting the Substance of Transactions

6

**This chapter covers:**
* The key concept of reporting substance
* Recognition of assets and liabilities
* Relationship of FRS 5 with other standards
* Disclosure requirements
* Linked presentation
* Offset
* Consignment stocks
* Debt factoring and invoice discounting
* Sale and repurchase agreements
* Other issues in FRS 5
* International Financial Reporting Standards

## 6.1   Background

### (a)  The Off Balance Sheet Finance Debate

For over twenty years, off balance sheet finance has been a significant financial reporting issue.

The publication in 1984 of SSAP 21, Leases and hire purchase transactions, marked an important step forward. Prior to SSAP 21 companies were not obliged to bring finance leased assets and related obligations into their balance sheets (see Chapter 14).

However, following the issue of SSAP 21, a number of loopholes still remained. Some companies succeeded in reporting transactions in accordance with their strict legal form in situations when this conflicted with commercial substance.

### (b)  Accounting Standards Board

The Accounting Standards Board put this subject high up its agenda and issued a Standard—FRS 5, Reporting the substance of transactions.

The Statement of Principles referred to in Chapter 4, underlines the principles of FRS 5.

## (c) FRS 5 – A Standard Based on General Principles

FRS 5 sets out general principles which are capable of being applied to a variety of transactions. In this respect, FRS 5 is different from other Standards. At the time of issue, most FRS 5 applications could be identified fairly readily. However, more less obvious applications of FRS 5 began to emerge as FRS 5 continued to play an increasingly central-stage role.

# 6.2    The Substance of Transactions

## (a) Reporting Substance

The basic message of FRS 5 is clear—paragraph 14 of the Standard requires that "A reporting entity's financial statement should report the substance of the transactions into which it has entered".

## (b) Commercial Effect and Legal Form

FRS 5 is aimed at "more complex transactions whose substance may not be readily apparent". The Standard states that

> "the true commercial effect of such transactions may not be adequately expressed by their legal form and, where this is the case, it will not be sufficient to account for them merely by recording that form ..." (Summary to FRS 5 para (b)).

A long-standing practical illustration of the "commercial effect over legal form" principle is the accounting treatment of fixed assets under hire purchase and finance lease arrangements.

A further illustration is debt factoring. Some companies factor debts as an alternative source of finance to a bank loan or overdraft. The legal form of the transaction is that the debts are "sold" or assigned over to the factoring company. However, in most debt factoring arrangements, the commercial effect is that the transaction is a financing one and not an asset disposal. Accordingly, FRS 5 would normally require monies received from the factoring company to be separately presented as a source of finance. However, in very restricted cases, linked presentation might be appropriate (see section 6.9).

# 6.3    Features of More Complex Transactions

Certain transactions of a more complex nature may include the following features:

## (a) Separation of Legal Title from Benefits and Risks

As an example, the legal title to a finance lease remains with the lessor although the risks and benefits associated with the asset pass to the lessee.

SSAP 21 requires the party having the benefits and risks relating to the under-lying property to recognize an asset in its balance sheet even though it does not have legal title.

### (b) Linking of Transactions

A transaction may be linked with others in such a way that the overall commercial effect can only be understood by considering the series as a whole. FRS 5 gives an example of a sale of goods where there is a commitment to repurchase. The repurchase price is set at costs (including interest) incurred by the other party in holding the goods. The transaction should be accounted for as a financial transaction—the original asset remains on the balance sheet whilst the "proceeds of sale" is accounted for as finance, i.e. as a balance sheet liability.

### (c) Inclusion of Options

The transaction may include options or conditions on terms that make it highly likely that the option will be exercised or the conditions fulfilled.

FRS 5 requires the commercial effect of the options or conditions to be assessed in order to determine what assets and liabilities exist.

## 6.4    Applying the Principles of FRS 5

### (a) General Principle

FRS 5, para 14 requires the accounts of a reporting entity such as a company to report the substance of the transactions into which it has entered. Para 14 extends this general principle as follows:

- All aspects and implications of a transaction should be identified. Greater weight should be given to those more likely to have a commercial effect in practice.
  For example, a legal agreement such as a consignment stock agreement may contain a large number of terms (see 6.11). It will be necessary to analyse these terms and decide which ones are important in practice. This analysis will form the basis of deciding the appropriate accounting treatment.
- A group of series of transactions that achieves or is designed to achieve an overall commercial effect should be viewed as a whole. For example, a sale of property where the seller is committed to repurchasing the property at a later date should be looked at in terms of its overall effect, not as two sepa-rate transactions (see 6.3(b)).

### (b) Application Notes

The FRS gives extensive criteria for identifying the substance of transactions as well as a lengthy appendix running to 67 pages with application notes on several areas including:

- consignment stock;
- sale and repurchase agreements;
- factoring debts;
- securitized assets;
- loan transfer;
- revenue recognition.

These application notes are referred to later in the chapter, or in Chapter 8 in the case of revenue recognition.

# 6.5   Recognition of Assets and Liabilities

## (a)  Recognition

This term refers to the process of incorporating an item into a primary statement, such as the balance sheet, under an appropriate heading. For example, if a company enters into a hire purchase arrangement, recognition refers to bringing a fixed asset and related creditor on to the balance sheet.

## (b)  FRS 5 Criteria

For an asset or liability to be recognized in the balance sheet, three criteria must be satisfied. These relate to:

- identification;
- existence;
- monetary measurement.

(FRS 5, paras 16 and 20).

### Identification test
Assets are defined as "rights or other access to future economic benefits controlled by an entity as a result of past transactions or events" (FRS 5, para 2).
    Liabilities are defined as "an entity's obligations to transfer economic benefits as a result of past transactions or events" (FRS 5, para 4).

### Existence test
This requires sufficient evidence of the existence of the item (including, where appropriate, evidence that a future inflow or outflow of benefits will occur) (FRS 5, para 20(a)).

### Monetary measurement test
This requires that the item can be measured at a monetary amount with sufficient reliability (FRS 5, para 20(b)).

Assets such as stock (FRS 10) and purchased goodwill (SSAP 22) would satisfy the three tests above. However, internally-generated goodwill would be unable to satisfy the monetary measurement condition, and so should not be recognized as an asset.

## (c) Examples

Some illustrations of how FRS 5 might be applied include:

- A finance lease – if this satisfied the SSAP 21 "risks and rewards of ownership" test (which is re-enforced by the FRS 5 "substance" test), the related asset and obligation would be included on the balance sheet.
- An operating lease, for example a contract hire arrangement – this would satisfy the FRS 5 tests above. In principle therefore, FRS 5 would require a "50% asset" (i.e. where the finance element of rentals is equivalent to, say, 50% of the overall cost of the asset) to come on the balance sheet together with the related obligation. However the more detailed requirements of SSAP 21 override in accordance with FRS 5, para 13. Operating leases – provided they satisfy the spirit as well as the letter of SSAP 21 should not be recognized, i.e. they will continue to remain off the balance sheet for the foreseeable future. (see also section 6.7).
- Consignment stocks of cars held by a dealer – in principle, this could go eitherway. Application Note A gives guidance as to whether the stock is an asset of the dealer at delivery (i.e. "recognition") or whether the stock is not an asset of the dealer at delivery (i.e. "no recognition"). This is referred to in detail later in this chapter.
- A company constructs a specialized item of machinery for its eventual use as a fixed asset. Once complete and ready for use, the item should be capable of satisfying the above recognition test. Direct costs together with a proportion of manufacturing overheads would be part of the measured "monetary amount".

# 6.6    De-recognition

## (a) De-recognition

This refers to ceasing to recognize an item in the balance sheet.

## (b) FRS 5 Criteria

Where a transaction satisfies both of the conditions below, the asset should cease to be recognized in the balance sheet:

- The transaction transfers to a third party all significant rights or other access to benefits relating to that asset.
- The transaction transfers to a third party all significant exposure to the risks inherent in those benefits (FRS 5, para 22).

## (c) Examples

- A straightforward sale of goods – the asset stock would be "de-recognized" and removed from the balance sheet. The transaction has passed access to benefits and exposure to risks on to the purchaser.
- Sale of goods with a commitment to repurchase – the first transaction cannot be considered in isolation, it is part of a "series of transactions ... designed to achieve an overall commercial effect". If the repurchase price is based on the original sale price plus interest, then from the viewpoint of both parties, the substance of the transaction is financing. The access to benefits and exposure to risks remain throughout with the original seller. Stock remains on the balance sheet, "de-recognition" is inappropriate. The so-called "income" received is dealt with as borrowings.
- A manufacturing company sells its fleet of 40 motor vehicles to a contract hire company. The vehicles are then leased back under a traditional contract hire arrangement. From the viewpoint of the seller the transaction satisfies the "de-recognition" test, for example the significant exposure to risks relating to residual value has been passed on to the contract hire company.
- Sale and operating leaseback of a freehold building, where the original seller retains a repurchase option – it will be necessary to assess whether the option terms make it "highly likely that the option will be exercised..." (FRS 5, para 47(c)). If this is the assessment, the sale will not result in a de-recognition and the property will remain on the balance sheet. The accounting treatment of a profit or loss on sale is dealt with in FRS 5, paragraphs 46 and 47.
- Sale and leaseback, where the lease is classified under SSAP 21 as a finance lease – clearly "de-recognition" is not appropriate. The treatment of profit or loss on sale is dealt with in SSAP 21.
- A trading company enters into a debt factoring arrangement – in principle this may or may not result in "de-recognition". In practice, the substance of most factoring arrangements is likely to be that of financing rather than disposal of assets, in which case "de-recognition" is not applicable. Significant exposure to risks of slow payment of debtors remains with the trading company. Slow payment results in higher finance charges paid to the factor. A further risk is that the amount received depends on the realization of the debtor balances. Debtors would remain on the balance sheet until cash is collected from the customer.
- Discounting of bills of exchange with recourse – when a company discounts bills receivable with a bank, it has not transferred the significant risks relating to possible non-payment by the original debtor. The company should, therefore, leave bills receivable on the balance sheet until the bill has matured and been collected by the bank. In other words, separate presentation should be adopted – similar to the treatment for most debt factoring arrangements.

*Illustration 1*

**Accounting policies (extract)**
*Accounting for the substance of transactions*
Where bills or leases are discounted with recourse to the company, then the transactions are brought onto the balance sheet within debtors and creditors.

**Notes (extracts)**

|  | Consolidated | |
|---|---|---|
|  | 19X5 | 19X6 |
|  | £'000 | £'000 |
| *Debtors* | | |
| Amounts falling due within one year: | | |
| Trade debtors | 118,683 | 113,839 |
| Amounts due from subsidiaries | – | – |
| Other debtors | 6,893 | 5,397 |
| Prepayments and accrued income | 5,079 | 5,504 |
| Bills and leases discounted with recourse | 20,354 | 21,241 |
|  | 151,009 | 145,981 |
| Amounts falling due after more than one year: | | |
| Amounts due from subsidiaries | – | – |
| Other debtors | 3,353 | 3,689 |
| Bills and leases discounted with recourse | 517 | 508 |
|  | 3,870 | 4,197 |
|  | 154,879 | 150,178 |
| *Creditors and provisions* | | |
| Amounts falling due within one year: | | |
| Trade creditors | 61,032 | 63,192 |
| Amounts due to subsidiary companies | – | – |
| Social security and payroll taxes | 5,182 | 6,190 |
| Other creditors | 20,389 | 17,349 |
| Accruals and deferred income | 26,096 | 27,351 |
| Bills and leases discounted with recourse | 20,354 | 21,241 |
| Repurchase obligations | 5,428 | 4,236 |
|  | 138,481 | 139,559 |

# 6.7   Relationship with Other Standards

## (a) General Rule

FRS 5, para 13 sets out the overriding rule:

> "Where the substance of a transaction or the treatment of any resulting asset or liability falls not only within the scope of this FRS but also directly within the scope of another FRS, a Statement of Standard Accounting Practice ("SSAP"), or a specific statutory requirement governing the recognition of assets or liabilities, the standard or statute that contains the more specific provision(s) should be applied".

## (b) Example – Relationship with SSAP 21

As regards SSAP 21, the leasing standard, concern has been expressed on the likely impact of FRS 5 on issues such as operating/finance lease classification;

and sale and leaseback arrangements, including those entered into some years ago.

Paragraph 45 of FRS 5 is the only part of the Standard which deals explicitly with leasing issues. This states:

> "The relationship between SSAP 21 "Accounting for leases and hire purchase contracts" and FRS 5 is particularly close. In general, SSAP 21 contains the more specific provisions governing accounting for stand-alone leases that fall wholly within its parameters, although the general principles of the FRS will also be relevant in ensuring that leases are classified as finance or operating leases in accordance with their substance. However, for some lease arrangements, and particularly for those that are merely one element of a larger arrangement, the FRS will contain the more specific provisions. An example is a sale and leaseback arrangement where there is also an option for the seller/lessee to repurchase the asset; in this case the provisions of Application Note B are more specific than those of SSAP 21".

This is further referred to in section 14.9.

### (c) Example – Relationship with SSAP 13

The accounting treatment of deferred development expenditure, satisfying the stringent SSAP 13 capitalization criteria, is a further illustration of the lay-off between the general principles of FRS 5 and the more specific provisions of another standard.

The general principles of FRS 5 would require such expenditure to be recognized in the balance sheet as an asset. However, para 13 of FRS 5 allows SSAP 13 to override and thus allows companies the option of capitalization or immediate write-off.

## 6.8    Disclosure Requirements

### (a) General Requirements

FRS 5 has two key paragraphs dealing with disclosure requirements for more complex transactions. Paragraphs 30 and 31 of the FRS state:

> "30 Disclosure of a transaction in the financial statements, whether or not it has resulted in assets or liabilities being recognised or ceasing to be recognised, should be sufficient to enable the user of the financial statements to understand its commercial effect.
>
> 31 Where a transaction has resulted in the recognition of assets or liabilities whose nature differs from that of items usually included under the relevant balance sheet heading, the differences should be explained".

### (b) Specific Applications

FRS 5 application notes deal with detailed disclosures on areas such as consignment stocks, sale and repurchase arrangements and debt factoring.

## 6.9 Linked Presentation for Certain Non-recourse Finance Arrangements

### (a) Applicability

Linked presentation is a very specific aspect of FRS 5 and is likely to apply to only a relatively few companies.

Linked presentation applies to a transaction that is in substance a financing transaction but where the financing effectively "ring-fences" the item. For example, where the transaction relates to debt factoring, the finance received will be repaid only out of the proceeds generated by the debtors. The company which has factored the debtors has a strictly limited exposure to loss—it is linked to a fixed monetary amount.

A linked presentation effectively shows the finance on the face of the balance sheet as a deduction from the gross amount of the item it finances.

### Illustration 2

Extract from annual report and accounts of Fundamental-e-Investments plc, year ended 30 September 2000.

**Consolidated balance sheet**

| | As at 30 September 2000 | | As at 30 September 1999 | |
|---|---|---|---|---|
| | £ | £ | £ | £ |
| Fixed assets | | | | |
| Tangible assets | | 185,329 | | 163,619 |
| Investments | | 100,000 | | 2 |
| | | | | |
| Current assets | | | | |
| Stocks | 1,183,436 | | 1,464,093 | |
| Debts factored without recourse: | | | | |
| Gross debts (after providing for credit protection fee and accrued interest) | 2,619,116 | | 2,354,844 | |
| Less: non-returnable proceeds | (2,228,173) | | (1,664,227) | |
| | 390,943 | | 690,617 | |
| Debtors | 586,709 | | 697,108 | |
| Cash at bank and in hand | 2,011,775 | | 145,144 | |
| | 4,172,863 | | 2,996,962 | |
| Creditors: amounts falling due within one year | (3,071,502) | | (1,554,587) | |
| Net current assets | | 1,101,361 | | 1,442,375 |
| Total assets less current liabilities | | 1,386,690 | | 1,605,996 |

**Principal accounting polices (extract)**

*Factoring arrangements*

Computer Component Marketing Limited, the trading subsidiary company, has entered into a factoring agreement. Debts approved by the Factor Company are assigned to it without recourse to the company. Non-refundable advances are made to Computer Component Marketing Limited by the factor company. A linked presentation of the relevant balances is therefore shown on the face of the balance sheet in accordance with the requirements of Financial Reporting Standard Number 5.

*13. Debts factored without recourse*
In addition to non-returnable proceeds received at the balance sheet date, additional unutilised funds amounting to £71,514, were available to draw upon with immediate effect from HSBC Invoice Finance (UK) Limited.

## *(b) Conditions*

A linked presentation can only be used if certain stringent criteria can be satisfied including the following:

- the finance will be repaid only from proceeds generated by the specific item it finances (or by transfer of the item itself) and there is no possibility whatsoever of a claim on the entity being established other than against funds generated by that item (or the item itself); and
- there is no provision whatsoever whereby the entity may either keep the item on repayment of the finance or re-acquire it at any time.

Additional conditions are contained in FRS 5, para 27. These are extremely stringent and likely to be difficult to satisfy in practice.

# 6.10 Offset

The general principle is that assets and liabilities should not be offset.

Debit and credit balances should be aggregated into a simple net item where:

- they do not constitute separate assets and liabilities, and
- the following three conditions are satisfied:
  - The reporting entity and another party owe each other determinable monetary amounts, denominated either in the same currency, or in different but freely convertible currencies.
  - The reporting entity has the ability to insist on a net settlement.
  - The reporting entity's ability to insist on a net settlement is assured beyond doubt.

*Illustration 3*

**Accounting Policies (extract)**

*Cash offsetting*
The Group has various arrangements with its bankers whereby loans taken from a bank are offset by cash deposits placed with the same bank in such a manner that the bank has the legal ability to insist on a net settlement in all situations of default. In those situations where the Group has an equal legal ability to insist on a net settlement, the loan is reduced by the amount of the cash deposit. In all other circumstances, the cash deposit and the loan are disclosed separately within the respective balance sheet headings, secured against each other.

# 6.11    Consignment Stocks

## (a) The Key Issues Involved

The trade most likely to be affected by this aspect of FRS 5 is motor dealer-ships. The manufacturer transfers motor vehicles to the dealer but retains legal title until, say, cash has been paid over. The key issue is to determine whether, at the point of physical transfer, the manufacturer has in substance passed on the risks and rewards of ownership to the dealer.

From the dealer's viewpoint, is the commercial substance of the transaction:

- a purchase of stock on extended credit terms; or
- are the vehicles simply being "loaned" by the manufacturer to facilitate a sale?

It is essential to determine whether, at the point of physical transfer, the manu-facturer has in substance passed on the risks and rewards of ownership to the dealership.

Risks of ownership would include obsolescence risks (models becoming out of date) and risks of slow movement (thus having to finance stocks prior to achieving a sale). Benefits of ownership would include fixing purchase price on delivery with opportunity to sell at a profit.

## (b) FRS 5 Guidance

FRS 5 Application note A includes the following table as guidance.

For example, if the features of the consignment stock arrangement are more in line with those in the right-hand column, this would indicate that the consignment stock should be included on the dealer's balance sheet.

| Indications that the stock is not an asset of the dealer at delivery | Indications that the stock is an asset of the dealer at delivery |
|---|---|
| Manufacturer can require the dealer to return stock (or transfer stock to another dealer) without compensation, or Penalty paid by the dealer to prevent returns/transfers of stock at the manufacturer's request. | Manufacturer cannot require dealer to return or transfer stock, or Financial incentives given to persuade dealer to transfer stock at manufacturer's request. |
| Dealer has unfettered right to return stock to the manufacturer without penalty and actually exercises the right in practice. | Dealer has no right to return stock or is commercially compelled not to exercise its right of return. |
| Manufacturer bears obsolecence risk, e.g.: − obsolete stock is returned to the manufacturer without penalty; | Dealer bears obsolescence risk, e.g.: − penalty charged if dealer returns stock to manufacturer; |

| Indications that the stock is not an asset of the dealer at delivery | Indications that the stock is an asset of the dealer at delivery |
|---|---|
| or<br>– financial incentives given by manufacturer to prevent stock being returned to it (e.g. on a model change or if it becomes obsolete). | or<br>– obsolete stock cannot be returned to the manufacturer and no compensation is paid by manufacturer for losses due to obsolecence. |
| Stock transfer price charged by manufacturer is based on manufacturer's list price at date of transfer of legal title. | Stock transfer price charged by manufacturer is based on manufacturer's list price at date of delivery. |
| Manufacturer bears slow movement risk, e.g.:<br>– transfer price set independently of time for which dealer holds stock, and there is no deposit. | Dealer bears slow movement risk, e.g.:<br>– dealer is effectively charged interest as transfer price or other payments to manufacturer vary with time for which dealer holds stock; or<br>– dealer makes a substantial interest-free deposit that varies with the levels of stock held. |

## (c) Disclosure requirements

(1) Where stock is regarded in substance as an asset of the dealer:

- Recognize stock on balance sheet of dealer with corresponding liability to the manufacturer. Comparative figures are required.
- Deduct any deposit paid from the liability, classifying difference as a trade creditor.
- Notes to the accounts should explain:
  - nature of arrangement;
  - amount of consignment stock included in the balance sheet;
  - main terms under which stock held including terms of any deposit.
- Where necessary comparative figures should be restated.

(2) Where stock is not regarded in substance as an asset of the dealer:

- Do not include stock on dealer's balance sheet until transfer of title has crystallized.
- Include any deposit under "other debtors".
- Notes similar to those in (1) above including the value of consignment stock held at year end.
- Note that comparative information should be given.

## (d) Illustrations

### Illustration 4

**Accounting polices (extract)**

*Stock*
Stock is valued at the lower of cost and net realisable value.

Stocks held on consignment are accounted for in the balance sheet when the terms of a consignment agreement and commercial practice indicate that the principal benefit of owning the stock (the ability to sell it) and principal risks of ownership (stockholding cost, responsibility for safe-keeping and some risk of obsolescence) rest with the Group. Consignment stocks not meeting those criteria are disclosed in the notes to the accounts but are not accounted for in the balance sheet.

Vehicles which are subject to repurchase agreements are included in stock at the lower of the agreed repurchase price and net realisable value, with the associated liability in creditors.

*18. STOCKS*

| | Group | |
| --- | --- | --- |
| | 20x1 | 20x0 |
| | £'000 | £'000 |
| Vehicles on consignment | 44,536 | 42,131 |
| Vehicles subject to Motability repurchase agreements | 8,101 | 15,444 |
| Cars and motorcycles | 59,249 | 42,535 |
| Parts, accessories and spares | 11,666 | 8,357 |
| Car rental fleet | 18,590 | 16,371 |
| Fuel, consumables and other stocks | 1,115 | 1,073 |
| | 143,257 | 125,911 |

**Note 20 (extract)**

CREDITORS: amounts falling due within one year

| | Group | |
| --- | --- | --- |
| | 20x1 | 20x0 |
| | £'000 | £'000 |
| Obligations relating to consignment stock | 44,536 | 42,131 |
| Obligations relating to Motability repurchase agreements | 7,896 | 8,073 |

**Note 21 (extract)**

CREDITORS: amounts falling due after more than one year

| | Group | |
| --- | --- | --- |
| | 2000 | 1999 |
| | £'000 | £'000 |
| Obligations relating to Motability repurchase agreements | 205 | 7,371 |

# 6.12 Debt Factoring and Invoice Discounting

## (a) Background

Debt factoring and invoice discounting are widely used methods of financing. Debt factoring is one of the topics dealt with in the application notes which are part of FRS 5.

The Association of British Factors and Discounters refer to these, in a 1994 booklet, terms as follows:

Factoring is the purchase by the factor and the sale by a company of book debts on a continuing basis, usually for immediate cash. The sales accounting functions are then provided by the factor who manages the sales ledger and collection of accounts under the terms agreed by the seller. The factor may assume the credit risk for accounts within agreed limits (non-recourse) or this risk may be retained by the seller.

Invoice discounting is the purchase by the discounter and the sale by a company of book debts on a continuing basis (occasionally selectively) for immediate cash. The sales accounting functions are retained by the seller and the arranged facility is usually provided on a confidential basis: credit protection can also be provided if required. Discounting is usually restricted to larger companies than those acceptable for factoring.

### (b) Key Issue

The key issue is to determine whether a particular debt factoring arrangement is:

- a sale transaction – unlikely in most cases as it would be necessary to demonstrate that all significant benefits and risks had been transferred to the factor; or
- a borrowing or financing transaction where the company's debts are used as collateral.

### (c) Evaluating the Treatment of Debt Factoring and Invoice Discounting Arrangements

FRS 5 suggests that two key questions should be asked (Application Note C, para C4):

- Does the seller have access to the benefits of the factored debts and exposure to the risks inherent to those benefits?
- Does the seller have a liability to repay amounts received from the factor?

In theory, the following are three possible responses:

- The seller has transferred all significant benefits and risks relating to the debts and has no obligation to repay the factor:
  - the appropriate accounting treatment is "de-recognition". This would remove the factored debts from the balance sheet and show no liability in respect of any proceeds received from the factor.
This treatment is likely to be appropriate only in very rare cases.

- The seller has retained significant benefits and risks relating to the debts. However, its downside exposure to loss is limited – there is no question of doubt on this:
  - the appropriate accounting treatment is "linked presentation". This would show the proceeds received from the factor as a deduction from the factored debts. The two elements and the net effect would be shown within a single asset caption.
- In all other cases, i.e. where debtors are used to obtain finance:
  - "separate presentation" is the appropriate accounting treatment. This shows the factored debt as an asset (as previously); and shows a corresponding

liability within creditors (this relates to the proceeds received from the factor).

Application Note C includes a table giving guidance as to appropriate treatment. In practice, for most factoring and invoice discounting arrangements, separate presentation is likely to be required.

In a typical with-recourse arrangement, the "seller" retains both slow payment risk (incurring higher finance charges paid to the factor) and bad debt risk.

In a non-recourse arrangement, the factor may be taking the bad debt risk by providing bad debt protection. However, where the factor's charges are linked to bank base rates and take into account speed of payment by debtors, the "seller" company has effectively retained a significant risk, i.e. risk of slow payment. Separate presentation will still be appropriate.

Confidential invoice discounting arrangements fall within the scope of FRS 5 and are subject to the same disclosure requirements in the shareholders' accounts.

## (d) Accounting and Disclosure Requirements

### De-recognition

- remove the factored debts from the balance sheet;
- no liability will be shown in respect of proceeds received from the factor;
- the profit and loss account will reflect the difference between the carrying amount of the debts and proceeds received on the sale of those debts to the factoring house.

### Linked presentation

- deduct proceeds received from gross amount of factored debts (after providing for bad debts, credit protection charges and any accrued interest) – show this offset on the face of the balance sheet;
- notes to the accounts should disclose:
  - the main terms of the arrangement;
  - the gross amount of factored debts outstanding at the balance sheet date;
  - the factoring charges recognized in the period, analysed as appropriate;
  - statement by directors that the entity is not obliged to support any losses, nor does it intend to do so;
  - statement that the provider of finance has agreed that it will seek repayment of finance only to the extent that sufficient funds are generated by the specific item it has financed and that it will not seek recourse in any other form.

### Separate presentation

- the gross amount of factored debts should be shown on the seller's balance sheet within assets;
- liabilities should include an amount in respect of proceeds received from the factor;

- the interest element of the factor's charges should be accrued and included in the profit and loss account;
- other factoring costs should be similarly accrued;
- the notes to the accounts should disclose the amount of factored debts outstanding at the balance sheet date.

Note also that CA 1985, Sch 4, para 48(4) requires disclosure of the aggregate amount of creditors in respect of which security has been given by the company, and the nature of the security.

### Illustration 5

Extract from annual report and accounts for the year ended 30 November 19X8.

*Note 13*

13 Debtors

|  | 19X8 £'000 | 19X7 £'000 |
|---|---|---|
| Trade debtors | 2,184 | 519 |
| Other debtors | 435 | – |
| Share capital unpaid (note 18) | 488 | – |
| Prepayments and accrued income | 343 | 77 |
|  | 3,450 | 596 |

Included within the trade debtors above are amounts of £1,027,000 covered under an invoice discounting facility.

*14 Creditors: amounts falling due within one year*

|  | 19X8 £'000 | 19X6 £'000 |
|---|---|---|
| Current portion of hire purchase and finance lease liabilities | 1,702 | 850 |
| Current portion of shareholder loan | – | 28 |
| Bank loans and overdrafts | 1,761 | 112 |
| Advances under invoice discounting facility | 621 | 278 |
| Trade creditors | 1,492 | 295 |
| Corporation tax | 96 | – |
| Other taxes and social security | 76 | 61 |
| Proposed dividends | 140 | 22 |
| Accruals and deferred income | 224 | 8 |
|  | 6,112 | 1,654 |

The advances under the invoice discounting facility are secured on trade debtors of the company, and the bank loans and overdrafts are secured on the assets of the company.

## 6.13 Sale and Repurchase Agreements

### (a) Background

Sale and repurchase agreements are arrangements under which assets are sold by one party to another on terms that provide for the seller to repurchase the asset in certain circumstances. This area can be complex, covering a diverse range of agreements. A key practical point is to be able to recognize sales agreements which include repurchase options or commitments. It will then be necessary to establish to what extent FRS 5 will be relevant.

## (b) Features

The main features of sale and repurchase agreements will include:

- Sale price – this may be:
  - market value;
  - another agreed price.
- Nature of the repurchase provision – possibilities are:
  - unconditional commitment for both parties;
  - an option for the seller to repurchase (a call option);
  - an option for the buyer to resell to the seller (a put option);
  - a combination of put and call options.
- The repurchase price – this may:
  - be fixed at the outset;
  - vary with the period for which the asset is held by the buyer;
  - be the market price at the time of repurchase.
- Other provisions – for example the use of an asset by the seller whilst in the ownership of the buyer.

## (c) Examples

Sale and repurchase agreements may cover a broad spectrum of possibilities including, for example:

- sale and leaseback of property with a commitment to repurchase at a future date;
- sale and leaseback of property with an option for the seller to repurchase at a future date;
- sale of new machinery with a commitment to repurchase in a few years' time in a substantially depreciated state.

## (d) Applying the Principles of FRS 5

### (i) Sale and leaseback of property with a commitment to repurchase

In a straightforward case, the substance of a sale and repurchase agreement will be that of a secured loan. An example of this would be where the seller has an unconditional commitment to repurchase the original asset from the buyer at the original sale price plus interest. In this case, the seller has retained all significant rights to benefits relating to the asset and all significant exposure to risk. The seller also has a liability to the buyer for the whole of the proceeds received. The "sales" arrangement should be accounted for by showing the original asset on its balance sheet together with a liability for the amounts received from the buyer.

## (ii) Sale and leaseback of property with a call option for the seller to repurchase

The key point to consider here is whether there is a genuine commercial possibility that the option will be exercised. In this situation the agreement gives the buyer no rights to require the seller to repurchase. An exception would be, for example, where the seller defaulted on the terms of the lease.

For this purpose, it is important to assume that the seller will act in accordance with its best economic interest, taking account of factors such as option price and value of property. For example, if there is no genuine commercial possibility that the option will fail to be exercised, the substance of the transaction is that of a secured loan with the benefits and risks of the asset remaining with the seller. The property and the related creditor should continue to appear on the seller's balance sheet.

## (iii) Sale of new asset and commitment to repurchase in a substantially depreciated state

The substance of the overall arrangement may be:

- sale of a new item of machinery; and
- a residual interest in the machinery – amounted for by including a stock item and associated creditor.

### Illustration 6

Extract for the year ended 30 September 19X5.

**Accounting policies (extract)**

*Accounting for the substance of transactions*
Where bills or leases are discounted with recourse to the company, then the transactions are brought onto the balance sheet within debtors and creditors. Where the company enters into commitments to repurchase equipment at specified dates, then the residual interest in the equipment is included within stock and the repurchase obligation is included within creditors.

**Note 8 – Stocks**

|  | 19X5 £'000 | 19X4 £'000 |
|---|---|---|
| Industrial | 40,157 | 38,824 |
| Materials handling | 31,900 | 25,260 |
| Capital equipment | 58,948 | 48,453 |
| Agricultural | – | 564 |
|  | 131,005 | 113,101 |

|  | 19X5 £'000 | 19X4 £'000 |
|---|---|---|
| Raw materials | 17,553 | 20,183 |
| Work in progress | 8,336 | 8,470 |
| Finished goods | 85,184 | 67,985 |
| Livestock | – | 142 |
| Residual interests in equipment | 19,932 | 16,321 |
|  | 131,005 | 113,101 |

**Note 10 – Creditors and provisions (extract)**

|  | 1995<br>£'000 | 1994<br>£'000 |
|---|---|---|
| Amounts falling due within one year: |  |  |
| Trade creditors | 61,032 | 63,192 |
| Amounts due to subsidiary companies | – | – |
| Social security and payroll taxes | 5,182 | 6,190 |
| Other creditors | 20,389 | 17,349 |
| Accruals and deferred income | 26,096 | 27,351 |
| Bills and leases discounted with recourse | 20,354 | 21,241 |
| Repurchase obligations | 5,428 | 4,236 |
|  | 138,481 | 139,559 |

**Note 12 – Creditors and provisions (extract)**

|  | 1995<br>£'000 | 1994<br>£'000 |
|---|---|---|
| Amounts falling due after more than one year: |  |  |
| Fair value provisions | – | 1,143 |
| Amounts due to subsidiaries | – | – |
| Pension provisions | 24,287 | 22,157 |
| Other creditors | 1,812 | 2,287 |
| Bills and leases discounted with recourse | 517 | 508 |
| Repurchase obligations | 14,504 | 12,085 |
|  | 41,120 | 38,180 |

The fair value provisions relate to the acquisition of ....

# 6.14 Further Complications

## (a) Quasi-subsidiaries

The area of quasi-subsidiaries is complex and is relevant to only a small proportion of listed companies. The summary to FRS 5 refers to quasi-subsidiaries as follows:

> "Sometimes assets and liabilties are placed in an entity (a "vehicle") that is in effect controlled by the reporting entity but does meet the legal definition of a subsidiary. Where the commercial effect for the reporting entity is no different from that which would result were the vehicle a subsidiary, the vehicle will be a "quasi-subsidiary". (FRS 5 summary para 1.)

## (b) Application Notes D and E

### (i) Application Note D – securitised assets

Application Note D describes securitisation as a means by which providers of finance fund a specific block of assets rather than the general business of a company. The assets that have been most commonly securitised in the UK are household mortgages. Other receivables such as credit card balances, hire purchase loans and trade debts are sometimes securitised, as are non-monetary assets such as property and stocks.

The Application Notes apply to all kinds of assets. In view of its specialised application, no further reference is made here.

*(ii) Application Note E – loan transfers*
Application Note E deals with the transfer of interest-bearing loans to an entity other than a special purpose vehicle. Again, no further reference is made here.

## (c) Application Note G, Revenue Recognition

This is referred to in Chapter 8.

# 6.15 International Financial Reporting Standards

There is no direct IFRS equivalent to FRS 5, but IAS 39 deals with recognition and de-recognition of financial assets and financial liabilities.

---

**Frequently Asked Questions**

1 If a transaction is unusual and would be potentially difficult for a user to understand its commercial effect, what is required in order to comply with FRS 5?
FRS 5 requires appropriate accounting to reflect the transaction's substance and disclose information which is "sufficient to enable the user of financial statements to understand its commercial effect". (paragraph 30).

2 What happens in the event of a conflict between the general principles of FRS 5 and the specific requirements of another standard?
The approach required by FRS 5 is to apply whichever standard contains the more specific provisions (para 13)—examples are operating leases where SSAP 21 applies and development costs where SSAP 13 applies.

3 How should a manufacturer account for an ordinary course of business sale of an asset such as machinery, where the sale agreement contains a clause requiring the manufacturer to repurchase at a specified future date?
FRS 5 sets out detailed guidance in the Application Note on sale and repurchase agreements which deals with repurchase commitments and call options which allow a "seller" to repurchase (see section 6.13 above).

---

# Converging UK GAAP with IFRS

---

**This chapter covers:**
* Requirements and options to adopt IFRS for different categories of company
* UK GAAP/IFRS comparison
* True and fair requirement
* Recent convergence developments
* UITF Abstracts based on international pronouncements

---

## 7.1 Terminology

The terms "International Financial Reporting Standards" (IFRS) and "International Accounting Standards" (IAS) are effectively interchangeable. The Companies Act 1985 and the relevant tax legislation refer to "IAS". However, the more widely used (and modern) term IFRS and is used in this book.

## 7.2 Recap

* Fully listed groups are required to adopt International Financial Reporting Standards (IFRS) in their *consolidated* accounts for accounts periods commencing on or after 1 January 2005. The European Regulation is mandatory for the *consolidated* accounts only;
* Companies listed on the Alternative Investment Market (AIM) are required by the London Stock Exchange to adopt IFRS for accounts periods commencing on or after 1 January 2007 (but may adopt earlier if they so choose);
* All other categories of companies are permitted (*but not required*) to adopt IFRS for accounts periods commencing on or after 1 January 2005, but may but may not adopt earlier.

## 7.3 Options for Members of a Group

The directors must ensure that the individual accounts of the parent company and each of its subsidiary undertakings are all prepared using the same financial reporting framework, except to the extent that in their opinion there are good reasons for not doing so.

This seemingly innocuous statement allows a number of possible combinations including:

- Consolidated accounts, parent company accounts and all UK subsidiaries prepared under IFRS;
- Consolidated accounts under IFRS; parent company and all UK subsidiaries prepared under UK GAAP;
- Consolidated accounts and parent company accounts under IFRS and all UK subsidiaries prepared under UK GAAP;

See the DTI's *"Guidance for British Companies on Changes to the Reporting and Accounting Provisions of the Companies Act 1985", paragraphs 4.13 to 4.16.*

## 7.4　Application to Different Categories of Company

| Type of company | Application of IFRS |
|---|---|
| Trading on OFEX* | For regulatory purposes, companies trading on OFEX are regarded as unlisted, and there is therefore no mandatory date for transition to IFRS. However such companies should consider strategic issues such as how late adoption of IFRS might be viewed in the market-place, particularly for those companies intending to move over to AIM or the full market. |
| UK subsidiaries of UK fully listed groups | All subsidiary companies within a group must adopt either UK GAAP or IFRS (see above). In practice, they are likely to adopt IFRS in order to ease the preparation of consolidated accounts under IFRS. |
| UK subsidiaries of foreign listed groups which are adopting IAS | Although UK company law will not require these subsidiaries to adopt IFRS, the overseas parent may require IFRS accounts for the purpose of preparing consolidated accounts. |
| Large private and unlisted PLCs | These companies can for the present choose whether and when they adopt IFRS. The decision may be affected by a number of considerations, including the desires of the major shareholder(s), whether the company has future plans for "going public" and its relations with suppliers and customers outside the UK. |
| SMEs | Similar considerations apply to SMEs as for larger unlisted companies. However, small companies presently adopting the FRSSE may wish to continue using the FRSSE pending the development of SME-IFRSs from the International Accounting Standards Board. |

*OFEX was established in October 1995 as a trading facility for unquoted and unlisted securities – it is regulated by the Financial Services Authority.

## 7.5　Comparison of UK GAAP and IFRS

The table below covers a number of topics and aims to give an overview of the main differences relating to accounts of individual companies. The table refers to a number of situations applicable to many individual unlisted companies and is not intended to be comprehensive. Issues relating to large groups are not referred to.

Paragraph references in brackets relate to the relevant UK or international standard. The differences reflect present rules and ASB/IASB intentions.

| Topic | UK GAAP treatment | IFRS treatment |
|---|---|---|
| Balance sheet format and terminology | Dealt with in CA 85: Schedules 4 & 8 | Dealt with in IAS 1 |
| Performance reporting | Profit and loss formats and terminology are dealt with in CA 85, Schedules 4 & 8 and FRS 3. | Income statement formats and terminology are dealt with in IAS 1. |
| | FRS 3 requires a Statement of total recognized gains and losses (FRS 3.27) | IAS 1 requires a Statement of changes in equity allows a choice of two formats: Columnar format statement *or* Statement of recognized income and expense (IAS 1.96, 97). |
| | FRS 3 includes a stringent definition of "discontinued operations" (FRS 3.4). | IFRS 5 refers to presentation of "discontinued operations" but the definition differs from that in FRS 3. |
| | FRS 3 requires *fundamental* errors to be accounted for by way of restatement (as though the error had never occurred) and prior year adjustment. The effects of *material* errors should be reflected in the profit and loss account without restatement (FRS 3.7, FRS 3.63). | IAS 8 prohibits the inclusion of *material* errors in the income statement (IAS 8.42). |
| Exceptional items | FRS 3 includes definitions for exceptional items (FRS 3.5). | IAS 1 does not refer to the term "exceptional item". |
| | FRS 3 requires all exceptional items to be charged or credited in arriving at operating profit (FRS 3.19) with three specific exceptions (FRS 3.20). | IAS 1 simply requires separate disclosure (either on the face of the income statement or in the notes) "when items of income and expense are material" (IAS 1.86) and gives examples of circumstances that would give rise to separate disclosure (IAS 1.87). |
| Extraordinary items | In theory permitted by FRS 3 (FRS 3.5, FRS 3.22) but in practice extinct. | IAS 1 prohibits use of extraordinary items (IAS 1.85). |
| Dividends paid and proposed | Equity and preference dividends (paid or proposed) are to be included in the profit and loss account (CA 85, Sch 4.7(b) for accounts periods which *commenced before 1 January 2005.* | Equity dividends paid must be dealt with in the statement of changes in equity (IAS 32.35). |

| Topic | UK GAAP treatment | IFRS treatment |
|---|---|---|
| | | Preference dividends paid (relating to preference shares classified as liabilities in accordance with IAS 32) shall be recognized as an expense in the income statement (IAS 32.35). |
| | SSAP 17 requires proposed dividends to be treated as adjusted post-balance sheet events (SSAP17.11). | *Equity* dividends declared after the balance sheet date shall not be recognized as a liability at the balance sheet date (IAS 10.11) but must be disclosed by way of note (IAS 1.125). |
| | Both of the above are superseded by FRS 25, Financial instruments —Presentation and disclosure (presentation paragraphs only) and FRS 21, Events after the balance sheet date, for accounts periods commencing on or after 1 January 2005. | |
| Cash flow statements | FRS 1 requires cash flows to be grouped under nine sub-headings (FRS 1.7). | IAS 7 requires cash flows to be grouped under three sub-headings (IAS 7.10). |
| | The statement should reconcile to cash (FRS 1.7). | The statement should reconcile to cash & cash equivalents (IAS 7.45). |
| | FRS 1 specifies a number of exemptions from its scope (FRS 1.5). | IAS 7 contains no scope exemptions (IAS 7.1). |
| | FRS 1 requires "net debt" disclosures (FRS 1.33). | IAS 7 specifies disclosure of breakdown of cash and cash equivalents, and reconciliation to Balance sheet (IAS 7.45, 48). |
| Revenue recognition | There is no comprehensive UK standard but ASB has issued an Application Note to FRS 5 providing detailed guidance on five specific areas.<br><br>UITF has issued Abstract 40 dealing with service contracts. | IAS 18, Revenue, includes detailed requirements and guidance.<br><br>IASB is currently developing a new standard to replace IAS 18. |
| Financial instruments —recognition and measurement | There is no comprehensive UK standard, although some aspects are covered by FRS 4 and SSAP 20.<br><br>FRS 26, subject to complex transitional arrangements, will not initially affect most unlisted companies. | Covered comprehensively by IAS 39. |

*Continued*

| Topic | UK GAAP treatment | IFRS treatment |
|-------|-------------------|----------------|
| | Under UK GAAP, derivatives are usually stated initially at historical cost (often £ nil). | IAS 39 requires fair value accounting with all gains and losses recognized in the profit and loss account (unless cash flow hedge accounting is applicable).<br><br>All derivatives must be recognized on the balance sheet (as debtors or creditors). |
| | Under UK GAAP, current asset investments are stated at lower of cost and NRV (CA85, Sch 4, paras 22, 23). | IAS 39 specifies different treatments for remeasurement, according to asset classification (IAS 39.46). |
| Financial instruments —presentation and disclosure | Some aspects of this are covered by FRS 4 (all companies) and FRS 13 (listed companies only).<br><br>FRS 25 will supersede much of FRS 4 for 2005 accounts. | Covered comprehensively by IAS 32 (currently under review by IASB). |
| | All preference shares are to be classified as share capital (CA85, Sch 4)—but Act has been amended for accounts periods which start on or after 1 January 2005, in line with FRS 25. | Preferences shares to be classified as *either* share capital *or* liabilities, according to their substance (IAS 32.15–18; IAS 32.AG25–26). |
| | Convertible loan stock is to be presented as liabilities until conversion to equity actually takes place (FRS 4.25–26). FRS 25 will change this for 2005 accounts. | On initial recognition, carrying amount to be allocated between liability element and equity element, and presented separately (IAS 32.28, AG30–35, IE34–36). |
| Deferred tax | In most cases, deferred tax may not be provided on revaluation surpluses, and gains on disposal where rollover relief is likely to be claimed (FRS 19.14–15). | Deferred tax must be provided on these "temporary differences" (IAS 12.15, 20). |
| | Deferred tax balance may be discounted (FRS 19.42). | Discounting is not permitted (IAS 12.53). |
| | Tax reconciliation required is to "current" tax (FRS 19.64(a)). | Tax reconciliation is to total tax expense [current tax plus deferred tax] (IAS 12.81(c)). |
| Retirement benefits | Where FRS 17 has been fully adopted, all actuarial gains and losses must be taken direct to reserves [presented in STRGL] (FRS 17.57). | IAS 19 originally required all such gains and losses to be taken to profit and loss account, either immediately or spread over a period (IAS 19.92, 93). |

| Topic | UK GAAP treatment | IFRS treatment |
|---|---|---|
| | | IAS 19 also has a complex 10% "corridor" option (IAS 19.92, 95).<br><br>ASB has amended IAS 19 to permit the immediate recognition of all actuarial gains and losses in a Statement of recognized income and expense [this option is likely to be widely used by UK companies]. |
| | Where FRS 17 has been fully adopted, deferred tax should be deducted from the respective retirement benefit asset or liability (FRS 17.49). | Deferred tax is dealt with in IAS 12—the deferred tax balance must be presented as a separate asset/liability. It may not be offset against the pension obligation/asset.<br><br>IAS 19 deals with a broader range of issues, including employee profit-sharing and termination benefits. |
| Goodwill (including purchased goodwill arising in the accounts of an individual company) | FRS 10 gives choice for positive goodwill between systematic amortization and carrying at unchanged amount subject to annual impairment review (FRS 10.15, 17).<br><br>Negative goodwill must be recognized in the profit and loss account over a specified period (FRS 10.48). | IFRS 3 prohibits systematic amortization but requires an annual review for impairment.<br><br>Negative goodwill should be credited to profit or loss as it arises. |
| Research and development costs | Where "development cost criteria" satisfied, policy option choice between capitalization and immediate write-off (SSAP 13.25). | Where IAS 38 criteria satisfied, capitalization is mandatory. |
| Investment properties | SSAP 19 requires investment properties to be revalued in the accounts each year at open market value (SSAP 19.11) with changes in market value taken to investment revaluation reserve, subject to limited exceptions (SSAP 19.13). | IAS 40 allows a choice between the "fair value model" and the "cost model" (IAS 40.30).<br><br>The fair value model requires property to be measured at its fair value reflecting market conditions at the balance sheet date (IAS 40.33, 38) with changes in value recognized in the profit or loss for the period (IAS 40.35).<br><br>The cost model is set out in IAS 16.30 and after recognition would require investment properties to be stated at cost less any accumulated depreciation and any impairment losses. |

*Continued*

| Topic | UK GAAP treatment | IFRS treatment |
|---|---|---|
| | SSAP 19 specifies particular requirements for investment properties held under operating leases. The cost of such leases should be capitalized and reported as a single asset. The asset should be remeasured at each subsequent balance sheet date at open market value. Such properties should be depreciated over the unexpired lease term where this period is twenty years or less (SSAP 19.10). | IAS 40 (revised) permits operating leases to qualify as investment property provided that: – the property must otherwise meet the definition of an investment property, and – the lessee must account for the lease as if it were a finance lease and measure the resulting asset using the fair value model (IAS 40.6, 25). |
| Property, plant and equipment—estimates of residual value | Residual value is defined as the net realizable value of an asset at the end of its useful economic life. Residual values are based on prices prevailing at the date of the acquisition (or revaluation) of the asset and do not take account of expected future price changes (FRS 15.2). | The residual value of an asset is the estimated amount that an entity would currently obtain from disposal of the asset, after deducting the cost of disposal, if the asset were already of the age and in the condition expected at the end of its useful life (IAS 16.6). |
| Revaluation of property, plant and equipment—determination of market value | FRS 15 requires the following bases (FRS 15.53): Non-specialized properties— existing use value; Specialized properties— depreciated replacement cost; Properties surplus to requirement—open market value. FRS 15, Appendix 1, contains RICS definitions. FRS 15 sets out strict rules regarding frequency of revaluations (FRS 15.44, 45). | IAS 16 requires revalued assets to be carried at fair value at date of revaluation, less accumulated depreciation (IAS 16.31). IAS 16 states that the fair value of land and buildings is usually determined from market-based evidence by appraisal that is normally undertaken by profes-sionally qualified valuer's (less guidance compared with FRS 15). ASB has commented on the implications of the above in the preface to FRED 29. IAS 16 requirements are less rigorous (IAS 16.34). |
| Leases of land and buildings | Treated as operating leases (SSAP 21.37). | Each of the elements of land and buildings must be considered separately for the purposes of lease classification (IAS 17.15). Where the land has an indefinite economic life, the land element is normally classified as an operating lease unless title is expected to pass to the lessee by the end of the lease term. |

| Topic | UK GAAP treatment | IFRS treatment |
|---|---|---|
| | | The buildings element will be classed as a finance lease or as an operating lease in accordance with the criteria in IAS 17. |
| Related party disclosures | FRS 8 allows exemption of certain intra-group transactions where consolidated accounts are prepared and publicly available (FRS 8.3 (c)) | There is no equivalent exemption (IAS 24.4) |
| | The definition of "materiality" is very broad and "is to be judged, not only in terms of their significance to the reporting entity, but also in relation to the other related party when that party is…" (FRS 8.20) | IAS 24 makes no specific reference to materiality other than the general point that IAS 24 should be read in the context of its objective (IAS 24.1) and … the Framework for the Preparation and Presentation of Financial Statements (paras 29 and 30 of the Framework refer). |

## 7.6 True and Fair Requirement

Under UK GAAP, Section 226A of CA 85 expressly refers to the true and fair requirement (see Chapter 2, Section 2.1(e)).

Section 226B requires that where the directors of a company prepare IAS individual accounts, they must state in the notes to those accounts that the accounts have been prepared in accordance with international accounting standards, and makes no explicit reference to the true and fair requirement.

Financial Reporting Review Panel has published a legal opinion on the effect of the IAS Regulation on the requirement for accounts to give a true and fair view (Press Notice 85, published June 2005).

The Press Notice states that the key points of the opinion are:

- Unlike the financial reporting standards of the ASB, IFRS are explicitly part of the law rather than being part of the "true and fair" requirement;
- Accounts must be fairly presented. Although the application of a IFRS is presumed to result in a fair presentation, it may be necessary, in extremely rare circumstances, for a company to depart from strict IFRS in the interests of fair presentation;
- Companies that continue to prepare accounts in accordance with UK national standards remain subject to the overriding requirement of the Act that accounts give a true and fair view, which, in all but highly exceptional cases, requires compliance with UK accounting standards.

[The above Opinion can be downloaded from the ASB section of FRC website]

## 7.7    Converging UK GAAP with IFRS – Recent Developments

As part of the process to harmonize UK GAAP with IFRS, ASB has issued a number of exposure drafts, several of which were converted into FRSs in November 2004. These are summarized in the table below.

International Accounting Standards/International Financial Reporting Standards from which these are derived are included in square brackets.

| Financial Reporting Exposure Drafts | Convergence developments |
|---|---|
| FRED 23 – Financial instruments: hedge Accounting [IAS 39] | FRS 26 – Financial instruments: measurement |
| FRED 24 – Effects of foreign exchange rates; Financial reporting in hyperinflationary economies [IAS 21/IAS 29] | FRS 23 – Effects of foreign exchange rates FRS 24 – Financial reporting in hyperinflationary economies |
| FRED 25 – Related party disclosures [IAS 24] | |
| FRED 26 – Earnings per share [IAS 33] | FRS 22 – Earnings per share |
| FRED 27 – Events after the balance sheet Date [IAS 10] | FRS 21 – Events after the balance sheet date |
| FRED 28 – Inventories; Construction and service contracts [IAS 2/IAS 11] | |
| FRED 29 – Property, plant and equipment; Borrowing costs [IAS 16] | |
| FRED 30 – Financial instruments: Disclosure and presentation; Recognition and measurement (plus various supplements) [IAS 32/IAS 39] | FRS 25 – Financial instruments: Disclosure and presentation FRS 26 – Financial instruments: Measurement |
| FRED 31 – Share-based payment [IFRS 2] | FRS 20 – Share-based payment |
| FRED 32 – Disposal of non-current assets and presentation of discontinued operations [IFRS 5] | |
| FRED 33 – Financial instruments: disclosures [IFRS 7] | |
| FRED 34 – Life Assurance [IFRS 4] | FRS 27 – Life Assurance |
| FRED 35 – Corresponding amounts* | FRS 28, Corresponding amounts |
| FRED 36 – Business combinations [IFRS 3] | |
| FRED 37 – Intangible assets [IAS 38] | |
| FRED 38 – Impairment of assets [IAS 36] | |
| FRED 39 – Amendments to FRS 12 and FRS 17 | |

*This relates to domestic UK company law issues and is not related to convergence developments (see Chapter 2).

The latest update of the ASB's Technical Plan was published on 22 June 2005 (www.frc.org.uk/asb/technical/techplan) (see Chapter 29). Note also ASB's Convergence Paper, published 21 December 2005 (see 29.4).

## 7.8   Urgent Issues Task Force Abstracts

A number of Abstracts, either published or about to be published, are derived from draft Interpretations issued by the IASB's International Financial Reporting Interpretations Committee (IFRIC). These include the following:

| Topic | IFRIC derivation | Current UK status | Date of publication by UITF |
|---|---|---|---|
| Emission rights | D1 | Draft Abstract | May 2003 |
| Retirement benefit schemes with a promised return on contributions or notional contributions | D9 | Draft Abstract | July 2004 |
| Waste electrical and electronic equipment | D10 | Draft Abstract | November 2004 |
| Members' shares in Co-operative Entities and similar Instruments | IFRIC 2 | Abstract 39 | February 2005 |
| Changes in contributions to employee share purchase plans | D11 | Draft Abstract | February 2005 |
| Reassessment of embedded derivatives | D15 | Draft Abstract | March 2005 |
| Scope of FRS 20 | D16 | Draft Abstract | June 2005 |
| Group and Treasury share transactions | D17 | Draft Abstract | June 2005 |

## 7.9   Extant Standards

Current International Accounting Standards (IASs) and International Financial Reporting Standard (IFRSs) are listed in Appendix 4.

---

**Frequently Asked Questions**

1  If an unlisted company adopts IAS, may it revert back to UK GAAP in a subsequent period?
No—if a company has prepared its accounts using IAS for a financial year, it cannot switch back to UK GAAP in subsequent financial year, apart from very restricted exceptions [Sections 226(5) and 227(6)].

2  Is a small company entitled to any exemptions under IFRS?
A small company may keep certain exemptions including:
  • audit exemption;
  • small companies will no longer be eligible under IFRS to file abbreviated accounts drawn up in accordance with Schedule 8A; however CA 85 Section 246 would allow small companies to deliver to the Registrar a full set of accounts minus Directors' report and profit and loss account.

- other Section 246 exemptions, for example Directors' report disclosures and directors' remuneration disclosures;
- staff numbers and costs;
- preparation of group accounts.

Size criteria will be measured by reference to numbers in the IFRS accounts. If it adopts IFRS, a small company will no longer be able to use the FRSSE (although SME IASs/IFRSs may be available at some future date).

*A cash flow statement will be required in accordance with IAS 7.*

3  Must an IFRS adopter use the term "revenue" in its Income statement, or may it continue to use the term "turnover"?

The term "revenue" will have to appear on the face of the income statement in accordance with paragraph 81 of IAS 1—there is no option under IAS 1 to use the term "turnover".

4  A parent company prepares both consolidated accounts and own accounts in accordance with IFRS. What does the company have to publish with the consolidated accounts regarding its own accounts?

The DTI's guidance (see 7.3 above) indicates that the current dispensation regarding publication of the parent company's own profit and loss account will continue to apply.

However, the other primary statements and note disclosures required by IAS will have to be given. This will therefore include the parent company's cash flow statement and its statement of changes in shareholders' equity.

# Revenue Recognition

## 8.1   Introduction

### (a)  Overview

Until comparatively recently, the topic of revenue recognition was low-profile. Enron and a number of other scandals and controversies changed all that. Revenue recognition is now high up the standard-setting agenda. This initial section considers some of the regulatory developments briefly. These are then examined in more detail in the remainder of this chapter.

### (b)  Companies Act 1985

The Act defines turnover as "...the amount derived from the provision of goods and services falling within the company's ordinary activities, after deduction of trade discounts ...".

Where customers (whether retail or wholesale) are offered goods at lower prices than would normally apply, turnover should be recorded at the lower amount received. This principle has not always been followed—some companies have previously reported turnover at "normal" selling price, with the discount included as a marketing expense. Examples of these are shown below.

## (c) UK GAAP

There is no comprehensive standard dealing with revenue recognition. In the past, former standard SSAP 2 on Accounting policies did include some principles, but these did not constitute a rigorous and coherent reporting framework. Hardly surprisingly, the result was inconsistent and unacceptable reporting in the UK. Some of the issues were picked up by the Financial Reporting Review Panel (see 8.6 below).

The ASB's Statement of Principles, referred to in 8.2 below, does contain some useful general principles.

In July 2001, the Accounting Standards Board published a Discussion Paper on Revenue recognition. The original intention was that this would eventually result in a comprehensive UK standard. However, this idea was dropped as soon as the International Accounting Standards Board announced its intention to develop a standard based on a new approach to determining revenue recognition. This project is still at a relatively early stage, but once a new standard has been put in place, IASB will withdraw IAS 18 (see 8.8 below).

In November 2003, as a short-term measure, the ASB issued Application Note G on revenue recognition which noted in its Preface:

> "... The Application Note has been prepared in response to the need for clarity in respect of questions that arise concerning the treatment of revenue...".

In November 2003 Press Notice announcing Application Note G, former ASB Chairman Mary Keegan commented that "Recent reports of questionable practice have highlighted the need for us to set out best practice...".

## (d) UITF Abstract 40

In late 2004, UITF had indicated that it was considering requests to issue guidance regarding revenue recognition in respect of contracts for professional services. A particular concern was the relationship between FRS 5, Application Note G and SSAP 9, Stocks and long-term contracts.

Issues being considered included:

- When should a contract to provide services be accounted for as a long-term contract?
- How should revenue and profit be recognized in contracts that are not long-term contracts?

Following consultation, UITF issued Abstract 40 in March 2005.

# 8.2   The Statement of Principles – Recognition in Financial Statements

Chapter 5 of the Statement, dealing with recognition starts by stating:

"If a transaction or other event has created a new asset or liability or added to an existing asset or liability, that effect will be recognised if:

(a) sufficient evidence exists that the new asset or liability has been created or that there has been an addition to an existing asset or liability; and
(b) the new asset or liability or the addition to the new asset or liability can be measured with sufficient reliability.

In a transaction involving the provision of services or goods for a net gain, *the recognition criteria above will be met on the occurrence of the critical event in the operating cycle involved...*" [emphasis added].

Later, Para 5.27 states that

> "... although the starting point for the recognition process may be the effect on assets and liabilities, *the notions of matching and the critical event in the operating cycle will often help in identifying these effects*" [emphasis added].

## 8.3   FRS 5, Application Note G

### (a) Introduction

As mentioned above, ASB had noted that questions continued to arise in relation to transactions affecting revenue recognition. It therefore issued guidance on a number of aspects of the topic. This guidance takes the form of Application Note G to FRS 5, Reporting the substance of transactions.

The Application Note sets out a number of basic principles, as well as detailed guidance on the following five areas, where inconsistencies have arisen in the past:

- Long-term contractual performance;
- Separation and linking of contractual arrangements;
- Bill and hold arrangements;
- Sales with rights of return;
- Presentation of turnover as a principal or agent.

The Application Note sets out basic principles which "*should be applied in all cases*", and is subject to a number of limited exceptions, in particular [where other standards or abstracts provide detailed requirements].

### (b) Basic Principles

A seller recognizes revenue under an exchange transaction with a customer when, and to the extent that, it obtains the right to consideration in exchange for its performance.

At the point of revenue recognition, the seller recognizes a new asset (usually a debtor).

When a seller receives payment from a customer in advance of performance, it recognizes a liability:

- This liability equals the consideration received and represents the seller's obligation under the contract;
- When performance takes place and the seller obtains right to consideration, the liability is reduced and the amount of the reduction reported as revenue.

A seller may obtain a right to consideration when some of its contractual obligations have been fulfilled. Revenue should be recognized to the extent that the seller has obtained the right to consideration through its performance.

Revenue should be measured at the fair value of the right to consideration.

Fair value is the amount at which goods or services could be exchanged in an arm's length transaction between informed and willing parties, other than in a forced or liquidation sale.

Turnover (often described as "sales" in the financial statements of a seller) is the revenue resulting from exchange transactions under which a seller supplies to customers the goods or services that it is in business to provide.

## (c) Controversy Over Application Note G

Some commentators have suggested that Application Note G marks a change to existing accounting practice. This does not appear to be what the Accounting Standards Board intended when it issued the Note.

The view held by many accountants, including the author, was that the Application Note did not in itself introduce new rules for valuing work in progress, at it was clearly stated that the Note did not conflict with SSAP 9. The "new rules" were in fact introduced by a subsequent statement—UITF Abstract 40 (see 8.4, below).

What Application Note G intended to do, and appears to have succeeded in achieving, is to stamp out dubious or unacceptable accounting practices. It is debatable whether many of these practices presented a true and fair view anyway, or in some cases even complied with the definition of turnover set out in the Companies Act 1985.

The Note provides guidance on five areas of which "Long-term contractual performance" is one. SSAP 9 contains long-standing and detailed notes in this area. SSAP 9 does relate to service contracts as the definition in paragraph 22 of SSAP 9 refers to "... a contract for ... the provision of a service ...".

The Application Note is quite clear:

> "Statement of Standard Accounting Practice 9, sets out requirements for accounting and disclosure under a long-term contract. The Application Note provides *additional guidance* on the recognition of turnover derived from such contracts, but *does not amend* the requirements of that accounting standard (para G14)" [emphasis added].

Paragraph G2 states that the Application Note does not apply to arrangements "which are dealt with more specifically elsewhere in this [i.e. FRS 5 itself] and other accounting standards" which clearly refers, *inter alia*, to SSAP 9.

## (d) Long-term Contractual Performance

The Application Note provides additional guidance on the recognition of turnover derived from such contracts. It does not amend the requirements of SSAP 9, Stocks and long-term contracts.

A contractual arrangement may require a seller to design, manufacture or construct a single substantial asset or provide a service for a customer which is significant to the business and which falls into different financial periods.

Any entity should assess how changes in a seller's assets or liabilities, and related turnover, that arise from its performance under an incomplete long-term contract should be recorded in the seller's financial statements.

Turnover should be recognized in respect of performance when and to the extent that the seller obtains the right to consideration. In applying this principle:

- Turnover recognized should be derived from an assessment of the fair value of goods or services provided to the reporting date as a proportion of the total fair value of the contract;
- This proportion may correspond with the proportion of expenditure incurred to total expenditure, but this will not always be the case;
- The stage of completion should reflect the extent to which the seller has obtained the right to consideration. Different stages of contracts may vary in their profitability.

Fair values should represent those applicable on inception of contract (except where contractual terms specify that changes in prices will be passed on to the customer).

Work-in-progress should continue to be measured at historical cost (unless net realizable value is lower). For long-term contracts which have reached the stage where it is appropriate to take profits, and where the seller has obtained the right to consideration (para G18), the asset recognized is "amount recoverable on contracts" which is a debtor and is therefore inclusive of profit, recognition of debtors. This is still historical cost as set out in the Companies Act 1985, Schedule 4, Section B, "Historical cost accounting rules". It is, therefore, wrong to suggest that accountants should now be valuing work in progress at "selling price".

### Illustration 1

Extract from annual report and accounts of IDS Group plc, year ended 31 December 2002.

**Accounting policies (extract)**

...

**Recognition of revenue**

The Group licenses software under non-cancellable licence agreements and provides services including maintenance, training and consulting. Software licence revenues are only recognised when persuasive evidence of an arrangement exists, the product has been shipped, fees are fixed and determinable and collectability is considered probable. Where customers are obligated to provide an upfront non-refundable payment, such payment (representing up to 25% of the licence) is recognised as revenue when collectable from the customer. The balance of licence revenue is recognised once the product has been installed.

Where there are extended payment terms of more than twelve months, revenue is recognised as payments fall due.

Revenue from short term development contracts is recognised once the services have been performed and delivered. Revenue from fixed fee contracts involving significant modification to or customisation of the basic software is recognised over the contract term, based upon the percentage of completion method. Foreseeable losses are recognised in the period in which the loss becomes known.

Maintenance revenues are deferred and recognised rateably over the maintenance period. Revenue from training and consulting services is recognised as such services are performed.

Revenue from services provided under computer bureau type arrangements, where invoicing is normally monthly, is typically recognised as it becomes due.

## (e) Separation and Linking of Contractual Arrangements

### (i) Situation

A single contractual arrangement may require a seller to provide a number of different goods or services (or "components") to its customers. Possible arrangements may include:

- Components unrelated and capable of being sold individually;
- Two or more components so closely related that their individual sale is not commercially feasible from the viewpoint of either party;
- A package of a number of goods or services provided in which the amount payable is set below the price at which the items would be sold individually.

### (ii) Required approach

Following performance under the contractual arrangement, the seller should determine which of the following two approaches is appropriate:

- Recognize a change in its assets or liabilities, and turnover, in respect of its right to consideration for each component on an individual basis ("unbundling"); or
- Combine two or more components, account for them as a single transaction, and recognize turnover on that basis ("bundling").

### (iii) "Unbundling"

Illustration

Sales of software and related maintenance services—with the following independent components:

- "Off the shelf" packaged software;
- Separately available support service, with helpline assistance;
- The customer has no commercial obligation or requirement to purchase the support service, and it is not needed in order for the software package to operate satisfactorily.

"Unbundling" is appropriate with separate recognition of turnover for each component.

### (iv) "Bundling"
#### Illustration

Sales of software and related maintenance services—interlinked components:

- Bespoke software;
- Maintenance (three years);
- Rights to future upgrades (three years).

The maintenance and upgrades are required in order to ensure that the software continues to operate satisfactorily throughout the period and are offered only by the supplier of the software.

The commercial substance of the agreement is that the customer is paying for a three-year service agreement comprising the above three components, all of which should be treated as linked.

"Bundling" is appropriate and turnover should be recognized on a long-term contractual basis.

### (v) Example of accounting policy note

Revenue from product sales is recognized on delivery of the equipment. Revenue from consultancy and other professional services is recognized as the services are performed.

Revenue from equipment rental, software support and hardware maintenance provided by the company is recognized rateably over the term of the agreement on a straight line basis. The unrecognized revenue is shown separately in the balance sheet as deferred income.

For contracts involving a combination of products and services, revenue is recognized on each element in accordance with the above policy, unless all elements are considered to be interdependent and not separately deliverable, when revenue is recognized based on the stage of completion. On major contracts extending over more than one accounting period, revenue is recognized based on the stage of completion when the outcome of the contract can be foreseen with reasonable certainty and after allowing for costs to completion.

## (f) Bill and Hold Arrangements

A seller enters into a contractual arrangement with a customer for the supply of goods where there is transfer of title but physical delivery is delayed to a later date.

It is important to determine whether the seller should either:

- Recognize turnover and a right to consideration, or
- Continue to recognize the goods as stock.

The goods cease to be the seller's assets and become the customer's assets when the seller transfers to the customer access to the significant benefits relating to the goods and exposure to the risks inherent in those benefits.

From the customer's perspective, the principal benefits include: right to obtain the goods as and when required; sole right to the goods for their sale to a third party, and the future cash flows from such a sale; and insulation from changes in prices charged by the seller (for example, arising from revisions to the seller's standard price list).

The principal risks include: slow movement (resulting in increased financing and holding costs) and risk of obsolescence; and being compelled to take delivery of goods that have become obsolescent or not readily saleable.

For changes in assets/liabilities and turnover to be recognized, the contractual arrangements between seller and customer should include *all* of the following characteristics:

- The goods should be complete and ready for delivery;
- The seller should not have retained any significant performance obligations other than the safekeeping of the goods, and their shipment when the customer requests this;
- The seller should have obtained the right to consideration regardless of whether the goods are shipped at the customer's request, to its delivery address.

Where rights of return are granted, the commercial substance of the related sales (including transfer of risk) should be considered. Separate guidance is provided regarding rights of return (see below):

- The goods should be identified separately from the seller's other stock and should not be capable of being used to fill other orders that are received between the date of the bill and hold sale and shipment of the goods to the customer; and
- The bill and hold terms should be in accordance with the commercial objectives of the customer and not the seller.

## (g) Sales with Right of Return

### (i) Terms of contractual arrangements

The terms of contractual arrangements may allow customers to return goods that they have purchased and either obtain a refund or be released from the obligation to pay.

Determine the effect of rights of return on a seller's recognition of changes in its assets/liabilities and turnover.

In some cases, "right of return" could oblige the seller to defer recognition of the sales transaction so long as the seller retains substantially all of the risks associated with the related goods.

The inclusion of rights of return in a contractual arrangement, compared with an otherwise identical arrangement without these rights, may affect both quantification of right to consideration, and the point at which that right should be recognized.

### (ii) Exclusion from sales value of estimated returns

Turnover should exclude the sales value of estimated returns. The seller may be able to reliably estimate the sales value of returns by reference to historical experience of comparable sales. Estimates of returns should be reviewed at each balance sheet date (taking account of changes in expectations and expiry of contractual rights of return).

Where the seller is unable to reliably estimate the expected value of returns, the maximum potential obligation (calculated in accordance with the contractual terms) should be excluded from turnover.

In some cases, the risk of return may be so substantial that all of the risks of the related goods remain with the seller and turnover should not be recognized. Any payments received should be included within creditors as payments in advance.

## Illustration 2

Extract from annual report and accounts of The Sage Group plc, year ended 30 September 2003.

**Accounting policies (extract)**

...

**(d) Revenue recognition**

Turnover represents amounts invoiced to third parties after deducting credit notes, allowances, trading discounts and sales tax. The Group derives revenue from software licences, postcontract customer support (PCS) and other products and services. PCS includes telephone support and maintenance updates. Other products and services include the sale of business forms and training.

Software licences—The Group recognises the revenue allocable to software licences and specified upgrades upon shipment of the software product or upgrade, when there are no significant vendor obligations remaining, when the fee is fixed and determinable and when collectability is considered probable. Where appropriate the Group provides a reserve for estimated returns under the standard acceptance terms at the time the revenue is recorded.

Postcontract customer support—Revenue allocable to PCS is recognised on a straight-line basis over the term of the PCS. Revenue not recognised in the profit and loss account under this policy is classified as deferred income in the balance sheet.

Other products and services—Revenue allocable to other products and services is recognised as the products are shipped, or services are provided.

## (h) Presentation of Turnover as Principal or Agent

### (i) Alternative arrangements

A seller may act on its own account (as "principal") when contracting with customers for the supply of goods or services in return for the right to consideration.

Alternatively a seller may act as an intermediary ("agent"), earning a fee or commission in return for arranging the provision of goods or services on behalf of a principal.

### (ii) Indicators
*Indicators of seller acting as principal*

- Performance of part of the services, or modification to the goods supplied;
- Assumption of credit risk; and
- Discretion in supplier selection.

### Indicators of seller acting as agent

- Seller has disclosed fact that it is acting as agent;
- Once customer's order confirmed with third party, seller has no further involvement in performance of ultimate supplier's contractual obligations;
- Amount seller earns is predetermined (fixed fee or percentage of amount billed to customer); and
- Seller bears no stock or credit risk.

### (iii) Reporting of turnover

Where the seller is acting as principal, turnover reported should be based on gross amount received/receivable in return for seller's performance under the contractual arrangement.

Where the seller is acting as agent, turnover reported should be based on commission receivable in return for seller's performance under the contractual arrangement.

### (iv) Disclosures

The Application Note *recommends* additional disclosures, where practicable, in cases where a seller acts as agent:

- The gross value of sales throughput as additional non-statutory information;
- A brief explanation of the relationship of recognized turnover to the gross value of sales throughput.

### Illustration 3

**Accounting policies (extract) – Turnover**

In the majority of cases, the company does not take ownership of the products or services being sold, and acts as agent, receiving a commission from the supplier of the products or services being sold. In these cases, turnover represents commission earned.

In a limited number of cases, the company acts as principal and purchases the goods or services for resale, and turnover represents the price at which the products or services have been sold.

### Illustration 4

Extract from annual report and accounts of ebookers plc, year ended 31 December 2002.

**Accounting policies (extract)**

**Turnover**

During the year, the presentation of negotiated fare turnover has been changed from a gross to a net basis. Negotiated fare tickets are tickets that are bought by the Group or other independent third parties to fulfil existing commitments to the Group's customers. The Group sells these tickets to consumers at fares determined by the Group, which are generally at a significant discount to published fares, that is, the fare at which the airline offers the ticket to the public. Accordingly, all turnover is now recorded at the margin earned rather than the amount invoiced to customers. The Directors believe that this change in presentation more accurately reflects the substance of the underlying transactions. All prior year information has been restated to reflect this method of presentation.

Gross sales is a memorandum disclosure and represents the total transaction value of all our services and hence includes the total amount paid by customers for the services provided by the Group, as opposed to the margin earned per the Group's turnover definition. The Group reports total transaction value since the Directors believe that it reflects more accurately the cash flows within the Group. It is also a widely used measure of company size within the travel sector.

Turnover in the Group consists largely of the margin on sales of discounted airfares on scheduled flights as well as other travel products and services. The Group recognises revenue at the time the reservation is ticketed as the customer generally does not have the ability to cancel tickets or obtain refunds after ticketing, and all amounts payable have been received. In cases where customers have the ability to cancel and obtain refunds after ticketing, the Group is able to estimate its refund obligations and such obligations are accounted for.

### Illustration 5

Extract from annual report and accounts of lastminute.com plc, year ended 30 September 2003.

**Accounting policies (extract)**

...

**Total Transaction Value ("TTV")**

TTV, which is stated net of Value Added Tax and associated taxes, does not represent the Group's statutory turnover.

Where the Group acts as agent or cash collector, TTV represents the price at which goods or services have been sold across the Group's various platforms. In other cases, (for example the reservation of restaurant tables, a flat fee is earned, irrespective of the value of goods or services provided. In such cases TTV represents the flat fee commission earned. Where the Group acts as principal, TTV represents the price at which goods or services have been sold across the Group's various platforms.

**Turnover**

Turnover represents the aggregate amount of revenue from products sold and is stated exclusive of recoverable VAT and associated taxes.

Where the Group acts as agent and does not take ownership of the products or services being sold, turnover represents commission earned less amounts due or paid on any commission shared. Where the Group acts as principal and purchases the products or services for resale, turnover represents the price at which the products or services have been sold across the Group's various platforms.

Turnover also includes advertising and sponsorship income which is recognised over the period to which it relates.

Travel turnover is recognised on the date of departure.

# 8.4    Contracts for Services and UITF Abstract 40

## (a)  UITF Abstract 40 – The Key Issue

The main issue addressed by Abstract 40 is "when the applicable accounting literature requires or allows *revenue* to be recognised as contract activity progresses [the "stage of completion method"] or on completion of the contract" [the "completed contract method"].

Note that the above refers to "revenue":
Under the *stage of completion method*, revenue would be recognized over the period of the contract

Revenue would be spread over the period of the contract even for a contract in its early stages where the outcome cannot be assessed with reasonable certainty before contract completion; in such a case, turnover would be recognized only to the extent of costs incurred [referred to in paragraph 10 of SSAP 9 as a zero estimate of profit].

Under the *completed contract method*, all contract revenue would be recognized only in the period when the contract was complete

When Application Note G, and the initial draft of Abstract 40 were published, many commentators considered that these requirements would not result in changes to long-standing practices regarding revenue recognition.

Advice offered by some of the professional bodies was to the effect that in the case of, for example an audit, a right to consideration might not arise until the audit engagement had been completed and the audit report delivered.

*Abstract 40 removes any remaining uncertainties on the subject, and makes it clear that revenue on service contracts should be accrued as contract activity takes place.*

## (b) UITF Abstract 40 – The Main Requirements (Paragraph References in Brackets)

*Scope*
Abstract 40 applies to all contracts for services and is mandatory for accounting periods ending on or after 22 June 2005 (22, 30).

Companies who use the June 2002 version of the FRSSE are exempt from Abstract 40. However, the "effective January 2005" version of the FRSSE incorporates the principles of Abstract 40. This version will apply for financial periods beginning on or after 1 January 2005 (early adoption is not permitted).

*Basic approach*
Revenue is recognized according to the substance of the seller's obligations under the contract (17).

Contracts for services should not be accounted for as long-term contracts *unless they involve the provision of a single service, or a number of services that constitute a single project* (24) [emphasis added].

Abstract 40 makes the following comments regarding contracts for services that do *not* fall to be accounted for as long-term contracts:

> "...contracts that require services to be provided on an ongoing basis rather than the provision of a single service...do not fall to be accounted for as long-term contacts under SSAP 9. For example, a contract to provided repetitive services (such as general

professional advice, accounting support, help-desk support, maintenance or cleaning) on an ongoing basis should not be accounted for as a long-term contract" (11).

A contract for services should be accounted for as a long-term contract where contract activity falls into different accounting periods and it is concluded that the effect is material (25).

The overriding consideration is whether the seller has performed, or partially performed, its contractual obligations. If it has performed some, but not all, of its contractual obligations, it is required to recognize revenue to the extent that it has obtained the right to consideration through its performance (16). This method is referred to as the "percentage of completion" method or "stage of completion" method (see also above).

### Where obligations are performed gradually over time

Where the substance of a contract is that the seller's contractual obligations are performed gradually over time, revenue should be recognized as contract activity progresses to reflect the seller's partial performance of its contractual obligations. The amount of revenue should reflect the accrual of the right to consideration as contract activity progresses by reference to value of the work performed (18, 26).

Paragraph 18 states that this is the case where the substance of the obligation is either: to provide the services of staff, i.e. where the seller earns the right to consideration as each unit of time is worked, where the amount of revenue is derived from the time spent or to require the seller to use its skills and expertise in carrying out acts that will take some time to perform, even when the output is encapsulated in a document such as a report. In such cases the amount of revenue will reflect the fair value of the services provided as a proportion of the total fair value of the contract, which will reflect the time spent and the skills and expertise that have been provided.

In assessing amount of turnover to be recognized, paragraph 9 (referring to Application Note G) states:
"…The amount of turnover recognised may be derived from the proportion of costs incurred only where it provides evidence of the seller's performance and hence the extent to which it has obtained the right to consideration…"
SSAP 9 provides further guidance in assessing the stage of completion.
For accountancy and legal firms, dependent on size and systems, stage of completion may be determined from time records and lists of work in progress.

### Right to consideration dependent on occurrence of critical event

Where the substance of a contract is that a right to consideration does not arise until the occurrence of a critical event, revenue is not recognized until that event occurs (19, 27). This only applies where the right to consideration is

conditional or contingent on a specified event or outcome, the occurrence of which is outside the control of the seller (19) (see Example 2, in (c) below).

*Uncertainty as to payment*
The amount of revenue recognized should reflect any uncertainties as to the amount which the customer will accept and be able to pay. It may be the case, for example, that even where the contract states that fees are to be calculated on a time basis, the customer will not accept that the time spent is reasonable (20, 28).

*SSAP 9 considerations*
Both Application Note G and Abstract 40 refer back to SSAP 9:
     "The Application Note …does not amend the requirements of that [SSAP 9] standard" (AN G, para G14);
     "In this Abstract, the term "accounted for as a long-term contract" refers to the method described in SSAP 9 …of recognising revenue as contract activity progresses" (Abstract 40, paragraph 2)
     SSAP 9 states:

---

Where the business carries out long-term contracts and it is considered that their outcome can be assessed with reasonable certainty before their conclusion, the attributable profit should be calculated on a prudent basis and included in the accounts for the period under review. The profit taken up needs to reflect the proportion of the work carried out at the accounting date and to take into account any known inequalities of profitability in the various stages of a contract… (paragraph 9);
     Where the outcome of long-term contracts cannot be assessed with reasonable certainty before the conclusion of the contract, no profit should be reflected in the profit and loss account in respect of those contracts, although in such circumstances, if no loss is expected it may be appropriate to show as turnover a proportion of the total contract value using a zero estimate of profit (paragraph 10);
     If it is expected that there will be a loss on a contract as a whole, all of the loss should be recognised as soon as it is foreseen… (paragraph 11).
     Appendix 1, SSAP 9 provides further guidance.

---

*Change of accounting policy*
A change in accounting policy resulting from adoption of Abstract 40 should be dealt with by means of a prior period adjustment. Where applicable, corresponding amounts should be restated (30).

## (c) Applying Abstract 40

*Example 1 – basic approach*
An unincorporated partnership has always previously valued work-in-progress at cost [i.e. the "completed contract method"]. Under its previous accounting

policy, cost has been determined from the work-in-progress recorded on the time ledger [hours worked multiplied by the relevant rates] and reducing this by time costs regarded as irrecoverable, time costs relating to the two equity partners and a provision to reduce chargeout rates of employees to cost.

A client has agreed a fee of £500 for the preparation of a set of accounts. At the year-end, the job is estimated as 80% complete and the value of time on the ledger is £450 and the cost of the work, determined on the basis referred to above amounts to £100.

Using 80% as a reasonable assessment of the stage of completion, revenue recognized in the current period is 80% of £500 i.e. £400. The balance sheet would include a debtor of £400, under the heading of debtors, amounts recoverable on contracts.

The following summarizes the impact of UITF Abstract 40 compared with the previous policy:

## Profit and loss account
### Extracts – 2005

|  | Old policy – Completed contract method £ | New policy – Abstract 40: Stage of completion method £ |
|---|---|---|
| Revenue | – | 400 |
| Costs | – | 100 |
| Operating profit | – | 300 |

### Balance Sheet extracts – 2005

|  | £ | £ |
|---|---|---|
| WIP (lower of cost & NRV) | 100 | – |
| Debtors (fair value) | – | 400 |
| Assets | 100 | 400 |
| Equity | 100 | 400 |

## Profit and loss account
### Extracts – 2006

|  | £ | £ |
|---|---|---|
| Revenue | 500 | 100 |
| Costs | (100) | – |
| – B/F |  |  |
| – current | (25) | (25) |
| Operating profit | 375 | 75 |

*Example 2 – contingent fees*

A client has retained a solicitor under a no-win-no-fee/conditional fee arrangement.

If the client wins the case, the client will pay the solicitor the basic charges plus a success fee of 50% of the basic charges.

If the client loses the cases, no charges or success fee will be payable.

This is an example of a contract where the substance is that a right to consideration does not arise until the occurrence of a critical event that is outside the control of the seller (i.e. solicitor). Revenue is not recognized until that event occurs.

So if judgement in favour of the client is received before the balance sheet date, revenue should be recognized based on charges plus 50% (i.e. equivalent to "fair value") and a debtor created ("amount recoverable on contracts").

If judgement has *not* been received by the balance sheet date, revenue should not be recognized until the following period. This would be the case even where judgement was received before the accounts were signed. However, related costs may be carried forward in the balance as work in progress (at lower of actual cost and NRV). A provision will be required if, at the time of signing off the accounts, there is evidence that costs will not be recoverable.

Similar principles would apply to a corporate finance transaction involving a "success fee".

*Example 3 – accounting policy note (compliant with Abstract 40)*
*Accounting policy note – revenue recognition*

Turnover represents revenue earned under a wide variety of contracts to provide professional services and advice to third parties.

Revenue is recognised as earned when, and to the extent that, the firm obtains the right to consideration in exchange for its performance under those contracts.

It is measured at the fair value of the right to consideration, which represents amounts chargeable to clients, including recoverable expenses and disbursements, but excluding Value Added Tax.

For incomplete contracts, an assessment is made of the extent to which revenue has been earned. This assessment takes into account the nature of the assignment, its stage of completion and the relevant contract terms.

Revenue in respect of contingent fee arrangements (over and above any minimum agreed fee) is recognised when the contingent event occurs and the recoverability of the fee is assured.

Unbilled revenue is included in debtors, under "amounts recoverable on contracts".

*Example 4 – accounting policy note (year of change)*
*Note 1 – Effect of the change in accounting policy (part of note)*

During the year ended 31 December 2005, the company adopted Urgent Issues Task Force Abstract 40, Revenue recognition and service contracts.

Revenue represents amounts chargeable to clients for professional services provided during the year, and is exclusive of value added tax. Revenue is now recognized as services are provided to clients based on the extent of performance of contractual obligations and the agreed rates for these services. To the extent that fees are recognised in advance of the client being billed they are included as debtors, amounts recoverable on contracts.

The previous accounting treatment recognised revenue on each client assignment when it was substantially complete.

The impact of this change in accounting policy on the profit on ordinary activities after taxation is to increase profit by £x. The restated profits after tax for 2004 are £y higher than the previously published figure.

# 8.5  Other Aspects of UK GAAP

## (a) Introduction

A number of UK standards deal with particular aspects of revenue recognition, particularly FRS 5 on reporting the substance of transactions, which refers to a number of complex transactions including sale and repurchase agreements. Also relevant are SSAP 21 on leasing, and SSAP 9 on stocks and long-term contracts and the UITF Abstract 26 (see (b) below).

FRS 5 is dealt with in Chapter 6 and the requirements of SSAP 21 dealing with the recognition of income from both operating leases and finance leases are dealt with in Chapter 14. Recognition of profits on long-term contracts is dealt with in Chapter 15.

## (b) UITF 26 – Barter Transactions for Advertising

UITF 26 deals with the accounting for transactions where advertising services are provided in exchange for advertising, for example where Internet companies exchange advertisements on each others' websites.

Turnover and costs relating to barter transactions for advertising should not be recognized unless there is persuasive evidence of the value at which, if the advertising had not been exchanged, it would have been sold for cash in a similar transaction.

The Abstract sets out detailed and stringent factors that need to be considered in judging the evidence of the value of exchanged advertising. However, the Abstract makes very clear that circumstances justifying recognition in the accounts are likely to be extremely rare. Essentially, persuasive evidence of the value of advertising exchanged will exist only where:

- the entity has a history of selling similar advertising for cash; and
- substantially all of the turnover from advertising within the accounting period is represented by cash sales.

Abstract 26 adds:

> "...Application of this Abstract is not mandatory for barter transaction for services other than advertising, although its principles may be relevant to such transactions".

## 8.6    Review Panel Press Notices

A number of Review Panel press notices have made specific reference to income recognition issues, including:

*(i) FRRP PN 65, Wiggins plc (Published March 2001)*
The Panel commented on the company's accounting policy for turnover which stated:

> "Commercial property sales are recognised at the date of exchange of contract, provided the Group is reasonably assured of the receipt of the sales proceeds" and said that "… this wording was similar to that used by many other companies and was not on the face of it objectionable…".

Later in the press notice, the Panel questioned whether it would be correct to recognise revenue in respect of two property transactions—the following have been extracted from the 8-page notice and refer to the general principles involved in the case, rather than specific detailed facts:

| | |
|---|---|
| 1. This contract was conditional on the company's subsequent fulfilment of a material condition – that planning permission had been obtained on terms satisfactory to the purchaser and without which the purchaser had certain rights not toproceed. | (1) The Panel's first concern was that if the company still has to perform a significant amount of work in order to satisfy the condition, it has not yet completed the earning process sufficiently to entitle it to recognise the revenue at the balance sheet date.<br><br>(2) The second concern is that if the outcome of a conditional contract is necessarily uncertain, and unless that uncertainty has been reduced to an acceptable level by the time that the accounts have been finalised, in general, the prudent course would be not to recognise the conditional contract until the condition is satisfied. |
| 2. This contract appeared to the Panel to have the characteristics of a financing deal rather than an outright sale and under FRS 5 should not be recognised until the risks and rewards of ownership pass at a future date. | The Panel considered that the substance of the contract reflected a development financed by the purchaser and retaining certain risks and rewards for the time being and should have been treated as a financing arrangement. |

*(ii) FRRP PN 54, Photo-Me International plc (Published September 1998)*
Certain sales of equipment had been made to group undertakings and

included in total turnover in the consolidated profit and loss account. Intercompany profit from such sales was eliminated from group profit.

However, the items were subsequently capitalised in the accounts of the individual purchasing companies. No adjustments were made on consolidation to reduce both turnover and cost of sales by the transfer amounts.

The company justified the treatment by invoking the true and fair override (see 2.1(g)) claiming that excluding such sates from turnover would understate the group's activities, thus failing to give a true and fair view.

The Panel held that the treatment in the consolidated accounts was contrary to the Companies Act 1985. The directors subsequently had to revise the comparative figures in the following year's accounts.

*(iii) FRRP PN 44, Associated Nursing Services plc (Published February 1997)*
This case involved the accounting treatment of a complex sale and leaseback transaction, in accordance with FRS 5. The transaction involved a 25-year lease, renewable for a further 25 years, and a call option held by the company.

The Panel's view, subsequently accepted by the directors, was that the nature of the transaction was such that not all the significant rights or other access to benefits relating to the asset in question and not all the significant exposure to the risk inherent in those benefits had been transferred to the purchaser. The asset should therefore have remained on the consolidated balance sheet and the sales "proceeds" included in borrowings.

*(iv) FRRP PN 33, Courts plc (Published June 1995)*
Under the company's then accounting policy for instalment and hire purchase transactions, the total amount due under long-term credit agreements was included in turnover and operating profit, and transfers were made to a deferred profit reserve. Following discussions with the Panel, the policy was revised so that turnover and operating profit included only the service charge income earned during the period.

# 8.7 Illustrations from Published Accounts

## (a) Introduction

Commentators have frequently complained about the lack of meaningful disclosures regarding recognition of both turnover and income. In some sectors, the need for extended revenue recognition policies is self-evident.

The illustrations below aim to give a view of UK GAAP as currently practised. The area is evolving rapidly—see, for example, several examples below involving changes of accounting policies.

The first illustrations cover specific aspects of revenue recognition. The two illustrations at the end of this section are good examples of extended revenue recognition policies.

## (b) "Gross" or "Net" Issues

The principal/agency issue was referred to above. Issues which have arisen in UK GAAP are:

### Illustration 6

Extracts from annual report and accounts of Uniq plc, year ended 31 March 2002.

**Accounting policies (extract)**

> "... The Group has changed its accounting policy in respect of turnover, to disclose turnover net of all discounts and allowances to customers, some of which were previously shown as an expense. Prior year turnover has accordingly been reduced by £176.7m..."

Extract from annual report and accounts of the Big Food Group plc, year ended 29 March 2002.

**Accounting policies (extract)**

A summary of the Group's principal accounting policies is set out below. Following the implementation of FRS 18, the Group has reviewed its accounting policies. The only significant effect is to restate the comparative amounts for turnover and cost of sales by a reduction of £329.2m for the 65 weeks ended 31 March 2001, reflecting the Group's revised policy of excluding sales incentives from turnover. Turnover and cost of sales for the 52 weeks ended 29 March 2002 would have been £293.3m higher without this change in policy. With the exception of this change the accounting policies have been applied consistently throughout the period and the prior period.

### Illustration 7

Extract from annual report and accounts of Somerfield plc, year ended 27 April 2002.

**Turnover**

Turnover represents external sales of goods and services during the period, net of value added tax. Where promotional activity is undertaken the "free sale" element is excluded from turnover.

### Illustration 8

Extract from annual report and accounts of Hays plc, year ended 30 June 2003.

**Accounting policies (extract)**

**Turnover**

...Certain Logistics contracts oblige the Group to purchase goods from third parties and sell them on to the customer at cost. As the Group is rewarded for the logistics services provided, and as the sale and purchases of the goods have no impact on the operating profit, the amounts invoiced on to customers and charged by suppliers for the sale and purchase of these goods are excluded from turnover and cost of sales. Stock, debtors and creditors relating to such transactions are included in the consolidated balance sheet.

### Illustration 9

Extract from annual report and accounts of W S Atkins plc, year ended 31 March 2003.

**Accounting policies (extract)**

**Turnover**

...Under certain service contracts, the Group manages customer expenditure and is obliged to purchase goods or services from third party contractors and recharge them to the customer at cost. The amounts charged by contractors and recharged to customers are excluded from turnover and cost of sales. Debtors, creditors and cash relating to these transactions are included in the Group balance sheet.

*Illustration 10*

Extracts from annual report and accounts of Universal Salvage plc, year ended 3 May 2003.

**Accounting policies (extract)**

. . .

**Turnover**

As part of the regular review of accounting policies, and cognisant of the convergence of United Kingdom Accounting Standards with International Accounting Standards, a change has been made in respect of turnover and cost of sales classification. In previous financial statements, the amounts recharged to insurers for recovery and storage when collecting vehicles from garages on their behalf have been included within turnover and cost of sales. It is the Board's view that these recharges do not represent revenue as the amounts recharged are not fees for services rendered. Previous period's figures have been restated to reflect this change (see note 2) which has no impact on profit or net assets.

. . .

**Turnover**

Turnover represents amounts receivable for goods and services provided in the normal course of business, net of trade discounts, VAT and other sales related taxes. The analysis of turnover, profit before tax and net assets by geographical market supplied has not been provided as substantially all of the Group's activity is undertaken within the United Kingdom and within one principal class of business.

Vehicle sales at auction are recognised in the financial statements when the hammer drops, which under the terms and conditions of sale is the point at which the legally binding contract is formed between the Group and the buyer. Where vehicles are sold on behalf of third parties, our vehicle handling fee is also recognised when the hammer drops following the completion of our service of disposal on behalf of our client.

Related service income such as delivery of vehicles and other services, such as vehicle logistic activities for third party clients, is recognised only when the associated service has been performed.

Scrap metal income from processing is recognised at the point, following the vehicle being crushed, the metal cubes have been weighed by third party fragmentors.

**Group finance director's review (extract)**

**Results (extract)**

...

Mainly as a result of the loss of Direct Line, turnover was lower at £61.3 million, compared to a restated 2002 turnover of £72.0 million. Recovery and storage charges, which are made by recovery agents and repair garages and are subsequently recharged and recovered from insurance companies, have now been netted off in cost of sales and no longer appear as turnover.

# 8.8    International Financial Reporting Standards

IAS 18, Revenue, applies to accounting for revenue arising from the following transactions:

- Sale of goods;
- Rendering of services;
- Use by others of entity assets yielding interest, royalties and dividends.

Revenue is recognized when it is probable that future economic benefits will flow to the entity and these benefits can be measured reliably.

Revenue is measured at the fair value of the consideration received or receivable.

Revenue from the sale of goods is recognized when the entity has transferred to the buyer the significant risks and rewards of ownership of the goods and the amount of revenue can be measured reliably.

Revenue for a transaction involving the rendering of services is recognized as work is performed. For services which will be provided beyond the balance sheet date, revenue should be recognized by reference to the stage of completion at the balance sheet date, provided a number of conditions can be satisfied.

IAS 18 requires disclosure of the accounting policies adopted for revenue recognition. This includes disclosure of the methods adopted to determine the stage of completion of *transactions involving the rendering of services*.

The standard also requires disclosure of the amount of each significant category of revenue recognized during the period.

---

**Frequently Asked Questions**

1  Does Abstract 40 apply only to professional services such as those provided by accountants, solicitors. Barristers and architects?
No—it applies to all contracts for services such as industrial cleaning, consultancy and advertising.

2  Must revenue on single project service contracts that straddle the year-end be spread over the period of the contract?
Yes—contracts relating to the provision of a single service must be accounted for as long-term contracts in accordance with SSAP 9. Revenue should be recognized as contract activity takes place.

3  How should revenue be determined in respect of goods which have been sold with a right of return?
Revenue (turnover) should exclude the sales value of estimated returns.

---

**Useful Website Addresses**

ICAEW website (www.icaew.co.uk)
This contains frequently asked questions on both accounting and tax aspects of Abstract 40 together with supporting materials.

ACCA website (www.accaglobal.com)
Technical Factsheet 128 on UITF Abstract 40.

The Consultative Committee of Accountancy Bodies has written to the Government regarding the tax problems that will be caused by UITF Abstract 40, requesting that any additional tax be spread over a period of ten years (see www.icaew.co.uk for details).

# Employee Benefits

> **This chapter covers:**
> * Key directors' remuneration disclosures for unlisted companies
> * Special disclosure concessions for small companies
> * Retirement benefits – CA 85 and FRS 17
> * International Financial Reporting Standards

## 9.1 Directors' Remuneration – Unlisted Companies (Other than those Claiming Small Company Exemptions under CA 1985 s246)

### (a) Introduction

The general statutory disclosure rules for directors' remuneration are set out in (c) below and in 9.2. Special concessions available to small companies are dealt with in 9.3 below.

Additional requirements for listed companies are briefly referred to in Chapter 23.

### (b) Emoluments

The term "emoluments of a director" includes salaries, fees, bonuses, expense allowances subject to UK income tax and the estimated money value of benefits in kind.

### (c) Basic Disclosures

These are set out in CA 1985, Schedule 6, and include:

* the aggregate amount of emoluments paid to or receivable by directors;
* the aggregate of contributions paid, or treated as paid, under a money purchase (defined contribution) scheme – other than contributions paid by the director;
* for either money purchase schemes or defined benefit schemes, the number of directors who are accruing benefits under the scheme.

Disclosures required relating to long-term incentive schemes are referred to in 9.2(b) below.

## (d) Compensation to Directors for Loss of Office

### (1) Meaning
In Schedule 6, para 8, references to compensation for loss of office include:

- compensation either in consideration for or in connection with a person's retirement from office;
- in cases of a breach of contract, payments made by way of damages for the breach or payments made by way of settlement or compromise of any claim in respect of the breach.

### (2) Disclosure requirements
The requirement is for disclosure of the aggregate amount of compensation paid to directors or past directors in respect of loss of office (note (1) above). This disclosure applies to directors collectively rather than individually.

The aggregate amount to be disclosed includes cash and the estimated money value of benefits otherwise than in cash.

The nature (but not value) of any non-cash benefits must be disclosed.

## (e) Highest Paid Director

Where the aggregate emoluments of the directors exceeds £200,000, information must be disclosed relating to the highest paid director. The £200,000 includes salaries, fees, bonuses, etc., but not pension contributions paid by the company (see also below where a company has long-term incentive schemes).

Disclosures required include:

- the highest paid director's emoluments;
- in a money purchase scheme, the company pension contributions attributable to the highest paid director;
- the amount of the highest paid director's accrued retirement benefits if he is a member of a defined benefit scheme. The amounts to be disclosed include, as at the year-end, both accrued pension and accrued lump sum. The amount should exclude money purchase benefits or benefits arising from voluntary contributions made by that director.

### Illustration 1

Unlisted company not entitled to small company exemptions.

**Note ... – Directors' emoluments**

*(i) The directors' emoluments were:*

|  | 20X1 £ | 20X2 £ |
|---|---|---|
| Aggregate emoluments | 295,670 | 285,345 |
| Company pension contributions to money purchase schemes | 24,760 | 22,570 |
| Compensation for loss of office | 48,700 | – |
|  | 369,130 | 307,915 |

| | Number 2001 | Number 2000 |
|---|---|---|
| *(ii) Number of directors who are accruing benefits under a money purchase scheme 4* | 4 | 4 |
| | £ | £ |
| *(iii) Emoluments of highest paid director* | | 3,965 |
| – Aggregate emoluments | 55,150 | 48,760 |
| – Company pension contributions to money purchase scheme | 4,830 | 3,965 |

*Assumptions*

- No directors exercised share options, or received amounts in respect of long-term incentive schemes;
- The company did not operate a defined benefit scheme.

# 9.2 Directors' Remuneration – Other Disclosures

## (a) Share Options

Unlisted companies are not required to disclose the aggregate of gains made by the directors on the exercise of share options. However, unlisted companies must disclose the number of directors who exercised share options.

Where disclosures have to be given concerning the highest paid director (see above), it is necessary to disclose whether the highest paid director exercised any share options.

## (b) Long-term Incentive Schemes

"Long-term incentive scheme" means any agreement or arrangement under which money or assets may become receivable by a director and which includes one or more qualifying conditions with respect to service or performance which cannot be fulfilled within a single year. The following are specifically excluded from the definition:

- bonuses, the amount of which falls to be determined by reference to service or performance within a single financial year;
- compensation for loss of office, payments for breach of contract and other termination payments;
- retirement benefits.

For unlisted companies, the following disclosures are required:

- the aggregate of:
  - the amount of money paid to or receivable by directors under long-term incentive schemes, and;
  - the net value of assets other than money and shares received or receivable under such schemes;
- the number of directors in respect of whose qualifying services shares were received or receivable under long-term incentive schemes.

For highest paid director disclosures, in determining whether the £200,000 threshold has been reached, it is necessary to add the amounts in para 9.2(d) below to the aggregate amount of emoluments:

- the amount to be disclosed for that director should include emoluments and any amounts received under long-term incentive schemes;
- whether any shares were received or receivable by that director in respect of qualifying services under a long-term incentive scheme.

## (c) Excess Retirement Benefits

This requirement relates to disclosure of the aggregate amount of excess retirement benefits of directors and past directors.

The Explanatory Note issued with the Regulations stated that "the effect of the paragraph is to require companies to disclose increases in the amount of retirement benefits paid to directors or past directors in excess of the amounts to which they were entitled when the benefits became payable unless those excess benefits were paid to all members of the relevant scheme on the same basis and were paid without recourse to additional contributions".

## (d) Payments to Connected Persons or Companies Controlled by the Director

Disclosable emoluments include the following cases of payments for making available the services of any person as a director: amounts paid to connected persons or to companies controlled by the director (Sch 6, para 10 (4)).

Any amounts relating to the above should be included as part of the directors' emoluments, but do not need to be separately disclosed.

"Connected persons" is a complex term—defined in CA 1985, s346, (Persons connected with a director) this includes:

- the director's spouse, child or step-child,
- a body corporate with which the director is associated,
- a trustee of a trust whose beneficiaries include the director, spouse, children, a body corporate with which he is associated,
- the partner of the director.

A body corporate with which the director is associated includes a company in which the director and other connected persons hold or control at least 20% of the equity share capital.

## (e) Payments to Third Parties (Other than Connected Persons)

CA 1985 requires disclosure of the aggregate amount of any consideration paid to or receivable by third parties for making available to services of any person as a director of the company. Note that this aggregate amount should be disclosed *separately* from other elements of remuneration (Sch 6, para 9).

For the purposes of the above, "third parties" means persons other than the director or persons connected with its director. (These are caught by Sch 6, para 10(4) at (d) above).

The aggregate consideration disclosed should include the estimated money value benefit of non-cash benefits. Disclosure is required of the nature of any such consideration (but not its value).

# 9.3 Directors' Remuneration – Small Companies Claiming Exemptions Under CA 1985, Part VII

## (a) General Considerations

The notes below assume such companies take advantage of the special provisions for small companies contained in section 246 of the Companies Act 1985. Note that these concessions do not automatically apply to small companies. The concessions only apply if the balance sheet contains a statement above the director's signature to the effect that the accounts are prepared in accordance with the special provisions of Part VII relating to small companies.

## (b) Disclosures Required

The following should be disclosed:

- the aggregate of emoluments paid to or receivable by directors and contributions paid, or treated as paid, under a money purchase (defined contribution) scheme, other than contributions paid by the director;
- for either money purchase schemes or defined benefit schemes – the number of directors who are accruing benefits under the scheme;
- compensation to directors for loss of office (see 9.1 above).

In addition, the emoluments of the highest paid director need not be disclosed even if the aggregate remuneration of all directors exceeds £200,000. This concession does not apply to other unlisted companies e.g. medium-sized.

### Illustration 2

Small company claiming maximum disclosure exemptions.

**Note...– Directors' emoluments**

*The directors' emoluments were:*

|  | 2000 £ | 1999 £ |
|---|---|---|
| Aggregate emoluments, including pension contributions | 52,670 | 49,385 |
| Compensation for loss of office | – | 26,700 |
|  | 52,670 | 76,085 |
| Number of directors accruing benefits under a *money purchase scheme* | *Number* | *Number* |
|  | 2 | 2 |

## (c) Special Considerations

Apart from the concessions referred to in 9.3(a) above, the only other concession is that small companies claiming exemption need not disclose the number of directors exercising share options and receiving shares under long-term incentive schemes.

Other requirements set out above in 9.2(c), (d) and (e) apply where relevant.

# 9.4    Retirement Benefit – Introduction

The first part of this chapter gives an overview of various pension arrangements and the related statutory disclosure requirements. The chapter then deals with SSAP 24, Accounting for pension costs, which was superseded in November 2000 by FRS 17, Retirement benefits. The changes in FRS 17 relate to defined benefit or final salary schemes. There are no changes to the accounting and disclosure requirements for defined contribution or money purchase schemes.

FRS 17 permits companies to implement the standard gradually. The full accounting requirements of FRS 17 do not have to be implemented in full until accounting periods commencing on or after 1 January 2005.

However, as a minimum, additional memorandum disclosures are required for accounts periods ending on or after 22 June 2001 and 2002. The relevant requirements are covered in the later part of the chapter.

# 9.5    Retirement Benefit – Companies Act 1985 Requirements

## (a) Pension Costs

Disclosure is required of the amount of "other pension costs so incurred" which forms part of the total of staff costs.

Pension costs is defined as including:

(1) contributions paid bythe company to a pension fund or insurance company;
(2) amounts set aside to a provision for employee benefits;
(3) any amount paid by the company in respect of pension payments without being set aside as under (2).

Note that "staff" includes directors provided that they are employed under contracts of employment.

## (b) Pension Commitments

Disclosure is required of pension commitments:

(1) any pension commitments included under any provision shown in the company's balance sheet; and

(2) any such commitment for which no provision has been made.

Note that particulars are also required of commitments relating to pensions payable to past directors of the company.

# 9.6   Funding of Pension Arrangements

Some of the main possibilities may be illustrated diagrammatically as follows:

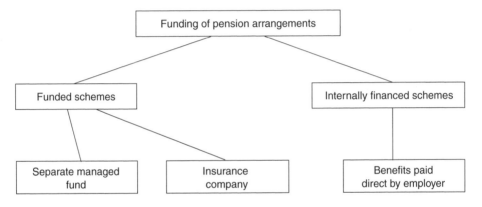

Two main groups of contractual schemes include defined contribution schemes and defined benefit schemes. Particular aspects of each may be contrasted as follows:

| Aspect | Defined contribution (money purchase) schemes | Defined benefit (final salary) schemes |
|---|---|---|
| (a) Benefit to employee? | Depends on funds available and performance of investments | May depend on employee's final pay prior to retirement |
| (b) Cost to employer? | Contributions payable in period (cost is easily measured) | Commitment is open-ended, final cost is often subject to considerable uncertainty |
| (c) Actuarial assumptions? | Not required | Crucial to calculation of pension costs in P/L ac |
| (d) Disclosures in annual accounts? | Relatively few | Extensive |

## 9.7 Accounting for Retirement Benefits – FRS 17: Introduction

Once FRS 17 has been fully implemented:

- Financial statements should reflect at fair value the assets and liabilities arising from an employer's retirement benefit obligations and any related funding.
- Operating costs of providing retirement benefits to employees should be recognized in the accounts period(s) in which the benefits are earned by employees.
- Related finance costs and any other changes in the value of the assets and liabilities should be recognised in the accounting periods in which they arise.
- Financial statements should contain adequate disclosure of the cost of providing retirement benefits and the related gains, losses, assets and liabilities.

## 9.8 FRS 17 – Transitional Provisions

In summary, the transitional arrangements (as amended) are as follows:

| Accounting periods ending on or after 22 June 2001 | Apply SSAP 24 accounting and disclosure requirements in *full*. Give FRS 17 memorandum balance sheet disclosures as at the current balance sheet date. |
|---|---|
| Accounting periods ending on or after 22 June 2002 | Apply SSAP 24 accounting and disclosure requirements in *full*. Give FRS 17 memorandum balance sheet disclosures for both the latest balance sheet date and for the previous one. Give FRS 17 memorandum profit and loss disclosures for the latest period only. |
| Accounting periods commencing on or after 1 January 2005 | Implement FRS 17 in full: <br> – make a prior year adjustment for a change in accounting policy, <br> – incorporate the FRS 17 numbers in the profit and loss account, balance sheet and statement of total recognised gains and losses, <br> – provide full FRS 17 disclosures, <br> – disregard SSAP 24 for *all* purposes. |

Prior to FRS 17, becoming mandatory in full, the following disclosure requirements applied in respect of defined benefit schemes:

- Nature of scheme (i.e. defined benefit).
- Date of most recent full actuarial valuation on which the amounts disclosed below are based.
- Contribution made in respect of accounting period and any agreed contribution rates for future years.

- For schemes which are closed and those for which the age profile of the active membership is rising significantly – the fact that under the projected unit method the current service cost will increase as the members of the scheme approach retirement.
- Main financial assumptions used at the balance sheet date, disclosing individually:
  - inflation assumptions,
  - rate of increase in salaries,
  - rate of increase for pensions in payment and deferred pensions,
  - rate used to discount scheme liabilities.
- Fair value of scheme assets at balance sheet date, analysed between classes, disclosing expected return for the period reported on and for the following period:
  - equities,
  - bonds,
  - other (e.g. property assets).
- Fair value of scheme assets (in aggregate), present value of the scheme liabilities and resulting surplus or deficit.
- Memorandum employee remuneration information in respect of the *current period only*:
  - current service costs,
  - any past service costs,
  - gains and losses on settlements or curtailments (e.g. where an employer has bought out pensions by making a payment to an insurance company or where some employees have been made redundant).
- Memorandum finance cost (income) information relating to the *current period only*:
  - interest cost,
  - expected return on scheme assets.
- Memorandum information regarding experience relating to assumptions made:
  - difference between expected and actual return on assets,
  - experience gains and losses arising on the scheme liabilities,
  - effects of changes in the demographic and financial assumptions underlying the present value of the scheme liabilities.
- Memorandum statistical information for the *current period only*:
  - difference between expected and actual return on assets, both as an absolute amount and as a percentage of the scheme assets at the balance sheet date,
  - experience gains and losses, both as an absolute amount and as a percentage of the present value of the scheme liabilities at the balance sheet date,
  - the total actuarial gains and losses expressed both as an absolute amount and as a percentage of the present value of the scheme liabilities at the balance sheet date.

## 9.9 FRS 17 – Full Implementation

For accounting periods commencing on or after 1 January 2005, FRS 17 must be implemented in full. SSAP 24 ceases to be applicable.

### (a) Defined Contribution Schemes

The pension cost should be reflected within the operating profit figure.

The pension cost charged to profit and loss account equals contributions payable to the scheme in respect of the accounting period.

Disclosures required are:

- Nature of scheme i.e. defined contribution,
- Cost for period,
- Any outstanding or prepaid contribution at balance sheet date.

### (b) Defined Benefit Schemes – Overview of Accounting and Disclosure Requirements

For 31 December 2005 year-ends onwards, the standard should be implemented in full and relevant amounts included in the balance sheet, the profit and loss account and the statement of total recognized gains and losses.

The changeover from SSAP 24 involves a complete change of accounting policy and is complex. Comparatives figures will need to be restated.

Key points to note in the first year of full implementation of FRS 17 are:

*(1) General*

- FRS 17 memorandum disclosure as for the previous year except that eventually a company will have to build up a five-year statistical summary covering the disclosure in the final bullet point in 9.8 above.
- Obtain full actuarial valuations at least three-yearly, updated at each balance sheet date (see below).

*(2) Balance sheet*
Include in the balance sheet one-line items for pension asset assuming a surplus) and pension reserve. These should be net of deferred tax.

The pension fund asset is calculated as the excess of the total market value of the scheme assets over the present value of the scheme liabilities; liabilities should be measured using the projected unit method.

*(3) Profit and loss account*
This should include the following charges or credits:

- current service cost and past service cost charged against operating profit,
- expected return on pension scheme assets,
- interest on pension scheme liabilities.

## (4) Statement of total recognized gains and losses (STRGL)
This should include actuarial gains and losses:

- actual return less expected return on pension scheme assets,
- experience gains and losses arising on the scheme liabilities,
- changes in assumptions underlying the present value of the scheme liabilities.

### Illustration 3

Extract from annual report and accounts of Uniq plc, year ended 31 March 2003.

**Note 32 – Pensions**

The Group operates pension schemes in the UK and overseas.

The main UK scheme is generally contributory for members and now has two sections, the defined benefit section and the defined contribution section. The defined benefit section was closed to new members generally in November 2002 and the defined contribution scheme was commenced in March 2003. Pension scheme assets in the UK are held in separate trust funds independent of the Group's finances other than in relation to unfunded over cap provision. Contributions are established according to funding rates advised by the scheme's actuary from time to time.

The Group also provides pensions under certain overseas schemes, some of which provide defined benefits for the majority of members. With the exception of the German pension scheme, which is an unfunded scheme, assets are held in separate trust funds independent of the Group's finances. The impact of all overseas schemes is included in the analysis below.

The FRS 17 valuations for all the Group's pension schemes were updated to 31 March 2003 by an independent qualified actuary in accordance with FRS 17. As required by FRS 17, the defined benefit liabilities have been measured using the projected unit method.

The following table sets out the key FRS 17 assumptions used for the schemes. Overseas plans are quoted as a weighted average based on liabilities. The assumptions used by the actuary are the best estimates chosen from a range of possible actuarial assumptions about the future which may not necessarily be borne out in practice.

**Assumptions**

|  | UK | | | Overseas | | |
|---|---|---|---|---|---|---|
|  | **2003** | 2002 | 2001 | **2003** | 2002 | 2001 |
|  | **%** | % | % | **%** | % | % |
| Inflation | **2.5** | 2.5 | 2.5 | **2.0** | 2.0 | 2.0 |
| Pension increases | **2.4** | 2.5 | 2.5 | **2.0** | 2.0 | 2.0 |
| Salary growth | **4.0** | 4.0 | 4.0 | **2.9** | 3.3 | 2.9 |
| Discount rate | **5.7** | 6.1 | 6.0 | **5.4** | 6.0 | 5.9 |
| Expected return for: |  |  |  |  |  |  |
| – Equities | **7.5** | 8.0 | 8.0 | **7.4** | 8.0 | 7.3 |
| – Bonds | **5.7** | 6.1 | 6.0 | **5.0** | 5.0 | 5.0 |
| – Other | **3.8** | – | 4.0 | **5.0** | 5.0 | 5.0 |

The table below sets out the fair value of assets, a breakdown of the assets into the main asset classes the present value of the FRS 17 liabilities and the deficit of assets below the FRS 17 liabilities (Which equals the gross pension liability). The fair value of the scheme's assets is not intended to be realised in the short term and may be subject to significant change before realisation. The present value of the scheme's liabilities is derived from cash flow projections over long periods and thus inherently uncertain. The significant decrease in the fair value of assets and present value of liabilities in the UK between 31 March 2001 and 31 March 2002 is due principally to the demerger of Wincanton on 17 May 2001.

| | UK £m | Overseas £m | Total £m |
|---|---|---|---|
| Fair value of assets 2003: | | | |
| – Equities | **203.9** | **1.7** | **205.6** |
| – Bonds | **196.8** | **6.5** | **203.3** |
| – Other | **0.6** | **1.6** | **2.2** |
| | **401.3** | **9.8** | **411.1** |
| Present value of liabilities | **(544.6)** | **(28.8)** | **(573.4)** |
| Gross pension liability | **(143.3)** | **(19.0)** | **(162.3)** |
| Deferred tax | **43.0** | **6.5** | **49.5** |
| Net pension liability at 31 March 2003 | **(100.3)** | **(12.5)** | **(112.8)** |
| Fair value of assets 2002: | | | |
| – Equities | 287.4 | 3.8 | 291.2 |
| – Bonds | 177.7 | 5.1 | 182.8 |
| – Other | – | 1.0 | 1.0 |
| | 465.1 | 9.9 | 475.0 |
| Present value of liabilities | (508.9) | (21.3) | (530.2) |
| Gross pension liability | (43.8) | (11.4) | (55.2) |
| Deferred tax | 13.1 | – | 13.1 |
| Net pension liability at 31 March 2002 | (30.7) | (11.4) | (42.1) |
| Fair value of assets 2001: | | | |
| – Equities | 742.8 | 3.9 | 746.7 |
| – Bonds | – | 5.2 | 5.2 |
| – Other | – | 0.8 | 0.8 |
| | 742.8 | 9.9 | 752.7 |
| Present value of liabilities | (778.5) | (19.9) | (798.4) |
| Gross pension liability | (35.7) | (10.0) | (45.7) |
| Deferred tax | 10.7 | – | 10.7 |
| Net pension liability at 31 March 2001 | (25.0) | (10.0) | (35.0) |

| **Movement in deficit during the year** | UK £m | Overseas £m | Total £m |
|---|---|---|---|
| **Year to 31 March 2003** | | | |
| Gross pension liability at start of year | **(43.8)** | **(11.4)** | **(55.2)** |
| Movement in the year: | | | |
| Current service cost | **(7.8)** | **(1.6)** | **(9.4)** |
| Curtailments and settlements | **2.1** | **–** | **2.1** |
| Contributions | **8.8** | **1.3** | **10.1** |
| Other finance income | **2.8** | **(0.7)** | **2.1** |
| Actuarial loss | **(105.4)** | **4.9** | **(110.3)** |
| Exchange adjustment | **–** | **(1.7)** | **(1.7)** |
| Gross pension liability at 31 March 2003 | **(143.3)** | **(19.0)** | **(162.3)** |
| **Year to 31 March 2002** | | | |
| Gross pension liability at start of year | (35.7) | (10.0) | (45.7) |
| Movement in the year: | | | |
| Current service cost | (13.0) | (1.7) | (14.7) |
| Curtailments and settlements | 5.9 | – | 5.9 |
| Contributions | 15.1 | 0.9 | 16.0 |
| Other finance income | 6.2 | (0.5) | 5.7 |
| Actuarial (loss)/gain | (37.7) | 0.1 | (37.6) |
| Wincanton demerger | 15.4 | – | 15.4 |
| Exchange adjustment | – | (0.2) | (0.2) |
| Gross pension liability at 31 March 2002 | (43.8) | (11.4) | (55.2) |

| Analysis of the amount recognised in the statement of total recognised gains and losses | UK £m | Overseas £m | Total £m |
|---|---|---|---|
| **Year to 31 March 2003** | | | |
| Actual return less expected return on pension scheme assets | **(91.4)** | – | **(91.4)** |
| Experience gains and losses arising on the scheme liabilities | **14.9** | **(0.3)** | **14.6** |
| Changes in assumptions underlying the present value of the scheme liabilities | **(28.9)** | **(4.6)** | **(33.5)** |
| Actuarial loss recognised in the statement of total recognised gains and losses | **(105.4)** | **(4.9)** | **(110.3)** |
| | | | |
| **Year to 31 March 2002** | | | |
| Actual return less expected return on pension scheme assets | (21.4) | – | (21.4) |
| Experience gains and losses arising on the scheme liabilities | (0.1) | 0.2 | 0.1 |
| Changes in assumptions underlying the present value of the scheme liabilities | (16.2) | (0.1) | (16.3) |
| Actuarial loss recognised in the statement of total recognised gains and losses | (37.7) | 0.1 | (37.6) |

| History of experience gains and losses | UK £m | Overseas £m | Total £m |
|---|---|---|---|
| **Year to 31 March 2003** | | | |
| Difference between the expected and actual return on scheme assets: | | | |
| Amount £m | **(91.4)** | – | **(91.4)** |
| Percentage of scheme assets | **(22.8%)** | **(0.5%)** | **(22.2%)** |
| Experience gains and losses on scheme liabilities: | | | |
| Amount £m | **14.9** | **(0.3)** | **14.6** |
| Percentage of the present value of scheme liabilities | **2.7%** | **(1.0%)** | **2.5%** |
| Total amount recognised in the statement of total recognised gains and losses: | | | |
| Amount £m | **(105.4)** | **(4.9)** | **(110.3)** |
| Percentage of the present value of scheme liabilities | **(19.4%)** | **(17.0%)** | **(19.2%)** |
| | | | |
| **Year to 31 March 2002** | | | |
| Difference between the expected and actual return on scheme assets: | | | |
| Amount £m | (21.4) | – | (21.4) |
| Percentage of scheme assets | (4.6%) | (0.1%) | (4.5%) |
| Experience gains and losses on scheme liabilities: | | | |
| Amount £m | (0.1) | 0.2 | 0.1 |
| Percentage of the present value of scheme liabilities | | 0.9% | |
| Total amount recognised in the statement of total recognised gains and losses: | | | |
| Amount £m | (37.7) | 0.1 | (37.6) |
| Percentage of the present value of scheme liabilities | (7.4%) | 0.5% | (7.1%) |

|  | Notes | 2003<br>**£m** | 2002<br>*(restated)*<br>*£m* |
|---|---|---|---|
| Profit/(loss) for the financial year | | **24.9** | (101.0) |
| Actuarial loss recognised on the pension schemes | 32 | **(110.3)** | (37.6) |
| Movement on deferred tax relating to<br>    actuarial loss on pensions | | **38.8** | 7.7 |
| Currency translation differences on<br>    foreign currency net investments | 24 | **4.2** | (0.3) |
| **Total recognised gains and losses for the year** | | **(42.4)** | (131.2) |
| Prior year adjustment | 31 | **(17.1)** | |
| **Total recognised gains and losses since<br>last annual report** | | **(59.5)** | |

## 9.10    International Financial Reporting Standards

The aim of IAS 19 is to prescribe the accounting and disclosure for employee benefits.

The Standard gives guidance on several  categories of employee benefits, the most important of which are:

- Short-term employee benefits;
- Post-employment benefits;
- Termination benefits.

### (a) Short-term Employee Benefits

This part of the standard refers to the  accounting treatment of profit-sharing and bonuses payable within twelve months after the end of the period in which the employees render the related service. It provides detailed  guidance in determining whether or not an entity has a legal or constructive obligation, as at the balance sheet date, to pay a bonus.

### (b) Post-employment Benefits

This part to retirement benefits such as pensions, as well as other post-employment benefits, such as post-employment life assurance and medical care.

The section on post-employment benefits deals with defined contribution pension schemes and defined benefit schemes.

Costs relating to defined contribution schemes will continue to be charged as incurred to the income statement, as was the case under both SSAP 24 and FRS 17.

As regards defined benefit schemes, the treatment  in IAS 19 of actuarial gains and losses differs from FRS 17. However, IASB published an amendment in December 2004 offering an option additional to those previously in IAS 19.

This would allow UK companies to recognize actuarial gains and losses *outside the income statement*, in a statement of recognized income and expense, similar to the treatment in FRS 17.

## (c) Termination Benefits

These should be recognized as a liability and an expense when, and only when, the entity is demonstrably committed to either:

- Terminate the employment of an employee before the normal retirement date, or;
- Provide termination benefits as a result of an offer made in order to encourage voluntary redundancy.

---

**Frequently Asked Questions**

1 Does FRS 17 change accounting/disclosure for contributions to money purchase schemes?
No—accounting and disclosure requirements are the same as was the case under SSAP 24.

2 When must FRS 17 be implemented in full for companies with defined benefit schemes?
FRS 17 is mandatory in full for accounts periods commencing on or after 1 January 2005.

3 Under FRS 17 do fluctuations in the market value of scheme investments have an immediate impact on profit or loss?
No—FRS 17 requires actuarial gains and losses to be taken directly to a Statement of total recognized gains and losses.

# Share-based Payment

## 10.1 Overview

### (a) Share-based Payment

This term refers to a wide range of situations where an entity grants shares, share options, and certain cash payments to directors and employees as part of their remuneration package and to suppliers as consideration for goods and services supplied to the entity. FRS 20 (see 10.5 below) includes a detailed and extensive definition of this term.

### (b) UK GAAP Requirements

The Urgent Issues Task Force has issued a number of Abstracts dealing with various aspects of this topic:

- Disclosure of directors' share options – Abstract 10 (subsequently withdrawn, but included in UKLA disclosure rules for fully listed companies);
- Accounting for Employee Share Ownership Plan (ESOP) trusts – Abstract 13, superseded by Abstract 38;
- Employee share schemes – Abstract 17 (revised on several occasions);
- National Insurance contributions on share option gains – Abstract 25;
- Date of award of employees of shares or rights to shares – Abstract 30;
- Employee benefit trusts and other intermediate payment arrangements – Abstract 32.

The first standard to deal with this subject comprehensively is FRS 20, Share-based payment, issued in April 2004.

FRS 20, and Abstracts 17, 25 and 38 are further referred to below.

## 10.2    Employee Share Schemes – UITF Abstract 17

### (a)  Background

The revised Abstract 17 was issued in December 2003 and should be read in conjunction with Abstract 38 "Accounting for ESOP trusts" which was issued at the same time. These Abstracts have been produced following the publication of Abstract 37 "Purchases and sales of own shares" and the revision to the Companies Act regarding treasury shares in SI 2003/1116.

The purpose of the Abstract is to deal with the question of the measurement and timing of charges to profit and loss accounts arising from employee share schemes. There is little practical change to the previous version of Abstract 17. Note that Abstract 17 is superseded by FRS 20, subject to transitional arrangements (see 10.2 (c) below).

### (b)  Accounting Treatment

#### (i)  Issue of shares

A charge should be made to the profit and loss account when a company issues shares to satisfy its obligations under share schemes. This charge should be based on the fair value of the shares issued.

The fair value is based on the market value of the shares at the date of the award (the date on which rights to the shares are granted). *No account should be taken of any movement in market value after the date of grant.*

Where the individual receiving the shares is required to contribute towards the cost of the shares, the charge is reduced by the amount of the contribution or exercise price.

If the grant is subject to performance criteria the charge should be arrived at after making a realistic estimate of the likely outcome. The overall cost (the difference between market value and exercise price) should be spread over the performance period. These estimates will be revised over the performance period and may result in variable amounts being recognized in the profit and loss account. If the award relates to an annual bonus, the charge should be reflected in the period to which the bonus relates.

If the grant terms include a provision that the employees should remain employed for a period after the end of the performance period before becoming unconditionally entitled to the shares, that extra period should not normally be included in the performance period. If there are no performance criteria, and the award does not relate to past performance, the cost should be written off over the period to the date when the employee becomes unconditionally entitled to the shares.

#### (ii)  Share options

A similar approach to the above should be adopted where share options are granted at values below market value at the date of grant.

## Illustration 1

A company sets up an unapproved share option scheme on 1 January 2003, when the market value of the company's shares is £5. Under the scheme a maximum of 10,000 shares are granted. The exercise price is £1, dependent on performance from 1 January 2003 to 31 December 2006.

Assume that the number of options expected to vest is estimated at each balance sheet date as follows:

- 31 December 2003 – 10,000 options
- 31 December 2004 – 9,000 options
- 31 December 2005 – 8,500 options

The amount to be "accrued" within shareholders' funds at each date would be as follows:

- 31 December 2003 – 1/3 of 10,000 × (£5–£1) i.e. £13,333
- 31 December 2004 – 2/3 of 9,000 × (£5–£1) i.e. £24,000
- 31 December 2005 – 8,500 × (£5–£1) i.e. £34,000

The charge to profit and loss account each year (charged in the relevant heading for staff costs) would be:

- 2003 – £13,333
- 2004 – £10,667
- 2005 – £10,000

*(a) Disclosure Implications*

**Accounting policies (extract)**

**Share options**

In accordance with the requirements of UITF 17, 'Employee Share Schemes', a charge is made in the profit and loss account for the difference between the fair value of the shares under option at the date of granting, and the exercise price. Where the award is conditional on certain performance criteria being met, this is reflected in the number of options on which the charge is calculated.

*Notes to the accounts (extracts)*
   Exceptional items included within administrative expenses:

   – Share options compensation expense...

   [Other reserves or profit and loss reserves would include effect of credit side of double entry (debit to profit and loss account, as above).]

*(b) Other Issues Arising from Granting of Share Options*
There are a number of disclosure issues which may arise according to the company's status:
   (i) UITF 25 could apply to any category of company, listed or unlisted, which had a share option scheme where options were granted post 6 April 1999 and which was not Inland Revenue approved (see 10.3(a) below).
   (ii) Companies Act 1985 disclosures – Sch 7, para 2B, requires disclosure for each director of share options granted or exercised during the year. These disclosures apply to both listed and unlisted companies, whether public or private.
   (iii) Companies Act 1985, Sch 4, para 40 requires disclosure of all share options, whether for directors or for staff. These should be disclosed in the notes to the accounts. Usual practice is to disclose this as part of the share capital note (see illustration above).

## Illustration 2

Extracts from annual report and accounts of Wyevale Garden Centres plc, year ended 28 December 2003.

**Accounting policies (extract)**

**Employee Share Schemes**

A charge is made to the Group Profit and Loss Account and a reserve created in capital and reserves to record the fair value of shares conditionally awarded under the Company's Long Term Share Incentive Plan.

**Group balance sheet (extract)**

|  |  | 2003 £'000 | 2002 £'000 |
|---|---|---|---|
| ... |  |  |  |
| **Capital and reserves** |  |  |  |
| Called up share capital | 17 | **13,948** | 13,910 |
| Share premium account | 18 | **78,515** | 78,167 |
| Revaluation reserve | 18 | **9,230** | 9,359 |
| Capital redemption reserve | 18 | **2,812** | 2,812 |
| Share scheme reserve | 18 | **616** | 488 |
| Merger reserve | 18 | **7,191** | 7,191 |
| Profit and loss account | 18 | **50,086** | 43,758 |
| **Shareholders' funds – equity** |  | **162,398** | 155,685 |

...

## Illustration 3

Extract from annual report and accounts of Wyevale Garden Centres plc, year ended 28 December 2003.

**Note 18 – Reserves (extract)**

**18 Reserves**

|  | Share premium £'000 | Revaluation reserve £'000 | Capital redemption reserve £'000 | Share scheme reserve £'000 | Merger reserve £'000 | Profit and loss account £'000 |
|---|---|---|---|---|---|---|
| **Group** |  |  |  |  |  |  |
| At 30 December 2002 | 78,167 | 9,359 | 2,812 | 488 | 7,191 | 43,758 |
| Transfer to profit and loss account | – | (100) | – | – | – | 100 |
| Transfer on property disposal | – | (29) | – | – | – | 29 |
| Arising on issue of shares | 348 | – | – | (48) | – | – |
| Share scheme charge | – | – | – | 176 | – | – |
| Share scheme award | – | – | – | – | – | 44 |
| Retained profits for the year | – | – | – | – | – | 6,155 |
| At 28 December 2003 | **78,515** | **9,230** | **2,812** | **616** | **7,191** | **50,086** |

Abstract 17 (revised) provides illustrative examples dealing with the accounting treatment in various scenarios.

## (c) Scope and Effective Date

The Abstract is mandatory for accounting periods ending on or after 22 June 2004 and supersedes the previous version of Abstract 17.

Abstract 17 (revised) applies to all share schemes, except Save-As-You-Earn schemes, including:

- Indirect schemes using convertible or exchangeable instruments such as warrants or options;
- Approved profit sharing schemes;
- All-employee share plans;
- Initial listings of companies where employees are given the opportunity to subscribe for shares, or rights to shares, at a discount to the float price payable by public investors.

Abstract 17 (revised) is relevant for all entities except those applying the Financial Reporting Standard for Smaller Entities.

> Please note that FRS 20 supersedes UITF Abstract 17 for the relevant effective date of FRS 20. For unlisted companies, this is no later than accounts periods commencing on or after 1 January 2006 (see 10.5(i) below).

# 10.3 National Insurance Contributions on Share Option Gains – UITF Abstract 25

## (a) Introduction

UITF 25 deals with a specific application of FRS 12 on provisions and contingencies, regarding an employer's future liability to National Insurance contributions on share option gains.

The Social Security Act 1998 brought in a NI charge on UK employers. The charge relates to gains made by employees on the exercise of share options issued under unapproved share option schemes (i.e. schemes not approved by the Inland Revenue):

- The charge applies to options granted on or after 6 April 1999.
- The gain is calculated as the difference between:
  - the share price at the date of exercise of the option, and
  - the exercise price paid by the employee.
- The charge applies to schemes where the shares are "readily convertible assets" (shares which can be sold on a stock exchange or shares for which there are arrangements in place that allow the employees to obtain cash for the shares).
- The rules of the scheme will usually set out special arrangements to enable the employer to recover from the employee any additional tax or National Insurance due.

## (b) Accounting Issues – Overview

Key issues are:

- whether the employer company should accrue for the estimated NI liability as from the date of grant of the option, and if so, what share price should be used for the calculation;
- to what extent the NI payable by the employer is recoverable from the employee;
- whether the accrual should be spread, for profit and loss account purposes, over the period from the date of the grant of the option to the date of completion of a performance period.

## (c) Accounting and Disclosure Issues – Detailed Considerations

### (1) Assessing the need for a provision

The Urgent Issues Task Force regards the granting of the option as a past obligating event under FRS 12. Although the future share price at the date of exercise of the option may be uncertain, UITF considers that the market price of the shares at the balance sheet date provides a reliable basis for making "…the best estimate of the expenditure required to settle the present obligation at the balance sheet date" (FRS 12, para 36).

- Provision should be made for NI contributions on outstanding share options that are expected to be exercised.
- The provision should be calculated at the latest enacted NI rate applied to the difference between the market value of underlying shares at the balance sheet date, and the option exercise price.
- The amount of the provision should be adjusted at subsequent balance sheet dates using the current market value of the shares.

### (2) Reimbursement by the employee
### (i) Agreement

The employer company will usually enter into an agreement with the employee to reimburse all or part of the employer's NI contributions. In such cases:

- A provision should be made for the full amount of NI to be paid;
- The expected reimbursement should be treated as a separate asset, but only if receipt is virtually certain;
- Net presentation is permitted for the profit and loss account only.

### (ii) Joint election

UITF 25, para 6, states that "… where there is a joint election by employer and employee under which the *liability* is *formally* transferred to the employee, there is no liability to appear in the employer's accounts".

### (3) Profit and loss account

- The provision, less any reimbursable amount recognized in the balance sheet, should be allocated over the period from the date of the grant to the end of the performance period.
- Where there is no performance period, full provision should be made immediately.
- Amounts provided for should be charged to profit and loss account as staff costs, except where they form part of capitalized staff costs (e.g. CA 1985 refers to own work capitalized and FRS 15, para 9(a) refers to labour costs of own employees).

## (d) Worked Example – Appendix to UITF 25

The company's year-end is 31 December.

A maximum of 10,000 share options are granted at 1 July 1999, when the market value is £1, at an exercise price of £1, dependent upon performance from 1 July 1999 to 30 June 2002. The options are exercisable from 1 July 2002 to 1 July 2003.

Employer's National Insurance contributions, currently at 12.2%, are payable on exercise of the options.

| Y/E 31 Dec | Market Value of Share | B/S Provision | P/L Charge (credit) |
|---|---|---|---|
| 1999 | £1.80 | Estimated max entitlement of option: $1/6 \times 12.2\% \times 10,000 \times (£1.80 - £1) = £163$ | £163 – £0 = £163 |
| 2000 | £3.00 | Estimated max entitlement of option: $1/2 \times 12.2\% \times 10,000 \times (£3.00 - £1) = £1,220$ | £1,220 – £163 = £1,057 |
| 2001 | £2.80 | Assuming 8,000 options will be exercised: $5/6 \times 12.2\% \times 8,000 \times (£2.80 - £1) = £1,464$ | £1,464 – £1,220 = £244 |
| 2002 | £2.20 | 6,000 options vested – but none had been exercised by 31/12/02: $12.2\% \times 6,000 \times (£2.20 - £1) = £878$ | £878 – £1,464 = (£586) |
| 2003 | £2.65 as at 17/5/03 | 6,000 options exercised on 17 May 2003: $12.2\% \times 6,000 \times (£2.65 - £1) = £1,208$ | £1,208 – £878 = £330 |

*Illustration 4*

Extract from annual report and accounts of lastminute.com plc, year ended 30 September 2003.

**Note 21 – Provisions for liabilities and charges**

| | *Share Option Provisions £'000s* | *Onerous contracts £'000s* | *Restructuring (see note 4) £'000s* | *Integration (see note. 4) £'000s* | *Other £'000s* | *Total £'000s* |
|---|---|---|---|---|---|---|
| At 1 October 2002 | 285 | 307 | 2,716 | – | 806 | 4,114 |
| Provided during the year | 1,083 | 3,329 | – | 858 | – | 5,270 |
| Utilised during the year | (54) | (1.907) | (2,716) | – | (806) | (5.483) |
| Released during the year | (9) | – | – | – | – | (9) |
| At 30 September 2003 | 1,305 | 1,729 | – | 858 | – | 3.892 |

The Group provides for National Insurance contributions on options granted under the unapproved share option scheme. A provision is made at a rate of 12.8% over the vesting period of the options on the difference between the period end share value and the grant price, being the Group's best estimate of the ultimate liability at each period end. This provision is utilised as options are exercised.

Provisions are recognised for onerous lease contracts and are based on the future charges of the leases over their remaining lease periods.

The restructuring provision related to costs associated with restructuring our French and Italian businesses.

The integration provision relates to costs associated with the integration of holiday autos. These costs primarily consist of a reduction in headcount, consolidation of properties and termination of certain contracts.

Others includes the provision for award minutes, which were utilised during the year.

**Accounting policies (extract)**

**Employee share schemes**

In accordance with UITF abstract 17 (revised 2000), Employee share schemes, the difference between the exercise price of share options granted under the Group's share option schemes and the fair market value of the underlying ordinary shares at the date of grant is provided for and charged to the profit and loss account on a straight-line basis over the period in which the options vest.

The Group provides for National Insurance contributions on options granted to UK employees on or after 6 April 1999 under its unapproved share option schemes in accordance with UITF abstract 25 National Insurance contributions on share option gains. The expected charge is allocated over the period in which the options vest on a straight-line basis.

# 10.4    Accounting for ESOP Trusts – UITF Abstract 38

## (a) Background

Abstract 38 was issued in December 2003 and replaces Abstract 13. It was produced following the publication of Abstract 37 "Purchases and sales of own shares" and the revision to the Companies Act regarding treasury shares in SI 2003/1116.

Abstract 38 deals with the question of when and how a sponsoring company should recognize the assets and liabilities of ESOP (Employee share ownership plan) trusts in their own accounts. It does not deal with expense recognition. A revised version of Abstract 17 has been issued covering that aspect.

The basic requirements of Abstract 13 remain unchanged. The main difference is the accounting treatment and presentation in the balance sheet.

## (b) Features of ESOP Trusts

ESOPs are often established to incentivise employees and to provide a vehicle to facilitate their shareholdings. The structures of ESOPs, and reasons for their existence vary but often contain the following features:

- The ESOP trust provides a warehouse for the sponsoring company's shares, for example by acquiring and holding shares that are to be sold or transferred to employees in the future;
- Where the ESOP trust borrows from a third party, the sponsoring company will usually guarantee the loan, i.e. it will be responsible for any shortfall if the trust's assets are insufficient to meet its debt repayment obligations;
- The company may also make regular contributions to the trust to enable the trust to meet its interest payments;
- Shares held by the ESOP trust are distributed to employees through an employee share scheme – this may be through the:
  - purchase of shares by employees when exercising their share options under a share option scheme;
  - purchase of shares by the trustees of an approved profit-sharing scheme for allocation to employees under the rules of the scheme;
  - transfer of shares to employees under another incentive scheme;
- Although the trustees of the ESOP trust must act at all times in accordance with the interests of the beneficiaries under the trust, most ESOP trusts (particularly those established as a means of remunerating employees) are specifically designed to serve the purposes of the sponsoring company, and to ensure that there will be minimal risk of any conflict arising between the duties of the trustees and the interest of the company. Where this is so, the sponsoring company has de facto control and there will be nothing to encumber implementation of its wishes in practice.

## (c) Accounting Treatment and Accounts Disclosures

The over-riding principle is that, as noted above, where the sponsoring company has de facto control of the ESOP's assets and liabilities they should be included in its own accounts. This will usually be the case when the trust has been set up for the purposes of an employee remuneration scheme. This follows the principles of FRS 5 "Reporting the substance of transactions".

The Abstract gives the following guidance on accounting treatment:

- Until such time as the company's own shares held by the ESOP trust vest unconditionally in employees, the consideration paid for the shares should be deducted in arriving at shareholders' funds;
- Other assets and liabilities (including borrowings) of the ESOP trust should be recognized as assets and liabilities of the sponsoring company;
- Consideration paid or received for the purchase or sale of the company's own shares in an ESOP trust should be shown as separate amounts in the reconciliation of movements in shareholders' funds;
- No gain or loss should be recognized in the profit and loss account or statement of total recognized gains and losses on the purchase, sale, issue or cancellation of the company's own shares;
- Finance costs and any administration expenses should be charged as they accrue and not as funding payments are made to the ESOP trust;
- Any dividend income arising on own shares should be excluded in arriving at profit before tax and deducted from the aggregate of dividends paid and proposed. The deduction should be disclosed if material.

The Abstract indicates that "sufficient information should be disclosed in the financial statements of the sponsoring company to enable readers to understand the significance of the ESOP trust in the context of the sponsoring company". This will usually include:

- A description of the main features of the ESOP trust including the arrangements for distributing shares to employees;
- The amounts of reductions to shareholders' funds and the number and (for companies that have shares listed or publicly traded on a stock exchange or market) market value of shares held by the ESOP trust which have not yet vested unconditionally in employees; and
- The extent to which these shares are under option to employees, or have been conditionally gifted to them.

*Illustration 5*

Extract from annual report and accounts of Computacenter plc, year ended 31 December 2003.

**Accounting policies (extract)**

...

In preparing the financial statements for the current year, the Group and Company have adopted UITF 38 'Accounting for ESOP trusts'. This abstract had no impact on the results for the period but shareholders funds have been reduced by £2,503,000 following the recognition of the ESOP trust within reserves.

**Note 23 – Reconciliation of shareholders' funds and movements on reserves (extract)**

| | Share capital £'000 | Share premium £'000 | Capital redemption reserve £'000 | Investment in own shares £'000 | Merger reserve £'000 | Profit and loss account £'000 | Total shareholders' funds £'000 |
|---|---|---|---|---|---|---|---|
| *Group* | | | | | | | |
| At 1 January 2002 | 9,281 | 68,710 | – | – | – | 143,825 | 221,816 |
| Prior year adjustment | – | – | – | (2,503) | – | – | (2,503) |
| At 1 January 2002 (restated) | 9,281 | 68,710 | – | (2,503) | – | 143,825 | 219,313 |
| Shares issued | 56 | 294 | – | – | – | – | 350 |
| Shares repurchased | (100) | – | 100 | – | – | (4,646) | (4,646) |
| Total recognised gains in the year | – | – | – | – | – | 38,270 | 38,270 |
| Equity dividends | – | – | – | – | – | (10,657) | (10,657) |
| At 31 December 2002 | 9,237 | 69,004 | 100 | (2,503) | – | 166,792 | 242,630 |
| Shares issued | 204 | 2,482 | – | – | – | – | 2,686 |
| Total recognised gains in the year | – | – | – | – | – | 50,463 | 50,463 |
| Equity dividends | – | – | – | – | – | (13,011) | (13,011) |
| **At 31 December 2003** | **9,441** | **71,486** | **100** | **(2,503)** | **–** | **204,244** | **282,768** |

...

Abstract 38 provides illustrative examples dealing with the accounting treatment in various scenarios.

### (d) Scope and Effective Date

The Abstract is mandatory for accounting periods ending on or after 22 June 2004. Earlier adoption is encouraged. On implementation corresponding amounts may need to be reclassified where applicable.

Abstract 38 is relevant for all entities except those applying the Financial Reporting Standard for Smaller Entities.

## 10.5  Share-based Payment, FRS 20

### (a) Share-based Payment and FRS 20

Following the issue by the International Accounting Standards Board of IFRS 2, the UK Accounting Standards Board issued an identical document, designated as FRS 20.

Please note that FRS 20 supersedes UITF Abstract 17 for the relevant effective date of FRS 20. For unlisted companies, this is no later than accounts periods commencing on or after 1 January 2006 (see 10.5(i) below).

FRS 20 deals with situations where entities grant shares or share options to:

- Directors, senior executives and other employees – as a feature of their remuneration package; and
- Suppliers – for example, as consideration for the provision of consultancy services or for the receipt of goods such as inventories, consumables, property, plant and equipment or intangible assets.

In FRS 20, the term "share-based payment transactions" refers to transfers of an entity's equity instruments by its shareholders to parties, including employees, that have supplied goods or services to the entity.

"Share-based payment transactions" includes the following three sub-categories:

| Equity-settled share-based payment transactions | Entity receives goods or services as consideration for equity instruments of the entity (including shares or share options). |
| --- | --- |
| Cash-settled share-based payment transactions | Entity acquires goods or services by incurring liabilities to the supplier of those goods or services for cash whose amount is based on the price (or value) of the entity's shares or other equity instruments. |
| Share-based payment transactions with cash alternatives | The entity receives or acquires goods or services and the terms of the arrangement provide either the entity or the supplier of those goods and services with a choice of whether the entity settles the transaction in cash or by issuing equity instruments. |

## (b) Scope of FRS 20

*Employee share purchase plans*

There is no exemption for "broad-based" or "all-employee" plans in which all (or virtually all) employees have the opportunity to buy a specific number of shares at a discounted price (i.e. at less than the fair value of the shares).

By contrast, UITF Abstract 17 on Employee share schemes, exempts from its scope Inland Revenue approved SAVE schemes and equivalent overseas schemes.

*Unlisted companies*

These are not exempt from FRS 20 but paragraph BC144 of the Basis for Conclusions on FRS 20; comments:

"...However, the Board acknowledged that there might be some instances in which an entity – such as (but not limited to) an unlisted or newly-listed entity – cannot estimate reliably the grant date fair value of share options granted. In this situation, the Board concluded that the entity should measure the share option at its intrinsic value, initially at the date the entity obtains the goods or the counterparty renders service, and subsequently at each reporting date until the final settlement of the share-based payment arrangement, with the effects of the remeasurement recognised in profit or loss…".

This is referred to in FRS 20, paragraph 24, and illustrated by numerical example in Implementation Guidance, paragraph 16, Example 10.

## (c) Overview of the Main Features of FRS 20

### (i) Basic measurement principle

The fair value of goods or services should be measured directly, unless that fair value cannot be estimated reliably in which case it should be measured by reference to the fair value of the equity instruments granted.

For equity-settled share-based payment transactions, the debit side of the entry is a charge to profit and loss account in determining operating profit.

The credit side of the double entry is an increase in equity (i.e. a separate component of equity shareholders funds).

### (ii) Transactions with employees (and others providing similar services)

The standard takes the view that it is not usually possible to estimate reliably the fair value of employee services received. Therefore the entity is required to measure (as at the grant date) the fair value of the equity instruments granted.

### (iii) Transactions with parties other than employees

These transactions could include the provision of consultancy or professional fees, as well as the receipt of inventories or property, plant and equipment. The standard makes a rebuttable presumption (which can be overturned in rare cases) that the fair value of these goods or services can be estimated reliably. Fair value is measured at the date the entity obtains the goods or the counterparty renders service.

### (iv) Taking account of vesting conditions

This refers to transactions with employees and others providing similar services. The vesting condition could, for example, be completion by the employee of a specified period of service (for example, three years), or satisfaction of a performance condition (such as achievement of a specified increase in company earnings), or both.

The vesting condition is taken into account by adjusting the number of equity instruments included in the measurement of the transaction amount.

### (v) Equity-settled share-based payment transactions

The standard refers to the "modified grant date method". Over the vesting period, the cumulative amount recognized in the income statement should be based on the number of equity instruments that actually vest.

The fair value of equity instruments granted should be based on market prices. If these are not available, fair value should be estimated using a valuation technique. The standard provides guidance on this. Fair value should also take account of the terms and conditions on which those equity instruments were granted.

*(vi) Cash-settled share-based payment transactions*
The standard requires the entity to measure the goods or services acquired, and the liability incurred, at the fair value of the liability.

Up until the liability is settled (in cash), the entity is required to remeasure the fair value of the liability at each reporting date and at the date of settlement. Any changes in value are recognized in the profit or loss for the period.

*(vii) Definition of fair value*
Fair value is defined in FRS 20, Appendix A, as:

"The amount for which an asset could be exchanged, a liability settled, or an equity instrument granted could be exchanged, between knowledgeable, willing parties in an arm's length transaction".

## (d) Recognizing Share-based Payment Transactions

Goods or services received or acquired in a share-based payment transaction shall be recognized when the goods are obtained or the services are received.

*(i) The debit side of the entry*
If the goods or services do not qualify for recognition as assets, they shall be recognized as expenses.

*(ii) The credit side of the entry*
This depends on the nature of the transaction:

- In an equity-settled share-based payment transaction, the corresponding credit is to equity;
- In a cash-settled share-based payment transaction, the corresponding credit is to liabilities.

## (e) Equity-settled Share-based Payment Transactions

*(i) General requirements*
The goods or services received, and the corresponding credit to equity, shall be measured directly at the fair value of goods or services received.

*(ii) Transactions with parties other than employees*
There shall be a rebuttable presumption that the fair value of the goods or services received can be estimated reliably.

*(iii) Transactions with employees (and others providing similar services)*
If the fair value of the goods or services received cannot be estimated reliably, their value shall be measured indirectly by reference to the fair value of the equity instruments granted.

This will usually be the case for transactions with employees and others providing similar services because it is not usually possible to measure directly the services received for particular components of the employee's remuneration package.

### Transactions with employees and others providing similar services

*Equity instruments granted which vest immediately:* In this situation, the counterparty is not required to complete a specified period of service before becoming unconditionally entitled to those equity instruments.

Therefore on grant date, the entity shall recognize full with a charge in arriving at profit or loss with a corresponding increase inequity.

*Equity instruments which do not vest until after a completed period of service:* The entity shall account for those services as they are rendered by the counterparty, with a corresponding increase in equity.

For example, if an employee is granted share options conditional upon completing three years' service, then the entity shall presume that the services to be rendered by the employee will be received over the three-year vesting period.

*Inclusion of performance conditions:* Share options may be granted on the achievement of a performance condition and remaining in the employment of the entity until that performance condition is satisfied.

The performance condition may be a *market condition* based on, say, a specified increase in the company's share price. Alternatively, the performance condition may be linked to achievement of, say, increases in earnings or sales targets.

The entity shall estimate the length of the expected vesting period at grant date, based on the most likely outcome of the performance condition:

- If the performance condition is a *market condition,* the estimate of the expected vesting period shall be consistent with the assumptions used in estimating the fair value of the options granted. The estimate shall not subsequently be revised.
- If the performance condition is not a *market condition,* where subsequent information indicates that the length of the vesting period differs from previous estimates, the entity shall revise its previous estimates.

*(iv) Determining the fair value of equity instruments granted*
Where transactions are measured by reference to the fair value of the equity instruments granted, fair value at the measurement date shall be based on

market prices taking into account the terms and conditions upon which those equity instruments were granted.

If market prices are not available, the entity shall estimate the fair value using a valuation technique to estimate what the price of those equity instruments would have been on the measurement date in an arm's length transaction between knowledgeable, willing parties.

For transactions with employees, "measurement date" is grant date. For transactions with parties other than employees, "measurement date" is the date the entity obtains the goods or the counterparty renders service.

FRS 20, Appendix B, gives guidance on measurement of fair value in different situations, including newly listed entities and unlisted entities.

*(v) Treatment of vesting conditions*
The different types of vesting conditions were referred to above.

*Vesting conditions other than market conditions*
These shall not be taken into account when estimating the fair value of the shares or share options at the measurement date.

However, vesting conditions *shall* be taken into account by adjusting the number of equity instruments included in the measurement of the transaction amount.

Ultimately, the amount recognized for goods or services received as consideration for the equity instruments granted shall be based on the number of equity instruments that *eventually* vest.

If the equity instruments fail to vest because of failure to satisfy a vesting condition, no amount will be recognized (i.e. charged to profit or loss) on a cumulative basis. For example, suppose share options will vest provided the employee works for the entity over the next three years. At the end of each of the first two years, the entity recognizes an amount for services received based on the best available estimate of the number of equity options expected to vest. This is revised in the light of subsequent information which indicates that the number of options expected to vest differs from previous estimates. If, say, the relevant employees left during the third year, and thus the options did not vest. In that case, the cumulative charge recognized over the three year period would be zero. So the totals charged to profit or loss in years one and two would then be credited back to profit or loss in year three.

FRS 20, Implementation Guidance, contains useful illustrations of calculations (see Examples 1–4).

*Market conditions:* Market conditions such as a target share price shall be taken into account when estimating the fair value of the equity instruments granted.

The entity shall recognize the goods or services received from a counter-party who satisfies all other vesting conditions. This applies whether or not the market condition is satisfied.

(see FRS 20, Implementation Guidance, Examples 5 and 6.)

### (vi) Events after vesting date

No adjustment shall be made to total equity after vesting date.

For example, suppose share options have been granted to an employee and will vest at the end of three years provided the employee remains with the entity until then. The share options have a life often years. Assuming the employee satisfies the three-year vesting condition, for each of the first three years, there will be a debit to profit or loss, with a corresponding credit to equity. These amounts cannot subsequently be reversed even if the employee does not exercise the options during the exercise period between years four and ten.

FRS 20, paragraph 23, also states:

> "...this requirement [i.e. "no subsequent adjustment to total equity after vesting date"] does not preclude the entity from recognising a transfer within equity, i.e. a transfer from one component of equity to another. For example, during the vesting period, the entity may make the relevant credit entry to a separately designated component of equity (for example, say, a "share scheme reserve"). There would be nothing to prevent the entity from making a subsequent transfer between this reserve and profit and loss reserves".

### (vii) Illustration where simple vesting conditions apply (the "modified grant method")

This illustration is based on Example 1, referred to above.

*Basic data:* An entity grants 100 share options to each of its 500 employees and vesting is conditional upon completion of three years' service.

The fair value of each share option is £15 (FRS 20, Appendix B, gives guidance on estimating fair value, and use of option pricing models).

The entity estimates, on the basis of weighted average probability, that 20% of employees will lose their rights to options as a result of failure to complete three years' service.

*Scenario 1 – everything turns out exactly as expected*

The entity will recognize the following amounts:

| Year | Calculation | Remuneration expense for period (debit to profit or loss) £ | Cumulative remuneration expense (credit to equity) £ |
|---|---|---|---|
| 1 | 50,000 options × 80% × £15 × 1/3 years | 200,000 | 200,000 |
| 2 | (50,000 options × 80% × £15 × 2/3 years) less £200,000 | 200,000 | 400,000 |
| 3 | (50,000 options × 80% × £15 × 3/3 years) less £400,000 | 200,000 | 600,000 |
| Total | | 600,000 | |

*Scenario 2 – estimates have to be revised*

*Year 1*

20 employees leave.

Estimate of total employee departures over the three-year period is revised from 100 employees (20%) to 75 employees (15%).

*Year 2*

A further 22 employees leave.

Estimate of total employee departures over the three-year period is revised from 75 employees (15%) to 60 employees (12%).

*Year 3*

A further 15 employees leave.

Total departures over the three years are 57 employees who forfeit their share option rights, leaving 443 employees entitled.

The entity will recognize the following amounts:

| Year | Calculation | Remuneration expense for period (debit to profit or loss) £ | Cumulative remuneration expense (credit to equity) £ |
|---|---|---|---|
| 1 | 50,000 options × 85% × £15 × 1/3 Years | 212,500 | 212,500 |
| 2 | (50,000 options × 88% × £15 × 2/3 years) i.e. £440,000 less £212,500 = £227,500 | 227,500 | 440,000 |
| 3 | (44,300 options × £15) i.e. £664,500 less £440,000 | 224,500 | 664,500 |
| Total | | 664,500 | |

*Note*: Had all remaining employees departed before the end of year 3, the cumulative charge to profit or loss over the three-year period would have been nil instead of £664,500. The credit to profit or loss in year 3 would have been £440,000.

#### (viii) Inability to obtain reliable estimate of fair value
FRS 20, paragraph 24, deals with a situation where the entity concludes that at the date of grant it cannot reliably estimate the fair value of the share options granted. Implementation Guidance Example 10 includes a numerical example with calculations. The basis of calculation is quite different from that in the intrinsic value method referred to in UITF Abstract 17, which does not require account to be taken of an increase in share price which takes place after grant date.

#### (ix) Other issues
The standard deals with a number of further complications including:

- Reload features – defined as a feature that provides for an automatic grant of additional share options whenever the option holder exercises previously granted options using the entity's shares, rather than cash, to satisfy the exercise price.
- Repricing of exercise price of options.
- Cancellation of options (other than a grant cancelled because of failure to satisfy vesting conditions).

The detailed requirements are not dealt with below. Numerical examples of the calculations are included in FRS 20, Implementation Guidance (see Examples 7–9).

### (f) Cash-settled Share-based Payment Transactions

#### (i) Example
The term is defined in (a) above. An example is where an entity grants share appreciation rights to employees as part of their remuneration package. The employees will become entitled to a future cash payment based on the increase in the entity's share price from a specified level over a specified period of time.

#### (ii) Requirements
The entity shall measure the goods or services acquired, and the liability incurred, at the fair value of the liability.

Subsequently, until the liability is settled, its fair value shall be remeasured at each reporting date and at the date of settlement.

Any changes in fair value shall be recognized in profit or loss for the period.

#### (iii) Recognition and measurement issues
If the share appreciation rights do not vest until the employees have completed a specified period of service, the entity shall recognize the services received, and a liability to pay for them, as the employees render service during that period.

The fair value of the share appreciation rights shall be calculated using an option pricing model, taking account of the terms and conditions on which the rights were granted, and extent to which service has been rendered to date (see FRS 20, Appendix B, which gives Application Guidance on the use of option pricing models).

## (g) Share-based Payment Arrangements with Cash Alternatives

Some share-based payment transactions contain terms which give one party a choice as to whether the entity settles the transaction in cash or by issuing equity instruments.

In some cases, the counterparty has the choice as to how the transaction is settled. In other cases, it is the entity who has the choice.

Cash alternatives are dealt with in FRS 20, paragraphs 34–43, and Implementation Guidance, paragraphs 1G20-22 and Example 13.

## (h) Disclosures

FRS 20 contains the following bold paragraph disclosure requirements:

An entity shall disclose information that enables users of the financial statements to understand the nature and extent of share-based payment arrangements (FRS 20.44).

An entity shall disclose information that enables users of the financial statements to understand how the fair value of the goods or services received, or the fair value of the equity instruments granted, during the period was determined (FRS 20.46).

An entity shall disclose information that enables users of the financial statements to understand the effect of share-based payment transactions on the entity's profit or loss for the period and on its financial position (FRS 20.50).

The standard contains detailed disclosure requirements in paragraphs 44 to 52. FRS 20, Implementation Guidance, includes illustrative disclosures (see IG 23 example).

## (i) Effective date and transitional provisions

An entity shall apply FRS 20 for annual periods beginning on or after 1 January 2005 for listed entities, and 1 January 2006 for unlisted entities.

There are detailed transitional provisions, including paragraph 53 which states:

> "For equity-settled share-based payment transactions, the entity shall apply this IFRS to grants of shares, share options or other equity instruments that were granted after 7 November 2002 and had not vested at the relevant effective date of this FRS (i.e. 1 January 2005 for listed entities, 1 January 2006 for unlisted entities)".

## 10.6    International Financial Reporting Standards

FRS 20 is identical to IFRS 2, apart from application of transitional arrangements.

---

**Frequently Asked Questions**

1  Are unlisted companies exempt from FRS 20?
   No—all companies with share-based payments arrangements fall within the scope of the standard.

2  Are sharesave schemes exempt from FRS 20?
   No—the exemption in UITF Abstract 17 is not contained in FRS 20.

3  When is  FRS 20 mandatory for unlisted UK companies?
   FRS 20 is mandatory in respect of accounts periods commencing on or after 1 January 2006.

---

# Taxation Including Deferred Tax

This chapter covers:
* Accounting for current tax – FRS 16
* Overview of deferred tax
* Accounting for deferred tax – FRS 19
* Deferred tax assets
* FRS 19 – disclosure requirements and illustrations
* SSAP 4 – Accounting for government grants
* SSAP 5 – Accounting for value added tax
* International Financial Reporting Standards

## 11.1 Accounting for Current Tax

### (a) Background

Advance corporation tax was abolished with effect from 6 April 1999. Large companies with taxable profits of at least £1,500,000 moved over to payment of tax on a quarterly instalments basis.

Small and medium-sized companies below this size pay the year's tax liability nine months after the year-end. Special tax rates, including marginal relief apply to these companies.

Following changes in the tax system, FRS 16, Current taxation, was issued.

### (b) Current Taxation

Current tax should be recognized in the profit and loss account for the period, except to the extent that it is attributable to a gain or loss that is, or has been, recognized in the statement of total recognized gains and losses (STRGL). This exception could relate to the tax effect of a change in accounting policy, dealt with as a prior period adjustment.

### (c) Gains and Losses Recognized in STRGL

Accounting Standards and/or CA 1985 require or permit certain gains or losses to be credited or charged direct to the STRGL.

Tax attributable to gains and losses recognized in the STRGL should itself be recognized in the STRGL. In exceptional cases, it may be difficult to determine the amount of such attributable tax. FRS 16 permits the attributable tax to be based on a reasonable pro rata allocation, or another allocation that is more appropriate in the circumstances.

## (d) Outgoing Dividends and Interest

Outgoing dividends paid and proposed (or declared and not yet payable), interest and other amounts payable are to be recognized at an amount that:

* Includes any withholding taxes;
* Excludes any other taxes, such as attributable tax credits, not payable wholly on behalf of the recipient.

*(FRS 16 defines withholding tax as tax on dividends or other income that is deducted by the payer of the income and paid to the tax authorities wholly on behalf of the recipient.)*

## (e) Incoming Dividends, Interest and Other Income

Incoming dividends, interest or other income receivable are to be recognized at an amount that:

* Includes any withholding taxes;
* Excludes any other taxes, such as attributable tax credits, not payable wholly on behalf of the recipient.

The FRS also requires that the effect of any withholding tax suffered should be taken into account as part of the tax charge.

## (f) No Adjustment for Notional Tax

Subject to (d) and (e) above, income and expenses should be included in the pre-tax results on the basis of the income or expenses actually receivable or payable.

No adjustment should be made to reflect a notional amount of tax that would have been paid or relieved in respect of the transaction if it had been taxable, or allowable for tax purposes, on a different basis.

## (g) Applicable Tax Rates and Legislation

Current tax should be measured at the amounts expected to be paid (or recovered) using the tax rates and laws that have been enacted or substantially enacted by the balance sheet date.

## (h) Disclosure Requirements

The following components of the current tax expense (or income) for the period should be separately disclosed in the profit and loss account and the statement of total recognized gains and losses:

(i) UK or Republic of Ireland tax (depending on the companies legislation in accordance with which the entity is reporting);
(ii) Foreign tax.
   • Provide analysis of both (i) and (ii) to distinguish tax estimated for the current period and any adjustments recognized in respect of prior periods.
   • Disclose domestic tax before and after double taxation relief.

## (i) Shadow Advance Corporation Tax (ACT) System

Because some ACT continues to be recoverable in the future under the shadow ACT system, detailed guidance is provided in FRS 16.

"Unrelieved ACT at the date of implementation of FRS 16", refers to any unrelieved advance corporation tax carried forward at implementation date for relief against future taxable profits. Such ACT should be recognized on the balance sheet only to the extent that it is regarded as recoverable.

Any change in the amount of ACT regarded as recoverable should be recognized as part of the tax expense (or income) for the period in the profit and loss account. It should be separately disclosed either on the face of the profit and loss account or by way of note.

Appendix II of FRS 16 provides detailed guidance for UK companies on the transitional arrangements for ACT, including the circumstances in which ACT can be regarded as recoverable.

# 11.2   Deferred Tax – Introduction

## (a) Accounting Profit and Tax – Adjusted Profit

In the UK, corporation tax is assessed on a company's tax-adjusted profit. It is unlikely that this will be the same as its accounting or reported profit.

*Illustration 1*

The tax computation of Gardens plc is as follows:

|                                          | £'000 | £'000 |
|------------------------------------------|------:|------:|
| Accounting profit (= reported profit)    |       |   800 |
| *Add* depreciation                       |   260 |       |
| Entertaining                             |   110 |   370 |
|                                          |       | 1,170 |
| *Less* capital allowances                |       |   440 |
| Taxable profit                           |       |   730 |

Assuming a corporation tax rate of 30%, corporate tax payable amounts to £219,000 (i.e. 30% × £730,000).

The difference between the two profit figures can be analysed between timing differences and permanent differences.

Timing differences reflect the fact that some items are recorded in different periods for tax as opposed to accounts purposes.

For example:

(1) Interest payable is treated for accounts purposes on an accruals basis. For tax purposes, interest payable is dealt with on a purely cash basis.
(2) Depreciation charges are allocated over accounting periods over the asset's useful life on an accruals basis. For tax purposes, the HMRC allows capital allowances rather than depreciation. Again, the difference is one of timing.

Permanent differences are usually items which are reflected in the accounts but which are totally disregarded for tax purposes. For example, entertaining expenditure relating to UK customers is charged in the accounts but is never allowed for tax purposes.

Deferred tax is concerned with timing differences. Permanent differences are outside the scope of deferred tax.

## (b) Tax Reconciliation

The tax assessed for the period is lower than the standard rate of corporation tax (assumed at 30%). The hypothetical tax charge based on the accounting profit may be reconciled to the actual tax charge as follows:

|  | £ |
|---|---|
| Accounting (reported) profit | 240,000 |
| £800,000 at 30% |  |
| Effects of: |  |
| Expenses not deductible for tax purposes |  |
| 30% × 110,000 | 33,000 |
| Capital allowances in excess of depreciation |  |
| 30% (440 − 260) | (54,000) |
| Current tax charge for the period | 219,000 |

(See also 11.5(e)(1) below.)

### Illustration 2

A company acquired a fixed asset on 1.1.X1 at a cost of £80,000. The company's depreciation policy is to depreciate over ten years on a straight-line basis, ignoring residual value. The profit after depreciation is £100,000 in each of the years 19X1 to 19X5. Assume the corporation tax rate is 30% and 25% writing-down allowances are available for tax purposes. No first year allowances are available.

Required: show the relevant extracts for both profit and loss account and balance sheet assuming deferred tax is provided in full on all timing differences.

**(1) Calculations**

*(i) Deferred tax*

|  | (1)<br>Accounts<br>NBV<br>£ | (2)<br>Tax<br>WDV<br>£ | Deferred tax<br>account (1)–(2)<br>times 30%<br>£ |
|---|---|---|---|
| Cost of asset 19X1 | 80,000 | 80,000 | 0 |
| Depreciation (Dep)/writing-down allowance (WDA) 19X1 | 8,000 | 20,000 | 3,600 |
| A/cs NBV/tax WDV 31.12.X1 | 72,000 | 60,000 | 3,600 |
| Dep/WDA 19X2 | 8,000 | 15,000 | 2,100 |
| A/cs NBV/tax WDV 31.12.X2 | 64,000 | 45,000 | 5,700 |
| Dep/WDA 19X3 | 8,000 | 11,250 | 975 |
| A/cs NBV/tax WDV 31.12.X3 | 56,000 | 33,750 | 6,675 |
| Dep/WDA 19X4 | 8,000 | 8,437 | 131 |
| A/cs NBV/tax WDV 31.12.X4 | 48,000 | 25,313 | 6,806 |
| Dep/WDV 19X5 | 8,000 | 6,328 | (502) |
| A/cs NBV/tax WDV 31.12.X5 | 40,000 | 18,985 | 6,304 |

*(ii) Corporation tax*

|  | 19X1<br>£ | 19X2<br>£ | 19X3<br>£ | 19X4<br>£ | 19X5<br>£ |
|---|---|---|---|---|---|
| Accounting profit | 100,000 | 100,000 | 100,000 | 100,000 | 100,000 |
| *Add* depreciation | 8,000 | 8,000 | 8,000 | 8,000 | 8,000 |
| *Less* capital allowances | (20,000) | (15,000) | (11,250) | (8,437) | (6,328) |
| Taxable profit | 88,000 | 93,000 | 96,750 | 99,563 | 101,672 |
| Corporation tax at 30% | 26,400 | 27,900 | 29,025 | 29,869 | 30,502 |

**(2) Extracts from financial statements**

*(i) Profit and loss account*

|  | 19X1<br>£ | 19X2<br>£ | 19X3<br>£ | 19X4<br>£ | 19X5<br>£ |
|---|---|---|---|---|---|
| Profit on ordinary activities before tax | 100,000 | 100,000 | 100,000 | 100,000 | 100,000 |
| Taxation: |  |  |  |  |  |
|   Corporation tax | 26,400 | 27,900 | 29,025 | 29,869 | 30,502 |
|   Deferred tax | 3,600 | 2,100 | 975 | 131 | (502) |
|  | 30,000 | 30,000 | 30,000 | 30,000 | 30,000 |
| Total tax charge as percentage of accounting profit | 30% | 30% | 30% | 30% | 30% |

Comment

Assuming no permanent differences, if deferred tax is provided in full, irrespective of the circumstances of the company, then the tax charge bears a relationship to reported profit.

*(ii) Balance sheet*

|  | 19X1 £ | 19X2 £ | 19X3 £ | 19X4 £ |
|---|---|---|---|---|
| Creditors – amounts falling due within one year: | | | | |
| Corporation tax | 26,400 | 27,900 | 29,025 | 29,869 |
| Provisions for liabilities and charges: | | | | |
| Deferred tax | 3,600 | 5,700 | 6,675 | 6,806 |

# 11.3   Accounting for Deferred Tax – FRS 19

## (a) Scope and Implementation

- FRS 19 applies to financial statements intended to give a true and fair view of the financial position and profit or loss for the period.
- There is exemption from FRS 19 for small companies applying the FRSSE (Financial Reporting Standard for Smaller Entities).

## (b) Overview

- Full provision is required for timing differences between the recognition of gains and losses for accounts and tax purposes respectively. The main exception to this rule is where fixed assets are revalued with no intention of sale without rollover relief.
- FRS 19 permits but does not require deferred tax assets and liabilities to be discounted.
- Extra disclosures are required to reconcile the actual tax charge in the accounts to the theoretical amount calculated by applying the relevant tax rate to the profit shown in the accounts (see 11.2(b) above).
- Disclosure is required of special circumstances affecting future tax charges or credits, for example tax losses carried forward.

## (c) Key Definitions

- *Deferred tax* – the estimated future tax consequences of transactions and events recognized in the financial statements of the current and previous periods.
- *Permanent differences* – differences between an entity's taxable profits and its results as stated in the financial statements that arise because certain types of income and expenditure are non-taxable or disallowable or because certain tax charges or allowances have no corresponding amount in the financial statements (e.g. disallowable entertaining expenditure).
- *Timing differences* – differences between an entity's taxable profits and its results as stated in the financial statements that arise from the inclusion of gains and losses in tax assessments in periods different from those in which they are recognized in financial statements. Timing differences originate in one period and are capable of reversal in one or more subsequent periods.

## (d)  Examples of Timing Differences

The main examples are:

- Capital allowances given for tax purposes; depreciation charged for accounts purposes.
- Pension liabilities accrued for accounts purposes; allowed for tax when contributions are paid.
- Interest costs or development costs capitalized for accounts purposes; treated as revenue expenditure and allowed as incurred for tax purposes.
- Intragroup profits in stock – unrealized at group level and reversed on consolidation.
- Fixed asset revalued in the financial statements; gain becomes taxable only when the asset is sold.
- Tax loss not relieved against past or present taxable profits – can be carried forward to reduce future taxable profits.
- Unremitted earnings of subsidiary and associated undertakings and joint ventures – recognized in the group results but subject to further taxation only if and when remitted to the parent undertaking.

## (e)  General Principles

(1) FRS 19 is based on an incremental liability approach i.e. deferred tax should be recognized in the balance sheet only where it meets the definition of asset or liability in its own right.

(2) A liability requires transactions and events to have given rise to obligations to pay tax in future as a result of past events that have occurred at the balance sheet date.

(3) Deferred tax should be recognized in respect of all timing differences that have originated but not reversed by the balance sheet date.

(4) Deferred tax should be recognized in the profit and loss account except where it relates to a gain or loss recognized in the statement of total recognized gains and losses (STRGL) in which case the deferred tax should be recognized in the STRGL.

(5) Deferred tax should not be recognized on permanent differences.

## (f)  Capital Allowances and Depreciation

Deferred tax should be recognized when capital allowances are received before or after depreciation is recognized in the profit and loss account (FRS 19.9).

Deferred tax should be reversed when all the conditions for retaining the allowances have been met—this may apply to certain industrial building allowances.

## (g) Revaluations and Disposals

Deferred tax should be recognized on timing differences arising when an asset is continuously revalued to fair value with changes in fair value being recognized in the profit and loss account—this situation is likely to be rare, (e.g. current asset investments "marked to market").

Deferred tax on timing differences arising when other non-monetary assets are revalued should not be recognized (e.g. property assets revalued under FRS 15) unless the reporting entity has at the balance sheet date both entered into a binding agreement to sell the revalued assets and has recognized the gains and losses expected to arise on sale.

Deferred tax on timing differences arising when non-monetary assets are revalued or sold should not be recognized if it is more likely than not that the taxable gain will be rolled over, becoming chargeable to tax only if and when the assets into which the gain has been rolled over are sold. This para does not apply to those assets falling within FRS 19 para 14 (e.g. current asset investments marked to market).

## (h) Unremitted Earnings of Subsidiaries, Associates and Joint Ventures

Tax payable (after taking account of double tax relief) should be provided on any future remittances of past earnings only to the extent at the balance sheet date that *either*:

- dividends have been accrued as receivable, or
- the subsidiary, associate or joint venture has entered into a binding agreement to distribute past earnings at a future date.

## (i) Applicable Tax Rate

Deferred tax should be measured at the average tax rates expected to apply in the periods in which the timing differences are expected to reverse based on tax rates and laws enacted or substantially enacted at the balance sheet date.

Where different tax rates apply to different bands of profit, use the average rate expected to be paid in the year in which the timing difference reverses.

In the UK "substantially enacted" means included in *either* a Bill passed by the House of Commons and awaiting only passage through the House of Lords and Royal Assent *or* a resolution having statutory effect that has been passed under the Provisional Collection of Taxes Act 1968.

# 11.4 Accounting for Deferred Tax – FRS 19: Deferred Tax Assets

## (a) General Rule

Deferred tax assets should be recognized to the extent that they are regarded as recoverable—i.e. more likely than not that there will be suitable taxable profits from which the future reversal of the underlying timing differences can be deducted.

## (b) Deferred Tax Assets that can be Recovered Against Deferred Tax Liabilities

A deferred tax asset may be regarded as recoverable to the extent that there is a deferred tax liability whose reversal will give rise to taxable profits.

## (c) Deferred Tax Assets that cannot be Recovered Against Deferred Tax Liabilities

Where such a liability above is insufficient, consider the likelihood of there being other suitable taxable profits:

### (1) Availability of evidence

The evidence required to support the recognition of a deferred tax asset relates to the specific circumstances that make it reasonable to forecast that there will be further profits against which the deferred tax assets can be recovered.

FRS 19, paras 28 to 32, give detailed guidance, including:

- All available evidence should be considered – particularly historical information about financial performance and position.
- The existence of unrelieved tax trading losses is strong evidence that there will not be suitable taxable trading profits in future against which the losses and other deferred tax assets can be recovered.
- Unrelieved trading losses and other deferred tax assets should only be recognised if there is other persuasive and reliable evidence available which suggests that suitable taxable profits will be generated in future.
- For unrelieved trading losses, such evidence may exist if the loss results from an identifiable and non-recurring cause and the entity has otherwise been consistently profitable over a long period.
- Equivalent guidance is given in respect of unrelieved capital losses.
- It may not be appropriate to recognise a deferred tax asset where it is expected that it will take some time for tax losses to be relieved and hence where recoverability is likely to be uncertain.

### (2) Disclosure implications

The amount of the deferred tax asset should be disclosed, together with the nature of the evidence supporting its recognition, in the following circumstances (FRS 19.62):

- where its recoverability is dependent on future taxable profits in excess of those arising from the reversal of deferred tax liabilities, and
- the entity has suffered a loss in either the current or preceding period in the tax jurisdiction to which the deferred tax asset relates.

### (3) Re-assessment of recoverability

Changes in circumstances from one balance sheet date to the next should be considered. For example, an improvement in trading conditions may make it more likely that a previously unrecognized tax loss will be recovered.

### Illustration 3

Extract from annual report and accounts of Ideal Shopping Direct plc, year ended 31 December 2002.

**Note 5 – Taxation on profit/(loss) on ordinary activities**

The tax credit represents:

|  | 2002 £'000 | 2001 £'000 |
|---|---|---|
| Corporation tax at 30% (2001: 30%) | 36 | – |
| Total current tax | 36 | – |
| Deferred tax: | | |
| Origination and reversal of timing differences | 849 | – |
| Adjustments in respect of prior year | (2,158) | – |
| Total deferred tax | (1,309) | – |
| Tax on profit/(loss) on ordinary activities | (1,273) | – |

The movement of £1,309,000 on deferred tax results principally in respect of the recognition of a deferred tax asset arising from the Company's cumulative tax losses. It is regarded as more likely than not there will be suitable taxable profits to permit the utilisation of such losses. The asset has been disclosed within other debtors falling due after more than one year because the directors cannot be certain as to the timing of the use of the losses.

There is no prior year adjustment in respect of FRS 19 because at 31 December 2001 there was not sufficient certainty that the company would utilise the losses.

...

**Note 13 – Debtors: amounts falling due after more than one year**

**The Group and the Company**

|  | 2002 £'000 | 2001 £'000 |
|---|---|---|
| Other debtors | 1,309 | – |

Other debtors comprise a deferred tax asset in respect of recoverable trading losses (see note 5 for further details).

## 11.5  Accounting for Deferred Tax – FRS 19: Disclosure Requirements

The main requirements are:

### (a) Accounting Policy Note

State accounting policy on deferred tax—including whether deferred tax balance is discounted or undiscounted.

State effect of changes to the accounting policy on deferred tax:

- reasons for change i.e. issue of FRS 19;
- effect of prior period adjustment on results for the preceding period;
- indication of effect of a change in accounting policy on the results for the current period.

## (b) Profit and Loss Disclosures (Including Notes)

- include all deferred tax recognized in the profit and loss account within the heading "tax on profit or loss on ordinary activities";
- within above heading, disclose separately material components of deferred tax charge or credit attributable to:
  - origination and reversal of timing differences,
  - changes in tax rates and laws,
  - adjustments to estimated recoverable amount of deferred tax assets arising in previous periods;
- where discounting policy has been adopted disclose changes in amount of discount deducted in arriving at the deferred tax balance.

## (c) Statement of Total Recognized Gains and Losses (STRGL)

Disclose tax charged or credited in STRGL indicating separate components as above.

## (d) Balance Sheet Disclosures (Including Notes)

### (1) Classification and disclosure on balance sheet

- classify net deferred tax liabilities as provisions;
- classify net deferred tax assets as debtors – as a separate subheading where material;
- offset deferred tax debit and credit balances to extent that they relate to taxes levied by same tax authority and arise in the same entity (or in a group of entities where the tax losses of one entity can reduce the taxable profits of another);
- disclose deferred tax liabilities and assets separately on the face of the balance sheet where amounts are so material that failure to disclose separately may cause a reader to misinterpret the financial statements.

### (2) Deferred tax note

- disclose total deferred tax balance (before discounting) analysed into timing difference categories;
- where discounting policy adopted, disclose impact of discounting and discounted amount of deferred tax balance;
- disclose movement on net deferred tax balance for current year showing separately:
  - amount charged or credited to profit and loss account,
  - amount charged or credited to STRGL,
  - movements arising from acquisition or disposal of businesses.

*(3) Deferred tax asset disclosures where losses incurred*

Disclose amount of asset and nature of supporting evidence where recoverability is dependent on future taxable profits and where losses incurred in current or preceding periods.

## (e) Special Circumstances Affect Current and Future Tax Charges

*(1) Current tax charge/credit reconciliation*

- disclose reconciliation of current tax charge/credit with that resulting from applying standard rate of tax to profit on ordinary activities before tax (see 11.2(b) above and illustrations 5 and 6 below);
- present reconciliation either in terms of monetary amounts or percentage rates;
- disclose basis on which standard rate of tax has been determined.

*(2) Deferred tax not recognized where assets revalued in the accounts or revaluations noted*

- disclose estimate of tax that could be payable or recoverable if assets sold at value shown;
- explain circumstances in which tax would become payable or recoverable;
- indicate amount that may become payable or recoverable in foreseeable future.

*(3) Assets sold or binding agreement to sell but deferred tax not recognized because of expectation of rollover relief*

- disclose conditions to be met to obtain rollover relief;
- disclose estimate of tax payable if conditions not met.

*(4) Deferred tax asset not recognized in the accounts*

Disclose amount not recognized and circumstances in which tax would be recovered.

*(5) Other deferred tax not recognized in the accounts*

Disclose nature of amounts, circumstances in which tax would become payable and recoverable and indication of amount.

*Illustration 4*

The following details relate to a company with a 31 March year-end.

**(i) Accounts and tax allowances summary**

|  | Accounts NBV £ | Tax WDV £ | Difference £ | At 30% £ |
|---|---|---|---|---|
| At 1.4.X0 | 1,700 | 880 | 820 | 246 |
| Additions | 1,100 | 1,100 | – | – |
| Depreciation/WDAs | (200) | (495) | 295 | 89 |
| At 31.3.X1 | 2,600 | 1,485 | 1,115 | 335 |
| Depreciation/WDAs | (300) | (371) | 71 | 21 |
| At 31.3.X2 | 2,300 | 1,114 | 1,186 | 356 |

**(ii) Accounting and disclosure – 20X2**

*(1) Accounting policy note – 20X2 accounts*
Deferred tax is provided in full in respect of taxation deferred by timing differences between the treatment of certain items for taxation and accounting purposes. The deferred tax balance has not been discounted.

No provision has been made for deferred tax on gains recognized on revaluing property to its market value as the company does not intend to sell the revalued assets.

*(2) Note... – Tax on profit on ordinary activities*

|  | 20X2 £'000 | 20X1 |
|---|---|---|
| Current tax |  |  |
| UK corporation tax on profits of the period | X | X |
| Deferred tax | 21 | 89 |
|  | XX | XX |

*(3) Provisions for liabilities and charges – deferred tax*

The deferred tax balance and movements during the year were as follows:

|  | £ |
|---|---|
| At 1 April 20X1 | 335 |
| Provided during the year | 21 |
| At 31 March 20X2 | 356 |

## Illustration 5

Extract from annual report and accounts of Hays plc, year ended 30 June 2003.

**Note 7 – Tax on profit on ordinary activities**

(a) Analysis of charge in period

| (In £'s million) | 2003 | 2002 |
|---|---|---|
| **Current tax** |  |  |
| United Kingdom corporation tax at 30% (2002 – 30%) for the year | 40.3 | 55.2 |
| Double taxation relief | (7.4) | (3.3) |
|  | 32.9 | 51.9 |
| Overseas taxation | 7.6 | 13.7 |
| Associated companies – current tax | 0.5 | 0.1 |
| Total current tax | 41.0 | 65.7 |
| **Deferred tax** |  |  |
| Origination and reversal of timing differences | (0.2) | (0.5) |
| Tax on profit on ordinary activities | 40.8 | 65.2 |

The exceptional items gave rise to a tax credit included above of £18.0 million (2002 – £6.4 million). No tax relief is assumed to arise on exceptional losses on disposal of businesses, the write off of goodwill or the impairment of tangible assets.

(b) Factors affecting the tax charge for the period
The tax assessed for the period is higher than the standard rate of corporation tax in the UK of 30%. The differences are explained below:

| (In £'s million) | **2003** | *2002* |
|---|---|---|
| (Loss)/profit on ordinary activities before tax | **(476.8)** | 147.6 |
| (Loss)/profit on ordinary activities before tax at the standard rate of UK corporation tax of 30% (2002 – 30%) | **(143.0)** | 44.3 |
| Factors affecting the charge for the period: | | |
| Capital allowances for the period in excess of depreciation | **0.8** | (0.5) |
| Permanent differences (principally goodwill amortisation and impairment) | **179.1** | 20.6 |
| Foreign tax charged at higher rates than UK standard rates | **1.1** | 1.2 |
| Other timing differences | **(1.3)** | (2.4) |
| Unrelieved overseas losses | **4.3** | 2.5 |
| Total actual amount of current tax | **41.0** | 65.7 |

(c) Factors that may affect future tax charges
Provision has not been made for taxation that would arise in the event of certain overseas subsidiaries and associated companies distributing the balance of their reserves as the earnings are continually reinvested and, accordingly, no tax is expected to be payable on them in the foreseeable future.

The Group's overseas tax rates are generally higher than those in the UK.

No provision has been made for deferred taxation on gains recognised on the sale of properties where potentially taxable gains have been rolled over into replacement assets. Such tax would only become payable if the properties were sold without being able to claim rollover relief. The total amount unprovided is £10.3 million (2002 – £10.2 million). At present it is not envisaged that any tax will become payable in the foreseeable future.

The Group provides for deferred tax assets if it is more likely than not that they will reverse in the future. Some of the Group's overseas operations, particularly those in Germany, have generated tax losses in the past, the future utilisation of which is uncertain. The Group has not recognised a deferred tax asset of £15.9 million (2002 – £10.2 million) in respect of tax losses of overseas companies.

**Note 19 – Provisions for liabilities and charges (extracts)**

| *(In £'s million)* | *Pensions* | *Deferred taxation* | *Property* | *Deferred employee benefits* | *Other* | *Total* |
|---|---|---|---|---|---|---|
| At 1 July 2002 | 6.9 | 16.5 | 2.5 | 10.3 | 47.4 | 83.6 |
| Exchange adjustments | 0.1 | 0.8 | – | 0.5 | 0.2 | 1.6 |
| Reclassification | – | – | 16.8 | – | (16.8) | – |
| Disposals | – | – | – | – | (0.9) | (0.9) |
| Charged to P&L account | 9.8 | – | 24.1 | 3.3 | 19.6 | 56.8 |
| Credited to P&L account | – | (0.2) | (0.6) | – | (0.3) | (1.1) |
| Utilised | (2.4) | – | (7.9) | (1.5) | (6.9) | (18.7) |
| **At 30 June 2003** | **14.4** | **17.1** | **34.9** | **12.6** | **42.3** | **121.3** |

. . .

Deferred taxation

| *(In £'s million)* | **2003 Provided** | **2003 Unprovided** | *2002 Provided* | *2002 Unprovided* |
|---|---|---|---|---|
| **The Group** | | | | |
| Accelerated tax allowances | **29.2** | – | 29.1 | – |
| Other timing differences | **(11.4)** | **(3.8)** | (12.6) | (4.3) |
| Overseas losses | **(0.7)** | **(15.9)** | – | (10.2) |
| Gain deferred by rollover | – | **10.3** | – | 10.2 |
| | **17.1** | **(9.4)** | 16.5 | (4.3) |

## Illustration 6

Extract from annual report and accounts of The Sage Group plc, year ended 30 September 2003.

Note 6 – Taxation on profit on ordinary activities

### (a) Analysis of charge in the period

| | Note | 2003 £'000 | 2002 £'000 |
|---|---|---|---|
| **Current tax** | | | |
| UK corporation tax before double taxation relief | | **24,961** | 26,652 |
| Double taxation relief | | **(3,825)** | (3,198) |
| UK corporation tax on profits of the period | | **21,136** | 23,454 |
| Adjustments in respect of previous periods | | **(2,264)** | (3,388) |
| UK current tax | | **18,872** | 20,066 |
| Overseas current tax on profits of the period | | **14,430** | 7,965 |
| Adjustments in respect of previous periods | | **(2,635)** | 1,937 |
| Overseas current tax | | **11,795** | 9,902 |
| Total current tax | | **30,667** | 29,968 |
| **Deferred tax** | | | |
| Origination and reversal of timing differences | | **16,154** | 12,505 |
| Adjustments in respect of previous periods | | **–** | (2,435) |
| Total deferred tax | 16(c) | **16,154** | 10,070 |
| | | **46,821** | 40,038 |

### (b) Factors affecting tax charge for the period
The following table reconciles the tax charge based upon applying UK corporation tax rates to the reported profit before taxation to the actual current tax charge disclosed above.

| | 2003 £'000 | 2002 £'000 |
|---|---|---|
| Profit on ordinary activities before taxation | **151,037** | 129,154 |
| Profit on ordinary activities multiplied by the standard rate of corporation tax in the UK of 30% (2002: 30%) | **45,311** | 38,746 |
| Effects of: | | |
| Expenses not deductible for tax purposes | **2,193** | 1,444 |
| Capital allowances (more than)/less than depreciation | **(352)** | 181 |
| Utilisation of tax losses | **(13,418)** | (12,686) |
| Tax amortisation of goodwill | **(2,032)** | – |
| Adjustments to tax charge in respect of previous periods | **(4,899)** | (1,451) |
| Higher tax rates on overseas earnings | **3,864** | 3,734 |
| **Current tax charge for the period** | **30,667** | 29,968 |

### (c) Factors that may affect future tax charges
There are tax losses which have not been recognised for deferred tax purposes. If sufficient suitable profits arise in the future, then these losses could be utilised and hence reduce the future tax charge.

Similarly, there are potential tax credits which have not been recognised due to the uncertainty over their availability. If these credits become available, then this would also reduce the future tax charge.

**Note 16 – Provisions for liabilities and charges**

**(a) Deterred tax liability/(asset) provided in the accounts comprises:**

|  | Group | | Company | |
|---|---|---|---|---|
|  | **2003** | *2002* | **2003** | *2002* |
|  | **£'000** | *£'000* | **£'000** | *£'000* |
| Accelerated capital allowances | **590** | 606 | – | – |
| Tax losses | **(17,002)** | (21,342) | – | – |
| Other short term timing differences | **(147)** | (7,570) | – | – |
|  | **(16,559)** | (28,306) | – | – |

The other short term timing differences include a deferred tax liability of £2,351,000 (2002: £319,000) in respect of tax amortisation of goodwill.

Of the above deferred tax asset, £10,485,000 will only be available to be utilised after more than 12 months.

**(b) Deferred tax liability/(asset) not provided in the accounts comprises:**

|  | Group | | Company | |
|---|---|---|---|---|
|  | **2003** | 2002 | **2003** | 2002 |
|  | **£'000** | £'000 | **£'000** | £'000 |
| Chargeable gains subject to rollover relief | **780** | 780 | – | – |
| Tax losses | **(5,493)** | (7,077) | – | – |
| Other short term timing differences | **(6,467)** | – | – | – |
|  | **(11,180)** | (6,297) | – | – |

The unprovided deferred tax relates mainly to tax losses. This potential asset has not been recognised as it is more likely than not that the losses will not be utilised in the foreseeable future.

**(c) Analysis of movement in the period:**

|  | Note | Group £'000 | Company £'000 |
|---|---|---|---|
| Deferred tax asset at 1 October 2002 |  | (28,306) | – |
| Exchange movements |  | 1,476 | – |
| Acquisitions of subsidiary undertakings |  | (5,883) | – |
| Deferred tax charge in profit and loss account | 6(a) | 16,154 | – |
| **Deferred tax asset at 30 September 2003** |  | **(16,559)** | – |

Deferred tax has been calculated at 30% (2002: 30%) in respect of UK companies (being the prevailing UK corporation tax rates at 30 September 2003 and 2002) and at the respective prevailing rates for the overseas subsidiaries.

# 11.6   Accounting for Government Grants

## (a) Introduction

The original version of SSAP 4 was issued in April 1974 and subsequently revised to take account of Companies Act changes as well as changes in government assistance and grants.

## (b) Scope

SSAP 4 covers all forms of government grants and assistance, including those from central government, local government and the European Community.

## (c) Basic Principles

Grants should be recognized in the profit and loss account so as to match them with the expenditure towards which they are intended to contribute.

Grants should not be brought into the accounts until conditions for receipt of the grants have been complied with and there is reasonable assurance that the grant will be received.

## (d) Capital-based Grants

Grants that are made as a contribution towards expenditure on fixed assets should be recognized over the expected useful lives of the related assets. Such grants should be accounted for by the deferred credit method and should not be netted off against the cost of the asset concerned (see section 12.12).

## (e) Grants for Achievement of Non-financial Objectives

An example would be a grant given on condition that jobs are created and maintained for a minimum period. Such a grant should be matched with the costs of providing jobs for that period.

## (f) Liability to Repay Grants

Potential liabilities to repay grants in specified circumstances should only be provided for to the extent that repayment is probable.

## (g) Disclosures

The following disclosures are required:

- the accounting policy adopted for government grants;
- the effects of government grants on the results for the period and/or the financial position of the enterprise;
- where the results of the period are affected materially by the receipt of forms of government assistance other than grants, the nature of that assistance and, to the extent that the effects on the financial statements can be measured, an estimate of those effects.

*Illustration 7*

**Accounting policies (extract)**

*Grants*

Grants received as a contribution towards specific expenditure on fixed assets are held in a deferred income account and recognised in the profit and loss account over the expected useful lives of the related assets.

Other grants received, including Regional Selective Assistance, are held in a deferred income account and recognised in the profit and loss account so as to match them with expenditure to which they are intended to contribute.

*Note 2 (extract)*
(d) Profit on ordinary activities before taxation is stated after
charging/(crediting):

| | *19X2* | *19X1* |
|---|---|---|
| Auditors' remuneration: | *£'000* | *£'000* |
| for audit services (including £30,000 in respect of the Company, 19X1: £30,000) | **105** | 75 |
| for non-audit services | **22** | 15 |
| Depreciation | **3,020** | 2,921 |
| Deferred grants | **(68)** | (67) |

# 11.7 SSAP 5 (Accounting for Value Added Tax)

Value added tax (VAT) is a tax on the final consumer and, therefore, the trader is normally merely acting as a collector on behalf of the Inland Revenue. Amounts due to and from the Inland Revenue will be included in creditors and debtors, and need not be disclosed separately.

Turnover shown in the profit and loss account should exclude VAT.

Irrecoverable VAT attributable to fixed assets should be treated as part of their cost. Capital commitments should also include irrecoverable VAT.

Irrecoverable VAT should be included in costs e.g. where the trader suffers VAT on his inputs but is exempted, either in whole or in part, on his outputs.

# 11.8 International Financial Reporting Standards

IAS 12 refers briefly to recognition of current tax liabilities and current tax assets, but most of the Standard is concerned with recognition and measurement of deferred tax liabilities and deferred tax assets. It is effectively the UK GAAP equivalent of FRS 16, Current tax, and FRS 19, Deferred tax.

## (a) Main features

The main features of IAS 12 are:

- A method of accounting for deferred tax described in the Standard as the "balance sheet liability method" – which focuses on "temporary differences" (as opposed to timing differences as in FRS 19);
- Temporary differences are differences between the tax base of an asset or liability and its carrying amount in the balance sheet;
- The focus is on the tax implications of assets and liabilities appearing in the balance sheet, rather than the tax implications of transactions charged or credited to profit and loss account;
- Deferred tax liabilities should be recognized for all temporary differences (subject to limited exceptions);
- Deferred tax assets should be recognized when it is probable that taxable profits will be available against which the deferred tax asset can be utilized;

- Deferred tax liabilities *must be recognized in respect of surpluses arising on fixed asset revaluations* (contrast with FRS 19);
- Deferred tax assets and liabilities should *not* be discounted (contrast with FRS 19);
- Extensive disclosure requirements, including an explanation of the relationship between tax expense and accounting profit in the form of a numerical reconciliation.

---

**Frequently Asked Questions**

1 Should deferred tax be provided in respect of revaluation surpluses under UK GAAP?
No—FRS 19 effectively prohibits provision of deferred tax on such surpluses except in very rare cases.

2 Must all UK companies provide a tax reconciliation?
Yes—all UK companies, except for those whose use the FRSSE, must provide a numerical statement which reconciles hypothetical tax (accounting profit times tax rate) to the current tax element of the tax charge.

3 Does SSAP 4 apply to grants other than those provided other than by government bodies or agencies?
Strictly these are outside the scope of FRS 4 but SSAP 4 provides guidance on best practice and should therefore its principles should be followed.

---

# 12 Tangible Fixed Assets, Including Impairment

**This chapter covers:**
* Fixed assets – definition and examples
* Coverage of FRS 15
* What goes into cost?
* Revaluation options
* Depreciation requirements
* Website development cost (UITF 29)
* Impairment and FRS 11
* Disposals
* Transfers from current assets to fixed assets
* Capital-based grants (SSAP 4)
* Investment properties (SSAP 19)
* International Financial Reporting Standards

## 12.1   Introduction

### (a) Scope of this Chapter

This chapter is concerned with tangible fixed assets, including investment properties and capital grants in relation to such assets. Chapter 12 deals with fixed assets under finance leases.

Intangible fixed assets are dealt with in Chapter 13, whilst fixed asset investments are covered in Chapter 17.

### (b) Relevant Regulations

Companies Act 1985, Schedule 4, deals with disclosure and accounting requirements—but not to the extent of coverage in related accounting standards such as FRS 15 and SSAP 21.

FRS 15, Tangible fixed assets, is the key standard in this area. Other key standards are:

* FRS 11, Impairment of fixed assets and goodwill – see 12.8 below.
* SSAP 21, Accounting for leases and hire purchase contracts (including guidance notes) – see Chapter 14.

- UITF 29 – Website development costs (see 12.7).
- SSAP 19, Accounting for investment properties – see 12.11 below.
- SSAP 4, accounting for government grants – see 12.12 below.

### (c) Definition of Tangible Fixed Assets

FRS 15 defines tangible fixed assets as:

> "Assets that have physical substance and are held for use in the production or supply of goods or services, for rental to others, or for administrative purposes on a continuing basis in the reporting entity's activities".

### (d) Fixed Asset Categories

Companies Act 1985, Schedule 4, specifies a minimum of:

(i)   land and buildings,
(ii)  plant and machinery,
(iii) fixtures, fittings, tools and equipment.

In practice, companies often take advantage of the option in the Companies Act 1985 to show the above items in greater detail. Additionally, the Act requires modification of wording where "the special circumstances of the business require such adaptation".

Examples of categories which incorporate modifications to the standard headings include:

*Illustration 1*

- Freehold land and buildings
- Long leasehold land and buildings
- Computer equipment
- Furniture, fixtures and equipment
- Short-term leasehold improvements
- Motor vehicles.

*Illustration 2*

- Freehold property
- Motor vessels
- Office equipment
- Motor vehicles.

# 12.2   Tangible Fixed Assets – Overview of FRS 15

### (a) Objective

The Summary to FRS 15 comments that:

> "... Its objective is to ensure that tangible fixed assets are accounted for on a consistent basis and, where a policy of revaluation is adopted, that revaluations are kept up-to-date".

## (b) Main Areas Covered in FRS 15

These include:

- determination of cost, i.e. what costs should or may be included in the carrying amount of the fixed asset;
- revaluations;
- depreciation and asset write-downs;
- disclosure requirements.

## (c) Scope and Operative Date

FRS 15 applies to all tangible fixed assets other than investment properties—SSAP 19 on investment properties is outside the scope of FRS 15.

# 12.3    Determining Cost

## (a) Initial Expenditure

A tangible fixed asset should initially be measured at its cost—the option to revalue at subsequent dates, and the conditions which follow from this, are referred to below in 12.5.

Some companies construct their own buildings or plant and machinery—FRS 15 gives guidance as to which costs should be included, and which should be excluded from the asset's carrying amount. In some cases, assets may need to be imported or installed on specially prepared sites—again, FRS 15 provides guidance on costs to be included.

Cost should include those costs that are directly attributable to bringing the asset into working condition for its intended use. This will include labour costs of own employees arising directly from the construction or acquisition of the specific tangible fixed asset. Administration and general overheads must be excluded.

Examples of directly attributable costs include:

- acquisition costs, e.g. stamp duty and import duties;
- site preparation and clearance costs;
- initial delivery and handling costs;
- installation costs;
- professional fees, e.g. legal, architects and engineers fees;
- estimated costs of dismantling and removing the asset and restoring the site, to the extent that it is recognized as a provision under FRS 12.

Costs associated with a start-up or commissioning period should be capitalized only where the asset is available for use, but incapable of operating at normal levels without such a start-up or commissioning period.

Paragraph 32 adds the following requirement relating to recoverable amount

"If the amount is recognised when a tangible fixed asset is acquired or constructed exceeds its recoverable amount, it should be written down to its recoverable amount" (see 12.8(b) below).

## (b) Subsequent Expenditure

The FRS sets out detailed rules as to the circumstances in which subsequent expenditure should be written off to profit and loss account as incurred, and when it should be capitalized:

### (1) Write-off as incurred

This is required when the expenditure is to ensure that the tangible fixed asset maintains its previously assessed standard of performance, e.g. repairs and maintenance expenditure, such as routine overhauling of plant or repainting a building.

### (2) Capitalization

Capitalization is required for expenditure which falls into one of three categories:

(i) Subsequent expenditure which provides an enhancement of the economic benefits of the tangible fixed asset in excess of the previously assessed standard of performance. This will include major modifications to fixed assets which are intended to increase productive capacity significantly.

(ii) Where a component of the tangible fixed asset that has been treated separately for depreciation purposes and depreciated over its useful economic life, is replaced or restored.

*Illustration 3*

Suppose a major item of plant costing £200,000 has a useful economic life of 20 years. The plant included a special motor whose life is expected to be 5 years after which it will need to be replaced. It is estimated that the cost element of the £200,000 attributable to the motor is £30,000.

Under FRS 15, the plant should be treated as two separate assets for depreciation calculation (but not disclosure) purposes. £170,000 (i.e. £200,000 less £30,000) should be depreciated over 20 years whilst £30,000 should be depreciated over 5 years.

On replacement of the motor element, any remaining part of the original cost should be written off.

(iii) Subsequent expenditure which relates to a major inspection or overhaul of a tangible fixed asset that restores the economic benefits of the asset that have been consumed by the entity and have already been reflected in depreciation. Note that the FRS provides detailed guidance in this area. This is particularly crucial for companies directly affected by the virtual prohibition of repairs provisions imposed by FRS 12.

*Illustration 4*

Happytours plc owns an aircraft which cost £30m and which has an economic useful life of 15 years. By law, the company is required to overhaul its aircraft once every three years. FAS 12 does not permit the company to build up a provision for future repairs (see FRS 12, Appendix iii Example 11B).

Suppose the cost of each major overhaul is estimated at £2.7m. For depreciation purposes, the initial cost of £30m should be split between:

- £27.3m depreciated over 15 years, i.e. £1.82m per annum;
- £2.7m depreciated over 3 years i.e. £0.9m per annum.

When the first overhaul bill of £2.7m is incurred, it should be capitalized and depreciated over 3 years i.e. a charge of £0.9 per annum.

### Illustration 5

Extract from annual report and accounts of Ryanair Holdings plc, year ended 31 March 2000.

**Statement of accounting policies (extract)**

*Tangible fixed assets and depreciation*
Tangible fixed assets are stated at costless accumulated depreciation. Depreciation is calculated to write-off the cost, less estimated residual value, of assets, other than land, on a straight line basis over their expected useful lives at the following annual rates:

| | |
|---|---|
| Plant and equipment | 20%–33.3% |
| Fixtures and fittings | 20% |
| Motor vehicles | 33.3% |
| Buildings | 5% |

Aircraft are depreciated over the estimated useful lives to estimated residual values.

**The current estimates of useful lives and residual values are:**

| Aircraft Type | Useful Life | Residual Value |
|---|---|---|
| Boeing 737-200's | 20 years from date of manufacture | US$1 million |
| Boeing 737-800's | 23 years from date of manufacture | 15% of original cost |

An element of the cost of an acquired aircraft is attributed on acquisition to its service potential reflecting the maintenance condition of its engines and airframe. This cost is amortized over the short period to the next check or the remaining life of the aircraft.

The costs of subsequent major airframe and engine maintenance checks are capitalized and amortized over the short period to the next check or the remaining life of the aircraft.

Advance payments and option payments made in respect of aircraft purchase commitments and options to acquire aircraft are recorded at cost and separately disclosed. On acquisition of the related aircraft these payments are included as part of the cost of aircraft and are depreciated from that date.

# 12.4 Capitalization of Interest

There is no requirement under FRS 15 for a company to capitalize finance costs. However, a company which chooses to have a capitalization policy must adhere to the restrictions imposed by FRS 15.

Paragraph 19 states:

"Where an entity adopts a policy of capitalizing finance costs, finance costs that are directly attributable to the construction of tangible fixed assets should be capitalised as part of the cost of those assets. The total amount of finance costs capitalised during a period should not exceed the total amount of finance costs incurred during that period".

The FRS gives extensive guidance to companies adopting this policy and imposes detailed rules and disclosure requirements.

It is not necessary for a specific loan to be taken out—FRS 15 permits the funds used to finance the construction of a tangible fixed asset to form part of the company's general borrowings.

However, one important restriction imposed by FRS 15 is that "... Capitalisation of finance costs should cease when substantially all the activities that are necessary to get the tangible fixed asset ready for use are complete....". This applies even if it is some time later before the asset comes into commercial use.

*Illustration 6*

Accounting policy (extract)
Interest costs incurred during the construction period on major fixed asset additions are capitalized and form part of the total asset cost. Depreciation is charged on the total cost including such interest.

# 12.5    Revaluation

## (a)  Basic Principles

The Companies Act 1985 offers UK companies the option of incorporating fixed asset revaluations into the double entry accounting system. This means, for example, that an individual company may carry some of its fixed assets in the balance sheet at historical cost, some at a 1995 valuation and some at a 1997 valuation.

FRS 15 seeks to require companies to adopt a structured approach to incorporating revaluations into the accounts. Tangible fixed asset revaluations should only be incorporated into a company's accounts where it adopts a formal revaluation policy which complies with the restrictions imposed by FRS 15.

Such a revaluation policy must be applied to individual classes of tangible fixed assets—it need not be applied to all classes of tangible fixed assets held. The separate classes shown in the Companies Act 1985 formats are:

- land and buildings;
- plant and machinery;
- fixtures, fittings, tools and equipment.

However, companies may adopt narrower classes where appropriate—for example, paragraph 62 suggests that in particular cases it may be acceptable to split land and buildings between specialized properties, non-specialized properties and short leasehold properties.

The term revaluation does not include the carrying amount of fixed assets which have been written down for impairment in accordance with FRS 11 (see 12.8 below). Also, it does not include assets stated at fair values, determined under FRS 7 following the acquisition of a business (see Chapter 26).

## (b) Frequency of Valuations

The basic rule in paragraph 43 states:

> "Where a tangible fixed asset is subject to a policy of revaluation its carrying amount should be its current value as at the balance sheet date".

Although FRS 15 does not insist on annual revaluations, the objective of a revaluation policy is to reflect current values as at the balance sheet date.

### (1) Usual approach

Paragraph 45 indicates that the Standard's requirements will be met by:

- a full valuation at least every five years, and
- an interim valuation in Year 3.

In situations where it is likely that there has been a material change in value, interim valuations should be carried out in years 1, 2 and 4 also.

### (2) Alternative approach

The FRS provides an alternative approach for portfolios of non-specialized properties. This is only likely to be acceptable in special cases, for example where the property portfolio either:

- consists of a number of broadly similar properties whose characteristics are such that their values are likely to be affected by the same market factors, or
- can be divided on a continuing basis into five groups of a broadly similar spread.

A full valuation may be performed on a rolling basis. This should be designed to cover all properties over a five-year cycle. Additionally, in cases where there has been a material change in value, an interim valuation should be performed on the remaining four-fifths of the portfolio.

## (c) Valuation Basis

Except for assets which are impaired, the following valuation bases should be adopted:

### (1) Non-specialized properties
Existing Use Value (EUV) plus notional directly attributable acquisition costs. Disclosure of Open Market Value (OMV) also required where materially different from EUV, together with reasons for difference.

### (2) Specialized properties
Depreciated replacement cost.

### (3) Properties surplus to requirement
Open market value, less directly attributable selling costs.

*(4) Tangible fixed assets other than properties*

Market value – where possible
Depreciated replacement cost – where market value not obtainable.

In cases where there is an indication of impairment, an impairment review should be performed in accordance with FRS 11 (see 12.8 below).

## *(d) Reporting Revaluation Gains and Losses*

*(1) Revaluation gain*
Where the gain is effectively a reversal of a revaluation loss on the same asset that was previously recognized in the profit and loss account (after adjusting for subsequent depreciation)—the gain should be recognized in the profit and loss account. Otherwise the gain should be recognized in the statement of total recognized gains and losses (STRGL).

*(2) Revaluation loss*
  (i) *Caused by consumption of economic benefits:* If the loss is caused by a clear consumption of economic benefits, it should be recognized in the profit and loss account.
  (ii) *Other cases:* In other cases, the loss should be recognized in STRGL until carrying amount reaches depreciated replacement cost.

Thereafter it should be recognized in the profit and loss account unless it can be demonstrated that the recoverable amount of the asset is greater than its revalued amount. In this event, the loss should be recognized in STRGL to the extent that the recoverable amount of the asset is greater than the revalued amount.

## *(e) Illustrations of Calculations*

*Illustration 7*

A company acquired an asset on 1.1.19X2 at a Cost of £100,000. The useful life of the asset was estimated as 10 years with a nil residual value at the end of that period. Depreciation is provided on a straight-line basis.

At 31.12.X4, the net book value of the asset is £70,000 (cost £100,000 less accumulated depreciation of £30,000). Suppose the asset is revalued at £84,000 and the remaining useful life still assumed to be seven years.

Revaluation surplus should be credited with £14,000 and the depreciation charge for 19X5 onwards should be £12,000 per annum (i.e. £84,000÷7).

(1) The depreciation charge in the profit and loss account should be related to the carrying amount in the balance sheet. Once a revaluation is incorporated in the balance sheet, depreciation charges relating to periods after this date should be based on revalued amount. In particular, no part of the depreciation charge should be set directly against reserves. In the above illustration, profit and loss account should be debited with £12,000. It would not be acceptable to debit £10,000 to profit and loss account and the remaining £2,000 to revaluation reserve (the so-called split depreciation method).

(2) The effect of the revaluation has been to increase the annual depreciation charge by £2,000 (i.e. £12,000 less £10,000).

(3) Each year (from 19X5 onwards) the company should make a transfer within reserves of £2,000 i.e. taking £2,000 out of revaluation reserve and into profit and loss reserves as follows:

|  | Profit and loss account | Revaluation reserve |
|---|---|---|
|  | £ | £ |
| Balance 1.1.X5 | X | 14,000 |
| Transfer within reserves | 2,000 | (2,000) |
| Retained profit 19X5 | X | X |
| Balance 31.12.X5 | X | X |

Each year £2,000 of the revaluation reserve becomes realized and thus forms part of distributable profit. At the end of the asset's useful life the part of the revaluation reserve relating to that asset should no longer exist.

(4) Depreciation charged prior to the revaluation should not be written back to profit and loss account except to the extent that it relates to a provision for permanent diminution in value which is subsequently found to be unnecessary, i.e. £14,000 must be credited to the revaluation reserve (as indicated above) and not profit and loss account.

## Illustration 8

### The details

A company owns a freehold building. The building is used by the company for its own operations and is therefore not to be treated as an investment property under SSAP 19.

At 1.1.X2, the relevant balances and allocation between land and buildings were:

|  | £ | £ |
|---|---|---|
| Land at cost |  | 150,000 |
| Buildings |  |  |
| Cost | 75,000 |  |
| Depreciation (8 years at 2%) | 12,000 | 63,000 |
| Net book value |  | 213,000 |

The building was revalued on the last day of the year at £320,000. The valuer allocated the valuation as follows:

|  | £ |
|---|---|
| Land | 230,000 |
| Buildings | 90,000 |
|  | 320,000 |

This revaluation is to be incorporated into the balance sheet at 31.12.X2. The remaining useful life of the building is left unchanged at 41 years.

Required: show the effect of the above information on the financial statements for the year.

### Workings

*(i) Calculation of surplus on revaluation*
Since the revaluation takes place on the last day of the year, the depreciation charge for the whole year is based on historical cost i.e. 2% × £75,000 = £1,500 (but note also 12.6(b), below).

For 19X3 and subsequent years, the depreciation charge will be $\frac{£90,000}{41}$ i.e. £2,195.

The surplus on revaluation may be calculated as follows:

|  |  | £ |
|---|---|---|
| Net book value at 31.12.X2 |  | 211,500 |
| (213,000–1,500) |  |  |
| Revaluation figure |  | 320,000 |
| So surplus on revaluation |  | 108,500 |
|  |  |  |
| Attributable: |  |  |
| Land (230,000–150,000) | 80,000 |  |
| Buildings (90,000–(63,000–1,500)) | 25,500 |  |
|  |  | 108,500 |

*(ii) Effect of revaluation on depreciation charge of subsequent years*

| Part of charge applicable to: | £ |
|---|---|
| Historical cost | 1,500 |
| Surplus 1/41 × £28,500 | 695 |
| Total charge | 2,195 |

**Effect on financial statements**

*(i) Fixed asset schedule (extract)*
  *Cost or revaluation*

|  | £ |
|---|---|
| Cost at 1.1.X2 | 225,000 |
| Adjustment on revaluation | 95,000 |
| Revaluation at 31.12.X2 | 320,000 |

*Depreciation*

|  | £ |
|---|---|
| At 1.1.X2 | 12,000 |
| Provided during the year | 1,500 |
| Adjustment on revaluation (13,500) | (13,500) |
| At 31.12.X2 | – |
| Net book value |  |
| 31.12.X2 | 320,000 |
| 31.12.X1 | 213,000 |

*(ii) Profit and loss account (extract)*

| Depreciation charge | 1,500 |
|---|---|

*(iii) Revaluation reserve account*

| Movement on account | 108,500 |
|---|---|

*(iv) Comparable historical cost figures (Companies Act 1985 disclosure)*

| Cost | 225,000 |
|---|---|
| Depreciation | 13,500 |
|  | 211,500 |

**Additional comments**

(1) The Companies Act 1985 requires information to be given regarding details of revaluations which took place during the year (e.g. name of valuer or qualification, basis of valuation).

(2) The part of the total revaluation reserve attributable to buildings (£28,500) may be amortized over the remaining life of the buildings (41 years) and dealt with each year as a transfer within reserves (as previously discussed).

## (f) Implications of FRS 15 Transitional Provisions

On implementation of FRS 15, companies carrying fixed assets at that time at a book value based on a previous revaluation less depreciation, were offered a choice by paragraph 104 of FRS 15:

- Option 1 – continue with a policy of incorporating revaluations into the balance sheet in accordance with the stringent requirements of FRS 15 (see 12.5(b))
- Option 2 – "freeze" the earlier revaluation figures and carry the assets in this and later balance sheet at this amount less subsequent depreciation. This involved specific disclosure, and the need to test the assets for impairment in accordance with FRS 11
- Option 3 – adopt a change of accounting policy, restating the assets from revalued amount to historical cost.

Different companies have dealt with this issue in different ways, and the consequent effects may be felt for some time to come.

# 12.6    Depreciation

## (a) Definition

Depreciation is defined in FRS 15 as the measure of the cost or revalued amount of the economic benefits of the tangible fixed asset that have been consumed during the period.

The definition continues:

> "Consumption includes the wearing out, using up or other reduction in the useful economic life of a tangible fixed asset whether arising from use, effluxion of time or obsolescence through either changes in technology or demand for the goods and services produced by the asset".

## (b) The Basic Requirement

FRS 15 refers to the fundamental objective of depreciation as ". . . to reflect in operating profit the cost of use of the tangible fixed asset (i.e. the amount of economic benefits consumed) in the period".

The depreciable amount of a tangible fixed asset should be allocated on a systematic basis over its useful economic life. The depreciation charge should be recognized as a charge against operating profit, even in cases where the asset has risen in value or been revalued at the end of the year.

Where an asset has been revalued, the depreciation charge for the current period should be based on the revalued amount and the remaining useful economic life. The FRS suggests that ideally this calculation should be based on the average value of the asset for the period. However, an acceptable alternative may be to use either opening or closing balance, provided the approach adopted is followed consistently (see example in 12.5 above).

## (c) Calculating Depreciation

The following three factors need to be taken into account:

- cost (or valuation when an asset has been revalued in the financial statements);
- the nature of the asset and the length of its expected useful life to the business having due regard to the incidence of obsolescence;
- estimated residual value.

*Residual value is defined as:*
The net realizable value of an asset at the end of its useful economic life. Residual values are based on prices prevailing at the date of acquisition (or revaluation) of the asset and do not take account of future expected price changes.

*Useful economic life is defined as:*
The useful economic life of a tangible fixed asset is the period over which the entity expects to derive economic benefit from that asset.

Useful life may be:

- predetermined, as in leaseholds;
- directly governed by extraction or consumption (e.g. mineral deposits);
- dependent on the extent of use;
- reduced by economic or technological obsolescence (e.g. specialized machinery manufacturing products for which there is no longer demand).

Useful life refers to useful economic life as far as the present owner is concerned and not the asset's total economic useful life.

Determination of useful life inevitably involves the exercise of judgement by management and should be reviewed annually. Where management considers that an original estimate of useful life needs to be revised, the unamortized cost of the asset should be charged to profit and loss account over the revised remaining useful life.

## (d) Choice and Application of Method

The method adopted should reflect as fairly as possible the pattern in which the asset's economic benefits are consumed by the entity. The method selected should also be appropriate to the type of asset and its use in the business.
Possible methods include:

(1) straight-line method;
(2) reducing balance method;
(3) output or usage method;

*(1) Straight-line (fixed instalment) method*
Under this method, cost (or valuation) less estimated residual value is allocated over the asset's estimated useful life on a straight-line basis.

*(2) Reducing balancing method*
The depreciation charge is calculated by applying a percentage rate to the accounts written down value of the asset.

## (3) Output or usage method

This method apportions the cost of a fixed asset in relation to the output or usage each year. The method may be useful where the output or usage varies significantly from one year to another.

### Illustration 9

A machine which cost £20,000 on 1.1.19X5 has an estimated life of three years. Its total life in machine hours is 2,700 hours, expected to arise as follows:

| | |
|---|---|
| 19X5 | 1,500 |
| 19X6 | 800 |
| 19X7 | 400 |
| | 2,700 |

Depreciation charges under this method (ignoring residual value) would be:

|  |  | £ |
|---|---|---|
| | | £ |
| 19X5 | $\dfrac{1,500}{2,700} \times £20,000$ | 11,111 |
| 19X6 | $\dfrac{800}{2,700} \times £20,000$ | 5,926 |
| 19X7 | $\dfrac{400}{2,700} \times £20,000$ | 2,963 |
| | | 20,000 |

### Illustration 10

Extracts from annual report and accounts of ebookers plc, year ended 31 December 2002.

**Accounting policies (extract)**

...

*Tangible fixed assets and depreciation*

Depreciation is provided to write off the cost less the estimated residual value of tangible fixed assets by equal instalments over their estimated useful economic lives as follows:

| | |
|---|---|
| Leasehold improvements | – the shorter of 20% per annum or over the life of the lease |
| Website development costs | – 50% per annum |
| Software and Computer and communications equipment | – 25–50% per annum |
| Fixtures, fittings and office equipment | – 15–20% per annum |

Website development costs capitalised relate to costs incurred in developing the Group's website during the year.

**Tangible fixed assets (extract)**

|  | Leasehold improvements £'000 | Website development costs £'000 | Software and computer and communications equipment £'000 | Fixtures, fittings and office equipment £'000 | Total £'000 |
|---|---|---|---|---|---|
| **Group** | | | | | |
| **Cost** | | | | | |
| At 1 January 2002 | 862 | 3,163 | 7,680 | 719 | 12,424 |
| Additions | 561 | 321 | 949 | 950 | 2,781 |
| Disposals | – | – | (30) | – | (30) |
| Foreign exchange | 17 | – | 66 | 49 | 132 |
| At 31 December 2002 | 1,440 | 3,484 | 8,665 | 1,718 | 15,307 |
| | | | | | |
| **Depreciation** | | | | | |
| At 1 January 2002 | 381 | 2,178 | 3,400 | 285 | 6,244 |
| Charge for year | 328 | 988 | 2,908 | 322 | 4,546 |
| Disposals | – | – | (30) | – | (30) |
| Foreign exchange | 174 | – | 87 | 470 | 731 |
| At 31 December 2002 | 883 | 3,166 | 6,365 | 1,077 | 11,491 |
| | | | | | |
| **Net book value** | | | | | |
| At 31 December 2002 | 557 | 318 | 2,300 | 641 | 3,816 |
| At 31 December 2001 | 481 | 985 | 4,280 | 434 | 6,180 |

## (e) Change of Method

A change from one method to another is permissible only on the grounds that the new method will give a fairer presentation of results and financial position.

A change of method does not constitute a change of accounting policy. The carrying amount should be depreciated over the asset's revised remaining useful life, starting with the period in which the change is made.

## (f) Asset with Two or More Major Components with Substantially Different Lives

Where the tangible fixed asset comprises two or more major components with substantially different economic lives, the FRS requires each component to be accounted for separately for depreciation purposes and depreciated over its individual useful economic life (see 12.3(b) above).

## (g) Subsequent Expenditure and the Materiality of the Depreciation Charge

### (1) Introduction

This is a particularly important aspect of FRS 15. The basic rule is set out in paragraph 86:

> "Subsequent expenditure on a tangible fixed asset that maintains or enhances the previously assessed standard of performance of the asset does not negate the need to charge depreciation".

### (2) The immateriality argument
Paragraph 90 states:

> "For tangible fixed assets other than non-depreciable land, the only grounds for not charging depreciation are that the depreciation charge and accumulated depreciation are immaterial. The depreciation charge and accumulated depreciation are immaterial if they would not reasonably influence the decisions of a user of the accounts".

### (3) Justifying non-depreciation
Paragraph 91 states:

> "An entity must be able to justify that the uncharged depreciation is not material in aggregate as well as for each tangible fixed asset. Depreciation may be immaterial because of very long useful economic lives or high residual values (or both). A high residual value will reflect the remaining economic value of the asset at the end of its useful economic life to the entity. These conditions may occur when:
> (a) the entity has a policy and practice of regular maintenance and repair (charges for which are recognised in the profit and loss account) such that the asset is kept to its previously assessed standard of performance; and
> (b) the asset is unlikely to suffer from economic or technological obsolescence (e.g. due to potential changes in demand in the market following changes in fashion); and
> (c) where estimated residual values are material:
>     (i) the entity has a policy and practice of disposing of similar assets well before the end of their economic lives; and
>     (ii) the disposal proceeds of similar assets (after excluding the effect of price changes since the date of acquisition or last revaluation) have not been materially less than their carrying amounts".

### (4) Impairment reviews
Paragraph 89 states:

> 'Tangible fixed assets, other than non-depreciable land, should be reviewed for impairment, in accordance with FRS 11, at the end of each reporting period when either:
> (a) no depreciation charge is made on the grounds that it would be immaterial (either because of the length of the estimated remaining useful economic life or because the estimated residual value of the tangible fixed asset is not materially different from the carrying amount of the asset); or
> (b) the estimated remaining useful economic life of the tangible fixed asset exceeds 50 years".

In principle, impairment reviews should be performed on an individual asset basis. Where this is not reasonably practicable, reviews should be performed for groups of assets, as part of income-generating units, in accordance with FRS 11.

In practice, the majority of companies now provide depreciation on buildings.

## (h) Review of Asset Lives and Residual Values

### (1) Asset lives

The economic useful life should be reviewed at each balance sheet date. If expectations are significantly different from previous estimates, the life should be revised. FRS 15 requires that the asset's carrying amount at the date of revision should be depreciated over the revised remaining useful economic life.

### (2) Residual values

Residual values, where material, should be reviewed at each balance sheet date. The review should take account of reasonably expected technological changes based on prices prevailing at the date of acquisition (or revaluation).

A change in its estimated residual value should be accounted for prospectively over the asset's remaining useful economic life, except to the extent that the asset has been impaired at the balance sheet date.

# 12.7 Website Development Costs

## (a) Overview

UITF 29 categorizes website development costs and specifies different treatments for each category.

- Planning costs – should be charged to profit and loss account as incurred.
- Application and infrastructure development costs – should be capitalized if the relationship between the expenditure and future economic benefits is sufficiently certain.
- Design and content costs – should be capitalized if the relationship between the expenditure and future economic benefits is sufficiently certain *and* if the costs lead to the creation of an enduring asset.
- Maintenance and operation costs – should be charged to profit and loss account as incurred.

## (b) Classification of Costs

The various cost categories identified in UITF 29 may be summarized as follows:

| Cost category | Examples |
|---|---|
| Planning costs | – Costs of undertaking feasibility studies<br>– Determining objectives and functionalities of the website<br>– Exploring ways of achieving the desired functionalities<br>– Identifying appropriate hardware and web applications<br>– Selecting suppliers and consultants |

| Cost category | Examples |
|---|---|
| Application and infrastructure development costs | – Obtaining and registering a domain name<br>– Buying or developing hardware<br>– Buying operating software relating to functionality of the site<br>– updateable content management systems<br>– e-commerce systems<br>– encryption software<br>– interfaces with other IT systems used by the entity |
| Design costs | – Development of design and appearance of individual website pages<br>– Creation of graphics |
| Content costs | Preparing, accumulating and posting the website content |
| Other costs | Costs of operating and maintaining website once it has been developed |

## (c) Accounting Treatment

In summary, the treatment required for each category is as follows:

| Planning costs | Charge to P/L as incurred |
|---|---|
| Application and infrastructure development costs | Capitalize as a tangible fixed asset provided the relationship between the expenditure and the future economic benefits is sufficiently certain. |
| Design costs/content costs | Capitalize as a tangible fixed asset provided the relationship between the expenditure and the future economic benefits is sufficiently certain but only to the extent that the costs create an enduring asset. This requires several stringent conditions to be satisfied, including:<br>– expenditure is separately identifiable<br>– the technical feasibility and commercial viability of the website have been assessed with reasonable certainty;<br>– the website will generate sales or other revenue directly;<br>– there is a reasonable expectation that the present value of the future cash flows will be no less than the amounts capitalized;<br>– adequate resources exist. |
| Other costs | Charge to P/L as incurred. |

# 12.8   Impairment

## (a) Introduction

### (1) Objective

The ASB developed FRS 11 because previously there was little guidance on how the "recoverable amount" of an asset should be measured and when asset write-downs should be recognized. FRS 11's objective is to ensure that:

- fixed assets and goodwill are recorded in the financial statements at no more than their recoverable amounts
- any resulting impairment loss is measured and recognized on a consistent basis
- sufficient information is disclosed in the financial statements to enable users to understand the impact on the financial position and performance of the reporting entity.

Please note—the comments in section 12.8 are relevant also to Chapters 13 and 27.

### (2) Scope

The Standard applies to all financial statements intended to give a true and fair view, and covers the following fixed asset categories:

- purchased goodwill recognized in the balance sheet in accordance with FRS 10;
- intangible fixed assets, including development costs recognized in the balance sheet in accordance with SSAP 13;
- tangible fixed assets, excluding investment properties;
- fixed asset investments, for example investment in subsidiaries in the parent company balance sheet.

Small companies who have adopted the Financial Reporting Standard for Smaller Entities (FRSSE) are outside the scope of the standard.

## (b) Definitions and Terminology

Terms such as "temporary diminution in value" and "permanent diminution in value" are not used by FRS 15. The FRS refers to impairment in value. FRS 11 definitions are as follows:

- Impairment: a reduction in the recoverable amount of a fixed asset or goodwill below its carrying amount.
- Recoverable amount: the higher of net realizable value and value in use.
- Net realizable value: the amount at which an asset could be disposed of, less any direct selling costs.
- Value in use: the present value of the future cash flows obtainable as a result of an asset's continued use, including those resulting from its ultimate disposal.

## (c) FRS 11 and Income-Generating Units (IGUs)

An income-generating unit is defined as a group of assets, liabilities and associated goodwill that generates income that is largely independent of the reporting entity's other income streams. The assets and liabilities include those directly involved in generating the income and an appropriate portion of those used to generate more than one income stream.

In principle, FRS 11 requires the calculation of value in use of a fixed asset to be estimated individually wherever this is practicable. However, where this is not practicable, FRS 11 states that value in use should be calculated at the level of income-generating units.

FRS 11 requires that IGUs should be identified by dividing the total income of the entity into as many largely independent income streams as is reasonably practicable in the light of information available to management. FRS 11 offers some guidance:

Identification of income streams is likely to follow the way management monitors and makes decisions about continuing or closing the different lines of business of the entity. For example, this could be by reference to major products or services.

For a small or medium-sized company, the IGU may be the company itself. For example, in the leisure sector, a group may be divided for FRS 11 purposes into, say, night clubs, bingo, restaurants and health clubs. For a UK retail group operating throughout Europe, a recently acquired German DIY chain may itself be regarded as a separate IGU. Much will depend on the group's internal procedures for monitoring profitability, cash flow and so on.

## (d) When does a Company or Group have to Carry Out Impairment Reviews in Accordance with FRS 11?

Both FRS 10 and FRS 11 need to be consulted in order to establish when impairment reviews are mandatory for a particular company or group. These Standards indicate that full impairment reviews must be carried out in any of the following situations:

- Where goodwill and intangibles are capitalized and amortized over more than 20 years
- Where goodwill and intangibles are amortized over a period of 20 years or less, a full impairment review will be required only in certain special cases:
  - a "first year review" which indicates that pre-acquisition projections have not been met (FRS 10, para 34(a))
  - subsequent years where events indicate impairment (FRS 10, para 34(b))
- Regarding fixed assets and goodwill generally – where events or changes in circumstances indicate that the carrying amount may not be recoverable (FRS 11, para 8).

The ASB's Press Notice on FRS 11, published in July 1998 stated:

"The measurement of an impairment can sometimes involve detailed calculations and, in the normal course of events, assets that are being depreciated in an appropriate manner are unlikely to become impaired. Consequently, FRS 11 does not require impairment reviews to be performed automatically each year. Rather, reviews are required only where there is an indication that assets might be impaired. The only exception is FRS 10's requirement to perform impairment reviews annually for goodwill that is being treated as having a very long or indefinite useful life".

FRS 11, para 9 states:

"... It is possible therefore, to rely on the use ot indicators of impairment to determine when a review for impairment is needed...".

FRS 11, para 10, gives a number of examples of changes in events or circumstances. These may indicate that impairment has occurred. FRS 11 suggests that the indicators below will trigger an impairment review only if they are relevant to the measurement of goodwill or fixed assets (tangible or intangible).

In brief summary, the examples include:

- current period operating losses/net cash outflows when considered in the context of past results and future expectations;
- significant decline in a fixed asset's market value during the period;
- evidence of obsolescence or physical damage to the fixed asset;
- significant adverse change in business or market, for example entrance of major competitor;
- significant adverse change in statutory or other regulatory environment in which the business operates;
- management commitment to undertake a significant reorganization;
- major loss of key employees.

## (e) FRS 11 Calculations

As indicated above, in cases where no indicator of impairment is present, it will not be necessary to carry out an impairment exercise.

Where the exercise has to be carried out, if recoverable amount (RA) is below carrying amount (CA), the fixed asset or goodwill should be written down. RA is higher of net realizable value (NRV) or value in use (VIU).

Where it is not practicable to calculate VIU at an individual asset level, VIU should be calculated at income-generating unit level. If this is the case, CA and NRV will also be calculated at IGU level.

## (f) Basic Steps in Outline – A Simple Situation

The calculations are potentially complex, and the results are likely to be sensitive to changes in assumptions. The steps below are simplified—the Standard and published commentaries should be referred to for detailed application. The comments below do not refer to further complications such as treatment of central costs and assets, revalued fixed assets, and effect of merging an acquired business with existing operations.

(1) Identify income-generating units (IGUs).
(2) Allocate carrying value of assets, goodwill and liabilities (excluding financing liabilities) to each IGU.
(3) Estimate expected future cash flows for each IGU – these should allow for allocation of central overheads but exclude the effect of cash flows relating to financing and tax.
   Cash flows should allow for capital expenditure unless it relates to improvement or enhancement of the IGU.
(4) Calculate present value of expected future cash flows for the particular IGU. The discount rate used to calculate the present value should be an estimate of the rate that the market would expect on an equally risky investment – FRS 11 gives guidance (see below).
   The discount rate should be calculated on a pre-tax basis.
(5) Calculate the impairment loss for the particular IGU by comparing carrying amount of the IGU with its recoverable amount.
   At this stage, it will be worth reworking the calculations using different assumptions e.g. regarding future cash flows and discount rates. This will help put the sensitivity of using alternative assumptions into context.
(6) Allocate the total impairment loss in the following sequence:
   (i) any specific assets where there is obvious impairment;
   (ii) any goodwill in the IGU;
   (iii) any capitalized intangibles in the IGU;
   (iv) tangible assets in the IGU on a pro rata or more appropriate basis.

## (g) Illustration

The following highly simplified illustration is intended as a general introduction of FRS 11. The company as a whole has been identified as the IGU. The cash flows are assumed to have stabilized following a period of decline, thus simplifying the present value calculations.

### Illustration 11

The company is a small manufacturing company which is emerging from a very difficult period of falling sales. Although not trading at a loss, the company has identified an indicator of impairment, such as significant adverse change in the market (see FRS 11, para 10) and is therefore carrying out an impairment exercise.
The company balance sheet in summary form shows:

|  | £'000 |
| --- | --- |
| Goodwill | 200 |
| Freehold property | 820 |
| Plant and machinery | 730 |
| Net current assets | 265 |
| Total | 2,015 |
| Financing – loans and shareholders funds | 2,015 |

Estimated future cash flows (assume for simplicity allows for capital expenditure and expected amounts unchanged each year, based on profit before interest and tax of £120,000 pa.

Discount rate estimated at, say, 7% pa (pre-tax) — calculated by reference to FRS 11, para 42.

*Outline approach*

| | | |
|---|---|---|
| Step 1: | The entire company is regarded as an appropriate IGU | |
| Step 2: | Allocate assets etc. – £2,015,000 | |
| Step 3: | Estimate future cash flows – £120,000 pa | |
| Step 4 and 5: | Calcuate present value of future cash flows using discount rate of 8%: £120,000/0.07 = £1,714,285 say £K 1715 | |
| Step 6: | Calculate impairment loss: £K 2015 – £K1715 = £K 300 | |
| Step 7: | Allocate impairment loss: Goodwill – write off in full £200,000 Allocate balance of £100,000 against plant and machinary, to write it down to £630,000. | |

*Assumptions:*
Property value is not less than £820,000
Stock, debtors etc are not stated in excess of net realizable value.

**Reviewing the assumptions**

What would have happened if the company was able to justify a discount rate of 6% on the grounds that the company was unlisted and its main source of borrowings were from the bank?

Using the same cash flows estimate, the present value of the cash flows (i.e. the value in use) would be £200,000 giving an impairment loss of £15,000. In this situation it is unlikely that the assets would be written down. This is subject to the acceptability of the revised assumptions.

## (h) Discount Rate

Paragraph 41 states that the discount rate used should be "… an estimate of the rate that the market would expect on an equally risky investment".

The rate should exclude the effect of any risks for which the cash flows have been adjusted.

The FRS suggests three possible ways of estimating the market rate:

- the rate implicit in market transactions of similar assets;
- the current weighted average cost of capital (WACC) of a listed company whose cash flows have similar risk profiles to those of the IGU;
- the WACC for the entity *but only if adjusted for the particular risks associated with the IGU.*

The discount rate should be calculated on a pre-tax basis. Paragraph 44 indicates that WACC will be a post-tax rate and gives guidance on how to convert to a pre-tax rate.

## (i) Monitoring of Subsequent Year Cash Flows

Where recoverable amount has been based on value in use, cash flows achieved in each of the five years following each impairment review should be compared with those forecast.

In some cases it will be necessary to re-perform the original impairment calculations using the actual cash flows achieved. This will apply where the cash flows are lower than forecast to such an extent their use could have required recognition of an impairment in a previous period.

### (j) Reversal of Past Impairment Losses

*(1) Tangible fixed assets and investments*
The reversal of past impairment losses is recognized when the recoverable amount of a tangible fixed asset or investment has increased because of a change in economic conditions or in the expected use of the asset.

*(2) Goodwill and intangibles*
Increases in the recoverable amount of goodwill and intangible assets are recognized only when an external event caused the recognition of the impairment loss in previous periods, and subsequent external events clearly and demonstrably reverse the effects of that event in a way that was not foreseen in the original impairment calculations.

### (k) Accounting

If the exercise indicates an impairment loss, this should be charged to the profit and loss account.

Remaining useful economic life and residual value should be reviewed and revised if necessary.

Revised carrying amount should be depreciated over revised estimate of remaining useful economic life.

### (l) Disclosure Requirements

The FRS includes a number of disclosure requirements in paragraphs 67 to 73. Paragraph 67 states that "Impairment losses recognized in the profit and loss account should be included within operating profit under the appropriate statutory heading, and disclosed as an exceptional item if appropriate...".

## 12.9    Disposal of Fixed Assets

Profit or loss on disposal is calculated by comparing:

- Net sales proceeds, and
- Carrying amount – whether carried at historical cost (less any provisions) or valuation.

*Illustration 12*

A company acquired a building in 19X2 at a cost of £120,000. The building was revalued in 19X6 at £250,000. The revaluation was reflected in the accounts and £130,000 credited to revaluation reserve as an unrealized surplus. The building was subsequently sold in 19X8 for proceeds of £400,000. Ignore depreciation.

The profit on sale may be calculated as follows:

£400,000–£250,000, i.e. £150,000. Assuming the profit on sale is to be regarded as an exceptional item, the profit and loss account would disclose an exceptional profit of £150,000. The amount of £130,000 hitherto included in revaluation reserve would then be transferred by means of a movement within reserves (i.e. no entry would be made in the actual profit and loss account) to profit and loss reserves.

# 12.10 UITF 5 – Transfers from Current Assets to Fixed Assets

## (a) Introduction

An asset, e.g. a trading property, may start off on acquisition as a current asset. Management may subsequently decide to retain the property as an investment property, held on a continuing basis as a fixed asset.

In these circumstances the UITF is concerned that the property might be transferred from current to fixed assets at book value, without regard to its value at the date of transfer. Management might then write-down the property by means of a debit to revaluation reserve, thus avoiding a charge to the profit and loss account.

## (b) UITF 5

(1) the effective date of transfer is the date of management's change of intent – this date should not be backdated;
(2) the current asset accounting rules (i.e. lower of cost and net realizable value) should be applied up to this date;
(3) the asset should be transferred at the lower of cost and net realizable value – if NRV is below cost, the diminution in value should be charged to the profit and loss account;
(4) subject to (3), the fixed asset will be held at either:
    (i) cost (under the historical cost accounting rules in CA 1985), or
    (ii) valuation (under the alternative accounting rules in CA 1985).

# 12.11 Investment Properties (SSAP 19)

## (a) Background

The general principle established by SSAP 12, and confirmed by the Companies Act 1985 and FRS 15, is that fixed assets with a restricted useful life should be subject to a depreciation charge.

The majority of fixed assets are used by the company for its own use in its business operations. However, certain types of property assets, referred to as investment properties, are held for their investment potential. Such properties have not usually been depreciated and have been excluded from the requirements of FRS 15.

The definition and accounting treatment of investment properties are covered by SSAP 19.

## (b) Definition

An investment property:

- *is* an interest in land and/or buildings in respect of which construction work and development work has been completed *and* which is held for its investment potential. It must be shown that the disposal of such a property would not materially affect any manufacturing or trading operations of the enterprise; and
- does *not* include:
  - property owned and occupied by the company for its own purposes;
  - property let to, and occupied by, another group company. (*Note:* this does not exclude property let to an associated company provided that rental income is determined on an arm's length basis.)

## (c) Accounting Treatment

The main features are as follows:

- A current value accounting system which reflects the fact that the main interest is in the current values of properties and changes therein.
- Investment properties should not be subject to periodic depreciation charges.

There is an important exception to this. Investment properties held or leases with less than 20 years to run at the balance sheet date should be depreciated. This is to avoid a situation which might otherwise occur whereby a company purchased a short lease, charged the amortization direct to reserves (investment revaluation reserve) but credited rentals received on the letting to profit and loss account.

- Investment properties (including those held on leases with less than 20 years to run) should be included in the balance sheet at their open market value.
- Changes in valuation from one balance sheet date to the next should be credited or debited to investment revaluation reserve (IRR).

These changes should be presented in the Statement of total recognized gains and losses (STRGL).

There is an important exception to this rule in cases where a deficit (or its reversal) on an individual property is expected to be permanent. In these cases:

- a deficit should be charged to profit and loss account
- a reversal of a previously recognized deficit (charged originally to profit and loss account on the grounds that it was believed to be permanent) should be credited to profit and loss account.

## (d) Disclosure

The following should be disclosed in the financial statements:

- names of valuers or particulars of their qualifications;
- basis of valuation;
- whether valuations have been made by employees or officers;
- prominent disclosure of investment properties, IRR and movements thereon;
- historical cost information relating to revalued assets.

## (e) Companies Act 1985 Implications

Under the Act, fixed assets with a limited useful economic life should be subject to periodic depreciation charges.

However, the Act also has a true and fair view requirement which overrides specific requirements. Should this apply (as it does with SSAP 19), a note to the accounts should give "particulars of that departure, the reasons for it, and its effect" (see also 2.1(g)). It is generally accepted that, in the case of SSAP 19, quantification is not meaningful and hence need not be given.

*Illustration 13*

### Note 12 – Tangible fixed assets (extract)

| Land and buildings include investment properties as follows | £'000 |
|---|---|
| **Valuation** | |
| At 1 April 19X4 | 93.3 |
| Additions | 41.4 |
| Reclassification | (1.0) |
| Revaluation surplus | 6.6 |
| **At 31 March 19X5** | **140.3** |

Investment properties were valued on the basis of open market value at 31 March 19X5 by the group's own professionally qualified staff.

In accordance with SSAP 19, no depreciation is provided in respect of investment properties. This represents a departure from the Companies Act 1985 requirements to provide for the systematic annual depreciation of fixed assets. However, these properties are held for investment, rather than consumption, and the directors consider that the adoption of the above policy is necessary to give a true and fair view.

# 12.12  Government Grants for Capital Expenditure

## (a) Introduction

SSAP 4 deals with accounting for government grants (see also 11.6(d)). The note below deals with the situation of a grant which is made as a contribution towards expenditure on fixed assets.

## (b) Standard Accounting Practice

SSAP 4 states that in principle two methods may be acceptable:

(1) To treat the amount of the grant as deferred income. The deferred income should be credited to profit and loss account over the expected useful economic life of the related asset on a basis consistent with the depreciation policy. This method is recommended as it accords with the requirements of the Companies Act 1985.

(2) To deduct the amount of the grant from the purchase price or production cost of the related asset, with a consequent reduction in the annual charge for depreciation. This method is not recommended as it is prohibited by the requirements of the Companies Act 1985.

*Illustration 14*

Manufacturers Ltd acquired an item of machinery on 1 January 19X3 at a cost of £100,000. The company received an investment grant of £20,000. The asset is to be depreciated over five years on a straight-line basis.

**Financial statements extracts**

*(i) Accounting policy note*
   Capital based investment grants are included in the accounts as deferred income and released to revenue over five years. being the estimated average useful life of the asset which attracted the grant.

# 12.13   International Financial Reporting Standards

IAS 16, Property, plant and equipment, deals with most of the recognition, measurement and disclosure issues covered by FRS 15, including: determination of cost; depreciation; impairment; revaluation. However, there are differences of detail between the two standards.

IAS 40, Investment property, offers a choice of two quite different accounting treatments—the fair value method, and the cost method.

After initial recognition, an entity that chooses the fair value model shall measure all of its property at fair value except for "exceptional cases" where the fair value is not reliably determinable.

A gain or loss arising from a change in the fair value of investment property *shall be recognized in profit or loss for the period in which it arises* (contrast with SSAP 19).

The cost model alternative follows the treatment in IAS 16, Property, plant and equipment, and measures investment property at historical cost less any accumulated depreciation and any accumulated impairment losses.

IAS 36, Impairment, sets out the procedures that an entity should apply to ensure that its assets are carried at no more than their recoverable amount.

If an asset (or group of assets) is carried in the balance sheet at more than its recoverable amount, the asset is described as impaired and the entity should recognize an impairment loss.

Recoverable amount is the greater of the amount to be recovered through the asset's use ("value in use") and the amount to be recovered through its sale ("fair value less costs to sell").

The standard links in closely with IFRS 3 (Business combinations) as the carrying amount of goodwill must be reviewed for impairment *at least annually*. IAS 36 also requires intangibles which are not being amortized to be reviewed for impairment at least annually.

---

**Frequently Asked Questions**

1 Is it acceptable under UK GAAP to assess revised RVs using current price levels?
No—for assets carried at historical cost less depreciation, the assessment should be based on price levels estimated at acquisition date. For assets carried at revalued amount less depreciation, the assessment should be based on price levels at the date of revaluation.

2 For property carried in the balance sheet at market value, how often should valuations be carried out?
At least every five years, with interim valuations between these dates.

3 Are companies with investment properties required to have external valuations?
No—SSAP 19 [paragraph 6].

 Intangible Fixed Assets,
Including Goodwill

---

**This chapter covers:**
* Regulatory framework
* Goodwill
  – FRS 10 requirements
* Intangibles (other than development costs).
  – the impact of FRS 10
* Research and development expenditure
  – SSAP 13
* International Financial Reporting Standards

---

## 13.1 Introduction

### (a) Statutory Headings

Companies Act 1985 Sch 4 includes the following sub-headings for intangible fixed assets:

* development costs;
* concessions, patents, licences, trade marks and similar rights and assets;
* goodwill.

### (b) Definition

FRS 10—Goodwill and intangibles, defines intangible assets as non-financial fixed assets that do not have physical substance but are identifiable and are controlled by the entity through custody or legal rights.

### (c) Regulatory Framework

### (1) Companies Act 1985

* format headings – these were referred to in (a) above.

- accounting rules – there are two important rules:
  - (i) intangibles such as concessions, patents, licences, trade marks and similar rights and assets may only be included in the balance sheet in either of the following situations:
    - the assets were acquired for valuable consideration and are not effectively part of goodwill, or
    - the assets were created by the company itself. (Note that the Companies Act 1985 prevents non-purchased or internally generated goodwill from being included on the balance sheet).
  - (ii) intangible assets (other than goodwill) may be included at their current cost. This alternative to historical cost is permitted by the alternative accounting rules of Schedule 4.

*(2) SSAPs and FRSs*

Accounting standards deal with research and development (SSAP 13), and goodwill and intangibles (FRS 10). These statements are referred to below.

## (d) Illustrations

The following are examples of some intangible fixed asset headings which have appeared in published accounts:

- goodwill;
- development costs;
- brand names;
- patents, trade marks and other product rights;
- trade values of retail outlets;
- betting office licences;
- know-how agreement;
- programmes, film rights and stores;
- newspaper titles;
- publishing copyright;
- publishing rights and titles, databases, exhibition rights and other similar intangible assets.

# 13.2   Accounting for Goodwill – FRS 10

## (a) Definitions

FRS 10 defines purchased goodwill as:

> "The difference between the cost of an acquired entity and the aggregate of the fair value of that entity's identifiable assets and liabilities".

Positive goodwill arises when the acquisition cost exceeds the aggregate of the fair values of the identifiable assets and liabilities.

Negative goodwill arises when the aggregate fair values of the identifiable assets and liabilities of the entity exceed the acquisition cost.

FRS 7, Fair values in acquisition accounting, gives guidance on determining fair values (see Chapter 26).

## (b) Classification of Goodwill

Possible types of goodwill may be illustrated diagrammatically as follows:

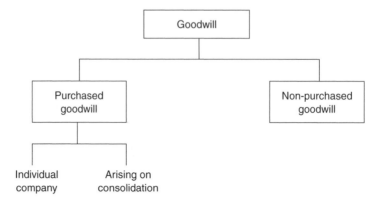

Non-purchased goodwill is sometimes referred to as inherent goodwill or internally generated goodwill.

## (c) Special Characteristics of Goodwill

Several features distinguish goodwill from other assets, including:

- goodwill cannot be sold as a separate asset apart from the rest of the business;
- the value of goodwill may fluctuate from day to day;
- the value and existence of goodwill are subjective;
- the value of goodwill has no reliable relationship to costs which may have been incurred in its creation.

## (d) FRS 10 – Overview

Purchased goodwill may result from:

(1) business combinations, involving the acquisition by a parent undertaking of a subsidiary undertaking, and accounted for by acquisition accounting;
(2) unincorporated businesses acquired by the reporting entity;
(3) investments accounted for using the equity method (FRS 9, Associates and joint ventures).

FRS 10 requires positive purchased goodwill to be capitalized, and included on the balance sheet under intangible fixed assets. Amortization requirements are referred to below, but for most companies, the maximum write-off period will be 20 years.

For small companies without subsidiaries, purchased goodwill will arise only as a result of (2) above. For parent companies heading up small groups, consolidation goodwill will arise only when consolidated accounts are prepared.

Negative goodwill must also be included in the fixed asset section of the balance sheet, under the intangible fixed asset sub-heading.

Internally generated goodwill should not be capitalized. This is consistent with the Companies Act 1985 which states that

> "Amounts representing goodwill shall only be included to the extent that the goodwill was acquired for valuable consideration".

The FRS applies to all intangible assets, except for:

- oil and gas exploration and development costs;
- research and development costs (covered by SSAP 13);
- any other intangible assets that are specifically addressed by another accounting standard.

## (e) Amortization Requirement – Positive Goodwill and Intangibles

The key point is whether or not goodwill and intangibles are regarded as having limited useful economic lives:

- if they are, they should be amortized on a systematic basis over those lives;
- if, however, they are regarded as having indefinite useful economic lives, they should not be amortized.

The general presumption, capable of being rebutted, is that useful lives should be limited to 20 years or less.

Some companies may wish to rebut this presumption and argue that:

 (i) useful economic life exceeds 20 years – for example, 40 years, or
(ii) useful economic life is indefinite.

The use of (ii) is likely to be uncommon for the majority of companies in view of the stringent conditions laid down in FRS 10.

## (f) Impairment Reviews: Goodwill and Intangible Assets Amortized over a Period of 20 Years or Less

Goodwill and intangible assets that are amortized over a finite period not exceeding 20 years should be reviewed for impairment (see FRS 11):

(1) at the end of the first full financial year following the acquisition – (referred to as "the first year review"), and, where applicable,
(2) in other periods, if events or changes in circumstances indicate that the carrying values may not be recoverable.

Where a first year review identifies an impairment, this could be due to:

- an overpayment;
- an event that occurred between the acquisition and the first year review;
- depletion between the acquisition date and the date of the first year review (where the amount exceeds the amortization charge).

The first year review may be performed in two stages:

(1) in all cases, identify any possible impairment by comparing post-acquisition performance in the first year with pre-acquisition forecasts used to support the purchase price;
(2) in specified cases only, it will also be necessary to carry out a full impairment review in accordance with the requirements of FRS 11 on impairment of fixed assets and goodwill. These cases are:
    - where the initial review indicates that the post-acquisition performance has failed to meet pre-acquisition expectations;
    - where any other previously unforeseen events/changes in circumstance indicate the carrying values may not be recoverable.

If the first year review does indicate the need for a write-down of the balance, the remaining carrying value should be amortized over a period not exceeding 20 years.

## (g) Impairment Reviews: Goodwill and Intangible Assets Amortized over a Period Exceeding 20 Years or not Amortized

This situation is likely to apply to relatively few companies. Goodwill and intangibles that are amortized over a period exceeding 20 years from the date of acquisition or are not amortized should be reviewed for impairment at the end of each reporting period.

Impairment reviews should be performed in accordance with the requirements of FRS 11 on impairment of fixed assets and goodwill (see 12.8).

## (h) Negative goodwill

### (1) Balance sheet positioning

Negative goodwill should be recognized on the balance sheet and separately disclosed. The required positioning is somewhat unusual—the negative goodwill should be disclosed in the asset section of the balance sheet, immediately below the goodwill heading. It should also be followed by a subtotal showing the net amount of the positive and negative goodwill.

### (2) Accounting treatment

Negative goodwill, of an amount not exceeding the fair values of the non-monetary assets acquired, should be recognized in the profit and loss accounts of the periods in which the non-monetary assets are recovered, whether through:

- depreciation, or
- sale.

Any negative goodwill in excess of the fair values of the non-monetary assets acquired, should be recognized in the profit and loss accounts of the periods expected to benefit.

# 13.3    Intangible Assets (Other than Goodwill)

## (a) Accounting Rules in FRS 10

Different rules apply according to how the intangible asset arose:

(1) Where an intangible asset is purchased separately from a business, it should be capitalized at cost.
(2) An intangible acquired as part of a business acquisition should be capitalized separately from goodwill provided its value can be measured reliably on initial recognition. Where the value of an intangible cannot be measured reliably, the intangible should be included within the part of the purchase price allocated to purchased goodwill.
(3) An internally developed intangible asset may be capitalized only if it has a readily ascertainable market value.

The term "ascertainable market value" is defined in paragraph 2 of the Standard, in a lengthy section which refers to a market where:

(i) the asset belongs to a homogenous population of assets that are equivalent in all material respects, and
(ii) an active market, evidenced by frequent transactions, exists for that population of assets.

Examples of intangibles that might meet these conditions include certain operating licenses, franchises and quotas.

By contrast, FRS 10 indicates that the following examples of "unique" intangibles are unlikely to satisfy the above test: brands, publishing titles, patented drugs and engineering design patents.

## (b) Amortization Requirement

As for goodwill, intangibles will usually require to be amortized over a period not exceeding 20 years.

However, it will be possible for companies to amortize over a longer period, or to charge no amortization. FRS 10 and FRS 11 set out demanding requirements for such situations.

## 13.4 UITF 27 – Revision to Estimates of the Useful Economic Life of Goodwill and Intangible Assets

### (a) Introduction

FRS 10 includes a rebuttable presumption that the useful economic lives of goodwill and intangibles are limited to periods of 20 years or less which is the practice adopted by the majority of companies.

Abstract 27 refers to the very specific situation where a company which has not previously amortized goodwill or intangibles now decides to start amortizing.

### (b) Requirements of FRS 10 and UITF 27

The key issue is that this change does not amount to a change of accounting policy requiring a prior year adjustment.

The Abstract states that

"... where estimates of the useful economic lives of goodwill or intangible assets are revised, the carrying value should be amortized over the revised remaining useful economic life ...".

It is also important to establish the company's reason for deciding to amortize and whether the goodwill or intangible asset has been impaired. Reference should be made, where appropriate, to the impairment indicators in para 10 of FRS 11.

## 13.5 FRS 10 Disclosure Requirements – Overview

The disclosure requirements of FRS 10 are very detailed and are contained in paragraphs 52 to 64 of the Standard. In brief summary, principal disclosures include:

- method used to value intangibles;
- balance sheet information for each of positive goodwill, negative goodwill and intangible assets, giving amounts of, and movements during the year on, cost or revalued amount and cumulative provisions for amortization or impairment;
- profit or loss on each material disposal of previously acquired business/ segment;
- methods for amortization of positive goodwill and intangibles, periods, reasons for choosing period;
- reason for rebutting 20 years presumption – where amortization period greater than 20 years or no amortization;
- true and fair override disclosures – where goodwill not amortized;
- details of revaluations of intangibles;
- periods in which negative goodwill is being written back to P/L;
- details of treatment of goodwill arising prior to implementation of FRS 10.

## 13.6 Accounting for Research and Development Expenditure

### (a) Background

The accounting treatment of research and development expenditure illustrates possible conflict between the accruals and prudence concept set out in former standard SSAP 2 Accounting policies.

On the one hand, R + D expenditure in the current period may lead to higher revenues (or lower costs) in subsequent periods than would otherwise have been the case.

On the other hand, there are considerable uncertainties regarding the amount of benefits (let alone whether such benefits will actually materialize) and the timing of benefits.

A general principle has been established in SSAP 13 which effectively requires expenditure to be written off as it arises unless its relationship to revenue of a future period can be established with reasonable certainty.

### (b) Definitions

#### (1) Pure (or basic) research

Experimental or theoretical work undertaken primarily to acquire new scientific or technical knowledge for its own sake rather than directed towards any specific aim or application.

#### (2) Applied research

Original or critical investigation undertaken in order to gain new scientific or technical knowledge and directed towards a specific practical aim or objective.

#### (3) Development

Use of scientific or technical knowledge in order to produce new or substantially improved materials, devices, products or services, to install new processes or systems prior to the commencement of commercial production or commercial applications, or to improve substantially those already produced or installed.

### (c) Examples of Research and Development Activity

#### (1) General principle

Research and development activity is distinguished from non-research based activity by the presence or absence of an appreciable element of innovation. If the activity departs from routine and breaks new ground it should normally be included; if it follows an established pattern it should normally be excluded.

(2) The following are examples of activities that would normally be included in research and development:
- experimental, theoretical or other work aimed at the discovery of new knowledge, or the advancement of existing knowledge;
- searching for applications of that knowledge;
- formulation and design of possible applications for such work;
- testing in search for, or evaluation of, product, service or process alternatives;
- design, construction and testing of pre-production prototypes and models and development batches;
- design of products, services, processes or systems involving new technology or substantially improving those already produced or installed;
- construction and operation of pilot plants.

(3) The following are examples of activities that would normally be excluded from research and development:
- testing and analysis either of equipment or product for purposes of quality or quantity control;
- periodic alterations to existing products, services or processes even though these may represent some improvement;
- operational research not tied to a specific research and development activity;
- cost of corrective action in connection with breakdowns during commercial activity;
- legal and administrative work in connection with patent applications, records and litigation and the sale or licensing of patents;
- activity, including design and construction engineering, relating to the construction, relocation, rearrangement or start-up of facilities or;
- equipment other than facilities or equipment whose sole use is for a particular research and development project;
- market research.

## (d) Accounting Treatment – Pure and Applied Research Expenditure

This expenditure should be written off as incurred since any possible future benefits are difficult to assess.

## (e) Accounting Treatment – Development Expenditure

Development expenditure may (not must) be capitalized as an intangible asset and amortized over period of time if all of the following conditions can be satisfied:

(1) There is a clearly defined project.
(2) The related expenditure is separately identifiable.

(3) The outcome of such a project has been assessed with reasonable certainty as to:
   (i) its technical feasibility; and
   (ii) its ultimate commercial viability considered in the light of factors, such as likely market conditions (including competing products), public opinion, consumer and environmental legislation.
(4) If further development costs are to be incurred on the same project the aggregate of such costs together with related production, selling and administration costs is reasonably expected to be more than covered by related future revenues.
(5) Adequate resources exist, or are reasonably expected to be available, to enable the project to be completed and to provide any consequential increases in working capital.

The basic principle is that development expenditure may be deferred to the extent that its recovery can reasonably be regarded as assured. It is also important to carry out an annual balance sheet date review of unamortized expenditure to ensure that the conditions referred to above are still capable of being satisfied. Irrecoverable expenditure should be written off immediately. Each project should be considered individually. Finally, consistency of accounting treatment between development projects should be paramount.

## (f) Capitalized Development Costs – Basis of Amortization

Amortization should start in the period in which commercial production of the product or process commences.

Development costs should be allocated over accounting periods by reference to:

(1) the sale or use of the product or process; or
(2) the period over which the product or process is expected to be sold or used.

## (g) Further Considerations

(1) The cost of fixed assets used for R + D purposes should be capitalized and depreciated.
(2) Expenditure in locating and exploiting mineral deposits does not come within the scope of SSAP 13.
(3) Where companies enter into a firm contract to carry out development work on behalf of third parties, or to develop and manufacture at an agreed price calculated to reimburse development expenditure, such expenditure should be included in work in progress.

## (h) Disclosure Requirements

The disclosure requirements of SSAP 13 are:

(1) the accounting policy should be stated and explained;
(2) movements on deferred development expenditure and the amount carried forward at the beginning and end of the period should be disclosed;

(3) deferred development expenditure should be separately disclosed under intangible fixed assets;

(4) the total research and development charge in the profit and loss account should be disclosed and analysed between:
    (i) current year expenditure;
    (ii) amounts amortized from deferred expenditure (but see (i) below).

### (i) Companies Act 1985 Implications

(1) Development costs may be capitalized in special circumstances (presumably those specified in SSAP 13). Disclosure is required of:
    (i) the period over which the costs are to be written off;
    (ii) the reasons for capitalizing the development costs.

(2) Costs of research may not be capitalized under any circumstances.

*Illustration – Accounting Policy disclosure*

*Intangible fixed assets*
Intellectual property represents the cost of acquisition of patents, trade marks and copyrights. Amortization is provided on intellectual property to write off the cost in equal annual instalments over its estimated economic life of 20 years.

*Development expenditure*
Development expenditure relating to specific projects intended for commercial exploitation is carried forward where the ultimate commercial viability has been assessed with reasonable certainty. Such expenditure is amortized over the period expected to benefit. Expenditure on pure and applied research is written off as incurred.

# 13.7   International Financial Reporting Standards

IAS 38, Intangibles, deals with accounting for those intangibles which are not specifically dealt with in another standard, and covers both measurement and disclosure issues.

Goodwill is dealt with in IFRS 3, Business combinations.

The treatment of research and development expenditure is covered by this standard. IAS 38 does not offer the flexibility offered by SSAP 13 as regards development costs.

No intangible asset arising from research (or from the research phase of an internal project) shall be recognized. Research expenditure shall be recognized as an expense when it is incurred. The standard gives examples of research activities.

IAS 38 requires that an intangible asset arising from development (or from the development phase of an internal project) **shall** be recognized if, and only if, an entity can demonstrate all of the following:

- The technical feasibility of completing the intangible asset so that it will be available for use or sale;
- Its intention to complete the intangible asset and use it or sell it;

- Its ability to use or sell the intangible asset;
- How the intangible asset will generate probable future economic benefits. Among other things, the entity can demonstrate the existence of a market for the output of the intangible asset or the intangible asset itself or, if it is to be used internally, the usefulness of the intangible asset;
- The availability of adequate technical, financial and other resources to complete the development and to use or sell the intangible asset;
- Its ability to measure reliably the expenditure attributable to the intangible asset during its development.

IAS 38 prohibits the recognition as intangible assets of the following:

- Brands;
- Mastheads;
- Publishing titles;
- Customer lists; and
- Items similar in substance.

The standard requires goodwill acquired in a business combination to be recognized as an asset from the balance sheet date, but prohibits the amortization of such goodwill. Instead, goodwill is to be tested for impairment annually (or more frequently in certain circumstances).

IFRS 3 does not use the term "negative goodwill". However, where the acquirer's interest in the net fair value of the identifiable assets, liabilities and contingent liabilities exceeds the cost of the business combination, the acquirer is required to reassess the identification and measurement of the acquiree's identifiable assets, liabilities and contingent liabilities and the measurement of the cost of the combination, *and* recognize *immediately in profit or loss* any excess remaining after that reassessment.

---

**Frequently Asked Questions**

1 Must positive goodwill be systematically be amortized under UK GAAP?
No—FRS 10 normally requires goodwill to be amortized over a period not exceeding 20 years, but allows a longer (or indefinite period) to be used in certain circumstances.

2 Can an internally-generated intangible be capitalized under UK GAAP?
Yes—but only if it has a "readily ascertainable market value". This means a market where the asset belongs to a homogeneous population of assets that are equivalent in all material respects, and an active market exists for that population of assets (FRS 10.2 gives brands and publishing titles as examples of intangibles which would not so qualify).

3 Can an intangible be revalued under UK GAAP?
Yes—but only if the intangible has a readily ascertainable market value.

# 14 Hire Purchase and Leasing

This chapter covers:
* Methods of financing asset purchases
* Hire purchase accounting
* Lessee accounting
  - background to SSAP 21
  - characteristics of finance leases
  - definitions and classification
  - methods of allocating finance charges
  - accounting entries
  - disclosures
* Interaction between SSAP 21 and FRS 5
* Lessor accounting
  - categories of lessors
  - operating leases
  - finance leases
  - methods of allocating earnings
  - accounting
  - disclosure
* Manufacturer/dealer lessor
* Sale and leaseback
* operating lease incentives (UITF 28)
* International Financial Reporting Standards

## 14.1  Introduction – Financing of Fixed Assets

A company may acquire the right to use a fixed asset over its useful life in one of a number of ways. These include:

(1) outright purchase for cash;
(2) outright purchase using the proceeds of a secured or unsecured loan;

(3) hire purchase (or lease purchase);
(4) finance leasing.

In the case of (1) and (2), legal title to the fixed asset is obtained at the date of purchase. In the case of (3), title is obtained when the final instalment has been paid and the option to purchase exercised. In the case of an agreement under a finance lease, as far as the United Kingdom is concerned legal title can never pass to the lessee.

# 14.2  Hire Purchase – Accounting for the Hirer

## (a) Introduction

Under a hire purchase agreement the owner of goods leases them to a person called the hirer, on the terms that the hirer shall pay to the owner a number of instalments, until a price has been paid, when the ownership of the goods will either pass automatically to the hirer, or he may exercise an option to purchase them by the payment of a stated small sum. Thus the property in the goods does not pass to the hirer until he has paid the last instalment or exercised his option to purchase.

## (b) Substance Over Form

Traditionally assets acquired under hire purchase agreements are brought into the balance sheet at cash price and depreciated over their useful economic life to the user. A corresponding obligation or liability is shown in the balance sheet. Payments to the hire vendor are allocated between capital and interest using some suitable basis. The capital part is used to reduce the balance sheet obligation, while the income part is debited to profit and loss account.

The justification for this treatment has been the substance over form argument: transactions and other events should be accounted for and presented in accordance with their substance and financial reality, and not merely with their legal form. Rights under hire purchase agreements, prior to the obtaining of legal title, are for most practical purposes equivalent to those of immediate legal ownership.

FRS 5 requires an entity's financial statements to reflect the commercial substance of the transactions into which the entity has entered (see Chapter 6, sections 6.2).

## (c) Apportionment of Hire Purchase Interest

The three main methods are:

(1) actuarial method;
(2) sum of the digits (rule of 78);
(3) straight-line method.

The basis of calculation and the respective merits of the various methods are dealt with in section 14.5.

### (d) Hire Purchase Agreements Terminated Prematurely

Agreements may be terminated prematurely, when the hirer:

(1) With the consent of the hire purchase vendor:
    (i) wishes to complete the purchase; he pays the remainder of the cash purchase price, and so much of the finance charge still outstanding, as the vendor may require, as consideration for his consent and as compensation for his loss of future interest; or
    (ii) sells or assigns the asset to a second hirer, who undertakes to pay the instalments as they fall due; or
(2) Fails to pay an instalment which falls due.

## 14.3   Lessee Accounting – Background

### (a) Introduction

A lease is a contract between a lessor and a lessee for the hire of a specific asset.

Traditional practice has been to charge lease payments to profit and loss accounts as incurred. Whilst this treatment is, for the time being, accepted for operating leases, it is not appropriate for those types of leases referred to as finance leases.

Operating leases usually involve the lessee paying a rental for the hire of an asset for a period of time which is substantially less than the asset's useful economic life. With an operating lease, the lessor retains most of the risks and rewards of ownership.

By contrast, finance leases usually involve payments by the lessee to the lessor of the full cost of the asset together with a return on finance provided. Although the lessee never obtains legal title, the lessee has substantially all the risks and rewards which are usually associated with ownership.

### (b) Typical Characteristics of a Finance Lease

Characteristics will vary between different leases. The following characteristics are provided by way of illustration:

(1) Lessor retains title to asset. At the end of the lease, the asset is returned to the lessor or the asset is disposed of by the lessee as agent for the lessor. The lease may specify that the lessee obtains a substantial part (e.g. 95%) of the proceeds as a rebate of rentals.
(2) Payments to the lessor during the primary period are substantial and non-cancellable.
(3) Payments to the lessor during the secondary period are nominal in amount ("peppercorn rent"). The lessee may be given the option during the secondary period to renew on an annual basis.

(4) Lessee has uninterrupted use of the asset as long as leasing payments are made (rewards of ownership).
(5) Lessee is responsible for insurance and maintenance (risks of ownership).
(6) Lessee indemnifies lessor for claims.
(7) Lessee cannot dispose of asset.

## (c) Capitalization of Finance Leases

SSAP 21 (Accounting for leases and hire-purchase contracts) accepts the traditional treatment of operating leases since it reflects both the economic substance and the legal form of the transaction.

However, SSAP 21 rejected the hitherto traditional treatment of finance leases and instead opted for capitalization. The effect of capitalization is to account for finance lease assets in a similar way to hire purchase assets.

There are two main arguments in favour of capitalization: substance over form, and the analysis of accounts argument.

### (1) Substance over form

Substance over form recognizes that a lessee's rights are for practical purposes little different from those of an outright purchaser. These rights represent an economic resource which is required in the business.

This argument is now expressed in terms of "reporting substance"—see Chapter 7 on FRS 5, Reporting the substance of transactions.

### (2) Analysis of accounts argument

The traditional treatment of finance leases charges the lease payments to profit and loss account as such payments are made. The finance for such leasing arrangements is excluded from the balance sheet, a practice usually referred to as off-balance sheet finance. This practice may materially distort the view given by the following ratios:

• Fixed assets as a proportion of total assets – since leased assets are excluded from the balance sheet.
• Debt/equity (or gearing) – since potentially large liabilities are built up off balance sheet.
• Return on capital employed (profit before interest and tax as a percentage of fixed assets plus net current assets).

SSAP 21 makes it clear that capitalization of finance leases should assist both external and internal users. External users may be assisted in making investment or credit decisions. Internal users such as managers may be in a better position to appraise divisional performance.

## (d) Problems of Capitalization Concept

Although the theoretical arguments have been forcibly advocated, certain problems remain. For example, the problem of distinguishing between finance leases and operating leases. Secondly, in some cases (such as where an asset could not be alternatively purchased for cash) it is not always clear how much should be capitalized at the outset of the lease. Leasing is presently under consideration by Accounting Standards Board.

### (e) Companies Act Implications

Two aspects should be considered:

- accounting treatment;
- disclosure requirements.

#### (1) Accounting treatment

The Companies Act 1985 does not define or distinguish between operating leases and finance leases. Thus, no accounting requirements are set out in the Companies Act.

#### (2) Disclosure requirements

Disclosure is required of:

(i) plant hire charges;
(ii) financial commitments which have not been provided for and which are relevant to assessing the company's state of affairs.

Note that non-cancellable operating leases of land and buildings are included here. Also included are finance lease commitments in so far as not reflected in the balance sheet (e.g. in the periods before which capitalization becomes mandatory under SSAP 21).

Finally, the overriding true and fair view requirements (see section 2.1(e)) should always be borne in mind.

## 14.4   Lessee Accounting – Classification

### (a) Hire Purchase Contracts

The accounting and disclosure requirements for finance leases generally apply equally to hire purchase contracts. Special points which relate to hire purchase contracts only will, however, be referred to separately.

### (b) Finance Leases

#### (1) Definition

A finance lease is a lease that transfers substantially all the risks and rewards of ownership of an asset to the lessee. This transfer is presumed to take place if, at the start of the lease, it can be shown that the present value of the minimum lease payments amounts to 90% or more of the fair value of the leased asset.

These terms are explained immediately below.

### (2) Explanation of terms

(i) *Present value:* This is obtained by discounting the minimum lease payments using the interest rate implicit in the lease as a discount factor.
(ii) *Minimum lease payments:*
 • Minimum payments over the remaining part of the lease term. These will relate essentially to the non-cancellable payments during the primary period.
 • If applicable, any residual amounts (at the end of the lease) which have been guaranteed by the lessee.
(iii) *Interest rate implicit in the lease:* This is the discount rate, which when applied at the outset of the lease, equates, the following:
 • the present value of the amounts which the lessor expects to receive and retain. These amounts will include the minimum payments in (ii) above together with any unguaranteed residual value not accountable to the lessee;
 • the fair value of the asset.
(iv) *Fair value of asset:* This is the price for which an asset could be exchanged in an arm's length transaction. This amount should be reduced by the amount of capital-based grants that such an asset would normally be entitled to.

### (3) Illustration 1

Langdale Ltd wishes to acquire the use of a new item of machinery. The company could purchase outright for cash of £16,200 or alternatively enter into a finance lease. The asset has an estimated useful life of ten years with a residual value of £800.

The terms of the finance lease are as follows:

(i) Primary period of five years – five rentals of £4,000 pa payable on first day of each year.
(ii) Secondary period – renewable on an annual basis for an indefinite period. Ignore secondary rentals.
(iii) Lessee responsible for insurance and maintenance.
(iv) At end of lease term, lessee entitled to 80% of proceeds of sale of asset as rebate of rentals.

**Step 1**
Calculate interest rate implicit in lease using a programmed calculator. To start with, identify the amounts which the lessor expects to receive and retain. These comprise:

(1) the lessee's minimum lease payments i.e. five lots of £4,000;
(2) unguaranteed residual value, less proportion accountable to the lessee i.e. 20% × £800 = £160.
It is then a question of determining what interest rate when applied to these amounts equates with a fair value of £16,200. This rate is determined as 12%.

|  | £ |
|---|---|
| *Check* £4,000 × 1.0 | 4,000 |
| £4,000 × 3.037 (annuity tables) | 12,148 |
| £160 × 0.322 (present value tables, year 10) | 52 |
|  | 16,200 |

**Step 2**
Calculate present value of minimum lease payments using a discount rate of 12%.

|  | £ |
|---|---|
| £4,000 × 1.0 (payment now) | 4,000 |
| £4,000 × 3.037 (annuity four years) | 12,148 |
|  | 16,148 |

**Step 3**
Compare with 90% of fair value of leased asset, i.e.
90% × £16,200 = £14,580

**Conclusion**
There is a presumption that the lease is a finance lease. It is unlikely that this presumption could be rebutted since the lease does transfer substantially all the risks and rewards of ownership to the lessee.

## (c) Operating Leases

An operating lease is defined as a lease other than a finance lease.

## (d) Unusual Situations

In exceptional circumstances, the above presumptions may be rebutted. For example in very unusual circumstances, a lease that would otherwise be classified as finance may instead be classified as operating. This could be so if it could be shown that the lease did not transfer to the lessee substantially all the risks and rewards of ownership. The converse might in exceptional circumstances also be true.

# 14.5　Lessee Accounting – Finance Leases and Hire Purchase Contracts

## (a) The Concept of Capitalization

Although a lessee never obtains legal title, in the case of finance leases the lessee's rights and obligations are such that the risks and rewards from the use of the asset are substantially (not, of course, identically) similar to those of an outright purchaser.

SSAP 21 makes it quite clear that what is capitalized (and included in the balance sheet as an asset) is not the asset itself but the lessee's rights in the asset. Also capitalized is the corresponding obligation to pay rentals.

However, the standard points out that from a practical viewpoint, these rights are substantially similar to those of an outright purchaser. The outcome of this is that these rights are effectively classified as finance lease assets and are included together with owned assets under the general balance sheet heading of tangible fixed assets. However, the leased assets should be distinguished from owned assets and the amount disclosed (see under lessee accounting disclosures).

## (b) Accounting Treatment

(1) *Calculation of initial amount to be recorded as asset and obligation*
(i) *Theoretical approach:* The amount to be capitalized should be the present value of the minimum lease rentals, discounted at the rate of interest implicit in the lease.

*Illustration 2*

Using the above example of Langdale Ltd. the amount to be capitalized would be £16,148.

(ii) *Practical approximation:* In many cases, the fair value of the asset will provide a reasonable approximation to the above. Clearly, in the example of Langdale, it would be acceptable to capitalize £16,200. In the subsequent illustrations, the amount to be capitalized will be taken as the fair value of the asset.

*(2) Depreciation of finance lease asset*
The asset should be depreciated over the shorter of:

(i) the lease term – this includes:
   – the period for which the lessee has contracted to lease the asset (i.e. the non-cancellable primary period); plus
   – any further secondary periods under which the lessee has an option to continue leasing the asset (possibly renewing on an annual basis) and where it is reasonably certain at the start of the lease that the lessee will exercise the option; or
(ii) the asset's useful life.

The guidance notes point out that in most cases residual value will be small, and so for the purpose of depreciation calculations may be taken as nil. In the case of Langdale, the straight-line depreciation would be 10% (16,200 – 80% × 800) i.e. £1,556 taking account of residual value or £1,620 ignoring it. The difference of £64 is clearly not material.

*(3) Allocation of rentals*
Rentals paid to the lessor should be apportioned between financial charge and repayment of obligation. Possible approaches to allocation of finance charges are explained below.

## (c) Allocation of Finance Charges

The key principle is that the total finance charge should be allocated to accounting periods during the lease terms so as to produce a constant periodic rate of charge on the remaining obligation outstanding.

Possible approaches include:
- Actuarial method – this accords exactly with the above requirement.
- Sum of the digits (rule of 78) – this is an approximation to the actuarial method. The sum of the digits method is regarded as a reasonable approximation

provided that the lease term is not very long (say, a primary period of less than seven years) and interest rates are not very high.

- Straight-line method – this does not produce a constant periodic rate of charge and is thus not normally regarded as acceptable. However, it may be used in practice in those situations where the total finance charges are not material.

Underlying calculations for each method are illustrated below.

## (d) Illustration of Calculations

### (1) Basic data

An item of plant and machinery with a useful life of ten years may be purchased outright for cash for £21,400. Alternatively, use of the asset may be obtained by means of a finance lease. Under this arrangement, the lessee would be responsible for insurance and maintenance and would be required to make five annual payments of £5,800 all payable in advance. After the primary period of five years, the lessee would have the option to continue leasing the asset for an indefinite period for a nominal ("peppercorn") rental. The amount of the rental may be ignored.

It is assumed that the fair value of £21,400 provides an acceptable approximation to the present value of the minimum lease payments discounted at the rate of interest implicit in the lease.

### (2) Depreciation calculation

If the straight-line method is used, and if residual value is ignored, the annual depreciation charge will be £2,140.

### (3) Finance charge – actuarial method

Total finance charge to be allocated to periods = excess of rentals paid over amount capitalized (i.e. £29,000 – £21,400 = £7,600).

The interest rate applicable is 18%. This may be calculated from annuity tables remembering that these tables assume the annuity is paid on the last day of each period.

Present value (£21,400 – £5,800) = £15,600
Annuity – four amounts of £5,800

$$\text{Annuity factor} = \frac{£15,600}{£5,800} = 2.69$$

From actuarial tables, interest rate is 18%.
The following table may then be constructed:

| Year | B/F £ | Rentals (in advance) £ | Finance charge at 18% £ | C/F £ |
|---|---|---|---|---|
| 1 | 21,400 | (5,800) | 2,808 | 18,408 |
| 2 | 18,408 | (5,800) | 2,269 | 14,877 |
| 3 | 14,877 | (5,800) | 1,634 | 10,711 |
| 4 | 10,711 | (5,800) | 889 | 5,800 |
| 5 | 5,800 | (5,800) | – | – |
| | | 29,000 | 7,600 | |

The column headed finance charge gives the debit to profit and loss account for each period (e.g. 18% (£ 21,400 – £5,800) = £2,808).

The carry forward column gives the balance sheet liability (obligation) at each year end.

For example, at the end of year 1, the total obligation is £18,408 of which £14,877 is non-current and the balance of £3,531 is current.

*(4) Finance charge – sum of the digits method*

The sum of the digits may be calculated by the formula $\dfrac{N(N + 1)}{2}$

where $N$ is the number of periods over which the finance charge is to be allocated. For example, in the above illustration, the obligation is deemed to be reduced to nil by the first day of year 5. Consequently, the finance charge is to be allocated over four periods.

The sum of the digits is (1 + 2 + 3 + 4) i.e. 10.

Alternatively, it may be calculated as $\dfrac{4(4 + 1)}{2} = 10$

The finance charge allocation is as follows:

| Year | | £ |
|---|---|---|
| 1 | 4/10 × £7,600 | 3,040 |
| 2 | 3/10 × £7,600 | 2,280 |
| 3 | 2/10 × £7,600 | 1,520 |
| 4 | 1/10 × £7,600 | 760 |
| Total | | 7,600 |

The obligation at each year end may be calculated by completing a table similar to that in (3) above.

*(5) Finance charge – straight-line method*

Annual finance charge $= \dfrac{£7,600}{4}$ i.e. £1,900.

# 14.6   Lessee Accounting – Operating Leases

Rentals under operating leases should be charged on a straight-line basis. This applies even if the payments are not made on this basis. No entry should be made in the balance sheet for either the right to use the asset or the obligation to pay rentals.

The standard requires the straight-line basis to be used unless "another systematic and rational basis is more appropriate". This could cover situations of rentals holidays where no payment is made during the first year in which the asset is in use. UITF 28, Operating lease incentives, provides further guidance in this area (see 14.16).

## 14.7 Lessee Accounting Disclosures Finance Leases

### (a) Fixed Assets

Two types of disclosure are possible:

(1) To disclose assets held under finance leases for each major class of asset, and to show:
- gross amounts of assets;
- accumulated depreciation;
- depreciation for the period.
(2) To integrate amounts for finance lease assets with those for owned assets. The only balance sheet information for leased assets would be the overall net book value.

*Illustration of (2)*

Using figures at the end of year 1 from the illustration above, the following note would appear at the foot of the fixed asset note:

The net book value of fixed assets of £x includes an amount of £19,260 in respect of assets held under finance leases and hire purchase contracts.

### (b) Obligations under Finance Leases

(1) Amounts of obligations related to finance leases (net of finance charges allocated in future periods) should be disclosed separately from other obligations and liabilities.
(2) The above information may be shown either on the face of the balance sheet or in the notes to the accounts.
(3) Net obligations under finance leases should be analysed between:
- amounts payable in the next year;
- amounts payable in the second to fifth years inclusive from balance sheet date;
- the aggregate amounts payable thereafter.
(4) The analysis above may be presented, either:
  (i) separately for obligations under finance leases.
    In this case, two alternatives are possible:
    - analysing the net obligations;
    - analysing the gross obligations and then deducting the future finance charges from the total;
              *or*
  (ii) where the total of finance lease obligations is combined on the balance sheet with other obligations and liabilities, by giving the equivalent analysis of the total in which it is included.

Note that whichever alternative is adopted, the obligation must be split between current and non-current for balance sheet presentation purposes.

In the above illustration, using figures from the actuarial method at the end of year 1, the total obligation of £18,408 would be included as follows:

Creditors: amounts falling due within one year £3,531

Creditors: amounts falling due after more than one year £14,877.

## (c) Profit and Loss Disclosures

The following amounts should be disclosed. For illustration purposes, figures have been taken from year 1 calculations from the earlier illustration of the actuarial method:

Profit is stated after charging:

|  | £ |
| --- | --- |
| Depreciation of assets held under finance leases and hire purchase contracts | 2,140 |
| Finance charges payable—finance leases and hire purchase contracts | 2,808 |

An additional note is required to comply with the Companies Act 1985:

Amounts charged to revenue in respect of finance leases and hire-purchase contracts are shown separately under the headings of depreciation (£2,140) and finance charges (£2,808) (total £4,948).

## (d) Additional Notes

(1) Disclosure is required for commitments existing at the balance sheet date for finance leases which have been entered into but whose inception occurs after the year end. (Inception of a lease is when the asset is brought into use or when the rentals first accrue, whichever is the earlier.)

(2) Accounting policies should also be disclosed. A suitable disclosure would be:

*Fixed assets held under leases:* Where assets are financed by leasing agreements that give rights approximating to ownership ("finance leases") the assets are treated as if they had been purchased outright and the corresponding liability to the leasing company is included as an obligation under finance leases.

Depreciation on leased assets is charged to profit and loss account on the same basis as shown above.

Leasing payments are treated as consisting of capital and interest elements and the interest is charged to profit and loss account using the actuarial method.

All other leases are "operating leases" and the relevant annual rentals are charged to profit and loss account on a straight-line basis over the lease term.

## 14.8 Lessee – Accounting Disclosures – Operating Leases

(a) The total of operating lease rentals charged as an expense in the profit and loss account should be disclosed and analysed between:
   – amounts payable in respect of hire of plant and machinery; and
   – operating leases.
(b) The lessee should disclose operating lease payments which he is committed to make during the next year, analysed between those in which the commitment expires:
   – within that year;
   – in the second to fifth years, inclusive; or
   – over five years from the balance sheet date.

Commitments in respect of leases of land and buildings should be shown separately from those for other operating leases.

### Illustration 3

This is taken from the guidance notes to SSAP 21.

At 21 December 19X7, the company had annual commitments under non-cancellable operating leases as set out below.

|  | 19X7 | | 19X6 | |
|---|---|---|---|---|
|  | Land and other buildings | | Land and other buildings | |
|  | £'000 | £'000 | £'000 | £'000 |
| Operating leases which expire: |  |  |  |  |
| Within one year | 30 | 100 | 25 | 90 |
| In the second to fifth years inclusive | 80 | 50 | 75 | 40 |
| Over five years | 120 | 20 | 110 | 10 |
|  | 230 | 170 | 210 | 140 |

The majority of leases of land and buildings are subject to rent reviews.

### Illustration 4

Accounting policy extract.

**Fixed assets held under leases**

Where assets are financed by leasing agreements that give rights approximating to ownership ("finance leases") the assets are treated as if they had been purchased outright and the corresponding liability to the leasing company is included as an obligation under finance leases. Depreciation on leased assets is charged to profit and loss account on the same basis as shown above. Leasing payments are treated as consisting of capital and interest elements and the interest is charged to profit and loss account. All other leases are "operating leases" and the relevant annual rentals are charged wholly to profit and loss account.

**Note 4 Profit on ordinary activities after taxation**

Profit on ordinary activities after taxation is after charging:

|  | 19X6 | 19X5 |
|---|---|---|
|  | £m | £m |
| Depreciation on owned assets including container usage | 165 | 144 |
| Depreciation on assets under finance lease | 18 | 21 |
| Auditors' remuneration – audit | 2 | 2 |
| – other services | 1 | 1 |
|  |  | 229 |

In addition, in 1995 fees of £1m were paid to the auditors in respect of acquisitions and were included as part of the cost of acquisitions.

| | | |
|---|---|---|
| Research and development costs | 21 | 18 |
| Operating lease rentals – property | 27 | 24 |
| – plant and equipment | 26 | 25 |

**13 Tangible fixed assets (extract)**

The net book value of plant and equipment held under finance leases was £89m (19X5: £ 101m)….

**25 Leasing commitments**

The future minimum lease payments to which the Group was committed as at the year end under finance leases were as follows:

|  | 19X6 | 19X5 |
|---|---|---|
|  | £m | £m |
| Within one year | 14 | 16 |
| Between one and five years | 35 | 39 |
| After five years | 13 | 19 |
|  | 62 | 74 |
| Less: Finance charges allocated to future periods | (19) | (23) |
|  | 43 | 51 |

The minimum annual lease payments in 1996, to which the Group was committed under non-cancellable operating leases as at the year end, were as follows:

|  | Property | | Plant and Equipment | |
|---|---|---|---|---|
|  | 19X6 | 19X5 | 19X6 | 19X5 |
|  | £m | £m | £m | £m |
| On leasing expiring: |  |  |  |  |
| Within one year | 1 | 2 | 5 | 5 |
| Between one and five years | 9 | 9 | 16 | 15 |
| After five years | 12 | 10 | – | – |
|  | 22 | 21 | 21 | 20 |

# 14.9  Lease Classification and FRS 5

FRS 5 does not change the accounting treatment of stand-alone operating leases and finance leases. However, para 45 of FRS 5 does state that "… the general principles of the FRS will also be relevant in ensuring that leases are classified as finance or operating leases in accordance with their substance."… (See also section 6.7(b).)

## 14.10   Lessor Accounting – Background

### (a) Categories of Lessors

Lessors may fall into any one of three categories:

(1) Companies such as finance houses which provide finance under lease contracts so as to enable a single customer to acquire the use of an asset for the greater part of its useful life. These leases will usually be finance leases.
(2) Companies which operate a business which involves the renting-out of assets for varying periods of time, usually to more than one customer (usually operating leases).
(3) Companies which are manufacturers or dealer lessors who use leasing to market their products. This could relate to either a finance lease or operating lease according to the criteria in SSAP 21.

### (b) Accounting Approach

(1) In the case of an operating lease, the lessor retains both the legal title and the risks and rewards of ownership of the asset. The risks of ownership include the possibility of reduced demand for the lease of the asset as well as the risk of obsolescence. An operating lease asset should be capitalized and depreciated.
(2) In the case of a finance lease, the substance of the transaction is similar to that of a secured loan receivable. Consequently, the asset is treated as a finance lease receivable.

## 14.11   Lessor Accounting – Operating Leases

### (a) Accounting Treatment

(1) Assets held for use in operating leases should be classified as fixed assets, being depreciated over their useful lives.
(2) Rental income should be recognized on a straight-line basis over the period of the lease. This applies even if the payments are not made on a straight-line basis. However, the standard does permit another systematic and rational basis to be used if this is more representative of the time pattern in which the benefits are receivable.

Turnover should comprise the aggregate rentals receivable in respect of the accounting period.

## (b) Lessor Profit and Loss Account

Using format 2, the relevant profit and loss extract would appear as follows:

| | £ | £ |
|---|---|---|
| | | X |
| Turnover | X | |
| Staff costs | X | |
| Depreciation | X | |
| Other operating charges | X | |
| Interest payable | X | (X) |
| Profit on ordinary activities before tax | | X |

## (c) Manufacturer/Dealer Lessor

Suppose a manufacturer/dealer enters into an operating lease. No sale has been made and so no immediate profit should be recognized.

If the asset has been manufactured, all reasonable manufacturing costs may be capitalized. If the asset has been acquired from a supplier, the purchased cost will be capitalized. The asset will be classified as a tangible fixed asset and depreciated over its useful life as far as the lessor is concerned.

Rental income will be credited to profit and loss account in the usual way.

# 14.12   Lessor Accounting – Finance Leases

## (a) Introduction to Accounting Treatment

### (1) Profit and loss account

The gross earnings from a finance lease comprise the excess of rentals received over the fair value of the asset. The way in which these earnings should be allocated over accounting periods is discussed below.

### Illustration 5

The relevant extract from a profit and loss account prepared under format 2 would be:

| | £ | £ |
|---|---|---|
| Gross earnings under finance leases | | X |
| Staff Costs | X | |
| Depreciation | X | |
| Other operating charges | X | |
| Interest payable | X | X |
| Profit on ordinary activities before tax | | X |

*Note*: The guidance notes to SSAP 21 suggest that the term "turnover" should not be used in view of the special nature of the company's business. A term such as "gross earnings under finance leases" may be appropriate.

However, it is considered that simply to disclose gross earnings would provide an incomplete measure of a lessor's activity. It is recommended that note disclosure should also be made of:

- aggregate rentals receivable under finance leases;
- cost of assets acquired for letting under finance leases.

*(2) Balance sheet*
The relevant asset should be described as finance lease receivables and included under the general heading of debtors. It will also be necessary to disclose by way of note the split of this total between amounts receivable within one year and those amounts receivable thereafter.

## *(b) Methods of Allocating Gross Earnings: Before-Tax Methods*

The three methods are:

- actuarial before-tax;
- sum of the digits;
- straight-line.

These methods are the mirror image of those previously considered for lessee accounting. The calculations are not referred to below but are described in the Guidance Notes to SSAP 21.

## *(c) Methods of Allocating Gross Earnings: After-Tax Methods*

*(1) Introduction*
These methods base their approach on the funds invested in the lease by the lessor. The earnings allocation is related to the net cash investment (NCI). NCI is defined as the net effect of the following:

- cost of asset;
- government grants;
- rentals received;
- taxation payments and receipts (including the effect of capital allowances);
- residual values at the end of the lease term;
- interest payments;
- interest received on cash surplus;
- profit taken out of the lease.

The before-tax methods assume that the cash received by way of rentals is applied exclusively towards payment of notional interest on borrowings and repayment of capital.

The after-tax methods recognize that cash received has many "calls" placed upon it. The following diagram illustrates some of the possibilities:

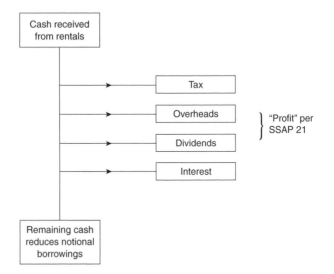

Cash is thus "diverted"—for example, each lease must make some notional contribution towards payment of general overheads and dividends to shareholders.

*(2) Possible approaches*
There are two main approaches, each consisting of several variants:

- actuarial method after tax;
- investment period method (1PM);
  (see Guidance Notes to SSAP 21)

# 14.13  Manufacturer/Dealer Lessor

Selling profit may be taken in full to profit and loss account in the period in which the agreement is entered into.

However, profit taken is restricted to the excess of the fair value of the asset over the manufacturer's or dealer's costs less any grants receivable by the manufacturer or dealer.

*Illustration 6*

A manufacturer constructs a machine at a cost of £20,000. He normally sells the machine for £25,000, giving a profit on sale of £5,000.

The manufacturer also offers the machine on a five year finance lease with a rental of £5,800 per annum (see the lessee accounting example above). This is equivalent to a capital cost of £21,400.

Profit on sale should be restricted to £1,400 (i.e. £21,400 less £20,000). The remainder of the profit is gross earnings and will be allocated over the lease term.

## 14.14   Lessor Accounting Disclosure Requirements

### (a) Introduction

Certain aspects of disclosure have already been referred to. For completeness, all the principal disclosure requirements of SSAP 21 are referred to below.

### (b) Operating Leases

Disclosure is required of:

- accounting policy for operating leases;
- aggregate rentals receivable in respect of an accounting period in relation to operating leases;
- gross amounts of assets held for use in operating leases and related accumulated depreciation charges.

### (c) Finance Leases and Hire Purchase Contracts

Disclosure is required of:

- net investment, at each balance sheet date, in:
  - finance leases;
  - hire purchase contracts;
- accounting policy for finance leases;
- aggregate rentals receivable in respect of an accounting period in relation to finance leases;
- cost of assets acquired for the purpose of letting under finance leases.

*Illustration 7*

**Accounting policies (extract)**

*(g) Contract hire income*
Contract hire income is credited to the profit and loss account so that income and expenditure are matched over the duration of the related contracts.

*(h) Deferred revenue*
In respect of instalment credit agreements where the interest and charges are added to the amount financed at the commencement of the agreement, unearned interest and charges are calculated on the 'rule of 78' which attributes an appropriate part of the interest and charges to instalments receivable after the date of the balance sheet.

*(i) Maintenance of contract hire vehicles*
Income received in respect of maintenance is deferred and subsequently credited to the profit and loss account so that it matches expenditure to be incurred over the duration of the related contracts.

*(j) Finance lease income and receivables*
Income from finance leasing contracts is credited to the profit and loss account in proportion to the funds invested. Finance lease receivables are stated in the balance sheet at the net investment in the leases after deduction of unearned charges.

## Illustration 8

**Accounting policies (extract)**

*(I) Contract hire fleet and rental fleets*
Contract hire fleet vehicles are capitalised and depreciated. Income and related costs in respect of the contract hire and rental fleet are recognised in equal monthly instalments over the terms of the contracts.

**Note II (extract)**

*Tangible fixed assets*

| Group | Land and Buildings Freehold £'000 | Short Leasehold £'000 | Plant and Equipment £'000 | Contract Hire and Rental Fleet £'000 | Total £'000 |
|---|---|---|---|---|---|
| Cost or valuation: | | | | | |
| Beginning of year | 30,593 | 276 | 34,443 | 11,185 | 76,497 |
| Additions | 1,395 | 14 | 6,272 | 949 | 8,630 |
| Disposals | – | (38) | (1,812) | (1,623) | (3,473) |
| Exchange adjustment | 756 | – | 832 | – | 1,588 |
| End of year | **32,744** | **252** | **39,735** | **10,511** | **83,242** |
| Depreciation: | | | | | |
| Beginning of year | 966 | 106 | 14,853 | 3,135 | 19,060 |
| Charged in year | 918 | 7 | 5,221 | 867 | 7,013 |
| Disposals | – | – | (417) | (768) | (1,185) |
| Exchange adjustment | (2) | – | (12) | – | (14) |
| End of year | **1,882** | **113** | **19,645** | **3,234** | **24,874** |
| Net book value: | | | | | |
| Beginning of year | 29,627 | 170 | 19,590 | 8,050 | 57,437 |
| End of year | **30,862** | **139** | **20,090** | **7,277** | **58,368** |

## Illustration 9

**Accounting policies (extract)**

*Instalment and hire purchase debtors*

The gross margin from sales on extended credit terms is recognised at the time of sale. The finance charges relating to these sales are included in the profit and loss account as and when instalments are received. The income in the Finance Division under instalment agreements is credited to the profit and loss account in proportion to the reducing balances outstanding.

**Note 18 (extract)**

18. Debtors

| | 20X2 Due within one year £m | 20X2 Due after more than one year £m | 20X1 Due within one year £m | 20X1 Due after more than one year £m |
|---|---|---|---|---|
| Group | | | | |
| Trade debtors: | | | | |
| Instalment and hire purchase debtors | **1,119.5** | **290.2** | 1385.5 | 541.1 |
| Provision for unearned finance charges | **(104.5)** | **(30.5)** | (153.7) | (53.4) |

|  | 1,015.0 | 259.7 | 1,231.8 | 487.7 |
| Other trade debtors | 265.8 | – | 320.1 | – |
| Total trade debtors | 1,280.8 | 259.7 | 1,551.9 | 487.7 |
| Book value of finance leases in lessor subsidiaries | 26.5 | 30.8 | 40.2 | 4.3.6 |
| Amounts owed by associated undertakings | 2.0 | – | 2.2 | – |
| Amount owed by joint venture | 43.1 | – | 34.1 | – |
| Taxation recoverable | 2.6 | – | 3.4 | – |
| VAT recoverable | 12.6 | – | 13.8 | – |
| Prepayments and accrued income | 158.1 | 20.5 | 68.7 | 6.2 |
|  | 1,525.7 | 311.0 | 1,714.3 | 537.5 |

# 14.15 Sale and Leaseback

## (a) Introduction

In commercial terms, sale and leaseback is one way in which a company may raise finance. A sale and leaseback transaction takes place when an owner sells an asset and immediately re-acquires the right to use the asset by entering into a lease with the purchaser.

For example, Northern Traders plc sells its freehold head office building, on which there was no fixed charge, to Merchant Finance plc thus raising cash. Merchant Finance plc could then lease the property back to Northern Traders who would continue to use the building for its own purpose. It would be necessary to determine for accounting purposes whether the lease was an operating lease or a finance lease. The concept of accounting for substance (see Chapter 7) is relevant here.

## (b) The Substance of the Transaction

In the case of a sale and leaseback of an operating lease, the substance of the transaction is that the seller-lessee has disposed of substantially all the risks and rewards of ownership of the asset and has realized a profit or loss on disposal.

In the case of a sale and leaseback of a finance lease, the substance of the transaction is the raising of finance secured on an asset which is held by the enterprise and not disposed of. Paragraph 153 of the guidance notes to SSAP 21 states:

> "... If the leaseback is a finance lease, the seller-lessee is in effect reacquiring substantially all the risks and rewards of ownership of the asset. In other words, he never disposes of his ownership interest in the asset, and so it would not be correct to recognize a profit or loss in relation to an asset which (in substance) never was disposed of ".

# 14.16 UITF 28 – Operating Lease Incentives

## (a) Introduction

When negotiating a new operating lease, or the renewal of an existing lease, a lessor will often provide some form of incentive to the lessee to enter into the agreement. This incentive may take the form of a cash payment direct to the lessor, a rent-free period or the assumption of costs that would otherwise be borne by the lessee (e.g. removal or fit-out costs).

## (b) The Need to Examine the Nature of the Incentive

The nature of incentives must be examined to establish if they are for the lessee's or the lessor's benefit. It is important that the accounts reflect the substance of the transaction.

*Examples*

- If a reimbursal relates to fixtures and fittings that are suitable only for the lessee, and do not add any value to the property, that is an incentive.
- However, if the payment is to install a new lift that will be operative beyond the lease term this may not be an incentive but an improvement to the property.

UITF 28 does not deal with incentives to surrender leases unless the lessor is making a payment to enable a lessee to vacate a property owned by another lessor. In this situation, it will be necessary to decide whether the payment equates to an incentive.

## (c) Accounting Treatment

The general principle is that incentives should be regarded as an integral part of the net payment for the use of the property. This is true regardless of the timing of cash flows or the precise nature of the particular incentive.

*Accounting by lessees*
Incentives should reduce the overall rental costs. They should be spread over the shorter of:

- The lease term; and
- The period from inception to the date when a market rental will be payable.

It is generally assumed that, where a lease provides for periodic reviews, any incentive will be spread over the period to the first review date. The straight-line basis should be used to spread the incentive unless some other systematic basis is more appropriate.

*Illustration 10*

Lessor Ltd is negotiating a 20-year lease with Lessee Ltd. The rent is subject to review at the end of years 5, 10 and 15.

An appropriate market rental for years 1 to 5 would normally be £200,000 per annum. However Lessor Ltd is prepared to accept a total rental for that period of £900,000. The "discount" of £100,000 could be presented in various forms:

(a) a reverse premium of £100,000;
(b) a contribution to fitting out costs of £100,000;
(c) a rent-free period for the first six months.

Whatever form the incentive takes, the annual charge for years 1 to 5 should amount to £180,000. This assumes that the rent review mechanism adjusts the rental to the prevailing market rate.

## Illustration 11

**Accounting policies (extract)**

*Operating lease rentals*
Rentals on operating leases are charged to the profit and loss account over the period of the lease. Premiums paid or received on the acquisition of short leasehold properties are transferred to the profit and loss account on a straight line basis over the period to the first rent review or over the length of the lease, as appropriate, commencing on store opening.

**Note 22 Leasehold property incentives**

*Rent free periods and reverse premiums*

| | Group £'000 |
|---|---|
| At 1 February 20X1 | 1,713 |
| Rent free periods and reverse premiums received during the year | 380 |
| Released to profit and loss account | (643) |
| **At 31 January 20X2** | 1,450 |

**(d) Illustrative example – Appendix to UITF 28**
The example assumes a lease for five years. It is assumed that a straight-line allocation basis is the most representative of the benefits. The accounting is illustrated from the perspective of the lessor. The lessee's expense would be equivalent to the lessor's income.

*Example 1 – First year rent-free, then four annual rentals of £500*

| Year | £ Income | | £ Cash | | £ Debtor | |
|---|---|---|---|---|---|---|
| | For year | Cumulative | Movement in year | Cumulative | Movement in year | Cumulative |
| 1 | 400 | 400 | – | – | 400 | 400 |
| 2 | 400 | 800 | 500 | 500 | (100) | 300 |
| 3 | 400 | 1,200 | 500 | 1,000 | (100) | 200 |
| 4 | 400 | 1,600 | 500 | 1,500 | (100) | 100 |
| 5 | 400 | 2,000 | 500 | 2,000 | (100) | – |

# 14.17 International Financial Reporting Standards

The approaches in IAS 17, Leases, and SSAP 21, Accounting for leases and hire purchase contracts, are similar in most respects. IAS 17 states that a lease is classified as a finance lease if it transfers substantially the risks and rewards incidental to ownership. A lease is classified as an operating lease if it does not transfer substantially all the risks and rewards incidental to ownership.

Under UK GAAP, a lessee is required to disclose, in addition to the amount charged in the year, the **yearly** amount of the payments to which the lessee is committed at the year end (i.e. the annual commitment). IAS 17 requires a lessee to disclose the total of future minimum lease payments, under non-cancellable operating leases, analysed by maturity of payments.

Where IAS 17 and SSAP 21 differ is the classification of leases of land and buildings. Under IAS 17, the land and buildings elements must each be considered separately for the purposes of lease classification.

IAS 17 (including the basis for conclusions section) contains considerable detail on this area. Where the land has an indefinite economic life, the land element is normally classified as an operating lease unless title is expected to pass to the lessee by the end of the lease term. The buildings element will be classed as a finance lease or as an operating lease in accordance with the criteria in IAS 17.

---

**Frequently Asked Questions**

1 Do operating leases have to be brought onto the balance sheet under UK GAAP? No—not under SSAP 21. However, there are long-running debates about the need to reflect all leasing commitments on the balance sheet but no changes in accounting treatment are imminent.

2 What is the spreading period for operating lease incentives?

Such incentives should normally be spread over the period up to the first rent review when full market rents come into effect.

3 Is the sum of the digits method of allocating finance charges in the accounts of lessees an acceptable method?
Yes—provided it represents a reasonable approximation to the actuarial method.

# Current Assets

This chapter covers:
* Main stock categories
* Acceptable methods
* Treatment of overheads
* Determination of net realizable value
* Definition of long-term contract
* Completed contract method v percentage of completion method
* Fundamental accounting concepts
* Determination of turnover and profits
* Disclosures for long-term contracts
* Amounts recoverable on contracts
* Loss making contracts
* Interpretation and analysis
* Debtor categories
* Start-up costs (UITF 24)
* Current asset investments
* Cash
* International Financial Reporting Standards

## 15.1  Stocks and Long-term Contracts – Overview

### (a) Principal Objectives of SSAP 9

SSAP 9 (Stocks and long-term contracts) seeks:

(1) to define practices of stock valuation;
(2) to narrow the differences and variations as between different companies;
(3) to ensure adequate disclosure in financial statements.

Aspects (2) and (3) are also covered by the Companies Act 1985.

## (b) Stock Categories

SSAP 9 stock categories may be illustrated diagrammatically as follows:

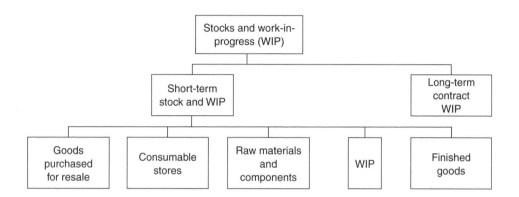

Section 15.2 of this chapter is concerned principally with short-term stocks while section 15.3 deals with long-term contract work-in-progress.

The Companies Act 1985 balance sheet formats refer to:

- raw materials and consumables;
- work-in-progress;
- finished goods and goods for resale;

but do not refer specifically to long-term WIP.

# 15.2    Short-term Stocks and Work-in-Progress

## (a) Basic Valuation Rule

The basis of stock valuation under both SSAP 9 and the Companies Act 1985 is that individual stock items (or groups of similar items) should be valued for accounts purposes at the lower of cost and net realizable value.

## (b) Elements of Cost

The overriding principle is that costs to be included in the stock valuation should relate to expenditure which has been incurred in the normal course of business bringing the product or service to its present location and condition.

These costs will include both purchase costs and conversion costs. Relevant cost elements are illustrated below:

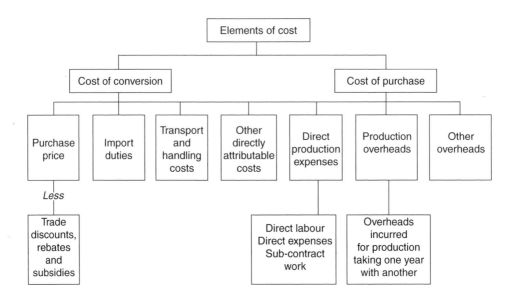

## (c) Net Realizable Value (NRV)

NRV is defined as actual or estimated selling price, net of any trade discount and after deducting any further costs expected to be incurred in completing, marketing, selling or distributing the product. Problems in determining NRV are discussed below in (e).

## (d) Cost Flow Assumptions

In a perfect world, when an item is sold the actual purchase or production costs of that item should be matched against sales in order to determine profit. This might be feasible for a garage selling cars but it is hardly practicable for a manufacturer of Widgets!

In the frequent situations where it is not practicable to relate actual expenditure incurred to specific stock items, an approximate method must be used. However, the standard requires management to ensure that whatever method is chosen provides the fairest practicable approximation to actual costs incurred in bringing the product to its present location and condition.

Possible approaches are referred to below and their acceptability or otherwise under SSAP 9 and the Companies Act 1985 referred to.

### (1) First-in-first-out (FIFO)

Under FIFO, cost of stocks and WIP is calculated on the basis that the quantities in closing stock represent the latest purchases or production. FIFO is a widely used stock valuation base and is acceptable under both SSAP 9 and the Companies Act 1985.

### (2) Last-in-first-out (LIFO)

Under LIFO, cost of stocks and WIP is calculated on the basis that the quantities in closing stock represent the earliest purchases or production. SSAP 9 states that LIFO cost of sales does not bear a reasonable relationship to actual costs obtaining during the period. For this reason, SSAP 9 does not usually regard LIFO as an acceptable valuation basis. However, the Companies Act 1985 permits the use of LIFO, as long as the directors consider it to be appropriate to the circumstances of the company. In practice, this provision has little practical importance in view of the restrictive terms of SSAP 9.

### (3) Average Cost (AVCO)

Under AVCO, cost of stocks and work-in-progress is calculated by applying an average price to the number of units on hand.

The average price may be computed in various ways, each of which may result in differing figures for closing stock. Possible approaches include:

- a continuous calculation (e.g. every six month, by means of computer program);
- a periodic calculation (e.g. six-monthly or yearly);
- a moving period calculation.

### (4) Other methods of stock valuation

These include:

### (i) Unit cost

Unit cost is the cost of purchasing or manufacturing identifiable units of stock. This method is acceptable because it goes directly to actual costs rather than some approximation thereof. This method is appropriate for stock items such as jewellery and motor vehicles.

### (ii) Base stock

Certain types of businesses e.g. sugar refiners, require a certain minimum physical quantity of stock for continuous operations. This stock must be identified in terms of a predetermined number of units of stock which are then valued for balance sheet purposes at a fixed unit value. Such stock may be classified under tangible fixed assets.

Any excess of physical quantities over this number is valued on the basis of some other method such as FIFO or AVCO. Should the number of stock units fall below the predetermined minimum, stocks are valued on the basis of fixed unit value.

The base stock method is permitted by the Companies Act 1985 provided that:

(a) the overall value is not material to assessing the company's state of affairs; and
(b) the quantity, value and composition are not subject to material variation.

SSAP 9 does not regard base stock as a generally acceptable basis, although base stock has been used on rare occasions.

### (iii) Replacement cost
Replacement cost is the cost at which an identical asset could be purchased or manufactured. Replacement cost is not acceptable under the historical cost convention, as it does not derive from actual costs incurred.

### (iv) Standard cost
SSAP 9, App 2 states that cost is calculated on the basis of periodically predetermined costs calculated from management's estimates of expected levels of costs and of operations and operational efficiency and the related expenditure.

Where standard costs are used they should be reviewed frequently to ensure they bear a reasonable relationship to actual costs obtained during the period, in which case the approach is acceptable under both SSAP 9 and the Companies Act 1985.

### (v) Selling price less margin
Some retail stores use selling price less an estimated profit margin as a means of valuing stocks. This is acceptable, provided it can be shown that the method gives a reasonable approximation to actual cost.

## (e) Problem Areas

Two particular problem areas regarding stock valuation are allocation of production overheads and determination of net realizable value.

### (1) Allocation of production overheads
Stock and work-in-progress should be valued for accounts purposes at the lower of cost and net realizable value. Cost should include all expenditure incurred in the normal course of business in bringing the product or service to its present location and condition.

These costs will include production overheads such as factory rent and rates and depreciation of plant and machinery, even though such costs accrue on a time basis.

Production overheads are defined in SSAP 9 as overheads incurred in respect of materials, labour or services, based on the normal level of activity taking one year with another.

In determining the normal level of activity SSAP 9, App 1 suggests that the following factors should be taken into account:

 (i) the volume of production which the facilities are intended to achieve;
 (ii) the budgeted level of activity for the current and following year;
(iii) the level of activity actually achieved in the current and previous years.

The following points may be added:

(a) It can be argued that in the present climate, key factors must be actual activity levels in current and previous years.

(b) The cost of unused capacity should be written off in the current year if the reduction in activity or trade of a company is considered to be permanent.

(c) Abnormal conversion costs (e.g. exceptional spoilage, idle capacity and other losses) should be excluded from stock valuation and should be charged to the profit and loss account of the period in which they are incurred.

Problems may also arise in determining whether particular overheads relate to the production, selling or administration function. Any arbitrary apportionment should reasonably have regard to the materiality of the amounts involved.

*(2) Determination of net realizable value*
*(i) Situations where applicable*
SSAP 9 refers to the following situations where net realizable value is likely to be below cost:

(a) increase in cost or fall in selling price;
(b) physical deterioration of stocks;
(c) marketing decisions to manufacture and sell at a loss;
(d) errors in production or purchasing.

In addition, SSAP 9 refers to the situation of stock held which is unlikely to be sold within the usual turnover period. The likely delay in realizing the stock increases the possibility of situations (a) to (c) occurring. This should be borne in mind when considering net realizable value.

*(ii) Considerations in determining NRV*
(a) *Formula approach:* It may be possible to determine NRV by using a formula and applying it to cost of items. The formula should be based on predetermined criteria which take account of age and movements of stock and estimated scrap values. The provision should then be reviewed in the light of any special circumstances which cannot be built into the formula.

(b) *Effect of finished goods valuation on raw materials:* If it is decided that finished goods stocks should be written down below cost, it is important that related raw material and sub-assembly stocks should be reviewed for possible write-down.

(c) *Post-balance sheet events:* Events between the balance sheet date and the date of approval of the financial statements by the directors should be taken into account in determining whether NRV is below cost.

In certain cases, it may not be necessary to reduce cost of raw materials to a lower figure of realizable value. These would be cases where the finished product could be sold at a profit after allowing for inclusion of raw materials at cost price.

## (f) Disclosure in Financial Statements

Disclosure requirements in the financial statements are specified in SSAP 9 and the Companies Act 1985. The disclosure requirements below relate to all stock categories with the exception of long-term contract work-in-progress.

### (1) Accounting policies

The accounting policies used to determine cost and net realizable value should be disclosed.

### (2) Analysis of stocks total

SSAP 9 requires that stocks and work-in-progress should be sub-classified in balance sheets or in notes to the financial statements in a manner which is appropriate to the business and so as to indicate the amounts held in each of the main categories. This is also effectively required by the Companies Act 1985.

### (3) Further disclosure

In addition to the above disclosures, the Companies Act 1985 requires a note, to the accounts disclosing the difference if material between:

(i)  the balance sheet value of stock;

(ii)  the comparable figure determined either on replacement cost at the balance sheet date or on the most recent actual purchase price or production cost (but purchase price or production cost may only be used if they appear to the directors to constitute the more appropriate standard of comparison).

### (4) Consignment stocks

These are dealt with in Section 6.11.

### Illustration 1 – Accounting policy: stocks

Stocks are stated at the lower of cost and net realizable value. In the case of raw materials, cost means purchase price including transport and handling costs, less trade discounts, calculated on a first-in first-out basis. For work-in-progress and finished goods, cost consists of direct materials, direct labour and attributable production overheads.

Net realizable value comprises the actual or estimated selling price (less trade discounts), less all further costs to completion, and less all costs to be incurred in marketing, selling and distribution.

### Illustration 2

Extract from annual report and accounts of Dixon Motors plc, year ended 31 December 2000.

**Note 18 – Stocks**

|  | | Group |
|---|---|---|
|  | 2000 | 1999 |
|  | £'000 | £'000 |
| Vehicles on consignment | 44,536 | 42,131 |
| Vehicles subject to motability repurchase agreements | 8,101 | 15,444 |
| Cars and motorcycles | 59,249 | 42,535 |
| Parts, accessories and spares | 11,666 | 8,357 |
| Car rental fleet | 18,590 | 16,371 |
| Fuel, consumables and other stocks | 1,115 | 1,073 |
|  | 143,257 | 125,911 |

The difference between the purchase price of stocks and their replacement cost is not material.

*Illustration 3*

Extract from annual report and accounts of Winchester Entertainment plc, year ended 31 March 2000.

**Accounting policies: stocks (extract)**

Stocks are stated at the lower of cost and net realisable value. In determining the cost of film and television project inventory, cost is taken as direct costs incurred for the production of or the acquisition of sales rights for film and television projects which includes finance charges and legal expenses, less any foreseeable losses. Interest on any loans taken out to fund specific production costs is capitalised until the date of completion. Film and television project inventory is appraised at each balance sheet date on a project by project basis and is amortised over a maximum amortisation period of ten years. In respect of the maximum amortisation period of ten years and the resultant carrying value at each balance sheet date due regard is given to the requirement for current assets to be held at the lower of cost and net realisable value. Net realisable value is calculated on a project by project basis having regard to the present value of estimated sales less further costs of completion and unrecoupable sales expenses.

# 15.3   Long-term Contracts

## (a) Definition

The definition of 'long-term contract' in SSAP 9 is as follows (emphasis added):

> "... a contract entered into for the design, manufacture or construction of a single substantial asset or the provision of a service (or of a combination of assets or services which together constitute a single project) where the time taken substantially to complete the contract is such that the contract activity falls into different accounting periods. A contract that is required to be accounted for as long-term by this accounting standard will usually extend for a period exceeding one year. However, a duration exceeding one year is *not an essential feature* of a long-term contract. Some contracts with a shorter duration than one year *should* be accounted for as long-term contracts if they are sufficiently material to the activity of the period that *not to record turnover and attributable profit would lead to a distortion of the period's turnover and results* such that the financial statements would not give a true and fair view, provided that the policy is applied consistently within the reporting entity and from year to year".

## (b) Implications

Contracts of less than twelve months' duration used to be automatically treated as short-term and had to be accounted for by the completed contract method, turnover and profits only being picked up in the year of completion.

SSAP 9 indicates that a true and fair view may require some contracts of less than 12 months duration to be treated as long-term contracts with turnover and profits being spread over the life of the contract. These could include contracts which possess the usual characteristics of long-term contracts, for example: detailed contract specification, some sub-contract work, staged payment terms and a fairly substantial time period.

A final point is that in these cases it is likely that the bulk of contract work will be completed by the time the financial statements are approved by the directors.

## Illustration 4

Fitters Ltd commenced a shop-fitting contract on 1 May 19X8 and completed it on 31 March 19X9. The accounts for the year ended 31 December 19X8 were approved by the directors on 1 October 19X9.

The contract price was £220,000 and costs amounted to £88,000 giving a total contract profit of £132,000.

Amounts invoiced and received were as follows:

|               | Invoiced £ | Received £ |
|---------------|-----------|-----------|
| Y.E. 31.12.X8 | 130,000   | 80,000    |
| Y.E. 31.12.X9 | 90,000    | 140,000   |
|               | 220,000   | 220,000   |

Assuming costs and contract activity accrue evenly on a time basis, how might the contract be reflected in the financial statements for the two years?

In theory, there are two approaches:

(1) the completed contract method; and
(2) the percentage of completion method.

Under method 1, turnover and profits would be reported in 19X9, the year of completion. Under the previous version of SSAP 9, this method would have been mandatory as the duration of the contract was less than twelve months.

Under method 2, turnover and profits would be spread over the life of the contract. Thus profits of £96,000 ($^8/_{11} \times 132,000$) would be reported in 19X8 and £36,000 ($^3/_{11} \times 132,000$) in 19X9.

The effect of the two methods on the financial statements for the two years would be as follows:

**(1) Completed contract method**

|                                  | 19X8 £  | 19X9 £  |
|----------------------------------|---------|---------|
| *Profit and loss account*        |         |         |
| Sales                            | –       | 220,000 |
| Cost of sales                    | –       | 88,000  |
| Gross profit                     | –       | 132,000 |
| *Balance sheet*                  |         |         |
| Creditors                        |         |         |
| Costs ($^8/_{11} \times 88,000$) | 64,000  | –       |
| Payments received on account     | 130,000 | –       |
|                                  | 66,000  | –       |
| Trade debtors                    |         |         |
| (130,000 – 80,000)               | 50,000  | –       |

**(2) Percentage of completion method**

|                           | 19X8 £  | 19X9 £ |
|---------------------------|---------|--------|
| *Profit and loss account* |         |        |
| Sales                     | 160,000 | 60,000 |
| Cost of sales             | 64,000  | 24,000 |
| Gross profit              | 96,000  | 36,000 |

|  | 19X8 | 19X9 |
| --- | --- | --- |
|  | £ | £ |
| *Balance sheet – debtors* |  |  |
| Amounts recoverable on contracts |  |  |
| (see below) (160,000 – 130,000) | 30,000 | – |
| Trade debtors (130,000 – 80,000) | 50,000 | – |
|  | 80,000 | – |

*Notes:*

(i) Amounts recoverable on contracts is treated in substance as a debt.

(ii) Under SSAP 9, the percentage of completion method may be claimed to give a truer and fairer view of profit and contract activity than the completed contract method and would be recommended in this case. The outcome of the contract would be apparent at the time the financial statements were approved by the directors.

## *Illustration 5*

**Accounting policies (extract)**

*Long term contracts*

The amount of profit attributable to the stage of completion of a long term contract is recognized when the outcome of the contract can be foreseen with reasonable certainty. Turnover for such contracts represents the value of work done in the year. Full provision is made for any losses which are foreseen.

*Short term contracts*

Contracts with a shorter duration than one year are accounted for as long term contracts if they are sufficiently material to the activity of the year that not to record turnover and attributable profit would lead to a distortion of the year's turnover and results such that the accounts would not give a true and fair view. Profit on other contracts is recognized on completion of the contract.

## *(c) Fundamental Accounting Concepts*

The four concepts specified in SSAP 2 (now superseded by FRS 18, see Chapter 3) are particularly relevant to the accounting treatment of long-term contracts.

Also of particular interest is the possible conflict between the accruals concept and the prudence concept.

(1) *Going concern concept*
In view of the time period for completion of many long-term contracts, adequacy of financial resources is particularly important.

(2) *Accruals concept*
Such a long-term contract may extend over several accounting periods: the accruals concept would require profits to be allocated over these periods.

The method described below (see (e)), which achieves this, is sometimes referred to as the percentage of completion method. The alternative view, that profit should not be included in profit and loss account until the contract is complete, is not considered appropriate for long-term contracts, as it could distort comparison of profits as between successive accounting periods. This latter approach is sometimes referred to as the completed contract method.

### (3) *Prudence concept*

In view of the considerable uncertainties surrounding the outcome of the contract, no profits should be recognized until such outcome can be assessed with reasonable certainty.

Clearly, the trade-off between the accruals concept and the prudence concept relies to a large extent on subjective judgement. FRS 18 places emphasis on "reliability" and is likely to restrict the importance of "prudence".

### (4) *Consistency concept*

It is essential that a company is consistent as between different contracts, and between successive accounting periods.

## (d) *Determining Turnover*

SSAP 9 states that for long-term contracts, turnover should be ascertained in a manner appropriate to the stage of completion of the contract, the business and the industry in which it operates.

SSAP 9, App 1, para 23 refers to two principal methods of ascertaining turnover:

(1) By reference to valuation of the work carried out to date (presumably balance sheet date). Under this method, sometimes referred to as the cost-based approach, all costs may be included in the profit and loss account as cost of sales with no costs left to be included in the balance sheet stock figure.
(2) By reference to valuation at specific points in the contract. Paragraph 23 refers to "... specific points during a contract at which individual elements of work done with separately ascertainable sales values and costs can be identified and appropriately recorded as turnover (e.g. because delivery or customer acceptance has taken place)".

The paragraph concludes that the Standard does not provide a definition of turnover in view of the different methods of ascertaining it. However, it does require disclosure of the means by which turnover is ascertained (see illustration in (h) below).

The standard also indicates that the question of how much turnover to recognize is independent of whether and how much profit should be taken. For example, in the case of a loss-making contract, turnover should be based on activity during the year. Loss provisions will be reflected in cost of sales.

## (e) *Calculating Profits – Two Possible Methods*

Where the outcome of the contract can be assessed with reasonable certainty before completion, the standard requires the prudently calculated attributable profit to be included in the profit and loss account.

SSAP 9 does not say how this should be calculated but there are two broad approaches:

(1) comparison of value of work to a particular date (often the balance sheet date) with costs incurred to that date;
(2) taking a proportion of estimated total profit over the life of the contract. This proportion should be calculated using an indicator of completion e.g. costs to date/estimated total cost or some appropriate physical measure, such as labour hours.

The terms of the contract may give a guide as to which method is more appropriate.

The calculation for method (2) may be carried out as follows:

*(i) Calculate estimated profit over life of contract:*

| | | |
|---|---:|---:|
| Total sales value of contract | | X |
| Total costs (including overheads) to date | X | |
| Total estimated further costs required to complete contract | X | |
| Estimated further costs of guarantee and rectification work | X | X |
| ∴ Total estimated profit on contract | | X |

*Note*: This procedure should be followed even if there is no intention of taking any profit to the credit of profit and loss account, since it may indicate the possibility of a contract turning in a loss. In this event, further investigation of figures is required.

*(ii) Calculate attributable profit (i.e. cumulative profit earned to date).*
Attributable profit (AP) = degree of completion % × total estimated profit.
Degree of completion (or indicator of performance) may be calculated in several ways including:

- costs incurred as proportion of total costs;
- surveys which measure work performed;
- completion of physical portion of contract work.

*(iii) Profit reported this year.*
This is calculated as attributable profit less profit taken up in previous years.

*Note:* The profit recognized this year will not necessarily represent the proportion of the total profit on the contract which corresponds with the amount of work carried out in the period. It is also likely to reflect the effect of changes in circumstances during the year which affect the total profit estimated to accrue on completion.

## (f) Further Factors to be Considered

The following points are referred to in SSAP 9:

(1) The profit taken up in a particular period should reflect the proportion of work carried out at the accounting date.

(2) Attributable profit is that part of total profit estimated to arise over the life of the contract which fairly reflects the proportion of work completed to date.

(3) There can be no attributable profit until the outcome of the contract can be assessed with reasonable certainty. SSAP 9 suggests that a company should define the earliest point for each particular contract before any attributable profit is taken up.

In the early stages of an apparently profitable contract it may not be possible to assess the outcome with reasonable certainty and the client thus decides to take no profit. However, progress after the end of the accounting period could be taken into account. An excessively prudent policy regarding taking of profit may not be acceptable as it may distort the truth and fairness of the accounts.

(4) If a company considers that the contract outcome can be assessed with reasonable certainty before the contract is completed, attributable profit should be taken up, but judgement should be exercised with prudence.

(5) In some contracts it will be necessary to take account of "known equalities of profitability in the various stages of a contract". For example, a contract may have four phases – A, B and D which are "own work" only and C which is a significantly less profitable phase consisting mainly of sub-contract work. Profit allocation between different periods should reflect these profitability variations.

(6) SSAP 9 recognizes that there are certain businesses which carry out contracts where the outcome cannot reasonably be assessed before completion. In these situations, profit should not be taken up prior to completion.

(7) Once it is expected that a contract will turn in a loss, full provision for the loss should be reflected in the current period financial statements.

*Illustration 6*

Contractors plc is engaged in a number of long-term contracts. The following summarised details refer to three particular long-term contracts which were in progress at 31 December 19X6.

|  | Contract A £'000 | Contract B £'000 | Contract C £'000 |
|---|---|---|---|
| Total contract price | 700 | 400 | 800 |
| Cost incurred to 31.12.X6 | 400 | 30 | 500 |
| Estimated total costs to complete (allowing for contingencies) | 790 | 300 | 570 |
| Progress payments invoiced | 390 | 40 | 600 |
| Amounts received relating to above progress payments invoiced | 350 | 20 | 450 |

To what extent should profits and losses be recognized up to 31 December 19X6? Dealing with each contract in turn:

*Contract A*

This contract indicates a foreseeable loss of £90,000. SSAP 9 requires the full amount of the loss to be reflected in the 19X6 financial statements. Clearly it is important to ensure that estimated total costs of £790,000 have been determined on a reliable basis.

Loss-making contracts are further considered in (I) below.

*Contract B*

This contract is expected to make a total profit of £100,000 (i.e. £400,000 less £300,000). However, since the contract is at a relatively early stage, it can be argued that the outcome of the contract cannot be assessed with reasonable certainty. On prudence grounds, therefore, the contract should be included in the balance sheet at cost of £30,000 less progress payments invoiced of £40,000. The £10,000 excess may be regarded as a creditor.

*Contract C*

This contract is expected to produce a total profit of £230,000. The contract is well advanced and it can be argued that its profitable outcome can be assessed with reasonable certainty. It is important to establish that estimated total costs of £570,000 have been arrived at on a reliable basis and allow for contingencies.

With the limited information available, the best way of determining attributable profit may be to use cost to date divided by expected total costs as an indicator of progress. On this basis, attributable profit would be calculated as:

$$\frac{£500,000}{£570,000} \times £230,000 = £201,755$$

say, £201,000

Clearly, given more information, other indications of progress might be available. A useful approach might be to use more than one method, each method providing a cross-check on the other.

The profit reported in current year profit and loss account would be attributable profit (£201,000 using the method above) less any profit recognized in previous years.

## Illustration 7

Contract 187 has a fixed contract price of £200,000. Total contract costs are estimated at £160,000 and thus total profits at £40,000.

At the end of 19X7, the contract is estimated to be 60% complete. The company's policy is to calculate attributable profit by applying degree of completion to estimated total profit. The effect on the 19X7 profit and loss account would be:

|  | £ |
|---|---|
| Turnover (60% × 200,000) | 120,000 |
| Cost of sales (60% × 160,000) | 96,000 |
| Gross profit (60% × 40,000) | 24,000 |

Suppose that costs incurred to complete in 19X8 amounted to £74,000 (as opposed to 40% × 160,000 = 64,000 expected). The effect on the 19X8 profit and loss account would be:

|  | £ |
|---|---|
| Turnover (40% × 200,000) | 80,000 |
| Cost of sales (actual costs) | 74,000 |
| Gross profit (balancing figure) | 6,000 |

*Note*: the profit recognized in 19X8 reflects the effect of changes in circumstances during 19X8 which affects the total profit on completion (see (m) on interpretation).

## (g) Variations and Claims

The appendix to SSAP 9 makes the following suggestions:

| Aspect | Suggested approach |
|---|---|
| Variations (additional work). | Make conservative estimate of effect on sales value. |
| Foreseen claims or penalties against guarantee contractor. | Ensure allowed for in further costs of and rectification. |
| Settlement of claims by contractor arising from circumstances not envisaged in the contract or arising as an indirect consequence of approved variations. | Only provide for in sales value if negotiations in advanced stage *and* written evidence of acceptability and amount. |

## (h) Disclosure Requirements for Long-term Contracts

The main disclosure requirements of SSAP 9 are as follows. The examples in (J) below illustrate some of the requirements.

(1) A suitable description for long-term contracts would be "at net cost less foreseeable losses and payments on account".

Net cost is effectively total costs incurred less amounts transferred to the profit and loss account in respect of work carried out to date.

(2) The policy for ascertaining turnover and attributable profit should be stated.

### Illustration of disclosure

STOCKS AND WORK-IN-PROGRESS

Stocks and work-in-progress are stated at the lower of cost and net realisable value. Cost includes direct materials and labour together with a proportion of production overheads.

Long-term contract work-in-progress is stated at costs incurred, net of amounts transferred to cost of sales in respect of work recorded as turnover. Profit on long-term contracts is taken as work is carried out provided that the final outcome can be assessed with reasonable certainty. Full provision is made for all known or expected losses as soon as they are foreseen.

TURNOVER

Turnover which is stated net of value added tax represents the value of services provided to third parties except in respect of long-term contract work-in-progress where turnover represents the sales value of work done in the year including amounts not invoiced.

(3) Specific disclosures for long-term contracts.

(i) If cumulative turnover (i.e. total turnover recorded since commencement of contract) exceeds total payments on account, the excess represents an "amount recoverable on contracts" and should be separately disclosed within debtors (see (i) below).

(ii) If payments on account exceed cumulative turnover (considering a particular contract) the excess is classified as a deduction from any balance on that contract in stocks. Any residual balance in excess of cost is classified with creditors.

(iii) Long-term contract balances should be separately disclosed within the balance sheet heading "stock". The following should be disclosed separately:
(1) net cost less foreseeable losses;
(2) applicable payments on account.

(iv) The amount by which the provision or accrual for foreseeable losses exceeds the costs incurred (after transfers to cost of sales) should be included within either provisions for liabilities and charges or creditors as appropriate.

## (i) Amounts Recoverable on Contracts

Appendix 3 of SSAP 9 points out that an "amount recoverable on contracts" may not have the contractual status of a debtor in strict legal form. The accruals concept should not preclude debtors and creditors from being recorded where this is necessary to reflect the substance of a transaction (see Chapter 6).

Counsel's opinion obtained by ASC (the former Accounting Standards Committee) confirmed that "amounts recoverable on contracts" should be classified under debtors and cannot be classified under stocks.

## (j) Example of Calculations and Disclosures

The following date relates to Hayseed plc, a construction company. Details relating to contract 467 are as follows. All figures are £'000.

|  | Year | | | |
|  | 1 | 2 | 3 | 4 |
| --- | --- | --- | --- | --- |
| Degree of completion at end of year | 25% | 60% | 85% | 100% |
| Contract price (as updated) | 800 | 850 | 900 | 980 |
| Estimated cost (as updated) | 500 | 560 | 650 | 730 |
| Estimated total profits | 300 | 290 | 250 | 250 |
| Costs to date (actual) | 135 | 350 | 570 | 730 |
| Payments on account (invoiced) | 160 | 490 | 790 | 980 |
| Payments on account (received) | 130 | 480 | 720 | 980 |

Attributable profit is calculated by applying a suitable measure or indicator of completion to the estimated total profit over the life of the contract. No profit is recognized by the company until a contract is at least 60% complete.

*Required*: Show how the above contract might be presented in the profit and loss account, balance sheet and notes of Hayseed for each of years 1 to 4 in accordance with SSAP 9 revised.

## Suggested solution

(1) *Workings*

(i)  Reported Profit

| Year | | £'000 |
|---|---|---|
| 1 | no profit (assume contract not sufficiently advanced to assess outcome of contract with reasonable certainty) | |
| 2 | (60% × 290,000) | 174 |
| 3 | (85% × 250,000 = 213,000) − 174,000 | 39 |
| 4 | (250,000 − 213,000) | 37 |
| | Total | 250 |

(Other methods of calculating attributable profit could include consideration of value of work done up to the balance sheet date.)

(ii) Cost of sales calculations

| Year | | £'000 |
|---|---|---|
| 1 | (25% × 500,000) | 125 |
| 2 | (60% × 560,000 = 336,000) − 125.000 | 211 |
| 3 | (85% × 650,000 = 552,000) − 336,000 | 216 |
| 4 | (730,000 − 552,000) | 178 |
| | Total | 730 |

(iii) Stocks at year end (costs not traded)

| Year | | £'000 |
|---|---|---|
| 1 | Cost incurred | 135 |
| | Transfer cost of sales | 125 |
| | Closing stock | 10 |
| 2 | Costs incurred | 215 |
| | | 225 |
| | Transfer cost of sales | 211 |
| | Closing stock | 14 |
| 3 | Costs incurred | 220 |
| | | 234 |
| | Transfer cost of sales | 216 |
| | Closing stock | 18 |
| 4 | Costs incurred | 160 |
| | | 178 |
| | Transfer cost of sales | 178 |
| | Closing stock | – |

*Note*: Alternative methods could include direct calculations of stock, transferring remaining costs to cost of sales.

(iv)  Turnover calculation

| Year | | £'000 | £'000 |
|---|---|---|---|
| 1 | No profit recognized, so base on cost of sales | | 125 |
| 2 | Cumulative turnover 60% × 850,000 less | 510 | |
| | recognized in year 1 | 125 | 385 |
| 3 | Cumulative turnover 85% × 900,000 less | 765 | |
| | recognized in years 1 and 2 | 510 | 255 |
| 4 | Cumulative turnover (=contract price) less | 980 | |
| | recognized in years 1, 2 and 3 | 765 | 215 |
| | Total | | 980 |

(v)  Balance sheet figures

(a)  Debtors – payments on account

| Year | | £'000 |
|---|---|---|
| 1 | (160,000 – 130,000) | 30 |
| 2 | (490,000 – 480,000) | 10 |
| 3 | (790,000 – 720,000) | 70 |

(b)  Other balances

| | Year 1 £'000 | Year 2 £'000 | Year 3 £'000 |
|---|---|---|---|
| Stock (cost not traded) | 10 | 14 | 18 |
| Debtors – amounts recoverable (510–490) | | 20 | |
| Creditors – applicable payments on account | | | |
| (160–125) | (35) | | |
| | | – | |
| (790–765) | | | (25) |
| Net total | (25) | 34 | (7) |

(vi)  The above amounts would be presented each year as follows:

Year
1    £25,000 (excess of payments on account over stock) in creditors
2    £14,000 in stock; £20,000 in debtors under sub-heading "amount recoverable on contracts"
3    £7,000 in creditors (as under 1 above)

(2)  *Extracts from financial statements*

(i)  Profit and loss account extracts

| | Year 1 £'000 | 2 £'000 | 3 £'000 | 4 £'000 | Total £'000 |
|---|---|---|---|---|---|
| Turnover | 125 | 385 | 255 | 215 | 980 |
| Costs of sales | 125 | 211 | 216 | 178 | 730 |
| Gross profit | – | 174 | 39 | 37 | 250 |

*Comment:* The actual contract profit of £250,000 is recognized as follows:

| Year | £'000 | % | Degree of completion |
|------|------|------|------|
| 1 | – | – | 25 |
| 2 | 174 | 69.6 | 35 |
| 3 | 39 | 15.6 | 25 |
| 4 | 37 | 14.8 | 15 |
| | 250 | 100.0 | 100 |

Hayseed does not recognize profit in the early stages of a contract on the grounds that the contract outcome cannot be assessed with reasonable certainty. This results in the recognition of a disproportionate amount of profit in year 2. In addition in year 3 the company has revised its estimate of expected total profit downwards from £290,000 to £250,000. This has resulted in the recognition of a relatively low proportion of profit in year 3 to the benefit of year 2.

(ii) Balance sheet extracts

| | Year 1 £'000 | Year 2 £'000 | Year 3 £'000 |
|------|------|------|------|
| Debtors – payments on account | 30 | 10 | 70 |
| – amounts recoverable on contracts | – | 20 | – |
| Stocks | – | 14 | – |
| Creditors | 25 | – | 7 |

## (k) Loss-making Contracts

Where a contract is expected to result in a loss, the total expected loss (not just the part which is deemed to have occurred to date) should be recognized in the financial statements as soon as it is foreseen.
The disclosure implications are as follows:

(1) The first step is to deduct the accrual or provision for foreseeable loss from the work-in-progress figure for that particular contract, thus reducing it to net realizable value.
(2) Any loss in excess of the work-in-progress should be classified either:
    (i)  as an accrual within creditors; or
    (ii) under provisions for liabilities and charges, depending on circumstances.

## (l) Contracts Expected to Result in Losses

Where it is expected that the contract as a whole will result in a loss, the whole amount of the loss should be accounted for as soon as it is recognized.
    Where unprofitable contracts are of such a magnitude that they can be expected to absorb a considerable part of the company's capacity for a considerable period, then the loss calculation should also reflect related overhead expenses expected to be incurred during the period to completion.

## Illustration 8

A company commenced work at the beginning of the year on a long-term contract. At the end of year 1 the following information is available:

|  | £ |
|---|---|
| Total contract price | 650,000 |
| Estimated costs to completion | 850,000 |
| Degree of completion | 40% |
| Costs to date | 350,000 |
| Progress payments invoiced | 290,000 |

*Required:* Extracts from financial statements for year 1.

**(1) Profit and loss account for year 1**

|  | £ |
|---|---|
| Turnover (40% × 650,000) | 260,000 |
| Cost of sales (350,000 + (850,000 − 350,000) − 60% × 650,000) | 460,000 |
| Loss | 200,000 |

*Note:* The foreseeable loss over the duration of the contract is £200,000 (£850,000 − £650,000). The full amount of this loss should be reflected in the profit and loss account in accordance with the accruals concept.

## Illustration 9

**Accounting policies**

*Turnover and recognition of profit and losses*
Turnover represents the value of work invoiced to customers, excluding value added tax plus the value of the work done but not invoiced on long-term contracts. Profits on contracts are only recognized after the final account has been agreed with the client or in the case of long-term contracts an interim account has been agreed and the outcome of the contract can be assessed with reasonable certainty. Provision is made in full for anticipated future losses on uncompleted contracts.

*Stocks and work-in-progress*
Stocks and work-in-progress are stated at the lower of cost, including an appropriate proportion of attributable overheads, and net realizable value less amounts received and receivable. Long-term contracts are included at net cost after deducting foreseeable losses and payments on account.

## Illustration 10

**Accounting policies**

*Income recognition*
Profit is recognized on houses when contracts are exchanged and building is substantially complete. Profit is recognized on commercial property developments or units of development when they are substantially complete and subject to binding and unconditional contracts of sale and where legal completion has occurred shortly thereafter. Where the sale price is conditional upon letting, profit is restricted by reference to the space unlet.

Profit in respect of construction is recognized when the contract is complete.

In the case of contracts that are regarded as long term, profit is recognized during execution provided a binding contract for sale exists and the outcome can be foreseen with reasonable certainty.

## Illustration 11

Extract from annual report and accounts of Bovis Homes Group plc, year ended 31 December 2000.

**Accounting policies (extract)**

*Stock and work in progress*
Development properties are recorded at cost. Ground rents are valued at various multiples of their gross annual income.

Land held for development, including land in the course of development until legal completion of sale, is recorded at cost and contains no addition for overheads.

Raw materials and consumables are recorded at cost as invoiced by suppliers.

Housing stocks, and properties taken in part exchange are valued at the lower of cost and net realisable value.

Work in progress is valued at prime cost of labour and materials with an addition for overheads other than those for general administration. Progress payments received and receivable from contracts are deducted from work in progress.

Provision is made, where appropriate, to reduce the value of stocks and work in progress to estimated realisable value.

**Note 13 – Stocks and work in progress**

| Group | 2000<br>£'000 | 1999<br>£'000 |
|---|---|---|
| Raw materials and consumables | 2,172 | 1,908 |
| Work in progress – housing | 119,048 | 88,066 |
| Part exchange properties | 27,288 | 13,485 |
| Land held for development | 309,567 | 256,231 |
| Development properties and ground rents | 510 | 585 |
| | 458,585 | 360,275 |

# (m) Interpretation and Analysis

Where a company is engaged in a significant amount of long-term contract activity, the relationship between aggregate figures for gross profit and turnover may be distorted by factors such as:

- contracts in early stages of completion where company policy is not to take any profit at that point;
- contracts whose outcome cannot be assessed with reasonable certainty before the conclusion of the contract;
- contracts where profitability varies significantly between different stages;
- loss-making contracts.

## Illustration 12

**Accounting policies (extracts)**

*4 Turnover*

Turnover comprises the sum of:

(a) deliveries made and services rendered during the year at fixed prices or at estimated prices where fixed prices are not agreed;

(b) price adjustments arising from revision of estimated prices or settlement of prices which in previous years were estimated;

(c) the estimated selling value of work done on major long-term development and similar contracts.

In the case of long duration contracts calling for a series of items to be delivered throughout the period of the contract, turnover is taken on each delivery.

Intra-group transactions are not included except as shown in the activity analysis and geographical analysis of turnover.

*5 Profit*

Profit is taken when turnover is recognised and, in the case of long duration contracts calling for a series of items to be delivered throughout the period of the contract, profit is taken on each delivery, based on the estimated overall profitability. Changes in estimates of overall profitability are adjusted against current year profits to the extent that they relate to current and prior year deliveries. Losses are provided for in full as soon as they become likely. Thus, profits for the year are not necessarily related to turnover, particularly if adjustments are made on very large contracts which account for a substantial part of turnover.

*9 Stocks*

(a) Work-in-progress, manufactured parts, raw materials and bought out stocks are valued at the lower of cost and estimated realisable value.

(b) Costs of manufactured parts and work-in-progress against customers' contracts comprise prime cost plus full overheads (including administration, distribution and selling expenses). The costs of other manufactured parts and work-in-progress comprise prime cost plus production overheads.

(c) Progress payments received from customers are deducted from stock and work-in-progress to the extent of the value of the work carried out and any excess is shown as customers' advances.

(d) Certain initial costs, including design, development, specific tooling and learning, on risk-sharing contracts, where final sales quantities are still to be determined, are carried forward and amortised over prudent estimates of sales. To the extent that such costs are not covered by firm orders they are shown as deferred costs in work-in-progress.

# 15.4 Debtors

## (a) Introduction

Companies Act 1985, Sch 4, Formats for debtors includes the following headings:

1. Trade debtors
2. Amounts owed by group companies
3. Amounts owed by related companies
4. Other debtors
5. Called up share capital not paid
6. Prepayments and accrued income

Separate disclosure is required of any parts of the above which are not considered to be recoverable within twelve months of the balance sheet date. (See UITF 4 below.)

## (b) Limitations of Companies Act 1985 Disclosures

For debtors, the Companies Act 1985 requires separate disclosure of amounts falling due after more than one year. Unlike creditors, however, this split does not show up on the face of the balance sheet. In the balance sheet formats the sub-total of net current assets may thus include an element of non-current debtors.

## (c) UITF 4 – Presentation of Long-term Debtors

In most cases the UITF Abstract accepts that it will be satisfactory to disclose the size of debtors due after more than one year by way of note.

The Abstract is particularly concerned with instances where the amount of the non-current debtor(s) is so material in relation to net current assets that its amount should be separately disclosed on the face of the balance sheet.

Examples of significant long-term debtors could include:

(1) part of the trade debtors of lessors (i.e. finance receivable);
(2) deferred consideration receivable relating to fixed assets investment sales.

## (d) Acceptable Disclosure Methods

*(1)* Analysis of debtors on the face of the balance sheet:

BALANCE SHEET EXTRACT

| Current assets | £ |
|---|---|
| Stocks | 186,000 |
| Debtors | |
| – due within one year | 112,530 |
| – due in more than one year | 42,500 |
| Bank balances and cash | 7,600 |
| | 348,630 |

(2) Disclosure related to the net current assets/liabilities figure:

BALANCE SHEET EXTRACT

| Current assets | £ |
|---|---|
| Stock | 186,000 |
| Debtors | 155,030 |
| Bank balances and cash | 7,600 |
| | 348,630 |
| Creditors: amounts falling due within one year | 195,780 |
| Net current assets (including amounts falling due after more than one year of £42,500 (1992–£X)) | 152,850 |

## (e) Start-up Costs (UITF 24)

*(1) Introduction*

Prior to UITF 24, FRS 15 addressed two issues:

(i) *Start-up costs which could be included in the costs of a tangible fixed asset*
Paragraph 14 of FRS 15 states:

> "...The costs associated with a start-up or commissioning period should be included in the cost of the tangible fixed asset only where the asset is available for use but incapable of operating at normal levels without such a start-up or commissioning period...".

## (ii) *Other start-up costs*

FAS 15, para 16, refers to start-up costs other than those which are costs of an essential commissioning period, and comments:

> "... there is no justification for regarding costs relating to other start-up periods, where the asset is available for use but not yet operating at normal levels, for example because of a lack of demand, as part of the cost of the asset. An example is the start-up period of a new hotel or bookshop, which could operate at normal levels almost immediately, but for which experience teaches that demand will build up slowly and fully utilisation or sales levels will be achieved only over a period of several months..."

FRS 15 gives no guidance on accounting for start-up costs that cannot be included in the cost of a tangible fixed asset. For some years a number of companies included start-up costs in prepayments, writing them off over a period.

UITF 24 takes the view that it is inappropriate to follow this accounting treatment as there is not a sufficiently certain relationship between the startup expenditure and any future economic benefits. Even before the issue of UITF 24, there was evidence of a number of companies changing their accounting policy for start-up costs to one of immediate write-off.

## (2) *Requirements of UITF 24*

Start-up costs should be accounted for on a basis consistent with the accounting treatment of similar costs incurred as part of the company's ongoing activities.

Start-up costs that do not meet the criteria for recognition as assets (under standards such as FRS 15, FRS 10 or SSAP 13) should be recognized as an expense when they are incurred. Such costs should not be carried forward as an asset.

## (3) *Disclosure implications*

- Start-up costs which fall within the definition of exceptional items should be disclosed as required by FRS 3.
- Companies (in practice, listed companies) are encouraged to give disclosures recommended by the ASB Statement on the Operating and Financial Review (paras 16–18).

## (4) *Examples of start-up costs*

UITF gives some guidance on interpretation of terminology and indicates that "start-up costs" should be "construed broadly" and include costs arising from one-time activities which relate to:

- opening a new facility;
- introducing a new product or service;
- conducting business in a new territory;
- conducting business with a new class of customer;
- starting some new operation.

## 15.5    Current Asset Investments

There is currently no UK standard which deals with accounting for current asset investments. However, the Companies Act 1985 requires that all current assets are stated in the balance sheet at the lower of cost and net realizable value.

On rare occasions, companies invoke the true and fair override to justify use of the marking to market method of valuation, where the investment is stated in the balance sheet at market value, and changes in market value are taken to the profit and loss account.

## 15.6    Cash

The Companies Act 1985, Schedule 8 Formats, include cash at bank and in hand as a separate heading. However, the Act does not define this category.

FRS 1, Cash flow statements, does include a definition of cash: Cash is essentially cash in hand and deposits repayable on demand with any qualifying financial institution, less overdrafts from any qualifying financial institution repayable on demand. Cash includes any cash in hand and deposits denominated in foreign currencies.

Clearly, this may not be the same number as that disclosed in the balance sheet, as the latter may include deposit accounts which FRS 1 regards as liquid investments. (FRS 1 requires that the notes to the cash flow statement enable users to reconcile the relevant numbers.)

## 15.7    International Financial Reporting Standards

### IAS 2, Inventories

This standard applies to all inventories with two main exceptions:

- Work in progress arising under construction contracts (dealt with in IAS 11);
- Biological assets relating to agricultural activity (live animals and plants) and agricultural produce at the point of harvest (dealt with in IAS 41).

The principles of IAS 2 are identical to those in SSAP 9—inventories within the scope of IAS 2 (except for certain inventories held by broker-traders) are measured in the balance sheet at the lower of cost and net realizable value.

The standard gives detailed guidance as to how cost should be determined. IAS 2 prohibits the use of the LIFO (Last-in-first-out) method of stock valuation.

IAS 2's disclosure requirements are more extensive than those of SSAP 9, for example, the standard requires disclosure of the amount of any write-down of inventories recognized as an expense in the period (i.e. when inventories held at the balance sheet date are written down below cost).

### IAS 11, Construction contracts

IAS 11 sets out the accounting treatment of revenue and costs associated with construction contracts. Contracts for the rendering of services are dealt with in IAS 18, Revenue.

A construction contract is a contract specifically negotiated for the construction of an asset or a combination of assets that are closely interrelated or interdependent in terms of their design, technology and function or their ultimate purpose or use. IAS 11 does not use the phrase "long-term"—but refers to "stage of completion of the contract activity at the balance sheet date".

Adoption of IAS 11 is unlikely to result in significant differences of recognition or measurement as compared with SSAP 9.

However, UK companies will need to note the provisions in IAS 11 relating to combining and segmenting construction contracts as these requirements are more extensive than those of SSAP 9.

UK companies following IAS 11 will have to disclose more by way of note as compared with existing practice under SSAP 9.

Balance sheet presentation as between stock, debtors and creditors is likely to differ for some companies, resulting in a change of accounting policy and restatement of previous year figures.

---

**Frequently Asked Questions**

1 Can work in progress relating to services provided be stated in the balance sheet at selling price?
No—work in progress relating to service contracts should be stated at the lower of cost and net realizable value. Once the point of revenue recognition has been reached, the asset to be recognized is a debtor ("amount recoverable on contracts"), valued at fair value (=selling price). This is illustrated in Chapter 8, Section 8.4(c) regarding application of Abstract 40.

2 Can start-up costs be capitalized?
Generally "no"—UITF Abstract 24 is extremely restrictive and sets out very demanding criteria before any such asset can be recognized in the balance sheet.

3 Is it acceptable to include current asset investments in the balance sheet at market value (assuming this is greater than cost)?
No—except in very restricted circumstances where "mark to market" approach adopted, invoking use of the "true and fair override". In future, FRS 26 when adopted will result in fair values for balance sheet carrying amounts of such investments.

# Loans, Provisions, Contingencies and Commitments

**This chapter covers:**
* Creditors and loans
* Provisions and contingencies
* Commitments

## 16.1 Introduction

This chapter includes an overview of Companies Act 1985 disclosure requirements, as well as classification and analysis of liabilities set out in FRS 4. Specific issues relating to FRS 4 are included in Chapter 17, together with international accounting developments regarding financial instruments.

## 16.2 Creditors and Loans

### (a) Companies Act 1985 Requirements

The balance sheet formats and disclosure requirements were referred to in Chapter 4 and may be summarized as follows:

(1) For each item shown under creditors, disclose:
    (i) aggregate amounts of debts repayable (other than by instalments) more than five years after B/S date;
    (ii) aggregate amount of debts repayable by instalments any of which fall due more than five years after the B/S date;
    (iii) for each item in (ii), the aggregate amount of instalments falling due after the five years.
(2) For each debt required to be disclosed within (1)(ii) above, disclose:
    (i) terms of payment or repayment and rate of interest payable; or
    (ii) if above statement would be of excessive length, a general indication of the terms of payment or repayment and rates of interest payable.

(3) For each item under creditors, supply:
   (i) aggregate amount of any debts in respect of which security has been given;
   (ii) indication of nature of securities given.
(4) Issues of debentures during the year – disclose:
   (i) reason for making issue;
   (ii) classes of debentures issued;
   (iii) for each class, amount issued and consideration received by company.
(5) Particulars of redeemed debentures which company has power to reissue.
(6) Where any of company's debentures are held by a nominee of or trustee for the company: state nominal amount of debentures and amount at which stated in the accounting records.
(7) Convertible debenture loans: amount of any convertible loans is required to be shown separately.

### (b) Classification and Analysis of Liabilities – FRS 4, Capital Instruments

FRS 4 requires that all capital instruments (except for shares) which contain an obligation to transfer economic benefits are classified as liabilities. The term "obligation" also includes a contingent obligation.

FRS 4 has been significantly amended for accounts periods which commence on or after 1 January 2005 (see 17.2 below).

FRS 4 has extended the disclosure requirements for analysis of maturity of debt. The notes should include an analysis between amounts falling due:

(1) in one year or less or on demand;
(2) between one and two years;
(3) between two and five years; and
(4) in five years or more.

Note that debt maturity should be determined by reference to the earliest date on which the lender can require repayment.

## 16.3   Provisions

### (a) Introduction

FRS 12 deals with measurement, accounting and disclosure requirements regarding provisions, contingent assets and contingent liabilities.

The FRS does not deal with provisions which are adjustments to the carrying amount of assets, such as those for depreciation, bad debts and stock.

Some existing standards deal in detail with particular types of provisions, for example:

- FRS 19 (deferred tax)
- SSAP 9 (long-term contracts)

FRS 12 does not apply to provisions that are already covered in greater detail by another FRS or SSAP.

## (b) Definitions – Provision

A provision is defined by FRS 12 as a liability of uncertain amount or timing. Liabilities are defined as obligations of an entity to transfer economic benefits as a result of past transactions or events.

Provisions can be distinguished from other liabilities such as trade creditors and accruals because there is uncertainty about the timing or amount of the future expenditure required in settlement:

- trade creditors are liabilities to pay for goods or services that have been received or supplied and have been invoiced or formally agreed with the supplier;
- accruals are liabilities to pay for goods or services that have been received or supplied but have not been paid, invoiced or formally agreed with the supplier, including amounts due to employees such as accrued holiday pay.

## (c) The Recognition Rules

One of the most crucial aspects of FRS 12 is how to determine when a provision should be recognized in the balance sheet. The FRS specifies that a provision should be recognized if *all* three conditions are met. If they are not, a provision should *not* be recognized. This latter situation might then result in a contingent liability disclosure.

The three conditions are:

(1) an entity has a present obligation (legal or constructive) as a result of a past event;
(2) it is probable that a transfer of economic benefits will be required to settle the obligation; and
(3) a reliable estimate can be made of the amount of the obligation.

Relevant to the above is the definition of obligating event—an event that creates a legal or constructive obligation that results in an entity having no realistic alternative to settling that obligation.

The FRS defines a *legal obligation* as an obligation that derives from a contract, legislation or other operation of law.

A *constructive obligation* is an obligation that derives from an entity's actions where:

(i) by an established pattern of past practice, published policies or a sufficiently specific current statement, the entity has indicated to other parties that it will accept certain responsibilities; and
(ii) as a result, the entity has created a valid expectation on the part of those other parties that it will discharge those responsibilities.

## (d) Examples of Applications

### (1) Future operating losses

The FRS is quite explicit—provisions should not be recognized for future operating losses. However, as indicated in (a) above, this does not override, for example, SSAP 9 where a company is expected to recognize in full losses anticipated to arise over the life of a long-term contract.

### (2) Onerous contracts

The standard defines an onerous contract as a contract in which the unavoidable costs of meeting the obligations under it exceed the economic benefits expected to be received from it.

If an entity has a contract that is onerous, the present obligation under the contract should be recognized and measured as a provision. The obligation is the lower of the cost of fulfilling it and any compensation or penalties arising from failure to fulfil it.

### Illustration 1

Extract from annual report and accounts of Boots Group plc, year ended 31 March 2003.

**Note 20 – Provisions for liabilities and charges (extract)**

|  | *Deferred taxation* | *Vacant property provisions* | *Closure or termination of operations* | *Total* |
|---|---|---|---|---|
| **Group** | *£m* | *£m* | *£m* | *£m* |
| At 1 April 2002 | 167.2 | 10.7 | – | 177.9 |
| Transfer from debtors (see note 14) | (7.8) | – | – | (7.8) |
|  | 159.4 | 10.7 | – | 170.1 |
| Currency adjustment | 3.1 | – | – | 3.1 |
| Profit and loss account | (23.5) | 1.0 | 45.7 | 23.2 |
| Acquisition of business | (7.1) | – | – | (7.1) |
| Disposal of business | (9.3) | – | – | (9.3) |
| Utilised | – | (2.1) | (9.0) | (11.1) |
| Transfer to debtors (see note 14) | 4.9 | – | – | 4.9 |
| **At 31 March 2003** | **127.5** | **9.6** | **36.7** | **173.8** |

The vacant property provisions represent recognition of the net costs arising from vacant properties and sub-let properties, the exact timing of utilisation of these provisions will vary according to the individual properties concerned.

The provision for closure or termination of operations relates to recognition of costs arising as a result of the Halfords disposal, the withdrawal from certain wellbeing services and the rationalising of the group's manufacturing facilities. The majority of the costs are expected to be incurred in the next two years.

## Illustration 2

Extract from annual report and accounts of IDS Group plc, year ended 31 December 2003.

**Note 17 – Provision for liabilities and charges**

| | Product rationalisation £'000 | Restructuring £'000 | Onerous leases £'000 | Business closure £'000 | Total £'000 |
|---|---|---|---|---|---|
| At 1 January 2002 | 59 | 413 | 246 | – | 718 |
| Arising during the year | | 6 | 486 | 236 | 728 |
| Utilised | (59) | (152) | (363) | (173) | (747) |
| Amounts written back | – | (186) | – | – | (186) |
| **At 31 December 2002** | – | **81** | **369** | **63** | **513** |

*Product rationalisation*
Provision was made in 2000 for costs arising as a result of the rationalisation of the Group's software product range. The Group utilised the remainder of this provision in 2003.

*Restructuring*
Provision was made in 2000 for the committed costs of restructuring the Group, as a consequence of the acquisition of DSI and DHSL in 2000 and the rationalisation of its software product ranges. Part of the provision has been released in the year, where amounts paid to customers have been less than originally provided. Although a significant amount of cost has been incurred in previous years relating to reductions in headcount and closure of a number of properties, the Group has committed costs of £81,000 that are expected to be incurred in 2003. These costs relate principally to property disposals and the costs associated with migrating customers off software products that are no longer supported.

*Onerous leases*
As part of the restructuring process undertaken in 2000 and 2001, a number of properties leased by the Group became redundant. The Group has successfully sublet the majority of these properties and has provided for the onerous period of the remaining vacant property, being the estimated amount of time that the property will be vacant prior to subletting. An increase has been made to the provision in the year, to account for a change in the original estimation of time that the property will be vacant. Provision has also been made where the rentals receivable from the sublease are less than the rentals payable under the head lease. £214,000 of the provision in place at the year end is expected to be utilised in 2003, with the remaining £155,000 expected to be utilised through 2007.

*Business closure*
The Group is withdrawing from its North American wholesale finance operations in Boston and will close its Boston office at the end of February 2003. The decision to close this office was made in June 2002 and therefore the anticipated net costs of run-fling this location, up to 28 February 2003, have been provided in these accounts and will be utilised in 2003.

## (3) Executory contracts

Executory contracts are contracts under which neither party has performed any of its obligations or both parties have partially performed their obligations to an equal extent.

Executory contracts are excluded from the scope of FRS 12, except where such contracts are onerous.

Paragraph 72 of FRS 12 states that "...many contracts (for example, some routine purchase orders) can be cancelled without paying compensation to the other party, and therefore there is no obligation...".

Supplier purchase contracts are thus outside the scope of FRS 12—liabilities for goods and services will only be recognized in the accounts when they are received. Likewise, capital commitments will also normally fall outside the scope of FRS 12.

### (4) Warranty and rectification provisions

FRS 12, Example 1, deals with warranty provisions and concludes that "a provision is recognised for the best estimate of making good under the warranty products sold before the balance sheet date". Paragraph 39 gives guidance on the measurement of a provision and states:

> "...Where the provision being measured involves a large population of items, the obligation is estimated by weighting all possible outcomes by their associated probabilities. The name for this statistical method of estimation is "expected value". Paragraph 39 includes a computational illustration".

### (5) Refunds policy

Appendix III of FRS 12 includes an example of a constructive obligation. Example 4, "Refunds policy", refers to a retail store which has a policy of refunding purchases by dissatisfied customers, even though it is under no legal obligation to do so. However, its policy of making refunds is generally known. The example applies the recognition rules and concludes that a provision should be made for the best estimate of the costs of the refund.

If the retail store returns such goods to its suppliers and claims reimbursement, paragraph 56 of FRS 12 prohibits the calculation of the provision on a "net" basis:

> "Where some or all of the expenditure required to settle a provision is expected to be reimbursed by another party, the reimbursement should be recognised only when it is virtually certain that reimbursement will be received if the entity settles the obligation. The reimbursement should be treated as a separate asset..."

However, netting off is permitted in the profit and loss account. Paragraph 57 states:

> "In the profit and loss account, the expense relating to a provision may be presented net of the amount recognised for a reimbursement".

### (6) Repairs and renewals provisions – relating to fixed assets which are owned

This aspect of FRS 12 has attracted considerable comment—not least because of concerns over the tax ramifications of a change in accounting treatment. A frequently-cited tax case, Johnston v Britannia Airways Ltd, held that a provision for future overhaul of jet aircraft could be charged in arriving at taxable profit.

FRS 12 prohibits setting up provisions for future repairs and maintenance in respect of assets which are owned (as opposed to leased—see below). The reason for this restriction is that no obligation exists at the balance sheet date.

Example 11B in FRS 12 illustrates the way that this type of expenditure must be dealt with. The example relates to an airline which is required by law to overhaul its aircraft once every three years. The example concludes:

> "...The costs of overhauling aircraft are not recognised as a provision for the same reasons as the cost of replacing the lining is not recognised as a provision in example 11A [FRS 12]. Even a legal requirement to overhaul does not make the costs of overhaul a liability because no obligation exists to overhaul the aircraft independently of the entity's future actions – the entity could avoid the future expenditure by its future actions, for example by selling the aircraft. Instead of a provision being recognised, the depreciation of the aircraft takes account of the future incidence of maintenance costs, ie an amount equivalent to the expected maintenance costs is depreciated over three years... (see 12.3, Illustration 4)"

The restriction above is further explained in paragraph 38, Appendix VII, FRS 12.

### (7) Repair/dilapidation provisions – relating to assets which are leased

*Example:* Suppose a company leases equipment on an operating lease. Under the terms of the lease, the company is required to return the equipment at the end of the lease in a well-maintained state. In previous years, the company has built up a provision for estimated restoration expenses. Estimated costs have been arrived at using an hourly charge applied to hours operated during the period.

The company is concerned as to how the provision will be affected by FRS 12, i.e. will it have to be written back by means of a prior year adjustment, with maintenance expenditure written off to profit and loss account as incurred.

FRS 12 is quite explicit that a mere intention to incur expenditure related to the future is not sufficient to create an obligation. This is not the case here as there is a present obligation as a result of a past event, i.e. the contractual obligation following from the signing of the lease. Provision should be made, therefore, for the obligation to restore the asset to the condition specified in the lease. The basis used until now for establishing the provision seems reasonable and appropriate. No accounting policy change is required.

*Comment:* The very last paragraph of FRS 12, paragraph 39 of Appendix VII, states:

> "... In some operating leases the lessee is required to incur periodic charges for maintenance of the leased asset or to make good dilapidations or other damage occurring during the rental period. The principle illustrated in example 11 [of FRS 12] does not preclude the recognition of such liabilities once the event giving rise to the obligation under the lease has occurred..."

*Illustration 3*

Extract from annual report and accounts of Charteris plc, year ended 31 July 2003.

**Note 14 – Provision for liabilities and charges**

| | *Group and Company* | | |
|---|---|---|---|
| | *Dilapidation costs* | *Deferred taxation* | *Total* |
| | *£'000* | *£'000* | *£'000* |
| 1 August 2002 | 26 | – | 26 |
| Transfer (to)/from profit and loss account | (1) | 7 | 6 |
| 31 July 2003 | 25 | 7 | 32 |

Dilapidation costs reflect provision for the cost of returning leased premises to the conditions in which they were first occupied and are expected to be fully utilised by 31 July 2004.

The provision for deferred tax comprises accelerated capital allowances of £32,000 less general timing differences of £25,000. At 31 July 2002, there was a deferred tax asset which is disclosed in note 11.

*(8) Reorganization and reconstruction provisions*

This aspect of FRS 12 receives extensive coverage—in both the main part of the Standard, and in the Appendices. Examples 5A and 5B deal with future costs relating to closure of a division.

## *(e) Measuring the Provision*

The FRS requires that the amount recognized as a provision should be the best estimate of the expenditure required to settle the present obligation at the balance sheet date.

Paragraph 39 states that:

> "Uncertainties surrounding the amount to be recognised as a provision are dealt with by various means according to the circumstances...".

Paragraph 39 then goes on to say:

> "... Where the provision being measured involves a large population of items, the obligation is estimated by weighting all possible outcomes by their associated probabilities".

The name for this statistical method of estimation is "expected value". The paragraph gives detailed guidance and includes an example of a numeral calculation using "expected value" and applying to a provision resulting from sales under warranty.

The FRS gives guidance on dealing with risks and uncertainties. It also deals with "present value" i.e. discounting of amounts to arrive at the provision in the current balance sheet. Paragraph 45 states:

> "Where the effect of the time value of money is material, the amount of a provision should be the present value of the expenditures expected to be required to settle the obligation."

Note that this is not an automatic requirement to discount, but the FRS does require provisions to be discounted where the effect is material.

## Illustration 4

Extract from annual report and accounts of Durlacher Corporation plc, year ended 30 June 2003.

**Note 20 – Provision for liabilities and charges (extract)**

|  | Reorganisation & reconstruction £'000 | Legal action £'000 | Other £'000 | Total £'000 |
|---|---|---|---|---|
| Group |  |  |  |  |
| Provisions at 1 July 2002 | (601) | – | (108) | (709) |
| Utilised during the period | 516 | – | 68 | 584 |
| Charged during the year | (712) | (600) | (104) | (1,416) |
| As at 30 June 2003 | (797) | (600) | (144) | (1,541) |

Before the year end the Directors decided that they would dispose of certain elements of the Private Client Stockbroking business and terminate the remainder and communicated that decision to the staff affected. A provision has been established in the respect of the Directors' best estimate of the redundancy and other termination costs. The obligations represented by the provision are expected to be settled within five months of the year end.

The Group has received a small number of complaints regarding the management of certain investment portfolios. Legal action has been served against the Company in respect of certain of the complaints while others have been referred to the Financial Ombudsman Service. Having carefully considered the Company's position and after taking legal advice on specific complaints the Directors have established a provision representing their best estimate of the liabilities likely to arise in respect of these complaints. The timing of any payment is dependent on how the cases develop.

The other provisions relate to redundancy and reorganisation costs which have been quantified on the basis of a commitment to pay the relevant parties. It is envisaged that these payments will be made in the course of the next financial year.

## (f) Changes in Provisions

Provisions should be reviewed at each balance sheet date and adjusted to reflect the best estimate.

Provisions should be reversed where it is "no longer probable that a transfer of economic benefits will be required to settle the obligation".

## (g) Uses of Provisions

A particular provision should be used only for expenditures for which the provision was originally recognized.

## (h) Disclosure

The following should be disclosed for each class of provision:

- the carrying amount at the beginning and end of the period;
- additional provisions made in the period, including increases to existing provisions;
- amounts used (i.e. incurred and charged against the provision) during the period;

- unused amounts reversed during the period;
- the increase during the period in the discounted amount arising from the passage of time and the effect of any change in the discount rate.

The FRS specifies that disclosure of comparative information is not required. For each class of provision, the following should be disclosed:

- a brief description of the nature of the obligation, and the expected timing of any resulting transfer of economic benefits;
- an indication of the uncertainties about the amount or timing of those transfers of economic benefit;
- where necessary to provide adequate information, an entity should disclose the major assumptions made concerning future events, as specified in paragraph 51 of the FRS, and the amount of any expected reimbursement, stating the amount of any asset that has been recognized for that expected reimbursement.

*Illustration 5*

Extract from annual report and accounts of Cable and Wireless plc, year ended 31 March 2003.

**Note 23 – Provisions for liabilities and charges**

| | Note | At 1 April 2002 £m | Additions/ (releases) £m | Amounts used £m | Foreign exchange and other movements £m | At 31 March 2003 £m |
|---|---|---|---|---|---|---|
| **Group** | | | | | | |
| Taxation, including deferred taxation | (i) | 493 | (31) | (380) | (15) | 67 |
| Pensions | (ii) | 36 | 9 | (5) | (1) | 39 |
| Redundancy | (iii) | 15 | 108 | (79) | – | 44 |
| Property | (iv) | 216 | 303 | (97) | (17) | 405 |
| Network | (v) | 60 | 159 | (34) | (3) | 182 |
| Other | (vi) | 18 | 75 | (67) | (3) | 23 |
| | | 838 | 623 | (662) | (39) | 760 |

| | Note | At 1 April 2002 £m | Additions £m | Amounts Used £m | At 31 March 2003 £m |
|---|---|---|---|---|---|
| **Company** | | | | | |
| Taxation, including deferred taxation | (i) | 203 | (5) | (197) | 1 |
| Pensions | (ii) | 14 | 4 | – | 18 |
| | | 217 | (1) | (197) | 19 |

*(i) Taxation, including deferred taxation*
The movement in the Group deferred tax balance from £105 million to £67 million (Company – £6 million to £1 million) during the year comprises £31 million credited in the profit and loss account (Company – £5 million) and £7 million relating to exchange and other movements (Company – £nil). The total deferred tax balance relates to excess capital allowances. The movement in the Group's other tax provisions from £388 million to £nil (Company – £197 million to £nil)

comprises utilisation of £380 million in respect of the tax settlement (Company – £197 million) and £8 million (Company – £nil) relating to exchange and other movements.

The deferred tax liability does not include an amount of £24 million (2002 – £58 million) of contingent tax liability arising on the reserves of overseas subsidiaries, joint ventures and associates which the Group does not expect to remit to the United Kingdom.

As at 31 March 2003, the Group had tax losses to carry forward of approximately £6,860 million (2002 – £2,588 million) against which no deferred tax asset has been recognised. A deferred tax asset is regarded as recoverable and therefore recognised only when, on the basis of all available evidence, it can be regarded as more likely than not that there will be suitable taxable profits from which the future reversal of the underlying timing differences can be deducted.

*(ii) Pensions*
The Group operates various unfunded pension plans. Provision is made for the expected cost of meeting the associated liabilities. In view of their long term nature, the timing of utilisation of these provisions is uncertain. Included within this provision is an amount of £4.7 million (2002 – £6.4 million) to cover the cost of former Directors' pension entitlements.

*(iii) Redundancy*
Provision has been made for the cost of redundancies announced during the year which are expected to be utilised within 12 months.

*(iv) Property*
Provision has been made for the best estimate of the unavoidable lease payments on vacant properties, being the difference between the rentals due and any income expected to be derived from their being sub-let. The provision is expected to be utilised over the shorter of the period to exit and the lease contract life. Provision has also been made for the difference between rentals on properties relating to businesses acquired during the previous financial year and their fair value at the date of acquisition. The provision is being utilised over the lease contract life.

*(v) Network*
Provision has been made for the best estimate of the unavoidable costs associated with redundant network capacity. The provision is expected to be utilised over the shorter of the period to exit and the lease contract life.

*(vi) Other*
Other provisions include £13 million relating to the disposal of the US discontinued businesses. It is expected that this provision will be utilised within 12 months. Other provisions also include £9 million relating to specific claims held against the Group's insurance subsidiary.

# 16.4 Contingencies

## *(a) FRS 12, Provisions and Contingencies*

FRS 12 defines contingent liabilities as:

(1) a possible obligation that arises from past events and whose existence will be confirmed only by the occurrence of one or more uncertain events not wholly within the entity's control; or

(2) a present obligation that arises from past events but is not recognized because:
   (i) it is not probable that a transfer of economic benefits will be required to settle the obligation, or
   (ii) the amount of the obligation cannot be measured with sufficient reliability.

The FRS distinguishes between provisions and contingent liabilities as follows:

Provisions are recognized as liabilities because they are present obligations where it is probable that a transfer of economic benefits will be required to settle the obligations.

Contingent liabilities are not recognized as liabilities because they are either possible obligations, or alternatively probable obligations that do not meet the recognition criteria, as indicated above.

## (b) Disclosures – FRS 12

The following disclosures are required for each class of contingent liabilities, unless the possibility of any transfer in settlement is remote:

(1) a brief description of the nature of the contingent liability, and
(2) where practicable:
    (i) an estimate of its financial effect;
    (ii) an indication of the uncertainties relating to the amount or timing of any outflow; and
    (iii) the possibility of any reimbursement.

Where information is not disclosed on the grounds that it is not practicable to do so, that fact should be stated.

## (c) Contingent Assets – FRS 12

A contingent asset is a possible asset that arises from past events and whose existence will be confirmed only by the occurrence of one or more uncertain future events not wholly within the entity's control.

An entity should not recognize a contingent asset.

Disclosure is required where an inflow of economic benefits is probable. Paragraph 94 states:

> "Where an inflow of economic benefits is probable, an entity should disclose a brief description of the nature of the contingent asset at the balance sheet date and, where practicable, an estimate of their financial effect, using the principles set out for provisions in paragraphs 36–55".

## (d) Companies Act 1985 Disclosure Requirements

The following should be disclosed regarding contingent liabilities:

• the amount or estimated amount of the contingent liability;
• its legal nature;
• whether any valuable security has been provided by the company in connection with that contingent liability and if so, what.

Disclosure is also required of:

- contracts for capital expenditure;
- pension commitments;
- any other commitments for which no provision is made in the accounts.

## (e) Typical Disclosure Items

The most common contingencies relate to guarantees given by the parent company e.g. in relation to borrowings from subsidiaries, and associated companies and house purchase schemes.

Other examples include:

- discounted bills of exchange;
- partly paid investments in other companies;
- law suits or claims pending.

### Illustration 6

Extract from annual report and accounts of Durlacher Corporation plc, year ended 30 June 2003.

**Note 25 – Contingent liabilities**

In a number of instances split capital investment trusts ("splits") have either failed or performed poorly in the past 18 months. The Financial Services Authority and the Financial Ombudsman Service are currently undertaking a review of the splits sector. There has also been speculation that legal action may be brought against a range of parties involved in the sector. No legal action has been served against the Company and in the event that the Company were to be included in any such proceedings these would be defended robustly. A review of the Company's exposure to clients deriving from their holdings of split trusts has been undertaken. Based on this review and the present progress of the regulatory proceedings the Board does not consider that any material provision is required. It is not possible to calculate the value of this contingent liability.

# 16.5  Commitments

The Companies Act 1985 requires disclosure as follows:

(1) Capital commitments:
 (i) contracts for capital expenditure not provided for;
 (ii) capital expenditure authorized by directors but not yet contracted for.
(2) Pension commitment particulars:
 Post balance sheet events 19.8
 (i) pension commitments included under any provision shown in the B/S;
 (ii) pension commitments for which no provision made;
 (iii) where applicable, separate particulars of pension commitments relating wholly or partly to pensions payable to past directors.

(See Chapter 9)

In addition SSAP 21 requires disclosure of leasing commitments (see Chapter 14).

## 16.6    International Financial Reporting Standards

IAS 37 and FRS 12 are virtually identical.

---

**Frequently Asked Questions**

1 Can there be an obligation in place before balance sheet date in respect of proposed equity dividends?
In general terms no, except in a very special situation where the relevant obligation is established by a shareholder resolution passed prior to the balance sheet date.

2 Should executory contracts be recognized in the balance sheet?
No—except where the contract is onerous.

3 Are private companies required to include a note to the accounts providing an analysis of debt split: less than one year; one–two years; two–five years; five years or more?
Yes—except for small companies who have adopted the FRSSE.

---

# Financial Instruments

This chapter covers:
* Definitions and terminology
* UK GAAP background
* Classification of shareholders' funds (FRS 4)
* Redemption of preference shares
* Accounting for debt (FRS 4)
* FRS 25 – Financial instruments: disclosure and presentation
* International Financial Reporting Standards

## 17.1 Overview

### (a) Definitions and Terminology

(Based on FRS 25, see below)

*Financial instrument:* A financial instrument is any contract that gives rise to both a financial of one entity and financial liability or equity instrument of another entity.

Financial instruments include both:

- primary instruments – such as receivables, payables and equity securities
- derivative financial instruments – such as forward exchange contracts interest rate swaps.

Commitments to buy or sell non-financial items are outside the definition, financial instruments.

*Financial assets:* A financial asset is any asset that is:

- cash;
- an equity instrument of another entity;
- a contractual right to receive cash or another financial asset from another entity;
- a contractual right to exchange financial instruments with another entity under conditions that are potentially favourable to the entity.

The term does *not* cover: physical assets (e.g. inventories, property, plant, equipment, leased assets); intangible assets; prepaid expenses.

*Financial liabilities:* A financial liability is any liability that is a contractual obligation:

- to deliver cash or another financial asset to another entity;
- to exchange financial assets or financial liabilities with another entity under conditions that are potentially unfavourable to the entity.

The term does not cover deferred revenue or warranty obligations because the probable outflow of economic benefits associated with these is the delivery of goods or services, rather than an obligation to pay cash or another financial asset.

*Derivatives:* A derivative is defined in International Accounting Standard 39 as a financial instrument or other contract with *all three* of the following characteristics:

- its value changes in response to the change in a specified interest rate, financial instrument price, commodity price, foreign exchange rate, index of prices or rates, a credit rating or credit index, or other variable (sometimes called the "underlying");
- it requires no initial net investment or an initial net investment that is smaller than would be required for other types of contracts that would be expected to have a similar response to changes in market factors;
- it is settled at a future date.

## (b) UK GAAP

Until recently, no single UK standard deals with issues regarding financial instruments: recognition, measurement, presentation and disclosure.

However, the following regulations are relevant:

- FRS 4, Capital instruments;
- FRS 13, Derivatives and other financial instruments: disclosure;
- Companies *Act 1985 rules* regarding valuation of investments (current assets and fixed assets – see 15.5 and 27.2;
- In view of FRS 13's restricted application to listed companies, together with convergence development, it is nor further referred to.

## (c) International Accounting Standards (IAS)

The International Accounting Standards Board has issued two standards dealing with financial instruments:

- IAS 39 on recognition and measurement;
- IAS 32 on disclosure and presentation.

These are now reflected in UK GAAP as FRS 26 and FRS 25, respectively.

## 17.2 FRS 4, Capital Instruments – Shareholders' Funds

### (a) Introduction

The stated aim of FRS 4 is "to secure clear and appropriate distinctions in the balance sheet between the various kinds of financial instruments and to ensure that their respective costs are properly reflected in the profit and loss account".

The term "capital instruments" refers to all instruments that are issued as a means of raising finance including:

- shares,
- debentures,
- loans and debt instruments,

options and warrants that give the holder the right to subscribe for or obtain capital instruments.

- FRS 25 Financial instruments – presentation and disclosure (see 17.4) supersedes parts of FRS 4 for accounts periods beginning on or after 1 January 2005.

**Please note that an appendix to FRS 25 includes "Amended text of FRS 4 'Capital Instruments'".** This is effectively what remains of FRS 4 after eliminating those parts such as classification of shareholders' funds which have been superseded by FRS 25.

### (b) Classification of Shares Under FRS 4

Shares must be classified either as equity or non-equity.

#### (1) Non-equity

These are defined as shares which possess any of the following three characteristics.

(i) Any of the rights of the shares to receive payments (whether in respect of dividends, in respect of redemption or otherwise) are for a limited amount that is not calculated by reference to the company's assets or profits or the dividends on any class of equity share.

(ii) Any of their rights to participate in a surplus in a winding up are limited to a specific amount that is not calculated by reference to the company's assets or profits and such limitation had a commercial effect in practice at the time the shares were issued or, if later, at the time the limitation was introduced.

(iii) The shares are redeemable either according to their terms, or because the holder, or any party other than the issuer, can require their redemption.

Thus, any shares that have a right to a dividend payment or to a redemption payment that is for a limited amount will be regarded as non-equity shares.

Participating preference shares are entitled to a fixed dividend plus a proportion of dividend paid on equity shares. This type of preference share is referred to in the Application Notes which states that such shares are non-equity in accordance with FRS 4. Paragraph 13 of FRS 4 defines the term "participating dividend".

*(2) Equity shares*

Equity shares are a residual category, i.e. shares other than non-equity shares.

**Note**

This aspect of FRS 4 has been superseded by FRS 25 which is mandatory for accounts periods beginning on or after 1 January 2005 (earlier adoption is prohibited).

## *(c) Balance Sheet Analysis of Shareholders' Funds*

The disclosure requirements of FRS 4 are as follows:

(1) the total amount of shareholders funds should be shown on the face of the balance sheet;
(2) the total in (1) should be analysed between:
    (i) amount attributable to equity interest; and
    (ii) amount attributable to non-equity interests.

The analysis may be given on the balance sheet or in the notes. If given by way of note the balance sheet caption should state that the total of shareholders funds includes non-equity interests.

A further analysis is required for (ii) above giving the total for each class of non-equity shares. Note, however, that FRS 4 does not require any of the individual components of shareholders funds such as share premium or revaluation reserve to be analysed between equity and non-equity interests.

*Illustration 1*

Part of balance sheet

|  | Note | £'000 | £'000 |
|---|---|---|---|
| Net assets |  | 11,446 | 10,240 |
| Capital and reserves | 16 | 1,774 | 1,774 |
| Called up share capital | 17 | 1,417 | 1,417 |
| Revaluation reserve | 17 | 581 | 581 |
| Other reserves | 18 | 7,674 | 6,468 |
| Profit and loss account Shareholders' funds |  | 11,446 | 10,240 |
| Attributable to equity shareholders |  | 11,360 | 10,154 |
| Attributable to non-equity shareholders |  | 86 | 86 |

These accounts were approved by the board of directors on... and were signed on its behalf by:

...

Director

## (d) Profit and Loss Account Disclosures (pre FRS 25)

The following profit and loss account information should be given:

(1) aggregate dividends for each class or shares giving sub-totals for:
    (i) dividends on equity shares;
    (ii) participating dividends (i.e. for participating preference shares the participating element of the dividend as opposed to the fixed element);
    (iii) other dividends on non-equity shares.
(2) any other appropriation of profit in respect of non-equity shares. This could relate to the annual build-up of the premium payable on redemption in some years time.

Where the above information is given by way of note, the P/L caption should make it clear that the above such amounts are included.

### Illustration 2

**Part of the profit and loss account**

|  | Note | £'000 | £'000 |
|---|---|---|---|
| Profit on ordinary activities before taxation | 6 | 1,621 | 579 |
| Tax on profit on ordinary activities |  | (5) | (123) |
| Profit for the financial year |  | 1,616 | 456 |
| Dividends paid and proposed (including non-equity) | 8 | (410) | (291) |
| Retained profit for the year |  | 1,206 | 165 |

**Note 8 – dividends**

|  | 1994 £'000 | 1993 £'000 |
|---|---|---|
| Non-equity shares |  |  |
|   Preference and pre-preference dividends paid | 4 | 4 |
| Equity shares |  |  |
|   Ordinary shares: |  |  |
|   Interim paid 10p (1993 – 5p) | 169 | 84 |
|   Final proposed 14p (1993 – 12p) | 237 | 203 |
|  | 410 | 291 |

## (e) Additional Disclosures for Non-equity Shares

For each class of non-equity shares, the notes to the accounts should give a brief summary of:

(1) rights to dividends;
(2) dates at which shares are redeemable and amounts payable on redemption;
(3) priority and amounts receivable on a winding-up;
(4) voting rights.

For shares with unusual rights and characteristics, further information may need to be given. The main sources for the above information will be the company's Articles (as amended, if appropriate) and any special agreements.

## Illustration 3

### Note 16 – share capital (part of note)

*5% pre-preference shares of £1 each*
The rights of the pre-preference shareholders include entitlement to receive a cumulative dividend, preferential to all other classes of shares, at a rate of 5% pa on the paid-up capital. The shareholders are entitled on a winding-up or otherwise to a repayment of paid-up capital, in priority to all other classes of shares.

At a general meeting, the voting rights of pre-preference shareholders are as follows: on a show of hands, one vote per member; on a poll, holders of pre-preference shares have nine votes per share compared with one vote for every ordinary share held by members.

*5% preference shares of £1 each*
The rights of the preference shareholders include entitlement to receive a cumulative dividend at the rate of 5% pa on paid-up capital. This dividend entitlement ranks after that of the pre-preference shareholders but is in priority to the other remaining classes of shares.

Except in restricted circumstances, the shares do not carry an entitlement to vote at a general meeting.

*"A" ordinary shares of £1 each*
These have the same rights as ordinary shares apart from voting rights. Except in restricted circumstances, the shares do not carry an entitlement to vote at a general meeting.

## (f) Redemption of Preference Shares at a Premium

FRS 4 requires the shares to be treated as follows:

(1) The preference shares will usually be classed as non-equity. The amounts attributable following issue are the net proceeds (i.e. cash received less issue costs).
(2) The total finance cost over the period up to redemption is the difference between:
   (i) proceeds on issue; and
   (ii) total payments to be made to the preference shareholders – either by way of dividends or payment on redemption.
(3) The finance cost should be allocated to each year's profit and loss account in a similar way to debt.
(4) Any difference between finance costs and dividends paid should be accounted for in the profit and loss account as an appropriation of profit.
(5) The balance sheet carrying amount should be increased by the finance cost for the period and reduced by payments.

## Illustration 4

(1) Basic data

Company issued 100,000 £1 6% preference shares on 20 December 20X3 at a premium of 5%. Issue costs were £3,000. The shares are redeemable on 31 December 20X3 at a premium of 10%.

The total finance cost is:

|  | £ |
| --- | --- |
| Net proceeds (105,000 – 3,000) | 102,000 |
| Redemption cost | 110,000 |
| Dividends (10 years × 6,000) | 60,000 |
| Total payments | 170,000 |
| Total finance costs | 68,000 |

The total cost of £68,000 should be spread over the ten years so as to give a constant rate on the carrying amount. Strictly this should be done using the actuarial method, with a financial calculator or computer package. For simplicity, however, assume a straight line method with an annual cost of £6,800 (£68,000 ÷ 10).

(2) The accounting entries are summarised below:
On issue of shares

|  | £ | £ |
| --- | --- | --- |
| Dr cash | 105,000 | |
| Cr preference share capital | | 100,000 |
| Cr share premium account | | 5,000 |
| Dr share premium account | 3,000 | |
| Cr cash | | 3,000 |
| Balance sheet extract 31 December 20X3 | | |
| Non-equity shareholders funds | | 102,000 |

*Notes*

(i) It is not necessary to give an analysis of the individual components of shareholders funds between equity and non-equity interests.
(ii) FRS 3 requires the £102,000 to be shown in the movement of shareholders funds statements.

Entries in each subsequent year

|  | £ | £ |
| --- | --- | --- |
| Dr profit and loss account (appropriation section) | 6,800 | |
| Cr redemption reserve (excess of premium on redemption over premium on issue (10,000 – 5,000) ÷ 10 | | 500 |
| Cr cash (dividend paid) | | 6,000 |
| Cr profit and loss reserve (issue costs £3,000 ÷ 10) | | 300 |

*Notes*

(i) The profit and loss account should distinguish between dividends on non-equity shares (£6,000) and other appropriations (£800).
(ii) The issue costs of £3,000 form part of the finance cost and so should be charged to profit and loss account over the life of the preference shares. However, as £3,000 has already been charged direct to reserve, reserves must be credited direct each year with a proportion of the £3,000.
(iii) At the end of 20X4, the total of non-equity shareholders funds to be disclosed by way of note is calculated as:

|  | £ |
| --- | --- |
| Carrying amount at 1.1.20X4 | 102,000 |
| Finance cost | 6,800 |
|  | 108,800 |
| less dividends paid | 6,000 |
| Carrying amount at 31.12.20X4 | 102,800 |

(iv) At the end of 20X3, this will have increased by £800 per annum (total: $9 \times £800 = £7,200$) to £110,000 which is the amount payable on redemption.

(v) As required by CA 85, a transfer of £100,000 should be made as a reserve movement out of distributable profits and into Capital Redemption Reserve (see 18.6 (g)).

# 17.3   FRS 4, Capital Instruments – Debt

## (a) Introduction

FRS 4 requires that all capital instruments (except for shares) which contain an obligation to transfer economic benefits are classified as liabilities. The term "obligation" also includes a contingent obligation.

In the case of convertible debt, FRS 4 specifically requires that conversion into shares should not be anticipated. Convertible debt must therefore be reported within liabilities, irrespective of the likelihood of conversion into shares (see below).

FRS 4 has extended the disclosure requirements for analysis of maturity of debt. The notes should include an analysis between amounts falling due:

(1) in one year or less or on demand;
(2) between one and two years;
(3) between two and five years; and
(4) in five years or more.

Note that debt maturity should be determined by reference to the earliest date on which the lender can require repayment.

## (b) Debt Redeemable at a Premium

FRS 4 sets out the following principles:

(1) Following the issue, debt should be stated at net proceeds (defined as fair value of consideration less issue costs).
(2) The total finance cost of the debt should be allocated over the period of the debt at a constant rate on the carrying amount. The finance cost is the difference between the proceeds on issue and the total payments to be made (either as annual interest charges or on redemption). The annual finance cost should be charged to profit and loss account.

In principle the allocation of finance costs between different periods should be done using the actuarial method (as for finance leases under SSAP 21).
(3) The balance sheet carrying amount each year will be calculated by adding the finance cost for the period to the opening balance and deducting the payments made for the period.

*Illustration 5*

A loan of £100,000 is taken out on 1 January 19X4. Annual interest of £5,900 is payable at the end of each year. The loan is repayable on 31 December 19X8 at a premium of £25,000. The effective periodic rate is approximately 10% pa (determined by using a financial calculator or computer package).

The relevant balance sheet and profit and loss account figures may be derived as follows:

| Year ending 31 December | B/S liability at beginning of year £ | P/L Finance cost (× 10%) £ | Cash paid £ | B/S liability at end of year £ |
|---|---|---|---|---|
| 19X4 | 100,000 | 10,000 | 5,900 | 104,100 |
| 19X5 | 104,100 | 10,410 | 5,900 | 108,610 |
| 19X6 | 108,610 | 10,861 | 5,900 | 113,571 |
| 19X7 | 113,571 | 11,357 | 5,900 | 119,028 |
| 19X8 | 119,028 | *11,872 | 5,900 | 125,000 |
| | | 54,500 | 29,500 | |

*Notes*

(1) *£ 11,872 is a balancing figure as the rate was not precisely 10%.

(2) The total finance cost of £54,500 is made up of annual interest payments totalling £29,500 plus premium on redemption of £25,000.

In some cases, the straight line method of allocating finance charges may give an acceptable figure within the limits of materiality—in this case £54,500 + 5 = £10,900 pa.

Note that this is a case where the sum of the digits method would not give acceptable figures.

## (c) Convertible Loan Stock

Convertible loan stock should usually be separately disclosed on the face of the balance sheet under the overall heading of creditors.

Conversion of loan stock into shares should not be anticipated, however probable this is. Finance costs should be allocated over the loan period on the assumption that the stock will never be converted.

If, subsequently, part of the loan stock is converted into shares, the "value" of the shares issued will be based on the carrying amount of the loan stock immediately prior to the conversion. Any excess of this amount over nominal value issued, will be credited to share premium account.

Note that the following disclosures are required:

- redemption dates;
- amount payable on redemption;
- number and class of shares into which the debt may be converted;
- dates or periods within which the conversion may take place;
- whether conversion is at the option of the issuer or at that of the holder.

FRS 25 supersedes the above parts of FRS 4 for accounts periods beginning on or after 1 January 2005. FRS 25 requires a split accounting treatment for convertible loan stock, allocating proceeds of issue between a liability element and an equity element. This is not further referred to in this text (for further deatils, see illustrative examples in FRS 25, paragraphs IE34 – IE50).

# 17.4 FRS 25 – Financial Instruments: Disclosure and Presentation

## (a) Objective

The objective of FRS 25 is to "enhance financial statement users' understanding of the significance of financial instruments to an entity's financial position, performance and cash flows".

## (b) Presentation Requirements

The presentation requirements of the standard deal with:

- Classification of financial instruments, from the issuer's perspective, into liabilities and equity;
- Classification of related interest, dividends, losses and gains;
- The circumstances in which financial assets and financial liabilities should be offset.

**The presentation requirements of FRS 25 superseded those of FRS 4—the new requirements are mandatory for all companies for *accounts periods beginning on or after 1 January 2005*. This change of accounting policy will require a prior period adjustment with restatement of comparative figures.**

## (c) Disclosure Requirements

The disclosure requirements of FRS 25 deal with:

- Risk management policies and hedging activities;
- Terms, conditions and accounting policies;
- Interest rate risk;
- Credit risk;
- Fair value;
- Other disclosures.

Unlisted companies are not required to implement the disclosure requirements of FRS 25 immediately—full implementation is not likely to be required prior to accounts periods commencing on or after 1 January 2007. However the whole of FRS 25 applies to companies who have implemented FRS 26, Financial instruments: recognition and measurement.

## (d) Presentation of Liabilities and Equity

On initial recognition, the issuer of a financial instrument shall classify the instrument, or its component parts, as a financial liability, financial assets or equity in accordance with the substance of the contractual arrangement and the definitions of a financial liability, a financial asset and an equity instrument (FRS 25.15).

Note that it is the financial instrument's substance, rather than its legal form, that governs its classification on the issuer's balance sheet:

- The classification is made on the basis of an assessment of the instrument's substance and without regard to probabilities of settlement when the instrument is first recognized.
- The critical feature in differentiating a financial liability from an equity instrument is the existence of a contractual obligation of one party to the financial instrument (the issuer) either to deliver cash or another financial asset to the

other party (the holder) or to exchange another financial instrument with the holder under conditions that are potentially unfavourable to the issuer.

Where such a contractual obligation exists, that instrument meets the definition of a financial liability regardless of the manner in which the contractual obligation will be settled.

Where a financial instrument does not give rise to a contractual obligation on the part of the issuer to deliver cash or another financial asset or to exchange another financial instrument under conditions that are potentially unfavourable, it is an equity instrument.

*Example 1*

Company A has preference shares classified in the balance sheet as non-equity shareholders' funds in accordance with FRS 4.

The preference shares carry a right to a cumulative fixed net dividend per share of 9% of the nominal value. The dividend payments are paid half yearly on 30 June and 31 December.

On a return of capital, the preference shareholders are entitled to a payment of the subscription price paid, plus a sum equal to arrears and accruals of dividend.

The preference shares will be redeemed by the company with five equal half yearly instalments of £66,666 and one final instalment of £66,670 payable half yearly in each year commencing on 31 December 2004.

The key issue is to determine *whether in substance* the preference shares are a financial liability or equity.

The substance of the contractual arrangements is that the preference shares contain two obligations:

The first is a financial liability to pay dividends—the company has no discretion over this [the possible lack of available distributable profits at a future date would make no difference to this analysis].

The second is that the company is obliged to repay the shares in accordance with a schedule of payments.

The preference shares should therefore be reclassified as a financial liability. In accordance with FRS 25.35, dividends relating to a financial instrument that is a financial liability shall be recognized as an expense in the profit and loss account.

*Example 2*

Company B's redeemable shares are non-voting and non-participating. The company may redeem all or part of the non-voting, non-participating shares at any time. The holders of non-voting, non-participating redeemable shares are not entitled to the payment of a dividend and may not vote at any general meeting of the company.

On a winding-up, the non-voting, non-participating redeemable shares in issue carry priority over the ordinary shares to the extent of capital paid up.

The redeemable shares are redeemable at par plus a capital redemption premium which is calculated at a rate of 8% per annum from date of issue up to a maximum of £40,000.

The substance of the contractual arrangements is that the preference shares no obligations—the company can exercise discretion over dividend payments as well as over redemption of capital.

Under FRS 25, the preference shares would fall to be classified as equity. No restatement would be required as regards the balance sheet.

However, the dividends paid would have to be debited direct to equity. Therefore, comparative profit and loss numbers would have to be restated.

## (e) Presentation of Interest, Dividends, Losses and Gains

*Classification and recognition issues:* Interest, dividends, losses and gains relating to a financial instrument, or a component that is a financial liability, shall be recognized as income or expense in profit or loss:

- Distributions to holders of an equity instrument shall be debited by the **entity directly to equity** (see example in 18.5 below);
- Dividend payments on shares classed as liabilities are classified as expenses in the same way as interest on a bond and recognized as expenses in profit or loss;
- Gains and losses associated with redemptions or refinancings of financial liabilities are recognized in profit or loss;
- Gains and losses associated with redemptions or refinancings of equity instruments are reported as changes in equity.

## (f) Offset

A financial asset and a financial liability shall be offset (with the net amount presented in the balance sheet) only when an entity currently has a legally enforceable right to set off the recognized amounts; *and* intends either to settle on a net basis, or to realize the asset and settle the liability simultaneously.

## (g) Implementation

The implementation date requirements for FRS 25 are complex.

The *presentation requirements* of FRS 25 will apply for accounting periods beginning on or after 1 January 2005 for *all* entities.

For unlisted companies, the *disclosure requirements* of FRS 25 will only be mandatory for entities who are adopting FRS 26. Unlisted entities who either are not required to or who choose not to adopt FRS 26, need not give the disclosure requirements in FRS 25.

# 17.5  International Financial Reporting Standards

FRS 25 converges UK GAAP with IAS 32. The differences between the two relate to implementation issues—in FRS 25 the paragraphs dealing with presentation are implemented sooner than those dealing with disclosure issues.

**Frequently Asked Questions**

1  A company has redeemable preference shares. These are redeemable in 2012 at a premium of 5%. Should the shares be classified as equity or liabilities?

   A preference share that provides for mandatory redemption by the issuer for a fixed or determinable amount at a fixed or determinable future date, or gives the holder the right to require the issuer to redeem the instrument at or after a particular date for a fixed or determinable amount, contains a financial liability. Provided that the dividend payment is also mandatory, the entire amount should be classified as a liability.

2  A company has preference shares which may be redeemed at the company's option at any time after five years. The shares carry a dividend coupon of 5% which must be paid each year provided that the company has sufficient distributable profits. Should the shares be classified as equity or liabilities?

   The company's obligation is limited to the payment of the dividend of 5% per annum. In theory the issue proceeds should be allocated between liability and equity. The liability portion would be calculated by reference to the present value of the stream of preference dividend payments, with the balance of proceeds allocated to equity.

   In practice, however, it is possible that the proceeds of issue is close to the present value of the dividend payment stream, so that the entire proceeds could be treated as a financial liability.

3  How should preference dividends paid be dealt with under FRS 25?

   If the preference shares are classified in the balance sheet as a liability, the preference dividend should be charged to profit and loss account as a finance cost. However, should the shares be classified as equity, the dividend paid would be taken direct to equity (as a movement on profit and loss reserves) and not recorded in the profit and loss account.

# 18 Shareholders' Funds and Dividends

**This chapter covers:**
* Share capital disclosure requirements
* Reserves categories
* Purchase and redemption of shares
* Distributable profits
* Purchases and sales of own shares
* FRS 25 – Financial instruments: Disclosure and presentation
* International Financial Reporting Standards

## 18.1   Introduction

Until comparatively recently, this topic attracted relatively little comment and discussion. The Companies Act 1985 set out disclosure requirements for share capital and reserves, whilst FRS 4 set out rules for distinguishing between equity shareholders' funds and non-equity shareholders' funds.

Recent developments include the new standard on Financial instruments: Disclosure and presentation, FRS 25 (see Chapter 17).

## 18.2   Share Capital Disclosures – Companies Act 1985

The Companies Act 1985 requires disclosure of:
(1) Authorized share capital.
(2) Allotted share capital:
    (i) where more than one class of shares allotted, number and aggregate nominal value of each class;
    (ii) amount of allotted share capital;
    (iii) amount of called-up share capital which has been paid up.

(3) Allotted redeemable shares:
    (i) earliest and latest dates on which company has power to redeem;
    (ii) whether redemption is mandatory or at option of company;
    (iii) premium, if any, payable on redemption.
(4) Shares allotted during the financial year:
    (i) reasons for making the allotment;
    (ii) classes of shares allotted;
    (iii) for each class of share:
        (a) number allotted,
        (b) aggregate nominal value,
        (c) consideration received by company.
(5) Options to subscribe for shares and any other rights to require allotment of shares to any person (including convertible loan stock):
    (i) number, description and amount of shares in relation to which right is exercisable;
    (ii) period during which it is exercisable;
    (iii) price to be paid for the shares allotted.

## Illustration 1

Extract from annual report and accounts of Wm Morrison Supermarkets plc, year ended 2 February 2003.

### Note 15 – Share capital (group and company)

|  | 2003 £'000 | 2002 £'000 |
|---|---|---|
| Authorised |  |  |
| Equity share capital |  |  |
| 2,000,000,000 ordinary shares of 10p each |  |  |
|   (2002 2,000,000,000) | 200,000 | 200,000 |
| Non-equity share capital |  |  |
| 50,000,000 5¼% cumulative redeemable |  |  |
|   convertible preference shares of £1 each |  |  |
| (2002 50,000,000) | 50,000 | 50,000 |
|  | 250,000 | 250,000 |
|  |  |  |
| Issued and fully paid |  |  |
| Equity share capital |  |  |
| 1,561,776,955 ordinary shares of 10p each |  |  |
|   (2002 1,543,854,430) | 156,178 | 154,386 |
| Non-equity share capital |  |  |
| 4,702,363 5¼% cumulative redeemable |  |  |
|   convertible preference shares of £1 each |  |  |
| (2002 9,262,475) | 4,702 | 9,262 |
|  | 160,880 | 163,648 |

Movement in period

| | Ordinary shares £'000 | 5¼% crc pref. shares £'000 | Share premium account £'000 |
|---|---|---|---|
| At 3 February 2002 | 154,386 | 9,262 | 7,708 |
| Options exercised | 260 | - | 2,100 |
| Preference shares converted | 1,532 | (4,560) | 3,028 |
| At 2 February 2003 | 156,178 | 4,702 | 12,836 |

The holders of the 5¼% cumulative redeemable convertible preference shares ('preference shares') are not entitled to attend or vote at general meetings of the company unless a dividend on those shares is six months in arrears, or any resolution is proposed either to vary the rights attaching to those shares or to wind up the company, in which event the said holder shall have one vote for each ordinary share into which the preference shares held would at that time be converted.

On a return of capital upon the liquidation of the company or otherwise the assets of the company available for distribution among the members shall be applied in repaying to the holders of the preference shares the amount paid up or credited as paid up thereon with an amount equal to any arrears and accruals of the fixed cumulative dividend to be calculated down to and including the date of commencement of the winding up whether or not such dividend has been declared or earned. Preference shares shall not entitle the holders thereof to any further or other right of participation in the assets of the company.

The preference shares can be converted at the option of the holder on the basis of 336 ordinary shares for every £100 in nominal amount of preference shares in the month of June in each year up to 2006. As over 75% of the preference shares originally issued have now been converted the remaining preference shares can be converted at the option of the company on the same basis within three months of the end of each conversion period. The company may redeem at par value preference shares at any time from 1 January 2007 and shall redeem at par value on 31 December 2009 the preference shares in issue on that date.

Particulars of contingent rights to the allotment of shares are set out in the directors' report (share options).

# 18.3    Reserves – Categories

The Act refers to the following reserves categories in the balance sheet formats:

## (a) Share Premium Account

When shares are issued at a premium, for cash or other consideration, the premium must be credited to a share premium account and dealt with according to Section 130 of the Companies Act 1985.

Section 130 permits a share premium account to be used for the following purposes only:

- A reduction of capital scheme (subject to the confirmation of the court);
- Paying up unissued shares of the company by way of a bonus issue to members of the company;

- Writing off: preliminary expenses; expenses of or commission paid on the issue of shares or debentures; discount allowed on the issue of debentures;
- Providing for the premium payable on the purchase or redemption of debentures;
- Providing for the premium on the purchase or redemption of shares (as permitted by the Companies Act 1985.

Section 131 deals with certain cases where shares are issued at a premium in connection with a share-for-share issue, and where the premium is treated as a merger reserve and not a share premium.

## (b) Revaluation Reserve

This reserve arises from a surplus on the revaluation of a tangible fixed asset, intangible fixed asset or a fixed asset investment.

## (c) Capital Redemption Reserve

This arises from the purchase or redemption of a company's shares (see 18.6(b)).

## (d) Other Reserves

Although not referred to as such in the Act, this may include an "Investment property revaluation reserve" (see 12.11(c)) and a merger reserve (see 26.4).

## (e) Profit and Loss Reserve

This is the accumulated balance which represents retained profits from the cumulative effect of each period's profit and loss account.

*Illustration 2*

**Note – Reserves**

|  | Capital Redemption Reserve Fund £'000 | Share Premium Account £'000 | Special Reserve £'000 | Revaluation Reserve £'000 | Profit and Loss Account £'000 | Total £'000 |
|---|---|---|---|---|---|---|
| (a) The Group | 50 | 30,129 | 10,411 | 938 | 86,876 | 128,404 |
| At 1 January 19X4 |  |  |  |  |  |  |
| Goodwill eliminated on current year acquisitions | – | – | (10,411) | – | (2,732) | (13,143) |
| Goodwill eliminated on acquisition made in the previous year | – | – | – | – | (453) | (453) |
| Arising on issue of shares | – | 9 | – | – | – | 9 |
| Retained profit for the year | – | – | – | – | 18,784 | 18,784 |
| At 31 December 19X4 | 50 | 30,138 | – | 938 | 102,475 | 133,601 |

(b) The Company

| | | | | | | |
|---|---|---|---|---|---|---|
| At 1 January 19X4 | 50 | 30,129 | 10,411 | 745 | 38,564 | 79,899 |
| Goodwill eliminated on current year acquisitions | – | – | (10,411) | – | (1,803) | (12,214) |
| Goodwill eliminated on acquisition made in the previous year | – | – | – | – | (453) | (453) |
| Arising on issue of shares | – | 9 | – | – | – | 9 |
| Retained profit for the year | – | – | – | – | 3,487 | 3,487 |
| At 31 December 19X4 | 50 | 30,138 | – | 745 | 39,795 | 70,728 |

# 18.4  Permitted Reserves Movements

These were referred to in 4.9(c).

# 18.5  FRS 25 – Financial Instruments: Disclosure and Presentation

FRS 25 was referred to in the previous chapter in relation to the classification of shares between equity and liabilities for accounts periods commencing on or after 1 January 2005. As indicated in that chapter, FRS 25 requires that distributions to holders of an equity instrument shall be debited by the entity directly to equity.

*Example*

The example below also deals with the changed treatment of proposed equity dividends as required by FRS 21, Events after the balance sheet date (see Chapter 20).

In line with the above changes to the Companies Act 1985, a new standard, FRS 25, Financial instruments: Disclosure and presentation, will be introduced into UK GAAP. This will supersede much of FRS 4, Capital instruments.

Amended paragraphs 12.1 requires a financial instrument to be classified in accordance with the substance of the contractual arrangement rather than its legal form.

Amended paragraph 12.6 requires dividends relating to a financial instrument that is a financial liability to be recognized as expense in profit or loss.

*Dividends paid to holders of equity shares must be debited direct to equity.*

Illustration – equity dividends paid and proposed: implementing FRSSE (effective January 2005)

The company has a 31 December year-end. The following extract is from its profit and loss account for the year ended 31 December 2004:

| | 2004 £ | 2003 £ |
|---|---|---|
| Profit on ordinary activities after tax | 421,500 | 398,650 |
| Dividends (note 9) | (180,000) | (155,000) |
| Retained profit for the financial year | 241,500 | 243,650 |

| | £ | £ |
|---|---|---|
| **Note 9 – Dividends** | | |
| Interim dividends paid | 75,000 | 60,000 |
| Final dividends proposed | 105,000 | 95,000 |
| | 180,000 | 155,000 |

The company is considering the likely impact on its 2005 accounts of FRS 21, Events after the balance sheet date (see Chapter 20) and FRS 25, Financial instruments: Disclosure and presentation.

For illustration purposes, suppose the profit after tax for 2005 amounts to £455,000 and the company pays an interim dividend in August 2005 amounting to £80,000, and proposes a final dividend of £120,000.

If an entity declares dividends to holders of equity instruments after the balance sheet date, the entity shall not recognize those dividends as a liability at the balance sheet date.

The Companies Act 1985 (as amended by Statutory Instrument 2947) requires disclosure by way of note of dividends paid and proposed (Schedule 4, new paragraph 35A; Schedule 8, new paragraph 35A).

Extracts from *pro forma* 2005 financial statements
*Profit and loss account extract*

|  | 2005 | 2004 restated |
|---|---|---|
|  | £ | £ |
| Profit before tax | 600,000 | 580,000 |
| Taxation | 145,000 | 158,500 |
| Profit for the financial year | 455,000 | 421,500 |

*Statement of total recognised gains and loss*

|  | 2005 | 2004 restated |
|---|---|---|
|  | £ | £ |
| Profit for the financial year | 455,000 | 421,500 |
| Unrealised surplus on revaluation of property | 72,000 | 41,000 |
| Total recognised gains and losses relating to the year | 527,000 | 462,500 |
| Prior year adjustment relating to proposed equity dividend (note 1) | 105,000 |  |
| Total gains and losses recognised since last annual report | 632,000 |  |

*Reconciliation of movements in shareholders' funds*

|  | 2005 | 2004 restated |
|---|---|---|
|  | £ | £ |
| Shareholders' funds at 1 January, as previously stated | 1,741,000 | 1,433,500 |
| Prior year adjustment relating to proposed equity dividend (note 1) | 105,000 | 95,000 |
| At 1 January as restated | 1,846,000 | 1,528,500 |
| Profit for the financial year | 455,000 | 421,500 |
| Dividends paid | (185,000) | (145,000) |
| Other recognised gains and losses relating to the year | 72,000 | 41,000 |
| Shareholders' funds at 31 December | 2,188,000 | 1,846,000 |

*Notes to the accounts*

*Accounting policies note*

......

**Note 1 – Accounting policies (extract)**

Prior year adjustment

During the year, the company adopted FRS 21, Events after the balance sheet date, and FRS 25, Financial instruments: Disclosure and presentation.

In previous years, equity dividends proposed by the Board of Directors were recorded in the financial statements and accrued as liabilities at the balance sheet date, and equity dividends paid and proposed were recorded in the profit and loss account.

This policy has been changed, and equity dividends proposed by the Board are not recorded in the financial statements until they have been approved by the shareholders at the Annual General Meeting. Equity dividends paid are dealt with as a movement on retained profits.

The change in accounting policy has been dealt with by way of prior year adjustment, and comparative accounts have been restated.

*Profit and loss reserves*

|  | £ |
|---|---:|
| Profit and loss account at 1 January 2005, as previously stated | 1,200,000 |
| Prior year adjustment | 105,000 |
| Profit and loss account at 1 January 2005, as restated | 1,305,000 |
| Profit for the financial year | 455,000 |
| Dividends paid (note 10) | (185,000) |
| Profit and loss account at 31 December 2005 | 1,575,000 |

**Note 10 – Dividends**

|  | £ |
|---|---:|
| Dividends paid: | |
| Final dividend in respect of 2004 | 105,000 |
| Interim dividend in respect of 2005 | 80,000 |
|  | 185,000 |

The Directors have proposed a final dividend in respect of 2005 amounting to £120,000. This will be recommended to the shareholders at the company's Annual General Meeting.

# 18.6 Purchase and Redemption of Shares – CA 1985 Rules

## (a) Redeemable Shares

A company limited by shares or a company limited by guarantee and having a share capital may issue redeemable shares (ordinary or preference) provided it is authorized to do so by its articles.

The Companies Act 1985, ss 159–161 specify the following additional conditions:

(1) redeemable shares may not be issued unless at the time of issue there are issued shares of the company which are not redeemable;

(2) redeemable shares may not be redeemed unless they are fully paid;

(3) the terms of redemption must provide for payment on redemption.

## (b) Financing the Redemption

The method of redemption is restricted to the following three possibilities:

(1) by the proceeds of a new issue of shares of any class; or

(2) out of distributable profits; or

(3) by a combination of (1) and (2).

Where shares are redeemed wholly out of profits, an amount equivalent to the nominal value of shares redeemed is to be transferred from distributable profits to a capital redemption reserve.

Where shares are redeemed wholly or partly out of the proceeds of a fresh issue of shares, a transfer to capital redemption reserve is required to the extent that the proceeds of the issue fall short of the nominal value redeemed (Companies Act 1985, s 170).

> CRR transfer = nominal value redeemed − proceeds of new issue of shares

## (c) Capital Redemption Reserve (CRR)

For the purposes of reduction of capital, the capital redemption reserve is treated as though it were paid-up share capital. However, the CRR may be applied in making a bonus issue of fully paid shares.

## (d) Premium on Redemption of Redeemable Shares

The basic rule is that any premium payable on redemption must be paid out of distributable profits of the company.

There is an exception to this rule, but it only applies if two conditions can both be satisfied:

(1) the shares to be redeemed were originally issued at a premium; and

(2) the redemption is to be financed by a fresh issue of shares.

In this situation, the premium or redemption may come out of share premium account (rather than distributable profits) but the amount of share premium account which may be used for this purpose is restricted to the lower of:

(i) the aggregate of premiums received on the original issue of the shares to be redeemed; and

(ii) the present balance on share premium account taking into account any premium relating to the fresh issue of shares.

## (e) Cancellation of Shares

Shares redeemed under the Companies Act 1985, ss 159–161 are to be treated as cancelled on redemption, and the company's issued share capital reduced accordingly.

However, the redemption of share capital is not to be taken as reducing the company's authorized share capital.

## (f) Purchase of Own Shares

A company limited by shares or a company limited by guarantee and having a share capital may purchase its own shares (including any redeemable shares) provided it is authorized to do so by its articles (Companies Act 1985, s 162).

However, a company may not purchase any of its shares if as a result of the share purchase there would be no member of the company holding shares other than redeemable shares,

There are three prescribed procedures for the purchase of shares by a company:

- off-market purchase;
- contingent purchase contracts;
- market purchase.

A detailed consideration of these, including necessary authorizations, is out side the scope of a financial accounting textbook.

All of the matters considered earlier relating to redeemable shares apply also to the purchase of own shares, except the terms and manner of purchase need not be determined by the articles.

## (g) Purchase or Redemption Out of Capital

*Example*
On 30 June 20X1, the company repurchased 25,000 ordinary shares held by F. Brown, a former director. The purchase consideration was cash of 155 pence per share.

The following must be disclosed in the directors' report (CA 85, Sch 7, part II):

- Number and nominal value purchased
- Aggregate consideration paid
- Reasons for purchase

*Suggested wording in directors' report*
On 30 June 200X the company purchased 25,000 £1 shares of the company for a consideration of £38,750 in accordance with S162 of the Companies Act 1985. The reason for the purchase was the retirement of a former director, Mr F Brown.

*Workings – journals*

|  | £ |  | £ |
|---|---|---|---|
| Dr ordinary share capital | 25,000 | Cr Cash | 38,750 |
| Dr profit and loss reserves | 13,750 |  |  |

(purchase at premium of 55 pence per share)

|  | £ |  | £ |
|---|---|---|---|
| Dr profit and loss reserves | 25,000 | Capital redemption reserve | 25,000 |

(statutory transfer)

*Disclosures in accounts*
- No effect on statement of total recognized gains and losses
- Movement of shareholders funds statement should include £216,000 as part of the movement for the year described as "purchase of shares during the year"
- Reserves note should include reserve movements following from the above journals.

*(1) Introduction*
This power is available to private companies only. Under no circumstances it is available to public limited companies.

The Companies Act 1985, ss 171–173 allow a private company limited by shares, or a private company limited by guarantee and having share capital, to make a payment out of capital provided it is permitted to do so by its articles.

The term "payment out of capital" essentially means a redemption or purchase of shares other than out of the company's distributable profit, or out of the proceeds of a fresh issue of shares.

*(2) Conditions*
  (i) The Act refers to the term permissible capital payment (PCP). This is the amount by which the purchase or redemption cost exceeds the total of available (i.e. distributable) profits, plus the proceeds of a fresh issue of shares made for the purpose of the redemption or purchase.
 (ii) The difference between the PCP and the nominal value of shares redeemed or purchased is to be dealt with as follows:
  - If the total of PCP, plus the proceeds of a fresh issue of shares, is less than the nominal value of shares redeemed or purchased, the amount of the difference is to be transferred to capital redemption reserve.
  - If the total of PCP, plus the proceeds of a fresh issue of shares, is more than the nominal value, the excess may be used to reduce any of the following:
    - capital redemption reserve;
    - share premium account;
    - fully paid share capital;
    - revaluation reserve.

(iii) The Companies Act 1985 specifies stringent legal conditions in connection with purchase or redemption out of capital. While the Act attempts to offer private companies greater flexibility than public companies, it is particularly concerned with the protection of creditors.

The legal conditions, a detailed consideration of which is outside the scope of this book, include:

- the approval by the members of the company by means of a special resolution;
- a statutory declaration of solvency by the directors with prescribed form and content and having annexed to it a special auditors' report;
- publicity for proposed payment out of capital; and
- rights of members or creditors to object.

*Illustration 3*

Private Ltd issued 1,000 £1 ordinary shares several years ago at par. Following the death of one of the major shareholders, the company now wishes to purchase 300 shares at a cost of £350. Distributable reserves amount to £270.

**(1) Basic calculations**

| (i) *Permissible capital payment (PCP)* | £ |
|---|---|
| Purchase cost | 350 |
| Distributable profits | 270 |
| PCP | 80 |

| (ii) *CRR calculation* | |
|---|---|
| | 300 |
| Nominal value purchased | 80 |
| PCP | 220 |

**(2) Journal entries**

| | £ | £ |
|---|---|---|
| Cash | | 350 |
| Share capital | 300 | |
| Distributable profits | 50 | |
| Distributable profits | 220 | |
| CRR | | 220 |

*Note*: share capital and non-distributable reserves have been reduced by £80 i.e. the amount of the permissible share capital payment.

| | Pre-purchase £ | Post-purchase £ |
|---|---|---|
| Share capital | 1,000 | 700 |
| CRR | – | 220 |
| Share capital and non-distributable reserves | 1,000 | 920 |

# 18.7 Distributable Profits

## (a) Overview

The Technical Release ("TR") updates guidance previously given in Technical Releases 481 and 482 issued in September 1982. The objective is to provide guidance on the determination of "realized profits" and "realized losses" for the purposes of the Companies Act 1985 ("CA 1985"). It does not however apply to the special circumstances of investment companies and insurance companies.

It is important to note that the guidance in the TR should not be used to question the lawfulness of previous distributions. However, existing reserves balances may need to be re-examined in the light of the guidance, before further distributions are made.

The TR reflects the law and accounting standards at 31 December 2002. New accounting standards only become relevant to distributions proposed in respect of periods when the change will first be recognized in the accounts.

The TR notes that the concept of realized profit is intended to be "dynamic, changing with the development of generally accepted accounting principles" and includes profits which ordinary language might not otherwise regard as realized. The TR makes particular reference to FRS 18, Accounting policies and includes definitions of key terms including "profit", "realized profit" and "realized loss" as well as terms specific to the TR such as "qualifying consideration".

## (b) Companies Act 1985 and Legal Considerations

The basic requirements are:

- A company shall not make a distribution except out of profits available for the purpose (s 263(1));
- Profits available for distribution are accumulated, realized profits (so far as not previously utilized by distribution or capitalization) less accumulated realized losses (so far as not previously written off in a reduction or reorganization of capital) (s 263(3));
- "Realized profits" and "realized losses" are such profits or losses as fall to be treated as realized in accordance with principles generally accepted *at the time when the accounts are prepared.*

## (c) Common Law

The TR makes two important points:

- A company cannot lawfully make a distribution out of capital;
- Directors are subject to fiduciary duties and when making a distribution should take into account additional considerations including whether the company will still be solvent following a proposed distribution.

## (d) Principles of Realization

Profits available for distribution are derived from a company's accounts. It is vital, therefore, that those accounts have been properly prepared in accordance with the law and generally accepted accounting principles.

The available profits may include amounts reported in the Statement of Total Recognized Gains and Losses and the Reconciliation of Movements in Shareholders' Funds as well as in the Profit and Loss Account. For example, a revaluation surplus becomes realized when the related asset is sold for "qualifying consideration" (see below).

FRS 18 says that profits should be treated as realized only when realized in the form of cash or "of other assets the ultimate cash realization of which can be assessed with reasonable certainty".

Transactions should be examined in terms of overall commercial effect and not in isolation, i.e. in accordance with FRS 5, Reporting the substance of transactions. Therefore a group or series of transactions must be viewed together to determine whether realized profits arise. Particular care should be taken over transactions which appear to be artificial, linked or circular.

# 18.8    International Financial Reporting Standards

FRS 25 converges UK GAAP with IAS 32. The differences between the two relate to implementation issues—in FRS 25 the paragraphs dealing with presentation are implemented sooner than those dealing with disclosure issues.

---

**Frequently Asked Questions**

1  How will equity dividends be accounted for under FRS 25 and what disclosures are required?
Equity dividends declared after the balance sheet date, these dividends shall not be recognized as a liability in the balance sheet;
Equity dividends paid shall be debited direct to equity;
The accounting policy note should state that financial liabilities and equity instruments are classified according to the substance of the contractual arrangements entered into;
The notes to the accounts should disclose the amount of dividends proposed or declared before the financial statements were authorized for issue but not recognized as a distribution to equity holders during the period (including amount per share).

2  Can a private company buy its own shares and hold in "treasury" without cancelling them?
No—this option is only available to fully listed companies and companies on the Alternative Investment Market [Statutory Instrument 2003/1116].

3  Does an unlisted company have to deal with the disclosure requirements of FRS 25 for accounts periods commencing on or after 1 January 2005?
No—provided it does not adopt FRS 26 an the fair value accounting rules in CA 85 on a voluntary basis.

 # Related Party Transactions

## 19.1   Introduction to FRS 8

### (a) Objective

The stated objective of FRS 8 is to "ensure that financial statements contain the disclosures necessary to draw attention to the possibility that the reported financial position and results may have been affected by the existence of related parties and by material transactions with them".

FRS 8 aims to achieve this objective by requiring:

(1) specified disclosures of transactions and balances with related parties; and
(2) disclosure of control, i.e. the name of the party controlling the reporting entity and, if different, that of the ultimate controlling party. This disclosure of control is required whether or not any transactions between the reporting entity and the controlling parties have taken place.

### (b) Scope

FRS 8 applies to all financial statements that are intended to give a true and fair view of a reporting entity's financial position and profit or loss for a period. Specific exemptions from disclosure are referred to below.

## (c) Small Companies

Shareholders' accounts of small companies, even those exempt from audit, are not exempt from FAS 8, but may adopt the Financial Reporting Standard for Smaller Entities (FRSSE)—see 22.4.

Small company abbreviated accounts must include the relevant CA 1985 disclosures but need not include those of FRS 8. However, abbreviated accounts of medium-sized companies are required to show a true and fair view and must therefore include the necessary disclosures.

# 19.2   Identifying Related Parties

## (a)   Introduction

The definition of related parties occupies two pages of the Standard and has two main strands:

(1) "deemed" related parties, i.e. those that are regarded as related parties irrespective of circumstances;
(2) "presumed" related parties, i.e. where it may be possible to present arguments which overturn the presumption.

## (b) Deemed to be Related Parties

These are specified in para 2.5 of FRS 8 as follows:

Two or more parties are related when at any time during the financial period:

(1) one party has direct or indirect control of the other party; or
(2) the parties are subject to common control from the same source; or
(3) one party has influence over the financial and operating policies of the other party to an extent that that other party might be inhibited from pursuing at all times its own separate interests; or
(4) the parties, in entering a transaction, are subject to influence from the same source to such an extent that one of the parties to the transaction has subordinated its own separate interests.

Control is defined by FRS 8 as

> "The ability to direct the financial and operating policies of an entity with a view to gaining economic benefits from its activities".

## (c) "Deemed" Related Parties – Further Guidance

So that there is no doubt whatsoever, FRS 8 adds that the following are to be regarded as related parties of the reporting entity:

(1) its ultimate and intermediate parent undertakings subsidiary undertakings and fellow subsidiary undertakings;
(2) its associates and joint ventures;

(3) the investor or venturer in respect of which the reporting entity is an associate or a joint venture;

(4) directors of the reporting entity and the directors of its ultimate and immediate parent undertakings; and

(5) pension funds for the benefit of employees of the reporting entity or of any entity that is a related party of the reporting entity.

## (d) Presumed to be Related Parties – Part 1

FRS 8 presumes the following to be related parties of the reporting entity unless "it can be demonstrated that neither party has influenced the financial and operating policies of the other in such a way as to inhibit the pursuit of separate interests":

(1) the key management of the reporting entity and the key management of its parent undertaking or undertakings;

(2) a person owning or able to exercise control over 20% or more of the voting rights of the reporting entity, whether directly or through nominees;

(3) each person acting in concert in such a way as to be able to exercise control or influence over the reporting entity; and

(4) an entity managing or managed by the reporting entity under a management contract.

FRS 8 defines the terms "key management" and "persons acting in concert" as follows:

*Key management:* Those persons in senior positions having authority or responsibility for directing or controlling the major activities and resources of the reporting entity.

*Persons acting in concert:* Persons who, pursuant to an agreement or understanding (whether formal or informal), actively co-operate, whether by the ownership by any of them of shares in an undertaking or otherwise, to exercise control or influence over that undertaking.

## (e) Presumed to be Related Parties – Part 2

The term related parties extends even further—it also catches certain individuals and entities who have a relationship with those "deemed" or "presumed" above.

FRS 8 presumes that the following are also related parties of the reporting entity: "members of the close family of any individual who falls under any of the categories in paras 16 to 18 above".

*Definition of "close family":* Close members of the family of an individual are those family members, or members of the same household, who may be

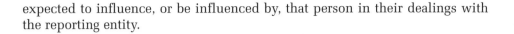

expected to influence, or be influenced by, that person in their dealings with the reporting entity.

*Illustration 1*

Harold is a director of ABC Ltd and holds 35% of the shares in the company. Harold's brother George is a controlling partner in a business which manufactures building materials. The partnership usually sells between 25% and 35% of its annual sales to ABC Ltd.

As regards ABC Ltd, Harold is deemed to be a related party.

Additionally, since George is a member of the close family of Harold, both George and the partnership which George controls are presumed to be related parties of ABC Limited.

## 19.3 Related Party Transactions – Definitions and Examples

### (a) Definition

FRS 8 defines "related party transactions" as: "the transfer of assets or liabilities or the performance of services by, to or for a related party irrespective of whether a price is charged".

### (b) Examples of Related Party Transactions – FRS 8

FRS 8 provides the following examples of related party transactions that could, subject to materiality, require disclosure by a reporting entity in the period in which they occur:

- purchases or sales of goods (finished or unfinished);
- purchases or sales of property and other assets;
- rendering or receiving of services;
- agency arrangements;
- leasing arrangements;
- transfer of research and development;
- licence agreements;
- provision of finance (including loans and equity contributions in cash or in kind);
- guarantees and the provision of collateral security; and
- management contracts.

## 19.4 Disclosure Requirements

FRS 8's disclosure requirements fall into two main categories:

(1) disclosure of control;
(2) disclosure of transactions and balances.

## (a) Disclosure of Control

The disclosure requirement applies where the reporting entity is controlled by another party. The following should be disclosed:

(1) the related party relationship;
(2) the name of the controlling party;
(3) the name of the ultimate controlling party (if different from 2).

This may result in the disclosure of controlling non-corporate persons, for example trusts, partnerships and individuals. In some cases, the name of the controlling party, or ultimate controlling party, may not be known. If this is so, that fact should be disclosed.

Note that the above disclosures are required even if no transactions have taken place between the controlling parties and the reporting entity.

## (b) Disclosure of Transactions and Balances

FRS 8 requires financial statements to disclose material transactions undertaken by the reporting entity with a related party. Disclosure is required whether or not a price is charged.
The following should be disclosed:

(1) the names of the transacting related parties;
(2) a description of the relationship between the parties;
(3) a description of the transactions;
(4) the amounts involved;
(5) any other elements of the transactions necessary for an understanding of the financial statements;
(6) the amounts due to or from related parties at the balance sheet date and provisions for doubtful debts due from such parties at that date; and
(7) amounts written off in the period in respect of debts due to or from related parties.

As regards (5), the explanation section of FRS 8 cites as an example the need to give an indication that the transfer of a major asset had taken place at an amount materially different from that obtainable on normal commercial terms. Note that there is no requirement to determine a fair value for such transactions (FRS 8, Appendix IV, para 20).

### Illustration 2

John is a controlling shareholder in XYZ Ltd. John's sister is a partner in a business which provides accountancy and consultancy services to XYZ Ltd.

John's adult son is a 60% shareholder in P Ltd which purchases a significant quantity of goods each year from XYZ Ltd.

Assuming the degree of influence normally expected from a close family relationship, the businesses run by the sister and son would be presumed related parties of XYZ Ltd.

As regards disclosures in XYZ Ltd., it will be necessary to disclose:
(1) the name of the controlling party, i.e. John;
(2) the names of the transacting related parties:
    (i) John's sister's partnership;
    (ii) John's son's company;
(3) description of the family relationship;
(4) a description of the transactions:
    (i) purchases of accountancy and consultancy services;
    (ii) sale of goods;
(5) amounts involved;
(6) year-end balances:
    (i) owing to the partnership;
    (ii) owing from the company.

## Illustration 3

For the whole year, the company was under the control of Mr Williams, a director, and members of his close family.

During the year, the company sold goods with a total value of £325,000 (1994 – £272,050) to a company controlled by Paul Williams, a son of the director. The transactions were in the ordinary course of business and at arm's length.

The balance owing to the company at the year-end was £36,500 (1995 – £21,700).

## Illustration 4

Extract from annual report and accounts of Wyevale Garden Centres plc, year ended 28 December 2003.

### Note 24 – Related party transactions

P H Williamson directly accent and indirectly controls 43% of Wyevale Holdings Limited and the wife of B A Evans, née Williamson, beneficially owns 8% of its share capital. During 2003 a subsidiary of Wyevale Holdings Limited, Wyevale Nurseries Limited, supplied 1% of all purchases by the Group for resale. The value of these purchases was £745,000 in 2003 (2002 £752,000) and the balance outstanding at 28 December 2003 was £108,000 (2002 £122,000).

## Illustration 5

Extract from annual report and accounts of Focus Solutions Group plc, year ended 31 March 2003.

### Note 20 – Related party transactions

The Group received consultancy and advisory services on an arm's length basis from Robert Hull & Co. Mr W R Hull, a director of the Company, is the proprietor of Robert Hull & Co. Purchases from Robert Hull & Co for the Group for the period ended 31 March 2003 were £68,000 (2002: £65,000), of which £68,000 (2002: £65,000) related to the Company.

Amounts due to Robert Hull & Co are disclosed below:

|  | Group | | Company | |
|---|---|---|---|---|
|  | 31 March 2003 £'000 | 31 March 2002 £'000 | 31 March 2003 £'000 | 31 March 2002 £'000 |
| Amount due to Robert Hull & Co | 8 | 9 | 8 | 9 |

The Group received consultancy and advisory services on an arm's length basis from DAMbusters. Mr R J M Jephcott, a former director of the Company, is the proprietor of DAMbusters. Purchases from DAMbusters for the Group for the period 1 April 2002 to 4 December 2002 were £nil (2002: £10,000), of which £nil (2002: £10,000) related to the Company.

The Group received the benefit of property rental on an arm's length basis from Mr J B Streets, the Chief Executive of the Company. Purchases from Mr J B Streets for the Group for the period ended 31 March 2003 were £9,000 (2002: £1,000), of which £9,000 (2002: £1,000) related to the Company.

Neither the Group nor the Company owed any amounts to Mr J B Streets in respect of property rental at 31 March 2003.

# 19.5 Companies Act 1985 – Directors' Interests in Contracts

## (a) Introduction

Directors have a general duty to disclose to the board of directors their interests in contracts. Once again, this aspect of the law is highly complex. Certain transactions caught within s 330 (loans, etc. to directors) may be unlawful, without more. Others, for example, substantial property transactions, may require the approval of the shareholders in general meeting.

This part of the notes is principally concerned with contracts for the provision of goods and services, including consultancy services, as well as contracts involving the transfer of property assets.

For private companies and unlisted plcs, the requirements to disclose are contained in Sch 6 of CA 1985.

Note also that references to directors are to include shadow directors.

## (b) Requirements to Disclose

Part 2 of Sch 6 requires the accounts to give particulars of "... any other transaction or arrangement with the company in which a person who at any time during the financial year was a director of the company had, directly or indirectly, a material interest".

## (c) Exemptions from Disclosure

The following are exempt:

(1) transactions between different companies where the director's interest arises purely from being a director of those companies;
(2) a contract of service between the company and a director (CA 1985 requires the company to make copies of such contracts available for inspection by members of the company);
(3) transactions and arrangements which were not entered into during the financial year and which did not subsist at any time during the year;
(4) transactions in which the director's interest is not material (if a majority of the other directors decide in a formal meeting it is not material this should be minuted);

(5) transactions in which a director has a material interest provided either:
    (i) the aggregate value did not exceed £1,000; or
    (ii) if it did exceed £1,000, it did not exceed the lower of £5,000 or 1% of the value of the company's net assets at the end of the period.

## (d) Details to be Disclosed

These include:

- the name of the director;
- the nature of the interest;
- the name of the person or company for whom the transaction or arrangement was made;
- the value of the transaction or arrangement.

These disclosures must also be included in abbreviated accounts filed with the Registrar.

# 19.6   International Financial Reporting Standards

IAS 24 is broadly similar effect to FRS 8, but there are differences of detail.

IAS 24 does not refer directly to materiality, but cross-refers to the IASB's "Framework". The definition in the Framework effectively asks "could the omission or misstatement influence economic decisions of users taken on basis of the financial statements?".

A key difference relates to exemptions from disclosure. FRS 8 allows certain exemptions for members of a group which prepares consolidated accounts. IAS 24 does not allow any exemptions to parent companies, venturers or investors who present separate accounts in accordance with IAS 27, nor to subsidiaries.

However, IAS 24 requires disclosures of transactions (including outstanding balances) to be made separately for each of a number of named categories (as opposed to named individual parties) as follows:

- The parent;
- Entities with joint control or significant influence over the entity;
- Subsidiaries;
- Associates;
- Joint ventures in which the entity is a venturer;
- Key management personnel of the entity or its parents;
- Other related parties.

**Frequently Asked Questions**

1  Under FRS 8, do transactions between subsidiary companies have to be disclosed as related party transactions in their individual financial statements?
Yes—if the group is small or medium-sized and group accounts are not prepared.
No—provided the subsidiaries are at least 90% owned within the group and the subsidiaries are included within consolidated accounts that are publicly available.

2  Are comparatives required in respect of directors' interests in contracts disclosures?
Yes—this is required by FRS 28 (see 2.1(d))

3  Do nil value transactions have to be disclosed?
Yes—provided they are material.

 Events after the Balance
Sheet Date

---

**This chapter covers:**
* SSAP 17 – Post balance sheet events
* FRS 21 – Events after the balance sheet date
* Examples of adjusting and non-adjusting events
* International Financial Reporting Standards

---

## 20.1   SSAP 17 – Post Balance Sheet Events

### (a) Introduction

SSAP 17 deals with post balance sheet events. The standard includes the following terms:

(1) Post balance sheet events are those events, both favourable and unfavourable, which occur between the balance sheet date and the date on which the financial statements are approved by the board of directors.
(2) Adjusting events are post balance sheet events which provide additional evidence of conditions existing at the balance sheet date. They include events which because of statutory or conventional requirements are reflected in financial statements.
(3) Non-adjusting events are post balance sheet events which concern conditions, which did not exist at the balance sheet date.

SSAP 17 is superseded by FRS 21 for accounts periods beginning on or after 1 January 2005.

### (b) Adjusting Events

These include two main categories:

(1) Events which provide additional evidence of conditions existing at the balance sheet date e.g. post balance sheet proceeds of obsolete and slow-moving stocks would help substantiate year-end stock provisions.

(2) Events which because of statutory of conventional requirements are reflected in financial statements. An example is dividends receivable from associated companies.

The financial effects of adjusting events should be reflected in the financial statements for the year under review.

In addition to the above, SSAP 17 requires adjustment of year-end amounts where a post balance sheet event indicates that the application of the going concern concept is no appropriate.

## Illustration 1

Extract from annual report and accounts of The Sage Group plc, year ended 30 September 2003.

### Note 26 – Post balance sheet events

On 24 October 2003 the Company announced that it had acquired Grupo SP, S.A., a leading provider of entry-level accounting software in Spain, for an enterprise value of £49.lm, to be paid in cash. SP had net cash of £6.6m upon acquisition, giving an equity value of £55.7m for the transaction.

On 14 November 2003 the Company completed the acquisition of the business and assets of Softline Limited ("Softline"); a company listed on the JSE Securities Exchange South Africa. The acquisition was for an equity value of £66.0 m, to be financed using the Company's existing debt facilities. Softline had net cash of £11.1m as at 31 March 2003, giving an enterprise value of £54.9m. Softline is a leading provider of business management software in South Africa and Australia.

## Illustration 2

Extract from annual report and accounts of Durlacher Corporation plc, year ended 30 June 2003.

### Note 14 – Acquisitions

On 17 March 2003 the Company acquired the entire share capital of Life Capital Limited for consideration comprising 74,000 shares in Durlacher Corporation plc, 100,000 warrants and deferred consideration contingent on future earnings. Life Capital Limited has been consolidated under the acquisition method of accounting. The following table sets out the book values of the identifiable assets and liabilities acquired and their fair value to the Group:

|  | Book value & fair value at the date of acquisition £'000 |
| --- | --- |
| Tangible fixed assets | 3 |
| Investments | 6 |
| Debtors | 3 |
| Total assets | 12 |
| Bank overdraft | (65) |
| Other creditors | (32) |
| Total liabilities | (97) |
| Net liabilities | (85) |

|                                              | £'000 |
|----------------------------------------------|------:|
| Consideration                                |       |
| Estimated deferred consideration             | 331   |
| Market value of 74,000 shares issued         | 59    |
| 100,000 warrants to subscribe for shares in  |       |
| Durlacher Corporation Plc at £1 per share    | 12    |
| Total consideration                          | 402   |
| Net liabilities acquired                     | 85    |
| Goodwill arising on acquisition              | 487   |

The deferred consideration is to be paid with cash, ranges from nil to £1.55 million and is dependent on actual revenues generated in the 18 months after acquisition by the business in force at the date of acquisition.

On the date the share warrants and shares were issued the share price was 80 pence per share.

**Post balance sheet event**

On 23 July 2003 Durlacher acquired the entire share capital of Web-angel plc. Had the transaction happened prior to the year end the consolidated balance sheet would appear as follows:

|                                         | Durlacher 30 June 2003 £'000 | Web-angel plc Date of acquisition £'000 | Durlacher Post-acquisition £'000 |
|-----------------------------------------|---------:|---------:|---------:|
| Intangible fixed assets                 | 475     | –       | 475     |
| Tangible fixed assets                   | 499     | 7       | 506     |
| Investments                             | 6       | –       | 6       |
| Total fixed assets                      | 980     | 7       | 987     |
| Current assets                          |         |         |         |
| Investments                             | 2,968   | –       | 2,968   |
| Debtors                                 | 3,065   | 4       | 3,069   |
| Cash and bank balances                  | 3,041   | 2,668   | 5,709   |
|                                         | 9,074   | 2,672   | 11,746  |
| Creditors: amounts falling due within one year | (3,904) | (314) | (4,821) |
| Net current assets                      | 5,170   | 2,358   | 6,925   |
| Total assets less current liabilities   | 6,150   | 2,365   | 7,912   |
| Creditors: amounts falling due after one year | (221) | – | (221) |
| Provisions for liabilities and charges  | (1,541) | –       | (1,541) |
| Net assets                              | 4,388   | 2,365   | 6,150   |
| Ordinary shares                         | 326     | 4,801   | 456     |
| Deferred shares                         | 28,330  | –       | 28,330  |
| Called up share capital                 | 28,656  | 4,801   | 28,786  |
| Share premium account                   | 18,072  | 331     | 17,941  |
| Capital reserve                         | –       | 608     | –       |
| Merger reserve                          | –       | –       | 3,901   |
| Profit and loss account                 | (42,340)| (3,375) | (44,478)|
| Equity shareholders' funds              | 4,388   | 2,365   | 6,150   |

Web-angel plc was purchased as a cash shell with no current trading. The goodwill on acquisition has therefore been charged to the profit and loss account in the year of acquisition. Further details of the transaction can be found in the circular recommending the offer by Durlacher for Web-angel plc.

## (c) Non-adjusting Events

The most common types of non-adjusting events are acquisitions or sales of subsidiaries, trading divisions or major investments. Share issues made or announced after the year end are a further possibility.

SSAP 17 also requires disclosure of a material post balance sheet event where it is the reversal or maturity after the year end of a transaction entered into before the year end, the substance of which was primarily to alter the appearance of the company's balance sheet (i.e. "window dressing" transaction).

# 20.2  FRS 21 – Events after the Balance Sheet Date

## (a) Overview

The objective of FRS 21 is to prescribe:

- when an entity *should* adjust its financial statements for events after the balance sheet date; and
- the disclosures that an entity should give about the date when the financial statements were *authorized for issue* and about events after the balance sheet date;
- that an entity should not prepare its financial statements on a going concern basis *if* events *after* the balance sheet date indicate that the going concern assumption is not appropriate.

The requirements remove the requirement to report proposed dividends in the profit and loss account. The ASB comments that this is "in accordance with the now generally accepted view that dividends declared after the balance sheet date should not be reported as liabilities".

Entities currently applying the FRSSE (effective June 2002) are exempt.

**FRS 21 supersedes SSAP 17 and is mandatory for accounts periods commencing on or after 1 January 2005. *Note that earlier adoption is not permitted.*** The reason is that related proposed changes to the Companies Act 1985 come into effect for accounting periods beginning on or after 1 January 2005. Compliance with the FRS before that date will not therefore be compatible with the law.

## (b) Definitions

### Events after the balance sheet date

These are defined as those events favourable and unfavourable that occur between the balance sheet date and the date when the financial statements are authorized for issue.

"Events" fall into two categories:

- Those that provide evidence of conditions that existed at the balance sheet date ("*adjusting events after the balance sheet date*"); and

- Those that are indicative of conditions that arose after the balance sheet date (*non-adjusting events after the balance sheet date*).

**When the financial statements are "authorized for issue"**

The term "authorized for issue" is not defined, but the standard notes that "...the process involved in authorising the financial statements for issue will vary depending upon the management structure, statutory requirements and procedures followed in preparing and finalising the financial statements."

The standard gives examples for determining "authorized for issue". In simple cases, the date will be when the board of directors reviews the financial statements and authorizes them for issue.

This date may well be important when dealing with the tax authorities, for example in justifying stock and bad debt provisions. FRS 21, like the existing SSAP 17, represents "UK GAAP".

## (c) Adjusting Events after the Balance Sheet Date

FRS 21 requires an entity to adjust the amounts recognized in its financial statements to reflect adjusting events after the balance sheet date.

FRS 21 gives the following examples of *adjusting events*:

- The settlement after the balance sheet date of a court case that confirms that the entity had a present obligation at the balance sheet date;
- The receipt of information after the balance sheet date confirming that an asset was impaired at the balance sheet date, or that the amount of a previously recognized impairment loss needs to be adjusted;
- The bankruptcy of a customer that occurs after the balance sheet date usually confirms that a loss existed at the balance sheet date on a trade receivable;
- The sale of inventories after the balance sheet date may give evidence about their net realizable value at the balance sheet date;
- The determination after the balance sheet date of the cost of assets purchased or the proceeds from assets sold, before the balance sheet date;
- The determination after the balance sheet date of the amount of profit-sharing or bonus payments, if the entity had a present legal or constructive obligation at the balance sheet date to make such payments as a result of events before that date [*Note – this example is not referred to in SSAP 17*];
- The discovery of fraud or errors that show that the financial statements are incorrect.

## (d) Non-adjusting Events after the Balance Sheet Date

An entity shall not adjust the amounts recognized in its financial statements to reflect non-adjusting events after the balance sheet date.

An example would be a decline in market value of investments between the balance sheet date and the date when the financial statements are authorized for issue.

FRS 21 gives the following examples of *non-adjusting events:*

- A major business combination after the balance sheet date;
- Announcing a plan to discontinue an operation;
- Major purchases and disposals of assets;
- The destruction of a major production plant by a fire after the balance sheet date;
- Announcing, or commencing the implementation of, a major restructuring;
- Major ordinary share transactions after the balance sheet date;
- Abnormally large changes after the balance sheet date in asset prices or foreign exchange rates;
- Changes in tax rates or laws enacted or announced after the balance sheet date that have a significant effect on current and deferred tax assets and liabilities;
- Entering into significant commitments or contingent liabilities;
- Commencing major litigation arising solely out of events that occurred after the balance sheet date.

The entity should not amend the balance sheet figures, although in some circumstances memorandum disclosures may be appropriate (see below).

## (e)  Dividends

This is the key area of change.

The new rule is that if an entity declares dividends to holders of *equity instruments* after the balance sheet date, the entity shall not recognize those dividends as a liability at the balance sheet date. Such dividends do not constitute a present obligation in accordance with FRS 12.

Such dividends will be disclosed in the financial statements by way of memorandum note (see example, 18.5).

## (f)  Going Concern

An entity shall not prepare its financial statements on a going concern basis if management determines after the balance sheet date either that it intends to liquidate the entity or to cease trading, or that it has no realistic alternative but to do so.

## (g) Disclosure

*Date of authorization for issue:* An entity shall disclose the date when the financial statements are authorized for issue and who gave that authorization.

*Updating disclosure about conditions at the balance sheet date:* If an entity receives information after the balance sheet date about conditions that existed at the balance sheet date, it shall update *disclosures* that relate to those conditions, in the light of new information.

*Preference shares:* The above requirement in FRS 21 does not affect those preference shares which are classified under FRS 25 as liabilities. Unpaid preference dividends due at the balance sheet date effectively represent obligations and should be included within creditors.

## 20.3   International Financial Reporting Standards

FRS 21 and IAS 10 are identical.

---

**Frequently Asked Questions**

1  What happens to proposed equity dividends for accounts periods beginning on or after 1 January 2005?
These should not be entered in the accounts until the shareholders have approved the payment of the dividend. Memorandum disclosure should be given by way of note.

2  Should bonuses be accrued if the amount to be paid is not determined until after the year-end?
Where the amount of profit-sharing or bonus payments is determined after the balance sheet date, the bonus may be accrued provided that the entity had a present legal or constructive obligation at the balance sheet date to make such payments as a result of events before that date.

3  Should revenue be included in the profit and loss account in "no win/no fee" situations where an event which confirms that the fee will be payable occurs after the balance sheet date but before the accounts are signed off?
No—the substance of the no-win, no-fee contract is that a right to consideration does not arise until the occurrence of a critical event which is outside the control of the seller. Revenue is not recognized until that event occurs (UITF Abstract 40, paragraph 19).

---

# Segmental Reporting

---

**This chapter covers:**
* Why segmental analysis is necessary
* Legal and UK Listing Authority requirements
* SSAP 25 disclosures for larger companies
* International Financial Reporting Standards

---

## 21.1 The Need for Segmental Analysis

International Accounting Standard 14 (Reporting financial information by segment) states:

> "Rates of profitability, opportunities for growth, future prospects and risks to investments may vary greatly among industry and geographical segments. Thus, users of financial statements need segment information to assess the prospects and risks of a diversified enterprise which may not be determinable from the aggregated data. The objective of presenting information by segments is to provide users of financial statements with information on this relative size, profit contribution, and growth trend of the different industries and different geographical areas in which a diversified enterprise operates, to enable them to make more informed judgements about the enterprise as a whole." [IAS 14, para 5.]

## 21.2 Companies Act 1985 Requirements

The Companies Act 1985 requires notes to accounts to give the following analyses:

(1) analysis of turnover between substantially different classes of business;
(2) analysis of profit or loss before tax between substantially different classes of business;
(3) analysis of turnover between substantially different geographical markets (determined by location of customers).

## 21.3    SSAP 25 – Segmental Reporting

SSAP 25, requires disclosure of segmental information, both by class of business segment and by geographical segment.

The disclosures specified by SSAP 25 extend well beyond those required by either the Companies Act 1985 (for all companies) or by the UK Listening Authority (for listed companies).

However, these additional disclosures are mandatory only for the following entities:

- a plc;
- an entity which has a plc as a subsidiary;
- a banking or insurance company or group;
- an entity which exceeds the criteria multiplied by 10 for defining a medium-sized company.

The full disclosures for the above entities are set out in section 21.7.

## 21.4    Terminology

SSAP 25 provides the following definitions of terms:

(a) A class of business is a distinguishable component of an entity that provides a separate product or service or a separate group of related products or services.
(b) A geographical segment is a geographical area comprising an individual country or group or countries in which an entity operates, or to which it supplies products or services.
(c) Origin of turnover is the geographical segment from which products or services are supplied to a third party or to another segment.
(d) Destination of turnover is the geographical segment to which products or services are supplied.

## 21.5    Disclosure Requirements

Entities referred to in section 21.3 above must disclose the following information:

(a) For each class of business and geographical segment:
- definition of class;
- turnover analysed between external customers and other segments;
- result before tax, minority interest and extraordinary items;
- net assets.
(b) Geographical segmentation of turnover by origin.
(c) Geographical segmentation of turnover to third parties by destination (or state, if appropriate, that this is not materially different from the figure in (b)).
(d) Where associates account for 20% or more of total results or net assets, segmental information regarding results and net assets of associates.

(e) Comparative figures (unless this is the first period for which segmental information has been provided).

(f) Where segment definitions or segment reporting policies have changed:
- nature of the change;
- reason for the change;
- effect of the change.

Previous year's figures should be restated.

## 21.6   Relaxations for Smaller Entities

Certain of the disclosures in section 21.5 above are not mandatory for smaller entities. These are:

- turnover derived from other segments;
- geographical segment analysis of results;
- analysis of net assets;
- geographical analysis of turnover by origin;
- associated company information.

The smaller entities which are exempt are entities that do not fall within any of the categories in section 21.3 above.

## 21.7   Summary of SSAP 25 Requirements

### (a) Disclosures by Classes of Business Segments: Overview

|  | "smaller" enterprises | plc's etc & "larger" enterprises |
|---|---|---|
| Definition of classes of business | M | M |
| Turnover: | | |
| total | O | M |
| Inter-segment | O | M |
| external (3rd parties) | M | M |
| Results | | |
| (before Int, Tax, MI) | M | M |
| Net assets | | |
| (FA&WC) | O | M |
| Associated undertakings (if significant): | | |
| segment results | O | M |
| net assets | O | M |

Note:
O = optional       FA = fixed assets
M = mandatory      WC = working capital

# (b) Disclosures by Geographical Segments (Markets): Overview

| | "smaller"<br>enterprises | plc's etc<br>& "larger"<br>enterprises |
|---|:---:|:---:|
| Definition of geographical segments | M | M |
| | | |
| Turnover: | | |
| by destination | | |
| external (3rd parties) | M | M |
| | | |
| by origin | | |
| total | O | M |
| inter-segment | O | M |
| external | O | M |
| | | |
| Results | | |
| (before Int, Tax, Ml) | O | M |
| | | |
| Net assets | | |
| (FA&WC) | O | M |
| | | |
| Associated undertakings | | |
| (if significant): | | |
| segment results | O | M |
| net assets | O | M |

*Note:*
O = Optional     FA = Fixed assets
M = Mandatory     WC = Working capital

## Illustration 1

Extract from annual report and accounts of Boots Group plc, year ended 31 March 2003.

**Note 1 – Segmental information**

| **(i) Turnover by business segment** | *Notes* | *2003*<br>*£m* | *2002*<br>*£m* |
|---|:---:|---:|---:|
| Health | | 1,716.4 | 1,633.5 |
| Beauty and Toiletries | | 1,891.9 | 1,770.9 |
| Other | | 676.1 | 667.7 |
| Boots The Chemists | | 4,284.4 | 4,072.1 |
| Wellbeing Services | | 262.5 | 231.0 |
| | | 4,546.9 | 4,303.1 |
| | | | |
| Boots Healthcare International | a | 430.1 | 385.5 |
| Boots Retail International | b | 35.6 | 40.3 |
| Group and other | c | 79.8 | 74.8 |
| | | | |
| Continuing operations | | 5,092.4 | 4,803.7 |
| Discontinued operation – Halfords | | 234.9 | 528.5 |
| | | | |
| **Turnover: group and share of joint ventures** | | 5,327.3 | 5.332.2 |

a  Boots Healthcare International also made inter-segmental sales of £30.3m (2002 £21.8m)
b  Boots Retail International also made inter-segmental sales of £1.4m (2002 £nil).
c  Group and other includes Boots Manufacturing third party sales of £68.1m (2002 £65.3m).

**(ii) Turnover by geographical segment**

|  | *Origin* 2003 £m | *Origin* 2002 £m | *Destination* 2003 £m | *Destination* 2002 |
|---|---|---|---|---|
| UK | **4,952.5** | 4,955.3 | **4,823.5** | 4,868.9 |
| Rest of Europe | **304.7** | 279.1 | **329.0** | 304.0 |
| Rest of World | **158.1** | 141.6 | **174.8** | 159.3 |
| Inter-segmental | **(88.0)** | (43.8) | – | – |
|  | **5,327.3** | 5,332.2 | **5,327.3** | 5,332.2 |

Included in the UK is turnover of £234.9m (2002 £528.5m) from discontinued operation – Halfords.

**(iii) Profit before interest by business segment**

|  | Notes | *Before exceptional items* 2003 £m | *Total* 2003 £m | *Before exceptional items* 2002 £m | *Total* 2002 £m |
|---|---|---|---|---|---|
| Boots the Chemist | a | **568.6** | **566.6** | 605.2 | 579.9 |
| Wellbeing Services |  | **(28.6)** | **(64.0)** | (33.1) | (33.1) |
|  |  | **540.0** | **502.6** | 572.1 | 546.8 |
| Boots Healthcare International |  | **70.1** | **70.1** | 66.7 | 56.5 |
| Boots Retail International |  | **(22.3)** | **(22.3)** | (24.1) | (35.3) |
| Group and other | b | **(66.2)** | **(58.2)** | (43.5) | (43.6) |
| Continuing operations |  | **521.6** | **492.2** | 571.2 | 524.4 |
| Discontinued operation – Halfords |  | **22.5** | **(100.7)** | 543 | 58,2 |
| **Profit before interest** |  | **544.1** | **391.5** | 625.5 | 582.6 |

a Boots The Chemists includes Digital Wellbeing Limited (DWL) operating loss of £14.7m. This includes share of joint venture loss of £11.8m (2002 £16.9m) which reflects DWL impairment of fixed assets amounting to £6.5m (2002 £nil). The comparative period also includes for the period up to 30 September 2001 bootsphoto.com losses of £17.3m, £10.4m of which was operating exceptional.

b Group and other includes £12.0m costs of rationalising the group's manufacturing facilities.

For an analysis of exceptional items see note 3.

**(iv) Profit before interest by geographical origin**

|  | *Before exceptional Items* 2003 £m | *Total* 2003 £m | *Before exceptional items* 2002 £m | *Total* 2002 £m |
|---|---|---|---|---|
| UK | **462.4** | **309.8** | 571.1 | 549.6 |
| Rest of Europe | **65.5** | **65.5** | 41.8 | 31.6 |
| Rest of World | **16.2** | **16.2** | 12.6 | 1.4 |
| **Total operating profit** | **544.1** | **391.5** | 625.5 | 582.6 |

Included in the UK is operating profit of £22.5m (2002 £54.3m) from discontinued operation – Halfords

| (v) Net assets by business segment | 2003 | 2002 |
|---|---|---|
| | £m | £m |
| Boots The Chemists | 1,811.1 | 1,714.4 |
| Wellbeing Services | 104.5 | 105.0 |
| | 1,915.6 | 1,819.4 |
| Boots Healthcare International | 418.3 | 388.6 |
| Boots Retail International | 17.6 | 26.2 |
| Other | 85.7 | 111.6 |
| Continuing operations | 2,437.2 | 2,345.8 |
| Discontinued operation – Halfords | – | 197.1 |
| Net operating assets | 2,437.2 | 2,542.9 |
| Unallocated net liabilities | (437.3) | (524.6) |
| | 1,999.9 | 2,018.3 |

Net operating assets include intangible and tangible fixed assets, investment in joint ventures, stocks, third party debtors and creditors. Unallocated net liabilities includes own shares, all taxation balances, dividend creditors and net debt.

| (vi) Net operating assets by geographical segment | 2003 | 2002 |
|---|---|---|
| | £m | £m |
| UK | 2,061.0 | 2,225.1 |
| Rest of Europe | 219.6 | 183.3 |
| Rest of World | 156.6 | 134.5 |
| | 2,437.2 | 2,542.9 |

Included in the UK are net operating assets of £nil (2002 £197.1m) from discontinued operation – Halfords.

# 21.8 International Financial Reporting Standards

IAS 14, Segment reporting, sets out disclosures required for reported business and geographical segments.

The standard is mandatory for entities whose equity shares are publicly traded, and by entities that are in the process of issuing equities in public securities markets.

The standard requires information to be reported for both business segments and geographical segments. Each entity must identify one basis of segmentation as primary and the other as secondary.

The dominant source and nature of an entity's risks and prospective returns should govern whether its primary segment reporting format will be business segments or geographical segments. Geographical segments may relate to location of production or location of customers.

In practice, business segments appear to be more frequently identified as primary than do geographical segments.

There are significant differences of detail between IAS 14 and UK GAAP SSAP 25. In some cases, SSAP 25 is more extensive than IAS 14, in other cases the reverse.

**Frequently Asked Questions**

1  Do companies using the FRSSE have to provide segment information?
   The FRSSE itself does not require segment information, but small companies are required by Schedule 8 to disclose the percentage of turnover which is exported.

2  Does CA 85 give any concessions from disclosure of segment information?
   Yes—if the directors consider that disclosures usually required would be seriously prejudicial to the interests of the company, that information need not be disclosed provided that the accounts state the *fact* that such information has not been disclosed.
   (CA 85, Sch 4, para 55)

3  Are all entities required to give disclosures relating to net assets?
   No—only Plcs, entities which exceed the criteria multiplied by 10 for defining a medium-sized company, entities which have a plc subsidiary, banks and insurance companies.

# 22 Accounting for Smaller Companies

This chapter covers:
* Overview of available exemptions
* Identifying small and medium-sized companies
* Shorter-form accounts for shareholders
* Financial Reporting Standard for Smaller Entities (FRSSE)
* Abbreviated accounts
* Audit exemption
* International Financial Reporting Standards

## 22.1 Reporting Requirements – an Overview

### (a) Companies Act 1985

The majority of CA 1985 accounting requirements apply equally to small and large companies. However, several important concessions are available for smaller companies and groups, for example:

(1) Small companies may present shareholders with a shorter form of accounts (see 22.3).

(2) Small and medium-sized companies may file abbreviated accounts of individual companies with the Registrar of Companies (see 22.7).

(3) Small and medium-sized groups may claim exemption from the preparation of group accounts (see 25.10).

(4) Most companies with a turnover not exceeding £5.6m and gross assets not exceeding £2.8m are entitled to exemption from statutory audit (see 22.12).

(5) Small companies may claim exemption from the preparation of cash flow statements under FRS 1 (see 5.1).

(6) Recent exemption referred to in 2.1(h) (6) (7) and 2.8(b).

## (b) Accounting Standards and UITF Abstracts

Small companies (as defined below for CA 1985 purposes) may adopt the Accounting Standards Board's "FRSSE" (Financial Reporting Standard for Smaller Entities), in which case they are exempt from all Standards and Abstracts. However, if a small company chooses *not* to adopt the FRSSE, it *must* follow all FRSs, SSAPs and UITF Abstracts (see 22.4(d) below).

# 22.2  Statutory Definitions

## (a) Small Company

A company is regarded as "small" for CA 1985 purposes provided it satisfies two sets of requirements:

(1) Two out of three of:
    (i) turnover not more than £5.6m
      (if the company's financial year is other than 12 months, the above limit must be adjusted proportionately);
    (ii) total assets not more than £2.8m
      (total assets means fixed assets plus current assets without deducting any liabilities);
    (iii) number of employees not more than 50.
(2) Legal status: whatever its size, a company cannot be regarded as small for these purposes if at any time during the year it falls within one of the following categories:
    (i) public company;
    (ii) banking, insurance or financial services company;
    (iii) a member of a group which includes a public company or a banking, insurance or financial services company.

*Illustration 1*

A Ltd is a small private company, part of the following group structure:

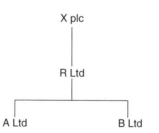

A Ltd is a member of an ineligible group (which includes X plc). A Ltd is not regarded as a "small" company for CA 1985 purposes.

## (b) Medium-sized Company

The respective limits for size are:

(i) turnover £24.8m;
(ii) total assets £11.2m;
(iii) number of employees 250.

The same considerations for legal status apply as for small companies.

## (c) Implications of Changing Size

Similar rules apply for both small and medium-sized companies. For clarity of explanation the notes below refer to small companies. The illustrative examples below, however, show the effect of changing size on the filling status of small and medium-sized companies.

A newly-incorporated company will qualify as small in its first year provided it meets the relevant criteria in that year. It will still qualify as small in year 2 even if it does not meet the size criteria in year 2.

An established company may qualify as small for abbreviated company accounts exemptions in one of four ways:

(a) small company size requirements satisfied this year and last year; or
(b) although small company size requirements not satisfied this year, they were satisfied in the two previous years (the one year of grace rule); or
(c) small company size requirements satisfied this year but not last year (however treated small last year for filing purposes on the basis of paragraph (b)); or
(d) small company size requirements satisfied last year but not this year (however, last year qualified as small as under paragraph (c)).

*Illustration 2 – long established company*

S refers to small company size.

|       | (a)   | (b)   | (c)   | (d)   |
|-------|-------|-------|-------|-------|
| 19X1  | S     | S     | S     | S     |
| 19X2  | S     | S     | S     | S     |
| 19X3  | Not S | S     | S     | Not S |
| 19X4  | S     | S     | Not S | S     |
| 19X5  | S     | Not S | S     | Not S |

The four columns refer to the four ways referred to above. In all cases, the company qualifies as small for 19X5.

## 22.3    Shorter Form of Accounts for Shareholders

### (a) Background

The Companies Act 1985 offers an opportunity for small (but not medium-sized) companies and groups. Directors may opt to circulate to shareholders a shorter form of directors' report and accounts. This exemption is quite distinct from the facility to file abbreviated accounts with the Registrar of Companies.

### (b) Minimum Information Required

For companies wishing to take maximum advantage of the concessions offered by CA 1985, the following is the minimum information which may be presented to shareholders:

(1) a shorter form of directors' report;
(2) a less detailed balance sheet;
(3) fewer notes to the accounts.

The concessions are dealt with below. Individual companies may take advantage of as many or as few of these concessions as they choose.

### (c) Special Considerations for Directors and Auditors

Where a company takes advantage of any or all of the exemptions above:

(1) The directors should make a statement immediately above the signature on the balance sheet, using wording similar to the following: These accounts have been prepared in accordance with the special provisions relating to small companies within Part VII of the Companies Act 1985.
(2) The directors' report should also include a similar statement under the heading "Small company exemption": "This report has been prepared in accordance with the special provisions of Part VII of the Companies Act 1985 relating to small companies".

### (d) Directors' Report Concessions

CA 1985 provides that certain disclosures, otherwise required in full form directors' reports maybe excluded in cases where a company has properly indicated that it has taken advantage of the exemptions.

The directors' report of a small company need not give any of the following information:

(1) a business review of the development of the business;
(2) recommended dividend and transfer to reserves;
(3) significant changes in fixed assets;
(4) for property assets, any substantial differences between market value and amount at which included in balance sheet;
(5) risk management objectives and policies;

(6) insurance effected for officers or auditors;
(7) miscellaneous disclosures:
    (i) particulars of important post-balance sheet events,
    (ii) indication of likely future developments in the business,
    (iii) indication of research and development activities.

Two other areas of disclosure would not be applicable to small companies in any event:

(1) health, safety and welfare at work disclosures;
(2) employee involvement disclosures.

## (e) The Shorter Form Balance Sheet

If a small company decides to take advantage of the exemptions, it may combine certain sub-headings which would otherwise be shown separately either on the face of the balance sheet or in the notes to the accounts.

## (f) Combined Sub-headings

"Plant and machinery", "fixtures, fittings, tools and equipment" and "payments on accounts and assets in course of construction" may be combined under a single heading: "Plant and machinery etc.".

## (g) Notes to the Accounts

A small company may take advantage of the special exemptions and *omit the following information* from the notes to the accounts:

(1) contingent right to allotment of shares;
(2) particulars of debentures issued during the year;
(3) the analysis of land and buildings between freehold/leasehold and long lease/short lease;
(4) separate disclosure of the provision for deferred tax from the provision for any other taxation;
(5) where the company has given a security in respect of creditors of the company, an indication of the nature of the securities given (para 48(4)(b)) (note that it will still be necessary to disclose the aggregate amount of the creditors for which security has been given);
(6) loans payable in more than five years – the terms of the repayment and the interest on the loan;
(7) aggregate of proposed dividends;
(8) detailed particulars of the tax charge;
(9) particulars of staff:
    (i) number employed and analysis,
    (ii) staff costs and analysis;
(10) any material difference between the stock figure in the balance sheet and the comparable figure on a replacement cost basis;

(11) analysis of turnover between different classes of business and geographical markets supplied; analysis of profit before tax between different classes of business (note that this segmented information may only be omitted if the notes disclose the percentage of turnover which has been supplied to geographical markets outside the United Kingdom—a negative statement is not required);

(12) Directors' remuneration disclosures need only include:

    (i) the aggregate of directors' emoluments and employers' pension contributions;

    (ii) the number of directors accruing benefits under either money purchase or defined benefit schemes;

    (iii) aggregate of amounts paid for compensation for loss of office.

## 22.4   The Financial Reporting Standard for Smaller Entities (FRSSE) – Overview

### (a) Who is the FRSSE Aimed at?

The FRSSE is aimed at companies which are regarded as small for *CA 1985* purposes (see 22.2 for conditions), as well as entities that would have qualified as small had they been incorporated under companies legislation.

Use of the FRSSE is optional. Companies who elect to use it are *exempt* from the requirements of Financial Reporting Standards (FRSs), Statements of Standard Accounting Practice (SSAPs) and Abstracts (issued by the Urgent Issues Task Force).

Companies who do not opt for the FRSSE *must comply in full* with all relevant FRSs, SSAPs and Abstracts.

### (b) Accounting Policy Disclosure

On implementation of FRSSE (effective June 2002), the financial statements should state that they have been prepared in accordance with the Financial Reporting Standard for Smaller Entities (effective June 2002). This should appear in the accounting policies note in both the full accounts and (where applicable) the abbreviated accounts.

*Illustration 3 – accounting policy note*

**Accounting policies – basis of accounting**

The accounts have been prepared under the historical cost convention and in accordance with the Financial Reporting Standard for Smaller Entities (effective June 2002).

### (c) Effect on Measurement of Profit or Assets?

With very minor exceptions, adopting the FRSSE will not affect the measurement of profit or assets, although it offers the opportunity of simplified calculations in some areas. The concessions offered by the FRSSE relate essentially to disclosure issues (see FRSSE, Appendix VI, "Simplifications – the FRSSE").

### (d) Transactions not Detailed in the FRSSE

Occasionally, small companies who have adopted the FRSSE will come into contact with transactions or events not dealt with in the FRSSE. Companies in this situation should "… have regard to other accounting standards and UITF Abstracts, not as mandatory documents, but as a means of establishing current practice".

For accounts periods which commenced before 1 January 2005, the "effective June 2002" version of the FRSSE must be used. For periods commencing on or after 1 January 2005, the "effective January 2005" version must be used (see 22.6).

## 22.5    Using the FRSSE – Accounting and Disclosure Issues

### (a) True and Fair View

Financial statements should present a true and fair view of the results for the period and of the state of affairs at the end of the period.

Regard should be had to the substance of any arrangement or transaction, or a series of such, into which the entity has entered. To determine the substance of a transaction it is necessary to identify whether the transaction has given rise to new assets or liabilities for the reporting entity and whether it has changed the entity's existing assets or liabilities.

The DTI is proposing to amend The Companies Act 1985 requires presentation of items within the balance sheet and the profit and loss account to have regard to the substance of the reported transaction or arrangement.

Two specific applications of this general principle dealt with in the FRSSE are consignment stock and debt factoring.

### (b) True and Fair Override

Where the true and fair override is invoked, the company should make a clear and unambiguous statement which gives:

- a statement of the treatment that would normally be required plus a description of the treatment actually adopted;
- a statement explaining why the prescribed treatment would not give a true and fair view;
- a description of how the position in the financial statements is different as a result of the departure: quantification is normally required except where quantification is already evident or whenever the effect cannot be reasonably quantified (note that directors should explain circumstances e.g. treatment of investment properties, below).

*Illustration of wording (4)*

**Extract from accounting policies note – investment properties**

Investment properties are accounted for in accordance with the Financial Reporting Standard for Smaller Entities (effective June 2002). No depreciation is provided in respect of such properties. Although the Companies Act 1985 would normally require the systematic annual depreciation of fixed assets, it is believed that this policy of not providing depreciation is necessary in order for the accounts to give a true and fair view, since the current value of investment properties, and changes in that current value, are of prime importance rather than a calculation of systematic annual depreciation. Depreciation is only one of the many factors reflected in the annual valuation, and the amount which might otherwise have been shown cannot be separately identified or quantified.

## (c) Accounting Policies

The FRSSE requires a statement that accounts have been prepared in accordance with the FRSSE. It is recommended that this statement appears *both* at the foot of the balance sheet and at the beginning of the statement of accounting policies.

There is a presumption that financial statements have been prepared in accordance with accounting principles (unless there is a statement to the contrary).

Where the relevant regulations offer a choice, companies should adopt those policies and estimation techniques that are most appropriate to its particular circumstances.

The FRSSE requires disclosure of:

- Accounting policies;
- Justification for changes in accounting policy;
- A description of any change to an estimation technique, where the effect is material. Additionally, the effect of the change on the results for the current period should be given, where practicable.

## (d) Exceptional and Extraordinary Items

*"Operating" exceptional items:* Apart from the three specified categories referred to below, all exceptional items should be included under the relevant statutory format heading and taken into account in arriving at operating profit. As an example, an abnormal loss on a long-term contract would (for companies using format 1) be included under the cost of sales expense caption.

Exceptional items may either be disclosed as a separate note or (where necessary for a true and fair view) shown separately on the face of the profit and loss account.

Each exceptional item must be adequately described so as to enable its nature to be understood.

*"Non-operating" exceptional items:* The three special cases—where exceptional items should be shown as separate line items below operating profit—are:

- Profits or losses on the sale or termination of an operation, for example the profit and loss on the sale of a business;
- Costs of a fundamental reorganization or restructuring which have a material effect on the nature and focus of the reporting entity's operations;
- Profits or losses on the disposal of fixed assets. This would include, for example, profits on the sale of freehold property but not profits and losses which are little more than marginal adjustments to depreciation previously charged.

*Extraordinary items:* The FRSSE refers to exceptional items as "extremely rare", and in practice should be avoided at all costs!

## (e) Statement of Total Recognized Gains and Losses

Where the only recognized gains and losses are those included in the profit and loss account, the FRSSE does not require a separate STRGL or any note.

Small companies adopting the FRSSE will still need a STRGL where, for example, an investment property revaluation has been reflected in the balance sheet, or where there has been a prior period adjustment in the period, to reflect a change of accounting policy.

## (f) Prior Period Adjustments

FRSSE defines these as material adjustments applicable to prior periods arising from changes in accounting policies or from the correction of fundamental errors.

Fundamental errors arise where financial statements of prior periods have been issued containing errors which are of such significance as to destroy the true and fair view and hence the validity of those financial statements.

They do not include normal recurring adjustments or corrections of accounting estimates made in prior periods.

An example of a fundamental error could include the discovery of a systems breakdown which had not been detected at the time but which came to light in the following year.

FRSSE requires prior period adjustments (PPA) to be accounted for by restating the comparative figures for the preceding period in the primary statements (i.e. balance sheet, profit and loss account, statement of total recognized gains and losses).

*Note* that only *fundamental* errors are accounted for in this way (i.e. by way of a "prior period adjustment"). Other material errors should be accounted for in the current period.

## (g) Tangible Fixed Assets

This section of the FRSSE covers all tangible fixed assets (TFAs) other than investment properties.

### (i) Capitalization of costs

Initially measure at cost, including all costs directly attributable to bringing the tangible fixed asset into working condition for its intended use.

Subsequent expenditure should be capitalized *only* if it is an improvement (enhances benefits in excess of previously assessed standard of performance), *or* replaces or restores a component that has been separately depreciated over its useful economic life.

### (ii) Subsequent write-down

Assets should be written down to recoverable amount if necessary—note that FRSSE refers to simplified impairment calculations.

### (iii) Revaluations

Where a revaluation policy has been adopted:

- Carrying amount should be market value (or best estimate thereof) at balance sheet date;
- Current value (lower of replacement cost and recoverable amount) may be used instead where directors believe market value is not an appropriate basis;
- Consistent revaluation policy required for all assets of similar nature;
- Values for certain TFAs (other than property) may be established by reference to active second-hand markets or appropriate publicly-available indices;
- Other TFAs (including properties) should be valued by an experienced valuer at least every five years and updated in the intervening years where it is likely there has been material change in value;
- Revaluation gains should be recognized in the Statement of total recognized gains and losses;
- Revaluation losses caused *only by changing market prices* should be recognized in Statement of total recognized gains and losses until carrying amount reaches depreciated historical cost.

### (iv) Depreciation

The requirements to charge depreciation should be applied to all tangible fixed assets other than investment properties.

A systematic depreciation method should be adopted, reflecting pattern of consumption of asset's economic benefits.

Tangible fixed assets which comprise two or more major components with substantially different useful economic lives should be accounted for and depreciated separately.

Useful lives and residual values should be reviewed regularly, and where adjustment is required, the carrying amount should be depreciated on a prospective basis.

The depreciation method should be changed only if new method will give a fairer presentation of results and financial position. A change in method should not be treated as a change of accounting policy. The carrying amount should be depreciated over the remaining useful life using the revised method. Disclosure is required of: effect of change on current period results; reason for change.

### (v) Disclosure implications

Give aggregate totals for (1) land and buildings (2) other tangible fixed assets of:

- Depreciation methods used;
- Useful economic lives or depreciation rates used;
- Financial effect (where material) of change during period in either estimate of useful economic lives or estimate of residual values.

## (h) Leasing

Lessee accounting principles are identical to those in SSAP 21 except that the FRSSE allows the use of the straight-line method for the allocation of finance charges.

The FRSSE requires separate disclosure of:

- Amounts relating to fixed assets held under finance leases or hire purchase – gross amounts of cost and accumulated depreciation, and aggregate depreciation charge for the period;
- The amounts of obligations related to finance leases, net of finance charges allocated to future periods;
- Operating lease payments that the lessee is committed to make during the next year, analysed into those commitments expiring within that year; those expiring in the second to fifth years inclusive, and those expiring over five years from the balance sheet date.

The FRSSE permits a number of disclosure concessions, including:

- No requirement to analyse obligations under finance leases;
- No requirement for lessees to disclose finance charges and operating lease rentals charged for the period;
- No requirement to analyse operating lease commitments between land and buildings and other operating leases.

## (i) Goodwill

Positive purchased goodwill should be capitalized and included in the fixed asset section of the balance sheet:

- The total amount should be depreciated over a period equivalent to its useful economic life, but this period must not exceed 20 years;
- The amortization charge should be taken into account in arriving at operating profit. Although not specified in the FRSSE, the annual charge would be included within administrative expenses (assuming profit and loss account format 1 is followed).

## (j) Other Intangibles (Other than Development Costs)

Intangibles purchased separately should be capitalized.

Intangibles purchased with a business should be capitalized provided that their value can be measured reliably.

Intangibles should be amortized over their economic useful life, again subject to a maximum period of 20 years.

A residual value may be built into the calculation, but only when the value can be established reliably.

## (k) Development Costs

The accounting principles are the same as those set out in SSAP 13.

The disclosure requirements are restricted to disclosing the amount of deferred development expenditure brought forward and carried forward. There is no requirement to disclose the movements during the year, or to disclose the charge to profit and loss account during the year.

## (l) Impairment

### (i) Simplification compared with FRS 11

FRS 11 is a lengthy and complex Standard. By contrast, the FRSSE deals with FRS 11—related areas extremely briefly.

One reason given by ASB for not incorporating more detailed requirements was:

> "... Formal, detailed rules regarding indications of impairment and the calculation of value in use are not as appropriate for smaller entities, by the very nature of their size. The greater flexibility allowed under the FRSSE enables smaller entities to use simpler calculations where appropriate, given that detailed projections are often not readily available and that in many cases the income-generating unit will be the entity itself. This approach should be more cost-beneficial..."

### (ii) FRSSE requirements

The FRSSE specifies rules for writing assets down to recoverable amount. The assets to which these rules apply include capitalized goodwill, tangible fixed assets (other than investment properties), intangible fixed assets and investments in subsidiaries.

Recoverable amount (RA) of an asset is defined as the higher of the amounts that can be obtained from:

- selling the asset – net realizable value (NRV), and
- continuing to use the asset in the business – value in use (VIU).

VIU is calculated as the present value of the future cash flows obtainable as a result of the asset's continued use, or a reasonable estimate of these.

Fixed assets and goodwill should be carried in the balance sheet at no more than RA. Write down will be required if the net book amount is considered not to be recoverable in full at the balance sheet date. This may be due to factors such as obsolescence or a fall in demand for a product.

A write down from net book amount to estimated recoverable amount will normally be charged to profit and loss account in determining operating profit.

The estimated recoverable amount should be depreciated over the goodwill or asset's remaining useful economic life.

## (m) Provisions and Contingencies

### (i) General requirements

The key rule is that a provision should be recognized when it is probable that a present obligation exists as a result of a past event, and that it will require a transfer of economic benefits in settlement that can be estimated reliably.

- Amount recognized should be the best estimate of the expenditure required to settle the obligation at the balance sheet date;
- Expenditures required to settle the obligation should be discounted to present value where the effect of discounting would be material;
- Where discounting is used, the unwinding of the discount should be included in the profit and loss account as a financial item, separately disclosed from interest (see discounting calculation in FRSSE, Appendix III);
- Where some or all of the expenditure required to settle a provision may be reimbursed by another party, the reimbursement should be recognized as a separate asset only when it is virtually certain to be received if the entity settles the obligation;
- Provisions should be reviewed at each balance sheet date and adjusted to reflect the current best estimate.

### (ii) Disclosure implications

There are no specific disclosure requirements included in the FRSSE, so requirements are contained in CA 1985.

### (iii) Contingent liabilities

Disclosure of the following is required except where the existence of the contingent liability is remote:

- A brief description of the nature of the contingent liability;
- An estimate of its financial effect (where practicable).

## (n) Current Taxation

The general rule on presentation is the same as for FRS 16—current and deferred tax should be recognized in the profit and loss account. The only exception is where the tax relates to a gain or loss dealt with in the Statement of total recognized gains and losses (for example, a prior year adjustment).

The FRSSE's disclosure requirements are less detailed than the equivalents in FRS 16. The key disclosure required by the FRSSE is to disclose separately the material components of the current and deferred tax charge or credit for the period.

The FRSSE omits much of the detail in FRS 16, for example requirements relating to tax rates for measurements purposes, and income and expenses subject to non-standard rates of tax.

## (o) Deferred Tax

### (i) General requirement

Consistent with the principles of FRS 19, the FRSSE requires deferred tax to be provided in full. This requirement is subject to a number of simplifications and relaxations compared with FRS 19.

### (ii) Measurement

The FRSSE states that deferred tax should not be recognized on either of the following:

- Revaluation gains and losses unless, by the balance sheet date, the entity has entered into a binding agreement to sell the asset and has revalued the asset to the selling price, or
- Taxable gains arising on revaluations or sales if it is more likely than not that the gain will be rolled over into a replacement asset.

The rules on recognition of deferred tax assets are similar but less detailed than those in FRS 19. The FRSSE states:

> "Unrelieved tax losses and other deferred tax assets should be recognised only to the extent that it is more likely than not that they will be recovered against the reversal of deferred tax liabilities or other future taxable profits (the very existence of unrelieved tax losses is strong evidence that there may not be "other taxable future profits" against which the losses will be relieved)".

In practice, recognition of deferred tax assets under the FRSSE should be no less onerous than under FRS 19. Users of the FRSSE may find relevant paragraphs of FRS 19, for example 28–30, helpful in applying the above requirements.

Other measurement issues dealt with in the FRSSE include:

- Deferred tax should be measured at the average tax rates that would apply when the timing differences are expected to reverse, based on tax rates and laws that have been enacted by the balance sheet date.

### (iii) Disclosures

As regards general disclosure issues, the FRSSE requirements are far less detailed than those in FRS 19 and specify disclosure of:

- The deferred tax balance and its material components;
- Movement between the opening and closing net deferred tax balances, with the movement analysed between its material components.

One specific requirement should be noted. Where assets have either been revalued in the accounts, or their market values disclosed in a note to the accounts, the FRSSE requires disclosure of the amount of tax that would be payable or recoverable if the assets were sold at the values shown.

*(iv) Circumstances affecting current and future tax charges*
The FRSSE continues to require disclosure of "... any special circumstances that affect the overall tax charge or credit for the period, or may affect those of future periods...".

This disclosure requirement is less onerous than the requirements set out in FRS 19. For example, FRS 19, paragraph 64(a) requires disclosure of "... a reconciliation of the current tax charge ... to the current tax charge that would result from applying a relevant standard rate of tax to the profit on ordinary activities before tax".

## *(p) Capital Instruments*

Much of the material in FRS 4 has been excluded from the FRSSE.
The FRSSE refers to:

- Principles for classifying financial instruments;
- Allocation of finance costs so as to reflect a constant rate on the carrying amount;
- Determination of the borrowings figure in the balance sheet;
- Treatment of arrangement fees.

## *(q) Related Party Transactions*

The FRSSE is very similar to FRS 8 (see Chapter 19).
The following must be disclosed:

- The identity of the controlling party or ultimate controlling party where these are not known (although the fact must be disclosed)
- The names of the transacting related parties
- A description of the relationship between the parties
- A description of the transactions
- The amounts involved
- Any other elements of the transaction necessary for an understanding of the financial statements
- The amounts due to or from related parties at the balance sheet date and provisions for doubtful debts due from such parties at that date
- Amounts written off in the period in respect of debts due to or from related parties
- Personal guarantees given by directors in respect of borrowings by the reporting entity.

The main concession compared with FRS 8 relates to materiality. The FRSSE does not require disclosure of transactions which are not material in terms of significance to the reporting entity, even if they are material to the other party.

## (r) Retirement Benefits

### (i) Recognition in the accounts

The cost of a defined contribution scheme equals the contributions payable to the scheme in respect of the period—whether the scheme is a self administered fund or takes the form of individual contracts with an insurance company.

The cost should be charged in arriving at operating profit.

### (ii) Disclosures

- The nature of the scheme (defined contribution);
- The cost for the period;
- Any outstanding prepaid contributions at the balance sheet date.

The FRSSE also requires disclosure of each material accounting policy.

### Illustration 5

**Pension costs**

The company contributes to defined contribution pension policies on behalf of the directors and certain other employees. The assets of the scheme are held separately from those of the company in independently administered funds. The pension cost charge in the accounts represents contributions payable by the company during the year.

### Illustration 6

**Pension costs**

The company makes contributions to personal pension schemes on behalf of directors and certain employees. The amount charged to the profit and loss account represents the amounts contributed during the period.

### (iii) Defined benefit (final salary) schemes

The ASB considers that relatively few small companies use defined benefit schemes. Consequently, the main body of the FRSSE does not include detailed rules for defined benefit schemes. Instead, companies with such schemes are referred to Appendix II of the FRSSE entitled "Accounting for retirement benefits: defined benefit schemes", which effectively represents simplified version of FRS 17.

# 22.6 Using the FRSSE (Effective January 2005) – Accounting and Disclosure Issues

## (a) Overview

The latest version of the FRSSE extends the existing content in the June 2002 version to incorporate the accounting requirements of companies legislation applicable to smaller companies (as amended by Statutory Instrument 2947).

The content has also been updated to reflect various changes in accounting standards and Abstracts since the publication of the June 2002 version, including UITF Abstract 40 on Revenue recognition and service contracts.

**The revised FRSSE is effective for accounting periods beginning on or after 1 January 2005. For legal reasons, earlier adoption is not permitted.**

## (b) Main Changes

The key areas of change relate to:

- Events after the balance sheet date (effect of FRS 21) – particularly regarding the treatment of equity dividends declared after the balance sheet date;
- The treatment of equity dividends paid;
- The new Companies Act 1985 requirement to have regard to the substance of a reported transaction or arrangement;
- Capital instruments (effect of FRS 25);
- Revenue recognition (Application Note G to FRS 5 and UITF Abstract 40);
- Start-up costs (UITF Abstract 34 on Pre-contract costs);
- Inclusion of Balance sheet and Profit and loss account formats;
- Inclusion of related CA 85 valuation rules and disclosure requirements;
- Inclusion of Directors' report disclosures.

New requirements (as opposed to the inclusion of existing CA 85 requirements) are referred to below.

## (c) Standards and Abstracts not Incorporated in the Revised Version

The requirements of the following standards and Abstracts have not been reflected in the proposed FRSSE revisions:

- FRS 20, Share-based payment;
- UITF Abstracts 31–33; 35-39.

## (d) Fair Value Accounting

The revisions to CA 85 introduces the option to fair value financial and certain other assets. The fair value rules for financial instruments will be dealt with in UK GAAP by means of a new standard FRS 26, Financial instruments: Recognition and measurement, based on IAS 39.

ASB has stated that it does not propose to introduce the fair value options into the FRSSE at this stage.

## (e) Events after the Balance Sheet Date

The revised FRSSE has amended the material previously included in the FRSSE.

The FRSSE states: "If an entity declares dividends after the balance sheet date, the dividends shall not be recognised as a liability at the balance sheet date" (paragraph 12.6).

This change in practice will come into effect in UK GAAP for financial years commencing on or after 1 January 2005 in line with FRS 21 and CA 85 changes. Early adoption is prohibited.

### (f) Having Regard to the Substance of a Reported Transaction or Arrangement

The new FRSSE incorporates the new Companies Act requirement to have regard to the substance of a reported transaction or arrangement, in determining how to present items in the profit and loss account and balance sheet.

One example of the impact of this requirement is that many preference shares will be shown as a liability in the balance sheet, and the related dividend payment as a finance cost in the profit and loss account (see "financial instruments", below).

### (g) Financial Instruments

In line with the above changes to the Companies Act 1985, a new standard, FRS 25, Financial instruments: Disclosure and presentation, will be introduced into UK GAAP. This will supersede much of FRS 4, Capital instruments.

Amended paragraphs 12.1 requires a financial instrument to be classified in accordance with the substance of the contractual arrangement rather than its legal form.

Amended paragraph 12.6 requires dividends relating to a financial instrument that is a financial liability to be recognized as expense in profit or loss.

Dividends paid to holders of equity shares must be debited direct to equity.

### (h) Revenue Recognition

The FRSSE incorporates the principles set out in paragraphs G4–G12 of Application Note G to FRS 5 (AN G).

Appendix III, paragraphs 29 to 34, also includes the "Consensus" part of Abstract 40 on Revenue recognition and service contracts (see Chapter 8, 8.4 for examples).

### (i) Start-up Costs

The existing section under this heading has been extended to include material on pre-contract costs, taken from UITF Abstract 34.

## 22.7    Abbreviated Accounts

### (a) Filing Concessions

Under the Companies Act 1985, smaller companies (as defined) may file less information with the Registrar of Companies than larger companies.

Smaller companies fall into two categories, each with a separate set of concessions. These categories are small and medium-sized respectively.

### (b) Qualifying Conditions

The Companies Act 1985 definitions of "small" and "medium-sized" were referred to in 22.2 above.

### (c) Parent Companies

A parent company will only be treated as small for CA 85 purposes if the group which it heads up is small.

### (d) Small Company Abbreviated Accounts

The minimum information which may be filed by a small company is as follows:

(1) A balance sheet in abbreviated form, containing only items designated in the formats by letters or roman numerals.
(2) Notes relating to the following matters:

- accounting policies;
- share capital;
- particulars of allotments of shares and debentures;
- particulars of debts
  - payable in more than five years
  - debts which are secured;
- loans and transactions with directors and officers;
- information on subsidiaries;
- ultimate parent company;
- movement on fixed assets;
- basis of translation of foreign currency amounts into sterling; corresponding figures.

*Note*: A small company need not file a profit and loss account, a directors' report and information regarding directors' emoluments.

## 22.8    Small and Medium-sized Groups

Exemption from the preparation of group accounts is dealt with in Chapter 25, section 25.10.

## 22.9    Concessions Offered by Particular Accounting Standards

As indicated above, small companies who adopt the FRSSE are exempt from all Standards and Abstracts.

For small companies who do *not* adopt the FRSSE, the following limited concessions are available.

### (a) FRS 1 (Cash Flow Statements)

Small companies (i.e. companies entitled to file abbreviated accounts as small companies) may claim exemption from preparing a cash flow statement.

### (b) FRS 2 (Accounting for Subsidiary Undertakings)

Small and medium-sized groups may claim exemption from the preparation of group accounts (see 25.10). FRS 2 merely repeats the exemption offered by the Companies Act 1985.

### (c) FRS 3 (Reporting Financial Performance)

No exemptions are offered to smaller companies as such. However, the circumstances of many such companies are such that certain FRS 3 disclosures will not be required.

### (d) SSAP 13 (Research and Development)

Certain of the disclosure requirements relating to total research and development expenditure need not be applied by an entity that:

(1) is not a plc or a special category company under s 257 (essentially banks and insurance companies); and
(2) satisfies the medium-sized company criteria multiplied by a factor of 10.

### (e) SSAP 25 (Segmental Reporting)

Small and medium-sized companies are exempt from several of the disclosure requirements of SSAP 25, segmental reporting (see 21.3).

### (f) FRS 14 (Earnings Per Share)

FRS 14 is mandatory for listed companies only.

## 22.10  Legal Considerations

### (a) Accounting Concessions

The concessions for shorter-form accounts, abbreviated accounts and group accounts exemption were referred to above.

## (b) Disclosure Concessions – Further Considerations

The Companies Act 1989 introduced a new requirement for companies to state in their accounts whether the accounts have been prepared in accordance with applicable accounting standards. Companies which depart from accounting standards will be required to disclose:

- particulars of any material departure from those standards;
- reasons for the departure.

Small and medium-sized private companies, as defined by the 1985 Act, are exempt from the above disclosure requirements.

Small and medium-sized companies are not required to disclose fees paid to their auditors for work other than audit work.

## (c) Filing of Accounts

All private companies (not just those which are small or medium-sized) have ten months to file accounts, compared with seven months for plcs.

## (d) Loans to Directors

The rules for loans to directors are less stringent for private companies than for plcs. These are not dealt with in this text.

## (e) Distributable Profit Rules

The rules for private companies are less stringent than those for plcs.

## (f) Share Purchases

Private companies are permitted to purchase or redeem shares out of capital, subject to compliance with CA 1985 requirements (see 18.6(g)).

# 22.11    Parent Companies

A parent company will only be treated as "small" for abbreviated accounts purposes if the group it heads up is small.

# 22.12    Audit Exemption

Certain small companies are entitled to exemption from audit. The size thresholds were increased for accounts periods on or after 30 March 2004, subject to special transitional arrangements. The main conditions in outline are:

- Turnover must not exceed £5.6m, and total assets (fixed assets plus current assets) must not exceed £2.8 million – this requirement is applied to each year for which exemption is claimed.

- As well as the above, the company must also be a small company under CA 1985 – this means, for example, that an established company must have satisfied the small company criteria for two consecutive years (see 22.2(c) above).

A small company which was a plc at the beginning of the year but which during the year converted to a private company would not be entitled to exemption (it does not satisfy the condition in 22.2(a) (2) above).

- Audit exemption is not available to certain categories such as financial services companies or unlisted plcs.
- A company must have an audit if requested by shareholders holding at least 10% of the share capital.
- Parent companies and subsidiaries that are part of a "very small group" are exempt from audit. Group turnover must not exceed £6.72m on a gross basis or £5.6m on a net (i.e. after elimination of inter-company items) basis. Limits for total assets are £3.36m on a gross basis, or £2.8m on a net basis.
- Exemption is automatically available to the majority of dormant companies an important change is the relaxation in the definition of "significant accounting transactions". This means that the payment of certain registration fees and late filing penalties will not result in a company losing its dormant status.

## 22.13   International Financial Reporting Standards

International Accounting Standards Board (IASB) proposes to issue SME standards—exposure drafts are expected in 2006. These are likely to focus mainly on disclosure concessions compared with full IFRS.

---

**Frequently Asked Questions**

1  Can a small unlisted PLC (turnover £1.5m and assets £800K) adopt the FRSSE?
No—it does not meet the CA 85 requirements for a small company.

2  Is a small company which uses the FRSSE exempt from the requirements of UITF Abstract 40 on revenue recognition?
No—although a FRSSE company is technically exempt from all UITF Abstracts, the requirements of UITF 40 are contained in the new version of the FRSSE for accounts periods ending on or after 1 January 2005.

3  Does a small company adopting the FRSSE have to disclose operating leasing commitments?
Yes—but it is not required to distinguish between commitments relating to land and buildings and other leasing commitments.

# Listed Company Reporting

**This chapter covers:**
* Who sets the rules?
* Companies Act 1985 changes
* Operating and Financial Review (OFR)
* Directors' Remuneration Report
* International Financial Reporting Standards (IFRS) specific to listed companies

## 23.1 Introduction

The purpose of this chapter is to provide a brief overview of the specific reporting requirements applicable to companies whose shares are publicly traded, and to indicate where the relevant rules can be found.

This book does not deal with the extensive reporting requirements specific to listed companies. For further information and commentary, reference should be made to detailed texts on the various subjects.

## 23.2 Fully Listed or AIM – Who Makes the Rules?

### (a) UKLA

Fully listed companies are subject to the Listing Rules of the Financial Services Authority, the UK Listing Authority—often referred to as the "Purple Book". This "book" is now in the form of a CD Rom. A key chapter of the Listing Rules is Chapter 9 on Continuing Obligations.

The London Stock Exchange is an EU "Regulated Market" and falls within the IAS Regulation (see Chapter 7 and below).

## (b) AIM Rules – the Alternative Investment Market

These are set by the London Stock Exchange and effectively make AIM an exchange regulated market, outside the scope of the IAS Regulation (see below).

## (c) The "IAS Regulation"

In June 2002, EU Member States adopted the Regulation on the Application of International Accounting Standards (*the "IAS Regulation"*).

---

This requires companies governed by the law of a Member State to prepare their *consolidated* accounts in conformity with international accounting standards if their securities are admitted to trading on a regulated market of any Member State. In the UK, this will apply to consolidated accounts of fully listed companies.

---

The IAS Regulation applies to each financial year *commencing on or after 1 January 2005.*

For example, a *fully* listed group with a 31 March year-end will have to apply IFRS to its full-year accounts to 31 March 2006.

## (d) The Financial Reporting Council (FRC)

FRC (see 2.2) is responsible for issuing and updating the Combined Code on Corporate Governance. The Code is available in pdf format on www.frc.org.uk/corporate.

# 23.3   Members of a Listed Group – UK GAAP or IFRS?

CA 85 requires the directors to ensure that the individual accounts of the parent company and each of its subsidiary undertakings are all prepared using the same financial reporting framework, except to the extent that in their opinion are good reasons for not doing so.

This allows a number of possible combinations including:

- Consolidated accounts, parent company accounts and all UK subsidiaries prepared under IFRS;
- Consolidated accounts under IFRS; parent company and all UK subsidiaries prepared under UK GAAP;
- Consolidated accounts and parent company accounts under IFRS and all UK subsidiaries prepared under UK GAAP.

See the DTI's *"Guidance for British Companies on Changes to the Reporting and Accounting Provisions of the Companies Act 1985", paragraphs 4.13 to 4.16).*

# 23.4    Directors' Remuneration – Additional Considerations

## (a) Companies Act 1985 Requirements

These were referred to in Chapter 9 and apply to all companies, listed and unlisted. However, certain concessions are available for small companies, whilst additional requirements apply to listed companies.

Illustrations of listed company disclosures, which reflect both Companies Act 1985 and requirements appear below.

## (b) Directors' Remuneration Report

CA 85, Section 234B requires the directors of a fully listed company to prepare a directors' remuneration report containing the information set out in Schedule 7A of CA 85. The disclosure requirements are extensive, covering almost 8 pages.

Key disclosure areas required include company policy on directors' remuneration and detailed information relating to each director on the following areas:

- Details of directors' services contracts;
- Detailed analysis of total remuneration;
- Share option details;
- Long-term incentive scheme details;
- Directors' pension provisions.

# 23.5    Operating and Financial Review (OFR)

## (a) Accounting Standards Board Statements

Follow the DTI's announcement in December 2005 to repeal the statutory requirement for an OFR, the Accounting Standards Board replaced Reporting Standard 1 with a Best Practice Reporting Statement.

## (b) Structure of RS 1

The statement contains:

- General principles;
- Disclosure framework;
- Key performance indicators (KPI);
- Practical implementation guidance.

The implementation guidance includes examples of a large number of KPIs. (The Reporting Statement is available on the FRC website).

## (c) The Disclosure Framework

The key elements of the disclosure framework are:

- The nature of the business (including a description of the market, competitive and regulatory environment and the objectives and strategies of the entity);
- The development and performance of the business – current year and in the future;
- Resources, principal risks and uncertainties and relationships that may affect long-term value;
- Position of the business, including description of capital structure; treasury policies and objectives; liquidity – current year and in the future.

## (d) The Companies Act 1985 (Operating and Financial Review and Directors' Report, etc.) Regulations 2005 [Statutory Instrument 2005 No. 1011]

The Regulations when issued made the OFR mandatory for fully listed companies. The rules were intended to be mandatory for financial years beginning on or after 1 April 2005.

The Government subsequently decided that it would no longer require quoted companies to produce an Operating and Financial Review, and that Regulations to repeal this requirement would come into effect on 12 January 2006.

The Regulations as revised will require all entities (other than small companies) to include a Business Review as part of the Directors' Report (see 2.8). For most listed companies, in practice the required information will be incorporated within an OFR.

The SI requires the OFR to state whether it has been prepared in accordance with relevant reporting standards (i.e. ASB's Reporting Standard 1). RS 1 states that "Compliance with this Reporting Standard will be presumed to constitute compliance with the [SI]".

In addition, the OFR must state whether it has been prepared in accordance with relevant reporting standards (i.e. ASB's Reporting Standard 1).

In the case of a quoted company, a directors' report need not contain any information included in the OFR.

# 23.6   Financial Reporting Review Panel (FRRP)

The activities of FRRP are referred to in Chapter 2 (Section 2.14).

## 23.7 International Financial Reporting Standards Specific to Listed Companies

### (a) IAS 14

IAS 14 sets out disclosures required for reported business and geographical segments. (see 21.8) The standard is mandatory for entities whose equity shares are publicly traded, and by entities that are in the process of issuing equities in public securities markets.

### (b) IAS 33 – Earnings per Share

The standard is mandatory for entities whose ordinary shares or potential ordinary shares are publicly traded, and entities that are in the process of issuing ordinary shares or potential ordinary shares in public markets.

An entity is required to present basic and diluted earnings per share (EPS) on the face of the income statement, with equal prominence for all periods presented.

EPS should be based on profit or loss from *continuing operations*, attributable to the ordinary equity holders of the parent entity.

Where an entity reports a *discontinued operation*, it is required to disclose basic and diluted EPS for the discontinued operation, either on the face of the income statement, or in the notes to the financial statements.

In addition to basic and diluted EPS measured in accordance with IAS 33, an entity may disclose amounts per share based on a reported component of the income statement. Basic and diluted amounts per share *relating to such a component* shall be disclosed with equal prominence and presented *in the notes* to the financial statements (not on the face of the income statement).

### (c) IAS 34 – Interim Financial Reporting

The standard sets out minimum content requirements for an interim financial report and principles for recognition and measurement.

It does not mandate which entities should be required to publish interim financial reports. It applies if an entity either chooses or is required to publish an interim financial report (for example, by the UK Listing Authority).

**Frequently Asked Questions**

1 Is the Combined Code on Corporate Governance mandatory for AIM companies?
No—the Purple Book Rules apply only to fully listed companies. However, AIM companies may adopt the Rules as best practice.

2 What is the reporting status of OFEX companies?
Technically speaking OFEX companies are treated as unlisted, although certain standards such as FRS 22 apply to companies whose shares are publicly-traded and these covers OFEX companies. OFEX companies may provide additional disclosures on a voluntary basis as a matter of best practice.

**Useful Website Addresses**

www.londonstockexchange.com
www.frc.org.uk
www.fsa.gov.uk
www.opsi.gov.uk
www.dti.gov.uk

# Limited Liability Partnerships

## 24.1   Introduction

### (a) Introduction

The Limited Liability Partnerships Act came into force on 6 April 2001, permitting a new form of corporate business association—the Limited Liability Partnership ("LLP"). Any new or existing firm of two or more persons can incorporate as an LLP.

Companies House describes the vehicle as "an alternative corporate business vehicle that gives the benefits of limited liability but allows its members the flexibility of organizing their internal structure as a traditional partnership".

Apart from tax considerations, the name of the vehicle is somewhat misleading—it is closer to a limited liability company than a partnership. The LLP is a separate legal entity offering limited liability to its members.

In an LLP, the equivalent of director is known as a "designated member" (see 24.2 (b) below).

The aim of this chapter is to provide an overview, and businesses considering this form of vehicle should seek appropriate legal and tax advice.

### (b) Overview of Legal and Tax Consideration

(1) *Legal status*
Similar to a limited company, an LLP can own its own assets (which can be the subject of fixed and floating charges) and enter into contracts.

Its members, in principle, have limited liability when acting on behalf of the LLP. Contractual claims by third parties will be against the LLP and not against its members.

(2) *Registration*
An LLP must be registered at Companies House using a prescribed form with a statutory fee. A certificate will then be issued by the Registrar. This certificate has the same effect as a company's Certificate of incorporation.

(3) *Members' agreement*
Members are advised to draw up an express written agreement. Should the members fail to draw up an agreement, the Limited Liability Partnerships Act 2000 effectively provides a default set.

The agreement is a private, but extremely important document for the benefit of the Members. It does not have to be registered at Companies House.

(4) *Tax*
LLPs are taxed quite differently from private companies. Whilst companies are assessed to corporation tax as separate legal entities, the members of LLPs are taxed as if in a partnership.

# 24.2    Legal and Administrative Matters

## (a) Members

The members are the people named on the incorporation document when the LLP is formed. The LLP must have at least two members.

Changes in membership (appointments and terminations of appointment) must be notified to the Registrar within 14 days of the change.

## (b) Designated Members

The LLP must have at least two "designated members". The incorporation document must say either:

- the partnership has specified individual designated members, or
- all members are designated members.

Changes of status must be notified to the Registrar.

## (c) Responsibilities of Designated Members

"Designated members" have the same rights and responsibilities towards the LLP as any other member. However, designated members are specifically responsible for:

- Appointing an auditor where one is needed (see below – a very small LLP may be entitled to audit exemption in the same way as a limited company)

- Signing the accounts on behalf of the members
- Delivering the accounts to the Registrar
- Notifying the Registrar of any changes of membership, address of registered office or name of the LLP
- Preparing, signing and delivering an annual return to the Registrar
- Acting on behalf of the LLP if it is wound up and dissolved.

# 24.3   Accounts and Audit

## (a) Accounting Records

LLPs are required to keep proper accounting records in the same way as limited companies.

## (b) Accounting and Disclosure Requirements

### (1) Introduction

An LLP is subject to the accounts and audit provisions of the Companies Act 1985, as modified by the Limited Liability Partnership Regulations 2001 (SI 2001/1090).

In May 2002, the Consultative Committee of Accountancy Bodies (CCAB) published a Statement of Recommended Practice (SORP) (see 24.4 below). An exposure draft of an amended SORP was published in September 2005 (see 24.6 below).

### (2) Content of accounts

These should comprise:

- A profit and loss account,
- A balance sheet signed by a designated member,
- An auditors' report (unless audit exemption is claimed),
- Notes to the accounts.

### (3) Profit and loss account

The profit and loss account must be drawn up in accordance with CA 1985 formats.

One exception to this—the line "Profit or loss for the financial year" is replaced by "Profit or loss for the financial year before members' remuneration and profit shares".

### (4) Balance sheet

In the normal CA 1985 balance sheet format, "capital and reserves" will be replaced by "members' interests and reserves". Details of aggregate movements on these will have to be given, disclosing:

- Capital contributed by members of the LLP,
- Money advanced to the LLP by members by way of loan,
- Money owed to members of the LLP in respect of profits,

- Any other amounts contributed to the LLP by its members,
- Aggregate of amounts contributed by members,
- Aggregate of amounts withdrawn by members.

*(5) Accounting standards*

LLP accounts will purport to give a true and fair view, and hence accounting standards will apply. This means, for example, that LLPs will have to give the disclosures required by FRS 8, Related party disclosures (see 24.4(g)).

*(6) Approval and signing*

The accounts must be approved by the members of the LLP and signed before they are sent to Companies House.

The balance sheet must be signed by a designated member.

Any statement concerning accounting, filing or audit exemptions (see below) must appear above this signature.

## (c) Filing of Accounts

Accounts must be filed with the Registrar within 10 months of the Accounting Reference Date.

## (d) Exemptions and Concessions

Concessions and exemptions in CA 1985 which are available to small and medium-sized companies are also available to small and medium-sized LLPs.

For example, a small LLP may draw up accounts for its members using the disclosure concessions in Part VII of CA 1985. It may also file with the Registrar abbreviated accounts consisting of an abbreviated balance sheet, notes and a special auditor's report (assuming the LLP is not audit exempt).

The size conditions are the same. For example, to qualify as a small LLP two of the following must be satisfied:

- annual turnover must be £5.6m or less,
- total assets (i.e. fixed assets plus current assets) must be £2.8m or less,
- average number of employees must be 50 or fewer.

The rules where company size changes from year to year are as in CA 1985 (see 22.2(c)).

The exemption from preparing consolidated accounts is also available to small and medium-sized groups headed up by an LLP. Essentially, the usual CA 1985 rules apply.

## (e) Audit Implications

LLPs will be subject to the same audit requirements as private limited companies. A small LLP may qualify for audit exemption—as for companies the LLP's annual turnover must not exceed £5.6m. Qualifying conditions are the same as for companies including appropriate statements above the signature of the designated member.

Auditors must be appointed annually by the designated members:

- The LLP's first auditor must be appointed before the end of the financial year for which they are appointed.
- In subsequent years the auditor must be appointed or re-appointed within two months of the approval of the accounts for the preceding financial year.

# 24.4  Statement of Recommended Practice (SORP)

## (a) Introduction

The Statement of Recommended Practice was issued in May 2002 by the Consultative Committee of Accountancy Bodies (CCAB).

A special feature of this SORP is that it applies to a new form of legal entity rather than to a specific industry or sector.

The preface to the Statement refers to the following as examples of trades or professions with member firms expected to seek LLP status:

- accountancy and legal professions,
- construction industry.

The SORP includes details, definitions, rules and interpretations and should be referred to in all practical applications.

## (b) Relationship to Accounting Standards

The SORP is intended to complement and not to replace SSAPs, FRSs and UITF Abstracts and should be read in conjunction with them.

In the event of a conflict, the standards and Regulations take precedence over the SORP.

## (c) Terminology

The SORP contains 11 different definitions. Three of particular importance are set out in summary form below:

| | |
|---|---|
| *Salaried remuneration of members* | Remuneration that is payable to a member such that it falls to be treated as a charge against profits and not an allocation of profits because it is an obligation which the members can claim from the LLP without any decision or agreement to divide profits having been taken. |
| *Allocated profit* | Profits allocated as a result of members deciding on a division of profits. |

| Unallocated profit | Profits that have been ascertained but not allocated because no decision has been made to divide them up. <br> Shown on balance sheet under "other reserves" pending decision to divide the profits among the members. |
|---|---|

## (d) Contents of the Annual Report

### (1) Financial statements

The contents will depend on whether the LLP is entitled to and takes advantage of the exemptions for small and medium-sized LLPs.

Subject to this, the financial statements will comprise:

- a profit and loss account (or, if applicable, a consolidated profit and loss account),
- a statement of total recognized gains and losses,
- a cash flow statement,
- a balance sheet (and, if applicable, a consolidated balance sheet),
- notes to the financial statement.

### (2) Other elements

These include:

- Statement of members' responsibilities,
- Report by a registered auditor (unless LLP claims audit exemption),
- Principal activities,
- Existence of branches outside the UK,
- Identity of designated members.

## (e) Format Issues – Profit and Loss Account

The main part of the profit and loss account will follow the same format as for a limited company.

However, the Regulations require the profit and loss account to disclose a total entitled "Profit or loss for the financial year before members" remuneration and profit shares' (this is the LLP equivalent of "profit or loss for the financial year").

The bottom part of the profit and loss account should appear as follows:

| | |
|---|---|
| [income less expenses] | X |
| Profit or loss for the financial year before members' remuneration and profit shares | X |
| Salaried remuneration of members | X |
| Profit or loss for the financial year available for division among members | X |

The ED of the SORP proposes changes to the above (see 24.6)

## (f)  Format Issues – Balance Sheet

The part of the CA 1985 balance sheet format dealing with "Capital and reserves" is replaced by the following items specific to LLPs. These must be shown separately on the face of the balance sheet:

- Loans and other debts due to members.
- Members' other interests – showing separate sub-totals for:
  - members' capital,
  - revaluation reserve,
  - other reserves.

Note that the SORP requires the balance sheet to disclose the net assets of the LLP. This is achieved by showing a sub-total of items from fixed assets down to "Loans and other debts due to members".

The items above should correspond to a specific note showing the movement on Members' interests—paragraph 31 of the SORP illustrates a detailed format which complies with the recommendations of the SORP.

Referring back to the definitions in 24.4(c) above, allocated profits are transferred from "Members" other interests' to "Loans and other debts due to members" whilst unallocated profits are included within "other reserves".

The ED of the SORP proposes changes to the above (see 24.6).

## (g)  The Application of Generally Accepted Principles to LLPs

The SORP deals in detail with recommendations and detailed guidance for each of the following issues:

### (1)  Retirement benefits payable to former members

- The requirement is for a provision to be set up at the date of the members' retirement in accordance with FRS 12.
- The provision should be based on the present value of the best estimate of the expected liability for future payments.
- The liability should be calculated in accordance with the principles of FRS 17.

### (2)  Taxation

Tax paid on members' remuneration is a personal liability of the members and should not be disclosed in the profit and loss account.

Such tax should be reflected within members' interests on the balance sheet.

### (3)  Stocks, long-term contracts and income recognition

- For stocks, the basic principle is that the cost of members' time and related overheads should be accounted for in accordance with SSAP 9, Stocks and long-term contracts.
- As regards calculating the cost of members' time involved in producing stock, the only elements which should be considered are those which would

be expensed in the profit and loss account. An example would be salaried members' remuneration.

- Long-term contracts should be accounted for in accordance with SSAP 9.

*(4) Merger and acquisition accounting*

- This section refers to a number of scenarios and considers the principles of FRS 6 in relation to each.
- The basic rule is that the accounting treatment for business combinations which include one or more LLPs should have regard to the substance of the combination.
- Acquisition accounting should be used when the conditions set out in FRS 6 to use merger accounting are not met. This could apply, for example, when one LLP acquires another.
- On the other hand, referring to group reconstructions, the SORP says:

> "The transfer of all or the majority of the assets, liabilities and business of a partnership into an LLP incorporated for that purpose should be dealt with as a group reconstruction except where the requirements of paragraph 13 of FRS 6 are not met, after taking account of the legal differences of an LLP. The intitial "opening" balance sheet should follow the accounting policies of the LLP."

- Further guidance is given in paras 76–81 of the SORP, dealing with "Considerations on transition from an existing partnership".

*(5) Provisions and other implications of FRS 12*

- LLPs should follow the principles of FRS 12.
- The comment is made that "... applying it fully may require a significant change in practice for existing partnerships that are incorporated as an LLP...".

*(6) Related parties*
The general requirements of FRS 8 apply.

## *(h) Legal Opinion*

The CCAB has obtained legal opinion on a number of matters relating to the profits of an LLP. This opinion is set out in Appendix 1 to the SORP.

## 24.5   Summary – Comparisons with Unlimited Partnerships and Limited Companies

|  | Unlimited partnerships | Limited liability partnership | Limited company |
|---|---|---|---|
| *Legislation* | Partnership Act 1890 | Limited Liability Partnership Act 2000 | Companies Act 1985 (as amended) |
| *Legal status* | No separate legal status apart from its members.<br><br>Partnership property must be held by specific partners on behalf of the partnership. | Separate legal entity which is not affected by changes in its membership.<br>May contract, sue and be sued in its own name and capacity.<br><br>Can hold property in its own right. | Separate legal entity which is not affected by changes in its membership.<br>May contract, sue and be sued in its own name and capacity.<br><br>Can hold property in its own right. |
| *Constitutional document* | Partnership agreement desirable – default provisions apply in absence of express provision. | Members' *agreement* desirable – default provisions apply in absence of express provision. | Memorandum and Articles are mandatory. |
| *Taxation status* | Partners assessed to income tax. | Members assessed to income tax. | Company assessed to corporation tax. |
| *Statutory book requirement* | No statutory requirement. | Mandatory. | Mandatory. |
| *Requirement to file accounts* | No statutory requirement. | Mandatory – file within 10 months of year-end. | Mandatory – file within 10 months of year-end. |
| *Audit requirement* | No statutory requirement. | Mandatory – unless entitled to audit exemption. | Mandatory – unless entitled to audit exemption. |
| *Management* | All partners can take part in management of business and enter into legally binding contract. | Every member can take part in the management of the business (but note "designated members") | Rights of management are delegated to directors who alone can act on behalf of and bind the company. |
| Liability of members | Unlimited. | Liability of each member is limited. | For limited liability company, liability limited to amount member has agreed to pay company for shares. |

## 24.6  Exposure Draft of Proposed Revised SORP

### (a) Introduction

The Consultative Committee of Accountancy Bodies (CCAB) issued an Exposure Draft of a SORP on Limited Liability Partnership on 30 September 2005 (see ICAEW website, TECH 56/05).

### (b) Changes Proposed to Existing SORP

The changes proposed to the May 2002 version result mainly from the issue of: FRS 25 – Financial instruments: Disclosure and Presentation; UITF 39 – Members' shares in cooperative entities and similar instruments; UITF 40 – Revenue recognition and service contracts. The ED also revisits post-retirement payments to former members.

　　The ED contains an Appendix with illustrative examples of balance sheets and profit and loss accounts (with numbers), with both "old" (pre-FRS 25/ UITF 39) presentation and "new" presentation. These illustrate the impact of significant changes regarding the presentation of Members' Interests in the balance sheet, and Members' remuneration in the profit and loss account.

### (c) Effective Date

Paragraph 94 states:

> "This SORP should be applied for accounting periods ending on or after 31 March 2006. Earlier application is encouraged. It should be noted that accounting standards should be applied from their mandatory date of application, which may be  earlier than the application date of the SORP".
>
> [Footnote 13 comments: "For example, FRS 25 applies to accounting periods beginning on or after 1 January 2005"]

## 24.7  International Financial Reporting Standards

There is no IFRS equivalent of the SORP—it is a purely UK legal vehicle.

　　However, the exposure draft of the SORP published on 30 September 2005 reflects international accounting developments recently incorporated into UK GAAP.

**Frequently Asked Questions**

1  Does an LLP have a choice of profit and loss account formats?
Yes—the same choice as for companies. However, the LLP SORP (including amendments proposed 30 September 2005) modifies the formats to reflect expense items which relate solely to SORPs (for example, Members' Remuneration).

2  Can LLPs use the FRSSE?
Yes—provided that they satisfy the small sized criteria.

3  Is a LLP with a turnover of £3m and assets of £2m entitled to audit exemption?
Yes—the qualifying criteria are identical to those for limited companies.

**Useful Website Addresses**

www.companies-house.gov.uk—for pdf of booklets: GBLLP1, GBLLP2, GBLLP3.

www.icaew.co.uk—for exposure draft of SORP (issued 30/9/05).

# 25 Accounting for Subsidiary Undertakings

## 25.1 Requirement to Prepare Consolidated Accounts

FRS 2 requires a parent undertaking to prepare consolidated accounts unless it claims one of the three exemptions referred to below. The consolidated accounts should include all subsidiary undertakings, consolidated on a line-by-line basis.

FRS 2 essentially adopts the definitions of parent undertaking and subsidiary undertaking introduced by the Companies Act 1985.

## 25.2 Definitions – Parent Undertaking and Subsidiary Undertaking

In the explanation below, "A" refers to the parent undertaking whilst "B" refers to the subsidiary undertaking.

An undertaking (A) is deemed to be a parent undertaking of another undertaking (B) in any of the five following cases:

(a) A holds a majority of the voting rights in B;
(b) A is a member of B and has the right to appoint or remove directors holding a majority of the voting rights at board meetings;

(c) A has the right to exercise a dominant influence over B;

(d) A is a member of B and controls alone, following an agreement with other shareholders or members, a majority of voting rights in B;

(e) A has a participating interest in B and either actually exercises a dominant influence over B or, A and B are managed on a unified basis. Note that a participating interest is a shareholding of at least 20%.

In practice most parent undertaking/subsidiary undertaking relationships are likely to fall within the first case i.e. whether or not A holds a majority of the voting rights in B. This case is also extended to sub-subsidiaries.

Situation (e) has also arisen in practice, but only in a small number of instances.

## 25.3    "Dominant Influence" and "Managed on a Unified Basis"

FRS 2 includes the following definitions:

### (a) Dominant Influence

Influence that can be exercised to achieve the operating and financial policies desired by the holder of the influence, notwithstanding the rights or influence of any other party.

a In the context of paragraph 14(c) and section 258(2)(c) *the right to exercise a dominant influence* means that the holder has a right to give directions with respect to the operating and financial policies of another undertaking with which its directors are obliged to comply, whether or not they are for the benefit of that undertaking.

b *The actual exercise of dominant influence* is the exercise of an influence that achieves the result that the operating and financial policies of the undertaking influenced are set in accordance with the wishes of the holder of the influence and for the holder's benefit whether those wishes are explicit. The actual exercise of dominant influences is identified by its effect in practice rather than by the way in which it is exercised.

### (b) Managed on a Unified Basis

Two or more undertakings are managed on a unified basis if the whole of the operations of the undertakings are integrated and they are managed as a single unit. Unified management does not arise solely because one undertaking manages another.

This definition does not include companies which are under common ownership only. There must be a connecting shareholding: one company must have a participating interest (i.e. a shareholding of at least 20%) in the other—see section 25.2(e) above.

## (c) Amendment to FRS 2

ASB issued a Press Notice in December 2004 indicating the following amendments to FRS 2:

- A change in the law, deleting references to "participating interest" in the definition of a subsidiary undertaking and introducing "the power to exercise or actually exercise, dominant influence and control";
- Extension of the exemption from the preparation of consolidated accounts for intermediate parent undertakings whose immediate parents are not governed by the law of an European Economic Area State; and
- Removal of the requirement for exclusion from consolidation of subsidiaries with dissimilar operations to the parent undertaking.

The amendment is effective for accounts periods commencing on or after 1 January 2005.

# 25.4    Accounting Policies

The consolidated accounts should be prepared on the basis of consistent accounting policies. This consistency may be achieved by either:

- using identical policies for all companies in the group; or
- putting through adjustments at the consolidation stage to ensure that the consolidated accounts reflect uniform and consistent policies.

In exceptional cases, it may be impracticable to use consistent policies. The Companies Act 1985 then requires disclosure of:

- particulars of the departure (which should refer to the different accounting policies used);
- the reasons for the departure;
- the effect of the departure.

# 25.5    Intra-group Items

## (a) Balances, Income and Expenses

Inter-company balances and inter-company income or expense items should be eliminated on consolidation.

## (b) Unrealized Profits

Profits or losses on inter-company transfers of assets should be eliminated in full to the extent that such assets are included in the consolidated balance sheet.

The amount of profit or loss eliminated should be allocated between group ownership and minority interest according to the ownership in the company which recorded the profit or loss.

# 25.6　Accounting Dates

## (a) Preferred Situation

Wherever practicable, all group companies should use the same accounting periods and year ends.

## (b) Permitted Alternatives

Where this is not possible, two alternative procedures may be applied:

(1) the option preferred by FRS 2 – the use of interim accounts prepared to the parent undertaking's accounting date;
(2) if (1) is not practicable – using the subsidiary undertaking's accounts made up to an earlier date, provided that is not more than three months earlier than the parent's balance sheet date.

## (c) Interim Accounts

### Illustration 1

Group accounts are to be prepared covering the year to 31 December 19X4. A particular overseas subsidiary has a 30 September year end. The results of the subsidiary may be included as follows:

(1) nine months' proportion of the audited annual accounts to 30 September 19X4;
(2) three months' specially prepared accounts up to 31 December 19X4;
(3) it will also be necessary to prepare an interim balance sheet at 31 December 19X4, purely for consolidation purposes.

### Illustration 2

**Extract from accounting policies**

*Basis of consolidation*
(i) The Group accounts consolidate those of the Company and its subsidiary undertakings for the period of 52 weeks (53 weeks when necessary) ending on the Sunday nearest 30 April, except that the Directors do not consider it appropriate for legal and fiscal reasons to change the accounting date of Frères Jacques SA from 31 December and so special financial statements have been prepared.

## (d) Consolidation at Different Dates

### Illustration 3

Suppose that the 30 September 19X4 accounts of a subsidiary are to be consolidated with the accounts of the remainder of the group made up to 31 December 19X4. Adjustments should be made for "abnormal transactions" arising in the three months to 31 December 19X4.
　There are two categories of such transactions which may require adjustment:

(1) significant (but normal) transactions with other group companies, for example, in the situation referred to earlier, a significant remittance of cash on 30 November 19X4 to the parent company;

(2) events such as major changes in exchange rates, major trade losses, and significant can fixed asset sales or discontinuance of business activities.

*Note:* ((b) above) the maximum gap permitted by the Companies Act 1985 between the parent's balance sheet date and the earlier date for the subsidiary is three months.

### Illustration 4

Extract from accounting policies.

**Basis of consolidation**

The Group accounts incorporate the accounts of West Cliff plc and its subsidiary undertakings. The accounts have been prepared for the period ended 30 September 19X5 except that the accounts of the overseas rental companies have for administrative reasons been prepared for the year ended 31 August 19X5; with account taken of any significant transactions in the intervening period.

FRS 2 and the Companies Act 1985 also specify additional disclosures for option (b)(2) relating to the particular subsidiary undertakings concerned. For each such subsidiary, the following should be disclosed:

- its name;
- its accounting date or period;
- the reasons for using a different accounting date or period for it.

# 25.7   Exclusion from Consolidation

## (a)  Where Exclusion of a Subsidiary from Consolidation is Mandatory

FRS 2 requires a subsidiary to be excluded from consolidation where:

(1) severe long-term restrictions substantially hinder the exercise of the rights of the parent undertaking over the assets or management of the subsidiary undertaking;
(2) the interest in the subsidiary undertaking is held exclusively with a view to resale and the subsidiary undertaking has not previously been consolidated;
(3) the subsidiary undertaking's activities are so different from those of other undertakings to be included in the consolidation that its inclusion would be incompatible with the obligation, to give a true and fair view.

The Standard makes it clear that exclusion on the grounds of different activities is likely to be rare. It takes the view that the usual approach will be for consolidation combined with segmental information possibly giving more information than that required by SSAP 25.

## (b)  Accounting and Disclosure

The Standard includes detailed requirements for both accounting and disclosure—these are outside the scope of this text.

From a practical viewpoint, exclusion from consolidation will usually be relevant only for certain larger quoted companies.

### Illustration 5 – held exclusively with a view to resale

**Accounting policies (extract)**

*Basis of consolidation*
The consolidated accounts have been prepared under the historical cost convention as modified by the revaluation of certain fixed assets and in accordance with applicable UK accounting standards.

A number of subsidiaries acquired as part of the acquisition of Portals Group plc have been excluded from consolidation because they are held exclusively with a view to subsequent resale. These subsidiaries, listed on page ..., are recorded as assets held for disposal within current assets and are held at the Directors' valuation of anticipated net sale proceeds discounted to their present value at the balance sheet date. These subsidiaries have retained a year end of 31 December.

The results of all of the other subsidiaries of the Company have been consolidated.

**Extract from balance sheet**

|  | *19X5* *Group* *£m* | *19X4* *Group* *£m* | *19X5* *Company* *£m* | *19X4* *Company* *£m* |
|---|---|---|---|---|
| **Fixed assets** | | | | |
| Tangible assets | 179.7 | 116.0 | 16.9 | 17.3 |
| Investments | 79.3 | 53.2 | 830.8 | 381.4 |
|  | 259.0 | 169.2 | 847.7 | 398.7 |
| **Current assets** | | | | |
| Stocks | 87.4 | 75.6 | – | – |
| Debtors | 179.2 | 117.9 | 14.4 | 29.1 |
| Assets held for disposal | 160.0 | – | – | – |
| Cash at bank and in hand | 106.4 | 375.3 | 13.3 | 259.6 |
|  | 533.0 | 568.8 | 27.7 | 288.7 |

**Note 13**

*Assets held for disposal*
Assets held for disposal represents the Group's investment in those companies listed as "Businesses held for resale" on page.... These companies, all of which were subsidiaries of Portals Group plc when the Group acquired Portals Group plc, are held exclusively with a view to resale. They are held at the Director's valuation of anticipated net sales proceeds discounted to their present value at 31 March 19X5.

## (c) Disproportionate Expense or Delay

A final point is that the Companies Act 1985 permits exclusion from consolidation where the information necessary for the preparation of group accounts cannot be obtained without disproportionate expense or delay.

It is important to note that FRS 2 does not permit this ground for exclusion for subsidiary undertakings that are individually or collectively material in the context of the group.

## 25.8    Minority Interests

### (a)  General Requirements

(1)  The aggregate of the minority interest proportion of net assets or liabilities of subsidiary undertakings should be separately disclosed in the consolidated balance sheet.
(2)  The consolidated profit and loss account should show separately:
  (i)  the aggregate of the profit or loss on ordinary activities attributable to minority interests;
  (ii)  the aggregate of any extraordinary profits or losses attributable to minority interests (this will usually be shown by way of note).

### (b)  Loss-making Subsidiaries

In cases where the company is still in a satisfactory position, the effect on the minority interest is:

(1)  In the consolidated profit and loss account, ignoring any other subsidiaries, the minority interest share of the loss will appear as a figure in brackets.
(2)  In the consolidated balance sheet, the minority interest will be equivalent to a percentage of net assets of the subsidiary. However, if a company continues to lose money, the minority interest in successive consolidated balance sheets will diminish.

### (c)  Subsidiaries with Negative Equity Interest

(1)  The first issue is whether a subsidiary with a negative equity interest (debit balance on reserves in excess of share capital) should be consolidated?
  (i)  If the going concern assumption can be justified, the subsidiary should be consolidated. To justify this, it will be necessary to demonstrate parent company guarantees, injections of fresh finance and so on.
  (ii)  If the parent company intends to abandon the subsidiary and to allow it to go into liquidation, it would be misleading to consolidate. It would, of course, be important to ensure the parent company had made adequate provision for previous guarantees given in respect of the subsidiary.
(2)  Suppose the going concern assumption is justified and the company is partly owned. How should minority interest be treated for consolidation purposes?

FRS 2 requires the group to make provision for 100% of the deficiency to the extent that it has any commercial or legal obligations to provide finance that may not be recoverable from the minority in respect of their share of the deficiency.

However, the explanation section to FRS 2 indicates that the normal route should be to recognize a debit balance for minority interest. The group should only provide for this debit balance in cases where it has a commercial or legal

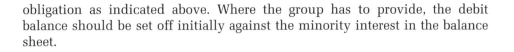

obligation as indicated above. Where the group has to provide, the debit balance should be set off initially against the minority interest in the balance sheet.

## 25.9 Individual Profit and Loss Account of Parent Company

A parent company which prepares group accounts need not publish its own profit and loss account provided the following conditions are satisfied:

(a) the individual profit and loss account must be approved by the board of directors;
(b) the group accounts must be prepared in accordance with the requirements of CA 1985 (as amended);
(c) the company's individual balance sheet must show by way of note the company's profit or loss for the financial year determined in accordance with CA 1985;
(d) the company's accounts must disclose the fact that the relevant exemption applies.

## 25.10 Exemptions from the Preparation of Group Accounts

### (a) Grounds for Exemption

Groups are exempt from preparing consolidated accounts in any of the following three cases:

(1) small and medium-sized groups (as defined by CA 1985);
(2) certain groups which are part of a larger group for which consolidated accounts are prepared (the EU parent exemption).

Both of the above exemptions are optional – full statutory consolidated accounts may be prepared if desired. Detailed conditions are set out in CA 1985.

(3) Groups which include only subsidiary undertakings falling into categories for which exclusion from consolidation is mandatory per FRS 2. These categories are: severe long-term restrictions and held exclusively with a view to subsequent resale.

Subsidiaries with different activities will usually be included in the consolidation.

## (b) Exemptions for Small and Medium-sized Groups

### (1) Definition of "small" and "medium-sized"

For accounting periods ending on or after 30 January 2004, the size thresholds have been increased. A group is counted as "small" if it satisfies two out of three of the following:

Turnover
- net                              £5.6m
- gross                            £6.72m

("Gross" means the aggregate of turnover figures for all group companies ignoring consolidation adjustments.)

Total assets
- net                              £2.8m
- gross                            £3.36m

(Again, "gross" is before taking account of consolidation adjustments; total assets is fixed assets plus current assets, before deducting any liabilities.)

Aggregate number of employees      50

For a medium-sized group, the respective figures are:

Turnover
- net                              £22.8m
- gross                            £27.36m
Total assets
- net                              £11.4m
- gross                            £13.68m
Employees                          250

**Note that the Company Law Reform Bill indicates that the Government intends to remove the exemption for medium-sized groups.**

In addition, to qualify for exemption the group must not be ineligible. Irrespective of size, a group is regarded as ineligible if any of its members is:

- a plc or a body corporate with the power to issue shares to the public;
- a banking company;
- an insurance company;
- an authorized person under the Financial Services Act 1986 i.e. a Financial Services Company.

### (2) Disclosure requirements

A parent company which claims exemption from the preparation of group accounts should give the following disclosures for each of its subsidiary under-takings:

- name, country of incorporation/registration, nature of business;
- classes of shares, proportion held;
- capital and reserves at the year-end;
- profit or loss for the year.

A parent company is also required to disclose the aggregate amount of its total investment in the shares of subsidiary undertakings. This amount is determined according to the equity method of valuation (see Chapter 27).

*Illustration 6*

XYZ Company Ltd
BALANCE SHEET (EXTRACT)

|  | 19X8 | 19X7 |
|---|---|---|
|  | £ | £ |
| Investments (at cost) | 322,000 | XX |

**Notes to the accounts (extract)**

*(i) Accounting policies*
Consolidation

1  The company has claimed exemption under Section 248 of the Companies Act 1985 from the preparation of group accounts on the grounds that the group is small/medium-sized.
2  The accounts present information about (parent) Ltd as an individual undertaking and not about its group.

*(ii) Investments*
Investments are stated at cost. The details of subsidiary undertakings are as follows:

| Name | Country of incorporation or registration | Class of shares held | Proportion % held | Capital and reserves at 31.12.X3 | Profit for year ended 31.12.X3 |
|---|---|---|---|---|---|
|  |  |  |  | £ | £ |
| A Ltd | England | Ordinary | 100 | 250,000 | 35,000 |
| B Ltd | England | Ordinary | 80 | 90,000 | 14,000 |

[Note: the required comparatives are not reproduced]

The disclosure in note 2, under consolidation, is required by FRS 2 (see (d) below).

In addition to the above, the profit and loss account and balance sheet formats set out in CA 1985, Sch 4 require separate disclosure of items such as:

• Income from shares in (group undertakings);
• Shares in (group undertakings);
• Loans to (group undertakings);
• Amounts owed by (group undertakings);
• Amounts owed to (group undertakings).

All of these items may be relegated to the notes to the accounts.

*(3) Filing requirements*

Where the above exemption applies, directors may be able to choose between:

• filing full group accounts; and
• filing individual accounts for the parent company and subsidiaries. In the case of these individual accounts the minimum required to be filed will depend on whether the company concerned is small or medium-sized.

A subsidiary may file abbreviated accounts as a small company provided it is small in size and is not a member of an ineligible group.

A parent company may only file abbreviated accounts as a small company if the group which it heads up is small.

### Illustration 7

A Ltd claims exemption from the preparation of group accounts on the grounds that the group is medium-sized.

The group structure and company size is as follows. For simplicity only turnover figures are given.

A Ltd (turnover £3.9m)

B Ltd
(turnover £1.5m)

C Ltd
(turnover £1.5m)

B Ltd and C Ltd may file abbreviated accounts as small companies.

Although A Ltd appears to be small, it is in fact classified by CA 1985 as medium-sized because the group it heads up has a turnover of £6.9m (i.e. 3.9 + 1.5 + 1.5) and thus exceeds the small company turnover of £2.8m (ignoring the asset and employee criteria).

### Illustration 8

P Ltd claims exemption from the preparation of group accounts on the grounds that the group is medium-sized. The group structure and company size are as follows:

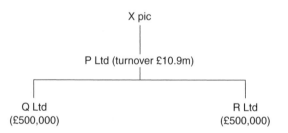

X plc

P Ltd (turnover £10.9m)

Q Ltd
(£500,000)

R Ltd
(£500,000)

P Ltd is entitled to the exemption as the combined size of P, Q and R is within the medium-sized threshold and the P group does not include any ineligible companies. However, none of P, Q and R can file abbreviated accounts as they are all members of an ineligible group (i.e. a group which includes a plc, X).

## (c) EU Parent (Part of a Larger Group) Exemption

### (1) Situations

The EU parent situation relates to certain parent companies included in the accounts of a larger group. In particular situations, an intermediate parent company whose own immediate parent is established under the law of a member state of the EU may be exempt from the requirement to prepare group accounts.

The situations are:

(i) where the company is a wholly owned subsidiary of that EU parent undertaking;
(ii) where that EU parent undertaking holds more than 50% of the shares in the company and where shareholders holding either more than 50% of the remaining shares in the company or 5% of the total shares in the company have not served notice requiring the preparation of group accounts.

*Illustration 9*

A  S.A. (French company)

100%

B  Ltd (incorporated in GB)

60%

C  Ltd (incorporated in GB)

B Ltd may be exempt from the requirement to prepare group accounts.

*(2) Conditions*

The exemption will only be given if detailed conditions are satisfied and additional disclosures given. In relation to the illustration above:

(i) B Ltd must be part of a consolidation of a larger group whose immediate parent (A S.A.) is established under the law of a member state of the EU.
(ii) The accounts of the A group are drawn up and audited in accordance with the law of the relevant country (i.e. France in the above illustration).
(iii) B Ltd in its individual accounts states:
  – that it is exempt from the obligation to prepare and deliver group accounts;
  – the name of the parent undertaking drawing up the consolidated accounts (i.e. A S.A.) and its country of incorporation.
(iv) B Ltd delivers to the Registrar a copy of the consolidated accounts of the larger group. If these are in a language other than English it is necessary to attach in addition a copy of those accounts translated into English.
(v) The parent company claiming the exemption must be an unlisted company.

### (3) Disclosures

The disclosure requirements are similar to those in (b) (2) above except that it is not necessary to disclose profit and loss for the financial year, and capital and reserves.

In addition, it is not necessary to give the aggregate amount of investments under the equity method of valuation provided the directors state that in their opinion the aggregate amount of the parent company's investment in the subsidiaries concerned does not exceed the related underlying assets.

The exemption will only be given if detailed conditions are satisfied and additional disclosures given. In relation to the illustration above:

  (i) B Ltd must be part of a consolidation of a larger group whose immediate parent (A S.A.) is established under the law of a member state of the EU.

 (ii) The accounts of the A group are drawn up and audited in accordance with the law of the relevant country (i.e. France in the above illustration).

(iii) B Ltd in its individual accounts states:
 - that it is exempt from the obligation to prepare and deliver group accounts;
 - the name of the parent undertaking drawing up the consolidated accounts and its country of incorporation.

(iv) B Ltd delivers to the Registrar a copy of the consolidated accounts of the larger group. If these are in a language other than English, it is necessary to attach in addition a copy of those accounts translated into English.

 (v) The parent company claiming the exemption must be an unlisted company.

## (d) Further Disclosure Requirements

Where a parent undertaking claims exemption from preparing group accounts for one of the three reasons referred to in (a) above, it must disclose by way of note:

(1) a statement that its accounts present information about it as an individual undertaking and not about its group; and

(2) a note of the grounds on which the parent undertaking is exempt from preparing consolidated accounts.

In addition, if the parent company claiming the exemption is itself part of a larger consolidation, it should disclose:

(1) the name of the parent undertaking of the largest group which includes P for which group accounts are prepared;

(2) the name of the parent undertaking of the smallest group which includes P and for which group accounts are prepared.

# 25.11    Significant Restrictions on Distributions

## (a)  FRS 2 Requirements

FRS 2 deals with cases where the parent undertaking's access to distributable profits is materially limited by significant statutory, contractual or exchange control restrictions on a subsidiary's distributions. FRS 2 requires disclosure of the nature and extent of the restrictions.

## (b)  Situations

Most of the situations envisaged are likely to relate to overseas subsidiaries, although situations involving UK subsidiaries could include:

(1)  profits capitalized by a subsidiary (for example, a bonus issue out of post-acquisition profits – see section 23.15);
(2)  post-acquisition profits which have been applied by a subsidiary against its pre-acquisition losses (see below).

## (c)  Example

The balance sheets of H Ltd and its wholly owned subsidiary, S Ltd at 31.12.X2 are as follows:

|  | H Ltd £ | S Ltd £ |
|---|---|---|
| Investment in S Ltd | 144 | – |
| Net assets | 1,156 | 340 |
|  | 1,300 | 340 |
| Called-up share capital | 1,000 | 200 |
| Profit and loss account | 300 | 140 |
|  | 1,300 | 340 |

At acquisition, the debit balance on S's reserves amounted to £32.

The usual consolidation procedures would calculate group revenue reserves as follows:

|  | £ |
|---|---|
| Reserves of H | 300 |
| Post-acquisition reserves of S (32 + 140) | 172 |
|  | 472 |

However, it would be misleading to include this amount without an accompanying note stating that of this amount, £32 was not available for distribution. This makes sense since the maximum dividend which S could pay would be £140 and this would have the effect of increasing H's reserves to £440.

## (d)  Note

### Illustration 10

**Note 33 – reserves (part of note)**

The Group profit and loss account includes £367.5m (19X2 – £344.7m) in respect of subsidiaries and associated companies operating overseas which, if distributed as dividends, would involve liabilities to additional United Kingdom taxation as reduced by appropriate double taxation relief and, in certain territories, additional overseas taxation. The funds representing the reserves of subsidiaries operating overseas are in the main permanently employed in the business and are unlikely to be distributed as dividends. Remittances from certain territories in which subsidiaries and associated companies operate require the permission of the exchange control authorities in those territories.

# 25.12    International Financial Reporting Standards

IAS 27, Consolidated financial statements and accounting for investments in subsidiaries, sets out the basic requirement for a parent company to present consolidated financial statements. These should consolidate investments in subsidiaries in accordance with the detailed requirements of the standard.

The inclusion of subsidiaries is based on the concept of consolidating financial statements of a group of entities under the control of a parent. Control is defined as the power to govern the financial and operating policies of an entity so as to obtain benefits from its activities (similar to UK GAAP).

IAS 27 does not deal with methods of accounting for business combinations and goodwill arising on a business combination—this is dealt with in IFRS 3.

Certain parent companies which are part of a group preparing consolidated financial statements, are exempt from presenting consolidated financial statements provided that they satisfy a number of very detailed conditions, including:

- Either the parent is itself a wholly-owned subsidiary *or* is a partially-owned subsidiary of another entity whose other owners do not object to the entity not preparing consolidated accounts;
- The parent debt or equity instruments are not publicly-traded ;
- The parent's ultimate parent (or any intermediate parent of the parent) produces consolidated financial statements available for public use.

Although IAS 27 does not refer to exemption from the preparation of group accounts for qualifying SME groups, this exemption will continue to be available under Section 248 of the Companies Act 1985.

---

**Frequently Asked Questions**

1 Can consolidated accounts include the results of subsidiaries made up to dates which are non-coterminous with the rest of the group?
Yes—although FRS 2 and Companies Act 1985 prefer coterminous year-ends "wherever practicable", they offer two options in respect of non-coterminous year-ends:
Preferably, interim financial statements for the subsidiary(ies) made up to the reporting date of the parent. Where this is not practicable, financial statements of subsidiaries made up to earlier dates (provided not more than three months earlier than the parent's reporting date) may be used.

**Frequently Asked Questions—cont'd**

2 Is it permitted to exclude from consolidation subsidiaries with activities which are dissimilar from the rest of the group?

In practice "no". CA 85, Section 229(4) requires exclusion from consolidation where the subsidiaries' activities are so different from those of the rest of the group that their inclusion would be incompatible with the obligation to give a true and fair view. However, the subsection concludes by stating that this does not apply "merely because some of the undertakings are industrial, some commercial and some provide services...".

In practice, the view taken today is that the issue is best solved by consolidating all subsidiaries and providing segmental information.

3 Under UK GAAP, can a parent company credit a dividend received from a subsidiary, paid out of pre-combination profits, to its profit and loss account?

Yes—except to the extent that it is necessary to provide for a diminution in the value of the investment in the subsidiary undertaking.

# Acquisition Accounting, Fair Values and Business Disposals

**This chapter covers:**
* Consolidation methods
* Date control passes
* Features of acquisition accounting
* Fair values – measurement and disclosures
* Merger reserve
* Changes in stake
* Share disposals
* Merger accounting
* International Financial Reporting Standards

## 26.1  Accounting for Business Combinations

### (a) Introduction

FRS 6, Acquisitions and mergers, sets out detailed criteria for determining the appropriate consolidation method for particular business combinations.

Those business combinations which satisfy the merger criteria must be accounted for using the merger accounting method of consolidation. FRS 6 anticipates that very few business combinations will satisfy the merger criteria. Merger accounting is dealt with in 26.10 below. No further reference to it is made in this chapter.

FRS 6 states that: "business combinations not accounted for by merger accounting should be accounted for by acquisition accounting ..."

### (b) Changes in the Composition of a Group

The phrase "changes in the composition of a group" can refer to purchases or sales of shareholdings in subsidiary undertakings.

A key point is the date of change. An undertaking becomes a subsidiary undertaking on the date when control passes to its new parent. An undertaking ceases to be a subsidiary undertaking on the date on which its former parent undertaking relinquishes its control.

Control is the ability of an undertaking to direct the financial and operating policies of another undertaking with a view to gaining economic benefits from its activities.

*Illustration 1*

**Accounting policies (extract)**

*Basis of consolidation*
The consolidated profit and loss account and balance sheet include the financial statements of the company and its subsidiary undertakings (subsidiaries) made up to 30 September. The results of subsidiaries sold or acquired are included in the profit and loss account up to, or from, the date control passes.

### (c) Becoming a Subsidiary Undertaking

Where an undertaking becomes a subsidiary undertaking the appropriate date will be the date of acquisition or the date of merger in accordance with the Companies Act 1985. The accounting treatment and disclosure requirements FRS 6 and the Companies Act 1985 are dealt with in this chapters.

### (d) Ceasing to be a Subsidiary Undertaking

Where an undertaking ceases to be a subsidiary undertaking, the consolidated profit and loss account should include:

(1) the results of the subsidiary undertaking up to the date that it ceases to be a subsidiary undertaking;
(2) any gain or loss arising on cessation (to the extent that these have not been already provided for in the consolidated accounts). (See section 26.8 below.)

## 26.2 Features of Acquisition Accounting

FRS 6 includes the following key features of acquisition accounting:

(a) identifiable assets and liabilities of the companies acquired should be included in the acquirer's consolidated balance sheet at fair value at date of acquisition;
(b) results and cash flows should be brought in from the date of acquisition;
(c) previous year figures for the reporting entity should not be adjusted;
(d) the difference between:
   (i) the fair value of the net identifiable assets acquired; and
   (ii) the fair value of the purchase consideration;
      is positive or negative goodwill.

## 26.3  Fair Values and Acquisition Accounting

### (a)  Definition

Fair value is defined by FRS 7 as the amount at which an asset or liability could be exchanged in an arm's length transaction between informed and willing parties, other than in a forced or liquidation sale.

### (b)  Fair Values and Goodwill Measurement

FRS 7 refers to positive or negative goodwill as the difference between:
• the cost of acquisition, and
• the fair value of the identifiable assets and liabilities acquired.

### (c)  Cost of Acquisition

The cost of acquisition should consist of:

• amount of cash paid;
• the fair value of other purchase consideration;
• expenses of acquisition.

If the consideration includes an element which is contingent on one or more future events, such as profit performance, the cost of acquisition should include the fair value of amounts expected to be payable in the future. Cost of acquisition may therefore be subject to subsequent revision.

### (d)  Fair Values of Identifiable Assets and Liabilities Acquired

FRS 7 specifies two general principles:

(1) the identifiable assets and liabilities should be those of the acquired entity that existed at the date of acquisition;
(2) the recognized assets and liabilities should be measured at fair values that reflect the conditions at the date of acquisition. Fair value is defined as the amount at which an asset or liability could be exchanged in an arm's length transaction between informed and willing parties, other than in a forced or liquidation sale.

The effect of the following should be excluded from the fair value calculation and treated as post-acquisition items:

(1) changes resulting from the acquirer's intentions or future actions;
(2) impairments or other changes, resulting from events subsequent to the acquisition;
(3) provisions or accruals for future operating losses or for reorganizations and integration costs expected to be incurred as a result of the acquisition. This exclusion applies irrespective of whether these relate to the acquired entity or to the acquirer. It is this aspect of FRS 7 which has been particularly contentious.

The standard gives guidance on the determination of fair values for the following specific categories:

- tangible fixed assets,
- intangible fixed assets,
- stocks and work-in-progress,
- quoted investments,
- monetary assets and liabilities,
- contingencies,
- business sold or held exclusively with a view to subsequent resale,
- pensions and other post-retirement benefits,
- deferred taxation.

*Illustration 2 – extracts from FRS 7 (paragraph numbers refer to FRS 7)*

**Extracts, FRS 7, Statement of Standard Accounting Practice**

*Tangible fixed assets*
9 The fair value of a tangible fixed asset should be based on:

(a) market value, if assets similar in type and condition are bought and sold on an open market; or
(b) depreciated replacement cost, reflecting the acquired business's normal buying process and the sources of supply and prices available to it.

The fair value should not exceed the recoverable amount of the asset.

*Stocks and work-in-progress*
11 Stocks, including commodity stocks, that the acquired entity trades on a market in which it participates as both a buyer and a seller should be valued at current market prices.

12 Other stocks, and work-in-progress, should be valued at the lower of replacement cost and net realisable value. Replacement cost is for this purpose the cost at which the stocks would have been replaced by the acquired entity, reflecting its normal buying process and the sources of supply and prices available to it - that is, the current cost of bringing the stocks to their present location and condition.

## (e) The Importance of Fair Value Adjustments

Wherever possible, any adjustments to asset values should be put through the books of the acquired company. Failing this, consolidation adjustments should be put through the group accounts in order to ensure that goodwill on consolidation is a meaningful figure and does not partly reflect undervaluation of assets such as freehold property.

## (f) Fair Value Disclosures

Detailed disclosures are set out in section 26.6 below. An important feature of these disclosures is the requirement by FRS 6 and CA 1985 for a fair value table.

In relation to a particular acquisition, FRS 6 requires the fair value table to show:

(1) the book values, as recorded in the acquired entity's books immediately before the acquisition and before any fair value adjustments;
(2) the fair value adjustments, analysed into:
    (i) revaluations;
    (ii) adjustments to achieve consistency of accounting policies; and
    (iii) any other significant adjustments, giving the reasons for the adjustments; and
(3) the fair values at the date of acquisition.

The table should disclose the amount of purchased goodwill or negative goodwill arising on the acquisition.
(See disclosure illustration in 26.6(f))

# 26.4   The Merger Reserve (CA 1985, s 131)

## (a) Section 131 and the Merger Reserve

FRS 6 does not deal directly with the accounting treatment of investments in the books of the parent company, although the matter is referred to in Appendix 1, FRS 6, note on legal requirements (see also section 26.9 below). However, the following provisions of the Companies Act 1985 are relevant:

### (1) Section 130
If a company issues shares at a premium, whether for cash or otherwise, a sum equal to the aggregate amount or value of the premiums should be transferred to a share premium account.

### (2) Section 131
This deals with the situation where the issuing company obtains at least 90% of the equity of another company. Section 130 does not apply to the premiums on any shares which are included in the consideration. Section 131 relief only applies to the issue of shares which take the holding to over 90%. "Merger reserve" is the title widely referred to in practice, although it is not used by the Companies Act 1985.

### Illustration 3

A already holds 15% of the share capital of company B. A issues 100,000 £1 ordinary shares (value £3) in order to obtain 80% of the share capital of B.
    The journal entry in the books of company could be as follows:

| | | | |
|---|---|---|---|
| *Debit* cost of investment in B | £300,000 | *Credit* OSC | £100,000 |
| | | Merger reserve | £200,000 |

The possible uses of the merger reserve in the individual accounts of the parent company are referred to in section 26.9 below.
    In the consolidated accounts, prior to FRS 10, it was fairly common for consolidation goodwill to be written off against the merger reserve. This accounting treatment is prohibited by FRS 10 for post-1998 acquisitions.

# 26.5   Acquisition Accounting Illustration

## (a) Basic Information

Panna Ltd and Rama Ltd decide to combine. Panna Ltd will issue 6,000 £1 shares in exchange for the entire share capital of Rama Ltd. The date of the combination is 30 September 19X3.

The draft financial statements of the two companies are as follows. No entries have yet been made in respect of the combination.

PROFIT AND LOSS ACCOUNT

for the year ended 31 December 19X3

|  | Panna £ | Rama £ |
|---|---|---|
| Turnover | 22,000 | 20,000 |
| Cost of sales | (8,000) | (6,000) |
| Distribution costs | (2,000) | (4,000) |
| Administrative expenses | (3,000) | (2,000) |
| Operating profit | 9,000 | 8,000 |
| Taxation | 4,500 | 4,000 |
| Profit after tax | 4,500 | 4,000 |
| Balance brought forward | 8,000 | 5,500 |
| Balance carried forward | 12,500 | 9,500 |

| Balance sheets at 31 December 19X3 | Panna £ | Rama £ |
|---|---|---|
| Tangible fixed assets | 16,000 | 11,000 |
| Net current assets | 13,500 | 9,500 |
|  | 29,500 | 20,500 |
| Called-up share capital (£1 shares) | 8,000 | 8,500 |
| Share premium | 4,000 | 1,500 |
| Revaluation reserve | 5,000 | 1,000 |
| Profit and loss account | 12,500 | 9,500 |
|  | 29,500 | 20,500 |

## (b) Acquisition Accounting Procedures

Assume the combination is accounted for using acquisition accounting.

For this purpose assume that the following additional information is provided:

(i)   The shares in Panna Ltd are issued at £5 per share.

(ii)  At 30.9.X3, the fixed assets of Rama Ltd have a fair value of £15,000.

(iii) The balances on share premium account and revaluation reserve are pre-acquisition.

(iv)  The balance on profit and loss account at 30.9.X3 was £8,500 (estimated by time apportionment).

## (1) Consolidated balance sheet procedures

Before setting out the working papers, it is necessary to record the issue of 6,000 shares at an issue price of £30,000. The shares are issued at a premium of £24,000. The journal entry in the books of Panna Ltd is:

| | | | |
|---|---|---|---|
| *Debit* cost of investment in | | *Credit* ordinary share capital | 6,000 |
| Rama Ltd (6,000 × £5) | 30,000 | *Credit* merger reserve | 24,000 |
| | | (see above) | |

Remember also that the goodwill calculation must reflect the undervaluation of fixed assets of £4,000 (i.e. £15,000 – £11,000) – see analysis below.

Consolidated fixed assets are £16,000 + £15,000 i.e. £31,000.

## (2) Analysis of equity

| | Total | Pre-acquisition | Post-acquisition P/L | Post-acquisition share premium | Post-acquisition revaluation reserve |
|---|---|---|---|---|---|
| | £ | £ | £ | £ | £ |
| Share capital | 8,500 | 8,500 | | | |
| P/L at acq. | 8,500 | 8,500 | | | |
|    since acq. | 1,000 | | 1,000 | | |
| Share premium | 1,500 | 1,500 | | – | |
| Revaluation | | | | | – |
|    per acs | 1,000 | 1,000 | | | – |
|    consol. adj. | 4,000 | 4,000 | | | |
| | 24,500 | 23,500 | | | |
| Cost of investment | | 30,000 | | | |
| Goodwill on consolidation | | 6,500 | | | |
| Panna's reserves | | | 12,500 | 4,000 | 5,000 |
| Consolidated B/S totals | | | 13,500 | 4,000 | 5,000 |

## (3) Consolidated balance sheet (acquisition accounting basis)

| | £ |
|---|---|
| Intangible fixed assets | 6,500 |
| Tangible fixed assets | 31,000 |
| Net current assets | 23,000 |
| | 60,500 |
| Called up share capital | 14,000 |
| Share premium account | 4,000 |
| Merger reserve | 24,000 |
| Revaluation reserve | 5,000 |
| Profit and loss account | 13,500 |
| | 60,500 |

## (4) Consolidated profit and loss account procedures

The key point to remember is that under amortization, only three months' results of Rama Ltd would be included. Strictly speaking, three months amortization of goodwill should be charged in arriving at operating profit. This has been ignored in this illustration.

The consolidated profit and loss account is as follows.

CONSOLIDATED PROFIT AND LOSS ACCOUNT
(ACQUISITION ACCOUNTING BASIS)

for the year ended 31 December 19X3

|  | £ |
|---|---|
| Turnover (22 + 5) | 27,000 |
| Cost of sales (8 + 1.5) | 9,500 |
| Gross profit | 17,500 |
| Distribution costs (2 + 1) | (3,000) |
| Administrative expenses (3 + 0.5) | (3,500) |
| Operating profit | 11,000 |
| Taxation (4.5 + 1) | 5,500 |
| Profit on ordinary activities after tax | 5,500 |
| Balance brought forward | 8,000 |
| Balance carried forward | 13,500 |

## 26.6 Acquisition Accounting Disclosures

The disclosure requirements of FRS 6 are extremely detailed and run to almost eight pages—the note below aims to provide an overview.

### (a) General Disclosures

The consolidated accounts should disclose:

(1) the names of combining entities (other than parent);
(2) that the combination is accounted for using acquisition accounting;
(3) date of combination.

### (b) Material Acquisitions

Details of the following are required for *each* material acquisition:

(1) composition and fair value of consideration given;
(2) a fair value table (see (d) below);
(3) details of reorganization and reconstruction provisions set up by the acquired entity in the twelve months prior to acquisition;
(4) details where fair values of assets and liabilities have been determined on a provisional basis;
(5) acquisition details required by FRS 3 (Reporting financial performance) and FRS 1 (Cash flow statements);
(6) details of certain costs incurred in reorganizing, restructuring and integrating the acquisition;

(7) details of certain post-acquisition exceptional profits or losses which have been determined using fair values at acquisition, for example disposals of fixed assets which were part of the company acquired;

(8) details of movements on provisions for costs related to an acquisition;

(9) details of profits relating to the acquired entity for periods up to the date of acquisition:
(i) current year up to date of acquisition;
(ii) previous year.

## (c) Minor Acquisitions

The disclosure referred to in (b) (1) to (8) but not (9) should be given on an aggregate basis for non-material acquisitions.

## (d) Fair Value Table

A fair value table should be provided for each material acquisition, and for non-material acquisitions in aggregate.

## (e) Substantial Acquisitions

Substantial acquisitions are defined as:

(1) for listed companies: class I or super class I transactions (see UITF 15 at (f) below);

(2) for other entities:
(i) where the net assets or operating profits of the acquired entity exceed 15% of those of the acquiring entity; or
(ii) where the fair value of the consideration given exceeds 15% of the net assets of the acquiring entity.

The disclosures below are required for all substantial acquisitions and also "in other exceptional cases where an acquisition is of such significance that the disclosure is necessary in order to give a true and fair view":

(1) summarized profit and loss/gains and losses information for the acquired entity from the beginning of the year up to the date of acquisition;

(2) profit after tax and MI of the acquired entity for the previous year.

## (f) UITF 15 – Disclosure of Substantial Acquisitions

FRS 6, Acquisitions and mergers, refers to specific disclosure requirements for "substantial acquisitions"—the definition of which refers to "class 1 or super class 1 transactions".

Some time after the issue of FRS 6, the Stock Exchange abolished the category of "class 1 transactions".

UITF 15 requires the FRS 6 reference to class 1 transactions to be interpreted as meaning "those transactions in which any of the ratios set out in the UK Listing Authority Listing Rules defining super class 1 transactions exceeds 15%".

## *Illustration 4*

Extract from annual report and accounts of the Sage Group plc, year ended 30 September 2003.

**Note 18 – Acquisitions**

**(a) Timberline Software Corporation**

On 19 September 2003 the Group completed the acquisition of Timberline Software Corporation ("Timberline") for a consideration of £63.7m (inclusive of £1.4m related costs). Total goodwill arising on the acquisition is £51.8m. The fair values of net assets acquired are based on provisional assessments pending final determination of certain assets and liabilities.

The assets and liabilities of Timberline at fair value were:

| | Book value £'000 | *Fair value adjustments* Alignment of accounting policies[1] £'000 | Other[2] £'000 | Fair value to Group £'000 |
|---|---|---|---|---|
| Intangible fixed assets | 5,711 | (5,711) | – | – |
| Tangible fixed assets | 13,246 | (30) | – | 13,216 |
| Stocks | 90 | – | – | 90 |
| Debtors | 3,346 | – | 2,228 | 5,574 |
| Cash | 7,759 | – | – | 7,759 |
| Creditors falling due within one year | (3,024) | – | – | (3,024) |
| Creditors falling due in more than one year | (226) | – | – | (226) |
| Deferred income | (11,552) | – | | (11,552) |
| | 15,350 | (5,741) | 2,228 | 11,837 |
| Cash consideration including cost (note 18(c)) | | | | 59,601 |
| Deferred consideration | | | | 4,053 |
| Total consideration | | | | 63,654 |
| Goodwill arising | | | | 51,817 |

*Notes:*

1 Alignment of accounting policies includes the write off of capitalised software development costs and alignment of the tangible fixed assets capitalisation policy.
2 Other adjustments include the recognition of a deferred tax asset.

Prior to acquisition the last full set of financial statements of Timberline was prepared for the year ended 31 December 2002 and showed a profit of US $1,757,000 after taxation and amortisation of capitalised software development costs.

The pre-acquisition results for Timberline for the period from 1 January 2003 to 19 September 2003 prepared under Timberline's accounting policies and principles prevailing prior to acquisition were as follows:

| | US £'000 |
|---|---|
| Turnover | 44,255 |
| Operating loss | (2,039) |
| Net interest receivable | 145 |
| Loss before taxation | (1,894) |
| Tax benefit | 3,195 |
| Profit after taxation | 1,301 |

Other than the profit for the period, there were no other gains or losses.

### (b) Other acquisitions made in the year

The following acquisitions, each for the entire share capital of the relevant company, were made during the year:

1 GFK Technology Limited was acquired on 2 December 2002 for a cash consideration of £1.4m (including costs). The fair value of assets acquired was £0.2m resulting in goodwill of £1.2m.
2 Concept Group was acquired on 7 January 2003 for a cash consideration of £5.2m (including costs), and a deferred element of £0.3m. The fair value of assets acquired was (£0.2m) resulting in goodwill of £5.7m.
3 KTS Group Inc. was acquired on 26 February 2003 for a cash consideration of £3.2m (including costs). The fair value of assets acquired was (£0.5m) resulting in goodwill of £3.7m.
4 Primus Software AG was acquired on 11 March 2003 for a cash consideration of £3.0m (including costs). The fair value of assets acquired was (£0.6m) resulting in goodwill of £3.6m.
5 Promis Software Limited was acquired on 20 March 2003 for a cash consideration of £0.2m (including costs). The fair value of assets acquired was (£0.1m) resulting in goodwill of £0.3m.
6 Winware AG was acquired on 10 April 2003 for a cash consideration of £1.7m (including costs). The fair value of assets acquired was £0.1m resulting in goodwill of £1.6m.
7 ATW Computer Services Limited was acquired on 4 September 2003 for a cash consideration of £1.8m (including costs). The fair value of assets acquired was £0.4m resulting in goodwill of £1.4m.

The assets and liabilities in respect of these acquisitions at fair value (based on provisional assessments pending final determination of certain assets and liabilities) were:

|  | Book value £'000 | Fair value adjustments Alignment of accounting policies[1] £'000 | Other[2] £'000 | Fair value to Group £'000 |
|---|---|---|---|---|
| Intangible fixed assets | 231 | (231) | – | – |
| Tangible fixed assets | 699 | – | – | 699 |
| Stocks | 121 | – | – | 121 |
| Debtors | 4,920 | (119) | 2,918 | 7,719 |
| Cash | 2,113 | – | – | 2,113 |
| Creditors falling due within one year | (8,489) | (9) | – | (8,498) |
| Deferred income | (2,870) | (5) | – | (2,875) |
|  | (3,275) | (364) | 2,918 | (721) |
| Cash consideration including costs (note 18(c)) |  |  |  | 16,480 |
| Deferred consideration |  |  |  | 273 |
| Total consideration |  |  |  | 16,753 |
| Goodwill arising |  |  |  | 17,474 |

*Notes:*

1 Alignment of accounting policies includes the write off of intangible assets and alignment of bad debt and deferred income calculations.
2 Other adjustments include the recognition of a deferred tax asset.

### (c) Analysis of net outflow of cash in respect of acquisitions

| Cash consideration: | £'000 |
|---|---|
| Timberline Software Corporation (note 18(a)) | 59,601 |
| Other acquisitions (note 18(b)) | 16,480 |
| Cash acquired | (9,872) |
|  | 66,209 |

**(d) Other**

During the year ended 30 September 2003 adjustments were made in respect of goodwill on prior year acquisitions of £485,000, due to additional acquisition payments of £837,000, increase to deferred consideration of £359,000 and increase in net assets of £711,000 following the re-appraisal of the fair value of assets and liabilities.

# 26.7    Changes in Stake

## (a) Situations

FRS 2 deals with the specific cases of:

- acquiring a subsidiary undertaking in stages (step-by-step or piecemeal acquisition);
- increasing an interest held in a subsidiary undertaking;
- reducing an interest held in a subsidiary undertaking.

## (b) Acquiring a Subsidiary Undertaking in Stages

The Companies Act 1985, Sch 4A, para 9 requires that a subsidiary's assets and liabilities should be included in the consolidated accounts at fair value as at the date that it became a subsidiary undertaking. This statutory requirement also applies where the group's interest in the subsidiary undertaking is acquired in stages.

*Illustration 5*

H Ltd acquired a controlling interest in S Ltd in two stages, as follows:

(1) 30.6.19X2 20% holding at a cost of £33,000 when the fair value of the net assets amounted to £150,000.
(2) 31.3.19X3 40% holding at a cost of £92,000 when the fair value of the net assets amounted to £190,000.

The CA 1985 computation of goodwill arising on consolidation is:

|  | £ |
|---|---|
| Cost of investment (33 + 92) | 125,000 |
| Group share of net assets at acquisition 60% × £190,000 | 114,000 |
| ∴Goodwill on consolidation | 11,000 |

FRS 2, para 89 refers to special cases, for example:

> "...in special circumstances, however, not using fair values at the dates of earlier purchases, while using an acquisition cost part of which relates to earlier purchases, may result in accounting that is inconsistent with the way the investment has been treated previously, and for that reason, may fail to give a true and fair view..."

One such case referred to by FRS 2 is where a group starts off with an interest which is treated as an associated undertaking. A further purchase of shares turns the undertaking into a subsidiary undertaking.

This is an example of a situation where the statutory calculation of goodwill would be misleading. FRS 2 therefore requires that goodwill should be calculated as the sum of goodwill arising from each purchase adjusted as necessary for any subsequent diminution in value.

*Illustration 6*

In the above illustration, assume that the 20% investment was treated as an associated undertaking (see chapter 27). At the date of purchase, the fair value of the company's net assets amounted to £150,000.

The FRS 2 calculation of goodwill is therefore:

|  | £ |
|---|---|
| 30.6.19X2 £33,000 – (20% × £150,000) | 3,000 |
| 31.3.19X3 £92,000 – (40% × £190,000) | 16,000 |
|  | 19,000 |

The goodwill in the consolidated accounts would therefore be £19,000. However, the above is a departure from the statutory requirement in CA 1985, s 227(6) which requires particulars of the departure, the reasons for it and its effect, to be disclosed by way of note.

The difference between the two goodwill figures of £8,000 (£19,000 – £11,000) forms part of group reserves (relating to the associated undertaking) (i.e. 20% (190,000 – 150,000)).

## (c) Increase in Stake in Undertaking that is Already a Subsidiary

Where a group increases its interest in an undertaking that is already a subsidiary, the subsidiary's assets and liabilities should be revalued to fair value. Goodwill arising on the increase in the interest in stake should be calculated by reference to those fair values.

*Illustration 7*

H Ltd acquires a 70% shareholding in S Ltd on 30.9.19X3 at a cost of £24,000 when the balance sheet of S Ltd was as follows. Assume that assets were already stated at fair value.

|  | £ |
|---|---|
| Net assets | 32,000 |
| Ordinary share capital | 10,000 |
| P/L reserves | 22,000 |
|  | 32,000 |

The effect on the consolidated balance sheet, leaving in goodwill for purposes of explanation would be:

|  | £ |
|---|---|
| Net assets | 32,000 |
| Goodwill £24,000 – 70% (£32,000) | 1,600 |
|  | 33,600 |
| Minority interest 30% × £32,000 | 9,600 |
| Cash paid | 24,000 |
|  | 33,600 |

On 30.11.19X5, H Ltd purchased a further 20% of the shares in S Ltd at a cost of £14,000. At that date, the balance sheet of S Ltd was:

|  | £ |
|---|---|
| Net assets | 42,000 |
| Ordinary share capital | 10,000 |
| P/L reserves | 32,000 |
|  | 42,000 |

The fair value of the net assets was estimated at £50,000.
Following FRS 2, the effect on the consolidated balance sheet at 30.11.19X5 would be:

|  | £ |
|---|---|
| Net assets | 50,000 |
| Goodwill (see below) | 5,600 |
|  | 55,600 |
| Minority interest |  |
| 10% × £50,000 | 5,000 |
| Group revaluation reserve |  |
| 70%(50,000–42,000) | 5,600 |
| Group P/L reserves |  |
| 70% (32,000 – 22,000) | 7,000 |
| Cash paid (24,000+14,000) | 38,000 |
|  | 55,600 |

|  | £ |
|---|---|
| Working – Goodwill calculation: |  |
| 30.9.19X3 | 1,600 |
| 30.11.19X5 |  |
| £14,000 – (20% × £50,000) | 4,000 |
|  | 5,600 |

## In support of the above treatment, FRS 2, para 90 states:

"...if the assets and liabilities were not revalued to fair values before calculating the goodwill arising on the change in stake, then the difference between the consideration paid and the relevant proportion of the carrying value of net assets acquired would be made up in part of goodwill and in part of changes in value..."

## Illustration 8

**Note 25 – Acquisitions and purchase of minority interest**

|  | Acquiree Book Values £m | Fair Value Adjustments £m | Total £m |
|---|---|---|---|
| Acquisitions |  |  |  |
| Tangible fixed assets | 2 | – | 2 |
| Intangible fixed assets | 1 | (1) | – |
| Current assets | 3 | – | 3 |
| Liabilities | (3) | – | (3) |

| | | | |
|---|---|---|---|
| Movement in net assets | 3 | (1) | 2 |
| Goodwill | | | 49 |
| Fair value of consideration | | | 51 |
| Cash acquired | | | (2) |
| | | | 49 |
| Purchase of minority interest | | | 147 |
| **Net cash consideration** | | | 196 |

Assets and liabilities are adjusted to fair values on external valuations and internal reviews. The principal acquisition was the purchase of XYZ plc on ... for a total cost of £48m.

The purchase of minority interest relates to the acquisition of the remaining 50% of ABC Ltd has been regarded as a subsidiary undertaking and its results have been consolidated into the Group results from ..., the date of the acquisition of an initial 50% controlling shareholding.

## (d) Reducing an Interest Held in a Subsidiary Undertaking

Where a group reduces its interest in a subsidiary undertaking, it should calculate any profit or loss arising as follows

| | £ | £ |
|---|---|---|
| Proceeds of sale | | X |
| The carrying amount of the net assets of that subsidiary undertaking attributable to the group's interest before the reduction | X | |
| *Less* the carrying amount attributable to the group's interest after the reduction | X | (X) |
| *Less* the appropriate proportion of goodwill not previously written off through P/L (per FRS 10, para 71) | | (X) |
| Profit (loss) on disposal | | X |

# 26.8   Accounting for Disposals of Shares in Subsidiary Undertakings

## (a) Date of Change

Under FRS 2, the date for determining when a subsidiary ceases to be a subsidiary is when its former parent relinquishes control.

The explanation section of FRS 2 gives guidance on how to determine this date, as this is an area which can give rise to difficulties in practice.

In the more straightforward cases the date is determined as follows:

(1) control transferred by a public offer – the date the offer becomes unconditional (usually because a sufficient number of acceptances have been received);

(2) control transferred by a private transaction – the date an unconditional offer is accepted.

## (b) Accounting Implications

The consolidated profit and loss account should include:

(1)  the results of the subsidiary up to the date that it ceases to be a subsidiary;
(2)  any gain or loss arising on cessation (i.e. gain or loss on disposal of shares).

## (c) Computation of Gain or Loss on Disposal

The gain or loss is calculated as follows:

|  | £ | £ | £ |
|---|---|---|---|
| Proceeds of sale |  |  | X |
| Carrying amount of net assets before cessation | (X) |  |  |
| Less carrying amount of net assets after cessation | X | (X) |  |
| Goodwill not written off through profit and loss account (see section (e) below) |  | (X) |  |
| Gain (or loss) |  |  | X |

## (d) Henry Group

*Illustration 9*

Until fairly recently, Henry Ltd owned two wholly-owned subsidiaries—Percy Ltd and Thomas Ltd.

Both subsidiaries had been acquired several years ago prior to the implementation in 1998 of FRS 10 when their reserves amounted to £25,000 and £4,000 respectively. Goodwill arising on consolidation had been written off immediately to profit and loss reserves.

Henry disposed of its entire shareholding in Thomas Ltd on 31 March 19X8 for cash proceeds of £92,000.

The draft accounts of the three companies for the year ended 31 December 19X8 were as follows:

### DRAFT PROFIT AND LOSS ACCOUNTS

|  | Henry Ltd £ | Percy Ltd £ | Thomas Ltd £ |
|---|---|---|---|
| Turnover | 650,000 | 80,000 | 50,000 |
| Operating expenses | (300,000) | (25,000) | (22,000) |
| Profit before tax | 350,000 | 55,000 | 28,000 |
| Dividend receivable | 12,000 | – | – |
| Taxation | (160,000) | (27,000) | (14,000) |
| Proposed dividends | (50,000) | (12,000) | (5,000) |
| Retained profit | 152,000 | 16,000 | 9,000 |
| Balance brought forward | 430,000 | 40,000 | 12,400 |
| Balance carried back | 582,000 | 56,000 | 21,400 |

The draft profit and loss account of Henry Ltd does not reflect the gain or loss on the sale of shares in Thomas Ltd.

DRAFT BALANCE SHEETS

|  | Henry Ltd £ | Percy Ltd £ | Thomas Ltd £ |
|---|---|---|---|
| Sundry net assets | 956,000 | 168,000 | 76,400 |
| Investment in Percy | 172,000 | – | – |
| Investment in Thomas | 84,000 | – | – |
| Dividends receivable | 12,000 | – | – |
|  | 1,224,000 | 168,000 | 76,400 |
| Called up share capital | 500,000 | 100,000 | 50,000 |
| Profit and loss account | 582,000 | 56,000 | 21,400 |
| Proposed dividends | 50,000 | 12,000 | 5,000 |
| Sale of investment in Thomas | 92,000 | – | – |
|  | 1,224,000 | 168,000 | 76,400 |

The key workings are as follows:

(1) Goodwill on consolidation arising on the acquisition of Percy and Thomas

|  | Percy £ | Thomas £ |
|---|---|---|
| Cost of investment | 172,000 | 84,000 |
| Share capital | (100,000) | (50,000) |
| Pre-acquisition reserves | (25,000) | (4,000) |
| Goodwill arising | 47,000 | 30,000 |

(2) Consolidated profit and loss reserves at 31 December 19X7

|  | £ |
|---|---|
| Henry | 430,000 |
| Percy (40,000 – 25,000) | 15,000 |
| Thomas (12,400 – 4,000) | 8,400 |
|  | 453,400 |
| Less goodwill written off direct to reserves (47,000 + 30,000) – pre FRS 10. | 77,000 |
| Balance at 31 December 19X7 | 376,400 |

(3) Gain or loss on disposal of shares—group accounts

|  | £ | £ |
|---|---|---|
| Proceeds of sale |  | 92,000 |
| Net assets at date of sale = shareholders funds at 31 March 19X8 |  |  |
| OSC | 50,000 |  |
| P/L b/f | 12,400 |  |
| 3 months profit after tax 3/12 × 14,000 | 3,500 | 65,900 |
|  |  | 26,100 |
| Less goodwill previously written off (see FRS 10, below) |  | 30,000 |
|  |  | (3,900) |

Note:

(1) The loss of £3,900 recorded in the group accounts may be reconciled to the profit of £8,000 (92,000 – 84,000) recorded in the parent company's accounts as follows.

The parent company profit and loss account records only dividends received whereas the group profit and loss account includes all attributable profits of subsidiaries whether paid out as dividends or retained:

|  |  | £ |
|---|---:|---:|
| Profit in accounts of parent company | | 8,000 |
| Post acquisition profits of Thomas included in group accounts | | |
| Reserves at acquisition | 4,000 | |
| Reserves at disposal | 15,900 | |
| Increase | | 11,900 |
| Loss in group accounts | | (3,900) |

(2) Tax on disposal of shares has been ignored.
   The group accounts may be completed as follows:

### CONSOLIDATED PROFIT AND LOSS ACCOUNT

#### for the year ended 31 December 19X8

|  | £ |
|---|---:|
| Turnover (650 + 80 + 3/12 × 50) | 742,500 |
| Operating expenses (300 + 25 + 3/12 × 22) | 330,500 |
| Operating profit | 412,000 |
| Loss on sale of shares (exceptional item per FRS 3) | (3,900) |
| Profit before tax | 408,100 |
| Taxation (160 + 27 + 3/12 x 14) | 190,500 |
| Profit after tax | 217,600 |
| Proposed dividends | (50,000) |
| Retained profit | 167,600 |

### CONSOLIDATED BALANCE SHEET

#### at 31 December 19X8

|  | £ |
|---|---:|
| Sundry net assets (956 + 168) | 1,124,000 |
| Less proposed dividends | 50,000 |
|  | 1,074,000 |
| Called-up share capital | 500,000 |
| Profit and loss account | 574,000 |
|  | 1,074,000 |

### PROFIT AND LOSS RESERVES

|  | £ |
|---|---:|
| Balance at 1 January 19X8 | 376,400 |
| Retained profit for the year | 167,600 |
| Goodwill written back to profit and loss account on disposal | 30,000 |
| Balance at 31 December 19X8 | 574,000 |

*Notes:*

(1)  The goodwill write back is in accordance with FRS 10 (see below).
(2)  The closing balance of £574,000 may be reconciled to the individual balances as follows:

|  | £ |
| --- | --- |
| Henry's P/L (582 + 8) | 590,000 |
| Percy's post-acq. (56 – 25) | 31,000 |
| Goodwill w/o against reserves (Percy) (pre-FRS 10) | (47,000) |
|  | 574,000 |

## (e)  Former UITF Abstract 3 – Goodwill on Disposal of a Business

### (1)  Scope

UITF 3 dealt with the computation and disclosure of the profit or loss on the disposal of a previously acquired business, subsidiary or associate. UITF 3 has been withdrawn, but its previous requirements are incorporated in the transitional provisions of FRS 10 (para 71).

### (2)  Computation

The profit or loss on disposal should include the attributable amount of purchased goodwill where this has not previously been charged through the profit and loss account.

In the illustration in (d), the goodwill relating to the earlier acquisition of Thomas of £30,000 had been charged direct to reserves, without any charge through the profit and loss account. Without the goodwill adjustment, the consolidated profit and loss account would simply have picked up £26,100 (i.e. £92,000 – £65,900). The double entry to record the adjustment was debit P/L 30,000, credit P/L reserves (reserve movement) 30,000.

Suppose, as an alternative, Henry group goodwill policy was one of amortization, with Thomas's goodwill written off over ten years. If the disposal was, say, four years after the acquisition the profit and loss accounts of the four years would each have been charged with £3,000 i.e. a total of £12,000. The required goodwill adjustment on disposal would then have been £18,000 (i.e. £30,000 total less £12,000 in respect of amounts amortized through P/L ac).

### (3)  Disclosure

The goodwill attributable to the business disposed of, and included in the P/L calculation should be disclosed on the face of the P/L or in a note.

Where it is impracticable to make a reasonable estimate of the purchased goodwill, the fact and the reasons should be disclosed.

### (4)  Other possibilities

The principles above are to apply also to cases where negative goodwill arises and to business closures.

*Illustration 10*

**Accounting policies (extract)**

*Goodwill*

The net assets of businesses acquired are incorporated in the consolidated accounts at their fair value to the Group. The difference between the price paid for subsidiary undertakings and the fair value of net assets acquired is taken direct to reserves. At the time of any disposal of a business the goodwill which arose at the time of acquisition is written back from reserves to calculate the profit or loss on disposal.

## (f) Part Disposal, Control Retained

Suppose a parent sells a 25% shareholding in a previously wholly-owned subsidiary.

Ignoring tax, the group's gain or loss on disposal would be calculated as follows:

|  | £ | £ |
|---|---|---|
| Proceeds of sale of 25% holding |  | X |
| Carrying amount of net assets before disposal | X |  |
| Less carrying amount × 75% of net assets after disposal | X |  |
|  |  | (X) |
|  |  | X |
| Less 25% of any goodwill, to extent that it has not been written off through P/L |  | (X) |
| Gain (loss) on disposal |  | X |

*Illustration 11*

Extract from annual report and accounts of Rentokil Initial plc, year ended 31 December 2000.

**Note 33 – Disposals**

The company disposed of 14 businesses during the year (as set out on page ...) for gross consideration of £616.2m, £605.4m after costs paid of £10.8m but before provisions and accruals of £4.0m.

|  | CONSOLIDATED 2000 £m |
|---|---|
| **Net assets** |  |
| Intangible assets | 1.8 |
| Tangible assets | 372.3 |
| Working capital | 97.4 |
| Debt | (10.2) |
| Other liabilities | (14.5) |
|  | 446.8 |
| Goodwill previously written off to reserves | 144.4 |
| Profit and loss on disposal | – |

| | |
|---|---:|
| Provisions and accruals | 4.0 |
| Net debt disposed | 10.2 |
| | 605.4 |

These businesses contributed £28.4m to net operating cash flow, paid £3.1m in respect of net returns on investments and servicing of finance and £1 1.2m in respect of taxation.

# 26.9 Realization of the Merger Reserve

## (a) The Problem of Pre-combination Dividends

Dividends paid out of pre-acquisition profits have in the past usually been treated as capital in the hands of the recipient company and not available for distribution to the recipient company's shareholders.

This view is still accepted where a subsidiary has been acquired other than by an issue of shares by the offeror. However, the view is now being challenged in the case of share-for-share issues. Consider the following illustration.

### Illustration 12

A and B are two identical companies. Their respective balance sheets are set out below.

Suppose that A issues 300 shares (deemed to have a value of £5 each) in order to acquire the entire share capital of B.

Two points may be made:

(1) The issue of shares falls within CA 1985, s 131 so if the investment is recorded at fair value of £1,500 (i.e. 300 shares issued valued at £5 each), the premium of £1,200 must be taken to a merger reserve and not to a share premium account.
(2) Under CA 1985, s 133, the investment in B may be recorded at nominal value issued ie at £300.

**Balance sheets**

| | A (before) | B (before) | A (after – s 131) | A (after – s 133) |
|---|---:|---:|---:|---:|
| | £ | £ | £ | £ |
| Sundry assets | 1,000 | 1,000 | 1,000 | 1,000 |
| Investment in B | – | – | 1,500 | 300 |
| | 1,000 | 1,000 | 2,500 | 1,300 |
| OSC | 300 | 300 | 600 | 600 |
| P/L | 700 | 700 | 700 | 700 |
| Merger reserve | – | – | 1,200 | |
| | 1,000 | 1,000 | 2,500 | 1,300 |

Now suppose B distributes its entire (and pre-acquisition) profit and loss account balance. How should this receipt be dealt with in the accounts of A?

(a) Where A's investment in B is recorded at £300 the former SSAP 23 appendix (accounts of the parent company) pointed out that "...where a dividend is paid to the acquiring or issuing company out of pre-combination profits, it would appear that it need not necessarily be applied as a reduction in the carrying value of the investment in the subsidiary".

Such a dividend received should be applied to reduce the carrying value of the investment to the extent that it is necessary to provide for a diminution in value of the investment in the subsidiary as stated in the accounts of the issuing company. To the extent that this is not necessary, it appears that the amount received will be a realized profit in the hands of the issuing company.

If A credits the dividend to its P/L ac, investment in B will remain at £300. This will be matched by B's remaining asset of £300 after the dividend payments (i.e. 1,000 – £700 = £300).

It is not necessary to provide for diminution in value.

(b) Where A's investment in B is recorded at £1,500—the appendix to the former standard SSAP 23 referred to situations where the parent company records the investment at fair value and pointed out:

it will in some cases ... be necessary for the parent company to credit to the investment the dividend paid out of the subsidiary's pre-combination profits.

Thus the dividend received of £700 should be credited to cost of investment of £1,500 leaving an adjusted carrying amount of £800.

The £800 is represented by:

| | |
|---|---:|
| Tangible assets of B | 300 |
| Non-purchased goodwill | |
| (1,500 – 1,000) | 500 |
| | £800 |

The balance sheets for company A may be compared as follows:

| | Situation (a) £ | Situation (b) £ |
|---|---:|---:|
| Sundry assets | 1,700 | 1,700 |
| Investment in B | 300 | 800 |
| | 2,000 | 2,500 |
| OSC | 600 | 600 |
| P/L | 1,400 | 700 |
| Merger reserve | – | 1,200 |
| | 2,000 | 2,500 |

Given that s 133 offers A a free choice of recording its investment in B at either £1,500 (fair value issued) or £300 (nominal value issued), it seems inconsistent that on the face of it A's distributable profit can be either £1,400 or £700.

With regard to (b), the appendix to the former standard SSAP 23 went on to say: In these circumstances, the question arises as to whether as a result of this treatment an equivalent amount of the merger reserve can legally be regarded as realised. No firm legal ruling on this is yet available.

Note the caution expressed; however FRS 6 returns to this aspect (see below).

These legal views appear to indicate that £700 of the merger reserve could be regarded as distributable, thus making total distributable reserves £1,400, i.e. the same as for situation (a).

## (b) FRS 6, Appendix 1, Legal Requirements

Some guidance is provided by way of an appendix to FRS 6.

*FRS 6, Appendix 1 – Note on legal requirements (extract)*

**Accounts of the parent company**

**15** The FRS deals only with the method of accounting to be used in group accounts; it does not deal with the form of accounting to be used in the acquiring or issuing company's own accounts and in particular does not restrict the reliefs available under sections 131–133 of the Companies Act.

**16** Where a dividend is paid to the acquiring or issuing company out of pre-combination profits, it would appear that it need not necessarily be applied as a reduction in the carrying value of the investment in the subsidiary undertaking. Such a dividend received should be applied to reduce the carrying value of the investment to the extent necessary to provide for a diminution in value of the investment in the subsidiary undertaking as stated in the accounts of the parent company. To the extent that this is not necessary, it appears that the amount received will be a realised profit in the hands of the parent company.

## Illustration 13

The Jack Simmons Group has recently disposed of a subsidiary. The subsidiary was originally acquired several years ago by means of a share-for-share exchange.

The shares originally issued as consideration were recorded at fair value, the premium of £250,000 being transferred to merger reserve. The consolidation followed acquisition accounting and goodwill of £60,000 was written off direct to merger reserve leaving a balance on merger reserve of £190,000.

The effect of the disposal on the reserves note for the company (following the legal advice in FRS 6 above) and the group (following FRS 10) would be as follows:

| The group | Merger reserve £ | Profit and loss account £ |
|---|---|---|
| At 1.1.19X8 | 190,000 | |
| Profit for the year | | X |
| Goodwill written back to merger reserve on disposal | 60,000 | |
| Merger reserve realized on sale of subsidiary | (250,000) | 250,000 |
| At 31.12.19X8 | – | X |
| The company | | |
| At 1.1.19X8 | 250,000 | X |
| Profit for the year | | X |
| Merger reserve realized on sale of subsidiary | (250,000) | 250,000 |
| At 31.12.19X8 | – | X |

# 26.10  Merger Accounting

## (a) Key Features

The key features of merger accounting are as follows:

(a) the financial statements of the combining companies are aggregated and presented as if the companies had been together since their respective incorporations;

(b) the full year's results of the combining companies must be included in the consolidated profit for the year even if the merger takes place during the year;

(c) comparative figures for both consolidated balance sheet and consolidated profit and loss account are restated as though the combining companies were together throughout the previous year.

## (b) When Merger Accounting is Mandatory

Business combinations meeting the stringent and detailed conditions set out in FRS 6, together with those in CA 1985, should be accounted for using merger accounting.

If these conditions are satisfied, merger accounting is mandatory. However, ASB anticipates that these conditions will be met on rare occasions only.

## (c) FRS 6, Accounting for Acquisitions and Mergers

In outline the FRS 6 conditions are as follows:

A combination meets the definition of a merger only if it satisfies the five criteria set out in paragraphs 6-11 of the FRS. These criteria relate to:

(1) the way the roles of each party to the combination are portrayed;
(2) the involvement of each party to the combination in the selection of the management of the combined entity;
(3) the relative sizes of the parties to the combination;
(4) whether shareholders of the combining entities receive any consideration other than equity shares in the combined entity;
(5) whether shareholders of the combining entities retain an interest in the performance of only part of the combined entity.

## (d) Companies Act Requirements

The following additional requirements must be satisfied before merger accounting can be used:

(1) that at least 90% of the nominal value of the relevant shares in the undertaking acquired is held by or on behalf of the parent company and its subsidiary undertakings;
(2) that the proportion referred to in paragraph (1) was attained pursuant to the arrangement providing for the issue of equity shares by the parent company or one or more of its subsidiary undertakings;
(3) the fair value of any consideration other than the issue of equity shares given pursuant to the arrangement by the parent company and its subsidiary undertakings did not exceed 10% of the nominal value of the equity shares issued; and
(4) that adoption of the merger method of accounting accords with generally accepted accounting principles or practice.

## (e) Merger Accounting – Applying the Rules

Where the group can satisfy the conditions referred to above and chooses to prepare consolidated accounts on a merger basis, the following principles apply:

(1) Where the carrying value of investment in a subsidiary (usually equivalent to nominal value of shares issued) is less than the nominal value of the

shares received from the offeree, the difference should be treated as a reserve arising on consolidation.

(2) Where the carrying value of investment in a subsidiary is greater than the nominal value of the shares received, the difference should be treated on consolidation as a reduction of reserves.

(3) In the consolidated profit and loss account, the full year's profits of the offeree should be included (note carefully).

(4) As regards comparative figures, these should be presented as if the companies had been combined throughout the previous period and at the previous balance sheet date (note very carefully).

The effect of these rules is shown in the illustration below.

(1) *The individual accounts of the parent company and section 133*

*Illustration 14*

Section 131 was referred to in section 26.4. Under s 131 the journal entry to record the parent's investment in the subsidiary would be:

| Credit cost of investment in B | £300,000 | Credit OSC | £100,000 |
| | | Merger reserve | £200,000 |

Section 133 refers to situations where the premium may be disregarded in determining the carrying amount.

In the above example, A could record its investment in B as follows:

| Debit cost of investment | £100,000 | Credit OSC | £100,000 |

Note two important points:

(1) the above statutory rules relate to the individual accounts of the parent company and not the consolidated accounts;

(2) in theory, company A may choose between recording the investment in B at £300,000 or £100,000 irrespective of whether it intends to present consolidated accounts on an acquisition basis or a merger basis.

In practice A would usually record the investment at £300,000 if it intended to consolidate using acquisition accounting, and £100,000 if it intended to consolidate using merger accounting.

*(2) Consolidation procedures – merger accounting*

*Illustration 15 (see information in section 26.5)*

(1) Carrying value in books of Panna Ltd of investment in Rama Ltd is £6,000 (i.e. nominal value of shares issued in exchange). Share capital of Panna Ltd is now increased to £14,000.

(2) Consolidated balance sheet workings:

| | £ |
| --- | --- |
| (i) Carrying value of investment | 6,000 |
| Nominal value received | 8,500 |
| Reserve arising on consolidation | 2,500 |

(ii) Reserve balances

|  | P/L £ | Share premium £ | Revaluation Reserve £ |
|---|---|---|---|
| Panna | 12,500 | 4,000 | 5,000 |
| Rama | 9,500 | 1,500 | 1,000 |
|  | 22,000 | 5,500 | 6,000 |

*Notes:*

(1) No distinction is made between pre-acquisition and post-acquisition reserves. The combining companies are treated as though they had operated as a combined unit since the date of incorporation.

(2) The fixed assets of the offeree company (Rama Ltd) are not revalued to determine fair value. This is not so with acquisition accounting.

The consolidated balance sheet under merger accounting principles is as follows:

|  | £ |
|---|---|
| Tangible fixed assets | 27,000 |
| Net current assets | 23,000 |
|  | 50,000 |
| Called-up share capital | 14,000 |
| Share premium account | 5,500 |
| Revaluation reserve | 6,000 |
| Capital reserve on merger | 2,500 |
| Profit and loss account | 22,000 |
|  | 50,000 |

(3) In preparing the consolidated profit and loss account, remember to bring in a full year's results for Rama Ltd even though the combination was on 30 September 19X3. Remember also that it is unnecessary (and inappropriate!) to adjust the reserves of Rama Ltd between pre- and post-merger.

### CONSOLIDATED PROFIT AND LOSS ACCOUNT
### (ON A MERGER ACCOUNTING BASIS)

for the year ended 31 December 19X3

|  | £ |
|---|---|
| Turnover | 42,000 |
| Cost of sales | 14,000 |
| Gross profit | 28,000 |
| Distribution costs | (6,000) |
| Administrative expenses | (5,000) |
| Profit on ordinary activities before tax | 17,000 |
| Taxation | 8,500 |
| Profit on ordinary activities after tax | 8,500 |
| Balance brought forward | 13,500 |
| Balance carried forward | 22,000 |

## (f) Group Reconstructions

One area where merger accounting may be appropriate is that of group reconstructions.

FRS 6 defines the term "group reconstructions" as including the following arrangements:

(a) the transfer of a shareholding in a subsidiary undertaking from one group company to another;
(b) the addition of a new parent company to a group;
(c) the transfer of shares in one or more subsidiary undertakings of a group to a new company that is not a group company but whose shareholders are the same as those of the group's parent;
(d) the combination into a group of two or more companies that before the combination had the same shareholders.

In the above cases FRS 6 permits the option of merger accounting but does not make it mandatory.

# 26.11    International Financial Reporting Standards

IFRS 3, Business combinations, covers

- The method of accounting for business combinations;
- Initial measurement of assets and liabilities acquired and assumed;
- Liabilities for terminating or reducing the acquiree's activities;
- The treatment of "negative goodwill";
- Accounting for goodwill.

IFRS 3 requires an entity to:

- Account for all business combinations within its scope by the purchase method;
- Identify an acquirer;
- Measure the cost of the business combination as the aggregate of the fair values of assets given less liabilities incurred plus the fair value of equity instruments issued plus any directly attributable costs;
- Recognize separately and measure initially at fair value, at the acquisition date the acquiree's identifiable assets, liabilities and *contingent liabilities* that satisfy specified recognition criteria as at that date (regardless of whether they had been previously recognized in the acquiree's financial statements);
- Recognize goodwill acquired in a business combination as an asset from the balance sheet date;
- Prohibits the amortization of goodwill acquired in a business combination, but requires such goodwill to be tested for impairment annually (or more frequently in certain circumstances);
- Where the acquirer's interest in the net fair value of the items recognized exceeds the cost of the combination (i.e. "negative goodwill"), requires the

acquirer to reassess the identification and measurement of the relevant items and to recognize immediately within profit or loss any excess then remaining;

- Disclose comprehensive information to enable users of the financial statements to make certain key evaluations, for example of changes in the carrying value of goodwill during the period.

---

**Frequently Asked Questions**

1 What standards require disclosures relating to acquisitions, apart from FRS 6?
FRS 1, Cash flow statements, requires a note to show a summary of the effects of acquisitions indicating how much of the consideration comprised cash. Material effects on amounts reported under each of the standard headings reflecting the cash flows of subsidiaries acquired should be disclosed as far as practicable.

FRS 3, Reporting financial performance, requires separate disclosure of the aggregate results of acquisitions down to operating profit level. The standard also requires disclosure of post-acquisition results for the period in which the acquisition occurs.

2 Is a fair value table required in the year subsequent to the acquisition?
If significant adjustments are made to provisional fair values, a fair value table is also required in the subsequent period (see comments of the Financial Reporting Review Panel in Press Notice 45).

3 Under UK GAAP, is it possible to avoid amortizing goodwill?
Yes, but only in special circumstances. FRS 10 contains a rebuttable presumption that the useful life of goodwill should be limited to 20 years or less. If companies can provide evidence to rebut this presumption, it is possible for goodwill to be carried in the balance sheet without amortization. In this situation, impairment reviews will need to be carried out annually.

---

 Associates and Joint
Ventures

---

**This chapter covers:**
* Categories of fixed asset investments
* Distinction between parent company accounts and consolidated (group) accounts
* Understanding the equity and gross equity methods
* Associates – definition, accounting and disclosures
* Joint ventures – definition, accounting and disclosures
* Situations where consolidated accounts not prepared
* Joint arrangements (JANEs)
* International Financial Reporting Standards

---

## 27.1 Introduction

The term fixed asset investments covers a broad spectrum including investments in subsidiaries, associates, joint ventures, joint arrangements and other investments which do not fit into any of the earlier categories.

The purpose of this chapter is to explain how fixed asset investments should be categorized, and how they should be accounted for and disclosed in accordance with FRS 9 to which reference should be made in complex cases.

It is always important to appreciate the distinction between the accounting treatment in the accounts of an individual company, i.e. the parent company, and the treatment in the consolidated or group accounts. For example, investments in subsidiaries will usually be stated at cost in the parent company's balance sheet, whilst the parent company's profit and loss account will include dividends received and receivable from subsidiaries. By contrast, the consolidated balance sheet will include the assets and liabilities of individual subsidiaries on a line by line basis, and the consolidated profit and loss account will include income and expenses, on a line by line basis, of the various subsidiaries.

## 27.2   Regulatory Environment – Overview

### (a) Companies Act 1985

Companies Act 1985 permits an individual investor company to carry a fixed asset investment using either the historical cost rules or the alternative accounting rules.

Under the historical cost rules, the investment is stated at historical cost, as reduced by any provision for permanent diminution in value or impairment. The Companies Act 1985 gives little guidance regarding impairment—detailed rules are contained in FRS 11 (see section 12.8). These rules could be relevant, for example where an investment relates to a subsidiary which has incurred trading losses over a prolonged period.

In practice, most groups adopt the historical cost rules for investments in subsidiaries, associates and joint ventures carried in the parent company's balance sheet.

The alternative accounting rules involve carrying investments at revalued amount. For example, a parent company may state an investment in a subsidiary as a proportionate amount of the subsidiary's underlying net assets. Any increase in the investment in the subsidiary figure from year to year would be credited to revaluation reserve, whilst a reduction would be debited to revaluation reserve (or profit and loss account, to the extent that the investment was written down below historical cost). Only a small minority of companies use the alternative accounting rules for fixed asset investments.

The Companies Act 1985 has comparatively few rules on the treatment in the consolidated accounts. Detailed rules are provided by Financial Reporting Standards such as FRS 2, Accounting for subsidiary undertakings, FRS 6, Acquisitions and mergers, and FRS 7, Fair values in acquisition accounting.

### (b) FRS 2, Accounting for Subsidiary Undertakings

FRS 2 deals with the criteria for deciding whether or not a particular investment should be classified as an investment in a subsidiary undertaking (see Chapter 25).

### (c) FRS 6, Acquisitions and Mergers and FRS 7, Fair Values in Acquisition Accounting

These provide detailed rules and guidance on how subsidiaries should be dealt with in consolidated accounts (see Chapter 26).

### (d) FRS 9, Associates and Joint ventures

The main objective of FRS 9 is to deal with two types of investments:

(1) associates – where the investor has a participating interest and significant influence;

(2) joint ventures – where the investor has a long-term interest and joint control.

FRS 9 deals also with a further investment category—a joint arrangement. The FRS 9 definitions are covered below, together with accounting and disclosure requirements.

## 27.3    Classification of Fixed Asset Investments

The Summary to FRS 9 gives a useful overview of the various investment relationships. In brief summary, these are listed below in descending order of control/influence:

(1) subsidiary – investor controls its investee;
(2) joint arrangement that is not an entity (JANE) – several entities participate in an arrangement to carry on part of their own trades or businesses;
(3) joint venture – investor holds a long-term interest and shares control under a contractual arrangement;
(4) associate – investor holds a participating interest and exercises significant influence;
(5) simple investment – does not qualify under one of the above categories due to either limited influence or fact that interest is not long-term.

The sections below deal in turn with associates, joint ventures and joint arrangements, and include practical illustrations from recently published accounts of listed companies. Subsidiaries are dealt with in FRS 2 (see Chapter 25).

## 27.4    Cost Method and Equity Method Compared – an Introduction

The definitions below are taken from FRS 9—the equity method is relevant for accounting for associates. The gross equity method, which is relevant for joint ventures is defined and dealt with in section 27.7 below.

### (a) Definition – Equity Method

A method of accounting that brings an investment into its investor's financial statements initially at cost, identifying any goodwill arising. The carrying amount of the investment is adjusted in each period by the investor's share of the results of its investee less any amortization or write off for goodwill, the investor's share of any relevant gains or losses and any other changes in the investee's net assets including distribution to its owners for example by dividend.

The investor's share of its investee's results is recognized in its profit and loss account.

The investor's cash flow statement includes the cash flows between the investor and its investee, for example relating to dividends and loans.

## (b) Example

### Illustration 1

The H group holds 30% of the share capital of Associate Ltd. The summarized profit and loss account of A Ltd showed the following position:

|  | £ |
|---|---|
| Turnover | 8,000 |
| Operating expenses | 3,500 |
| Operating profit | 4,500 |
| Taxation | 2,000 |
|  | 2,500 |
| Dividends proposed | 1,000 |
| Retained profit | 1,500 |

The summarized balance sheet of A Ltd was as follows:

|  | £ |
|---|---|
| Fixed assets | 9,500 |
| Current assets | 1,500 |
| Creditors due within one year | (1,000) |
| Creditors due in more than one year | (3,000) |
|  | 7,000 |
| Ordinary share capital | 2,000 |
| Profit and loss account | 5,000 |
|  | 7,000 |

The shares were purchased five years ago at a cost of £1,100 when A's reserves amounted to £1,000.

### (1) Consolidated profit and loss account (extracts)

The consolidated profit and loss account is shown under the three following assumptions:

(i) H group has no investment in A Ltd (assumed figures are used);
(ii) A group accounts for its investment in A Ltd using the cost method (the traditional method of accounting for fixed asset investments);
(iii) H group accounts for its investment in A Ltd using the equity method.

For simplicity no information is given as regards subsidiary companies of company H. Assume, however, that H is required by law to prepare consolidated accounts.

| | Consolidated profit and loss account | | |
| --- | --- | --- | --- |
| | Situation (i) | Situation (ii) | Situation (iii) |
| Turnover | 30,000 | 30,000 | 30,000 |
| Operating expenses | (8,000) | (8,000) | (8,000) |
| Dividends receivable | – | 300 | – |
| Share of profit of investment | – | – | 1,350 |
| Profit on ordinary activities before tax | 22,000 | 22,300 | 23,350 |
| Tax | | | |
| Group | (11,000) | (11,000) | (11,000) |
| Share of investee's tax | | | (600) |
| Profit after tax | 11,000 | 11,300 | 11,750 |
| Dividends | 5,000 | 5,000 | 5,000 |
| Retained profit | 6,000 | 6,300 | 6,750 |

*Notes:*

(1) Under the cost method, only the share of dividend receivable (30% × £1,000 = £300) is included.

   Under the equity method, a proportionate share of profit before tax (30% × £4,500 = £1,350) and a proportionate share of tax (30% × £2,000 = £600) are included.

(2) The cost method does not include the group's proportion of the retained profits of the associate (30% × £1,500 = £450). This accounts for the difference between the two retained profit figures.

(3) The difference between the two approaches could have a significant effect on earnings per share (which is based on profit after tax).

## (2) Consolidated balance sheet (extracts)
### (a) Fixed asset investments

*(i) Cost method*
Investment will be stated at cost of £1,100

*(ii) Equity method*
The investment will be stated as follows:

| | £ |
| --- | --- |
| Investment in associate | |
| Share of net assets | 2,100 |
| Goodwill arising on acquisition less amortization | 150 |
| | 2,250 |

**Workings:**

| | |
| --- | --- |
| (i)  Share of net assets | |
| 30% × £7,000 | 2,100 |
| (ii) Goodwill less amortisation | |
| Arising on acquisition of Associate Limited: | |
| Cost of investment | 1,100 |
| Proportion of net assets at acquisition | |
| 30% (2,000 + 1,000) | 900 |
| | 200 |
| Unamortized portion $^{15}/_{20} \times 200 =$ | 150 |

*Note:* treatment of amortization follows FRS 10 (see FRS 9, paragraph 31(a)).

**(b) Reserves**

(i) *Cost method*
Group reserves will include dividends received and receivable from associates.

(ii) *Equity method*
Group reserves will also include share of post-acquisition profits, less an adjustment for amortization of goodwill, i.e. £1,150.

**Workings:**

|  | £ |
|---|---|
| Reserves of A |  |
|    At year end | 5,000 |
|    At acquisition | 1,000 |
|  | 4,000 |
| Proportionate share 30% × £4,000 | £1,200 |
| Less amortisation of goodwill ($5/20 \times 200$) | 50 |
|  | 1,150 |

# 27.5   Investments in Subsidiaries

## (a) Individual Accounts of the Parent Company

The accounting treatment was referred to in section 27.2 above.

## (b) Accounts of the Group

Subsidiaries are normally consolidated in the usual way unless:

(1) the parent company is exempt from the preparation of group accounts for one of the reasons discussed in section 25.10;
(2) the subsidiary is required to be excluded from consolidated accounts for one of the reasons discussed in section 25.7.

# 27.6   Associates

## (a) Definition

FRS 9 defines an associate as

> "... an entity (other than a subsidiary) in which another entity (the investor) has a participating interest and over whose operating and financial policies the investor exercises a significant influence ...".

## (1) Participating interest

This is defined in FRS 9 as

> "... an interest held in the shares of another entity on a long-term basis for the purpose of securing a contribution to the investor's activities by the exercise of control or influence arising from or related to that interest ...".

FRS 9 emphasizes that the investor's interest must be a beneficial one and the benefits expected to arise must be linked to the exercise of its significant influence over the investee's operating and financial policies.

"... an interest in shares ..." includes an interest convertible into an interest in shares or an option to acquire shares.

Companies Act 1985 provides that a holding of 20% or more of the shares of an entity is to be presumed to be a participating interest unless the contrary is shown. This presumption is rebutted if either the interest is not long-term or it is not beneficial.

### (2) Exercise of significant influence

This is defined in FRS 9 as follows:

The investor is actively involved and is influential in the direction of its investee through its participation in policy decisions covering aspects of policy relevant to the investor, including decisions on strategic issues such as:

(i) the expansion or contraction of the business, participation in other entities or changes in products, markets and activities of its investee, and
(ii) determining the balance between dividend and reinvestment.

Companies Act 1985 provides that an entity holding 20% or more of the voting rights in another entity should be presumed to exercise a significant influence.

## (b) Accounting – Individual Accounts of Investor

The investment in the associate should be stated in the balance sheet at either cost less any amounts written off or at valuation.

Dividends received and receivable should be included in the profit and loss account.

## (c) Accounting – Consolidated Accounts of Investor

### (1) Equity method

Investments in associates should be included in the consolidated account using the equity method of accounting.

### (2) Key elements

The main aspects of the equity method are:

(i) it is a method of accounting that brings an investment into its investor's accounts initially at cost, identifying any premium arising;
(ii) the balance sheet carrying amount is adjusted in each period by:
  – the investor's share of the results of its investee (less any amortization or write-off for goodwill in accordance with FRS 10);
  – the investor's share of any relevant gains or losses;

- any other changes in the investee's net assets including distributions to its owners, for example by dividend;
(iii) the profit and loss account picks up the investor's share of the investee's results;
(iv) the cash flow statement includes the cash flows between the investor and its investee (for example, relating to dividends and loans).

## (d) Summary – Comparison of Accounting in the Parent Company and the Consolidated Accounts

|  | Parent company accounts | Group (consolidated) accounts |
|---|---|---|
| **Balance sheet** |  |  |
| (i) Fixed assets – shares in associates | Usually at cost of investment less any amounts written off (in some cases shown at a valuation). | Total of: (i) group share of net assets (other than goodwill); (ii) group share of goodwill in associates' balance sheet; (iii) premium (discount) on acquisition of shares. |
| (ii) Reserves profit and loss account | Dividends received and receivable by investing group. | Include also group share of retained post-acquisition profits. |
| Revaluation reserve | N/A | Include group share of post-acquisition revaluation reserve of associates. |
| Profit and loss account | Dividends received and receivable. | Group share of profits less losses of associates. |

## (e) Disclosure Requirements

The key disclosure requirements are as follows (special considerations for significant holdings in associates are referred to in section 27.14).

### (1) Consolidated profit and loss account
The main requirements of FRS 9 are as follows:

(i) the profit and loss account may give a memorandum turnover figure which combines group and associate turnover, provided that the share of associate turnover is clearly distinguished;

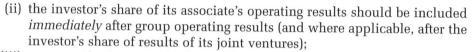

(ii) the investor's share of its associate's operating results should be included *immediately* after group operating results (and where applicable, after the investor's share of results of its joint ventures);

(iii) any amortization or write-down of goodwill relating to the acquisition of the associate should be charged at the point above and separately disclosed;

(iv) the investor's share of any "non-operating" exceptional items (i.e. exceptional items required by FRS 3 to be shown below operating profit), or of interest, should be shown in the usual profit and loss position, but separate from the amounts for the group;

(v) the investor's share of tax should be included within the group amounts but separately disclosed in the notes to the accounts;

(vi) the note giving segment information for turnover and profit may likewise bring together group and associate figures, provided that the distinction between the two is made clear.

*(2) Consolidated statement of total recognized gains and losses*

The investor's share of the total recognized gains and losses of its associates should be included in the consolidated gains statement under the appropriate headings, separately disclosed if material.

*(3) Consolidated balance sheet*

(i) The investor's consolidated balance sheet should include the investor's share of the net assets of its associates as a separate item under the fixed asset investment heading.

(ii) The carrying amount should include goodwill arising on acquisition of associates (less amortization and write-downs), separately disclosed.

*(4) Consolidated cash flow statement*

The investor's consolidated cash flow statement should include dividends received from associates. This should be shown as a separate item positioned between operating activities and returns on investments and servicing of finance.

# 27.7   Joint Ventures

*(a) Definitions*

FRS 9 defines a joint venture as:

> "An entity in which the reporting entity holds an interest on a long-term basis and is jointly-controlled by the reporting entity and one or more other ventures under a contractual arrangement…".

In many cases, the contractual arrangement will be evidenced through a shareholders' agreement.

"A reporting entity jointly controls a venture with one or more other entities if none of the entities alone can control that entity but all together can do so and decisions on financial and operating policy essential to the activities, economic performance and financial position of that venture require each venturer's consent." (FRS 9, paragraph 4.)

The summary to FRS 9 indicates that the joint venture agreement can override the rights normally conferred by ownership interests with the effect that:

(1) acting together, the venturers can control the venture and there are procedures for such joint action;
(2) each venturer has (implicitly or explicitly) a veto over strategic policy decisions.

There is usually a procedure for settling disputes between ventures and possibly, for terminating the joint venture.

## (b) Accounting Individual Accounts of Investor

The investment in the joint venture should be stated in the balance sheet at either cost less any amounts written off, or at valuation.

Dividends received and receivable should be included in the profit and loss account.

## (c) Accounting – Consolidated Accounts of Investor: the Gross Equity Method

Joint ventures should be reflected in the consolidated accounts by a modified form of equity accounting referred to as the "gross equity method". FRS 9 defines this as:

"A form of the equity method under which the investor's share of the aggregate gross assets and liabilities underlying the net amount included for the investment is shown on the face of the balance sheet and, in the profit and loss account, the investor's share of the investee's turnover is noted".

The gross equity method is similar to the equity method used for associates and dealt with above, subject to the differences noted below under disclosure requirements.

## (d) Disclosure Requirements

The disclosures are similar to those required for associates, subject to the differences below:

### (1) Consolidated profit and loss account

The investor's share of the turnover of its joint venture should be disclosed, but not as part of group turnover—again illustrated in the example above.

### (2) Consolidated balance sheet

The balance sheet should show separately the investor's share of gross assets and gross liabilities, which then subtotal to give the investment in joint ventures, based on the net equity amount. It is assumed (although not explicitly stated in FRS 9) that this will include any unamortized goodwill relating to the joint venture.

### (3) Supplemental information for joint ventures

The general rule is that any supplemental information given for joint ventures, whether it relates to the consolidated balance sheet or the consolidated profit and loss account, must be shown clearly separate from amounts for the group and must not be included in the group totals.

# 27.8   Acquisitions and Disposals

## (a) Acquisitions

PAS 7 fair value principles apply to determining the fair value of the purchase consideration, the fair value of the underlying assets and liabilities of the investee, and the goodwill arising. Goodwill should be dealt with in accordance with FRS 10 (para 31(a)).

Where an investment in an associate or joint venture is acquired in stages, the principles set out in paragraphs 50 and 51 of FRS 2 should be followed (FRS 9, para 41).

## (b) Disposals

Where an interest in an associate or Joint venture is disposed of, the profit or loss on disposal should be calculated after taking account of any related goodwill that has not been written off through the profit and loss account.

Special rules apply where an investment in an associate or joint venture is acquired or disposed of in stages (FRS 9, para 41 refers again to FRS 2).

# 27.9 Commencement or Cessation of an Associate or Joint Venture Relationship

## (a) Effective Date

This date is crucial in determining when equity accounting can start and when it must cease:

| Event | Effective date |
|---|---|
| Investment becomes associate. | Date on which investor holds a participating interest and exercises significant influence. |
| Investment ceases to be associate. | Date on which investor ceases to fulfil either element above. |
| Investment becomes a joint venture. | Date on which investor has a long-term interest and begins to control entity jointly with other venturers. |
| Investment ceases to be a joint venture. | Date on which investor ceases to have joint control. |

## (b) Carrying Amount – Entity Ceases to be Associate or Joint Venture

The initial carrying amount of any interest retained is based on the percentage retained of the final carrying amount for the former associate or joint venture at the date the entity ceased to qualify as such, including any related goodwill.

The carrying amount determined above should be reviewed, where required by FRS 11, for impairment and if necessary written down to its recoverable amount.

# 27.10 Loss-making Associates and Joint Ventures

## (a) General Rule

The investing company should continue to record changes in the carrying amount for each associate or joint venture, even if applying the equity/gross equity method results in an interest in net liabilities rather than net assets.

Where an interest in net liabilities arises, the amount recorded should be shown as a provision or liability.

## (b) Special Case

There is one exception to the above that is where there is sufficient evidence that an event has irrevocably changed the relationship between the investor and the investee indicating the investor's inevitable and irreversible withdrawal from its investee.

This evidence would include:

- A public statement by the investor that it is withdrawing plus a demonstrable commitment to the process of withdrawal, or
- Evidence that the direction of the operating and financing policies of the investee is to become the responsibility of the investee's creditors (including its bankers) rather than its equity shareholders.

# 27.11  Joint Arrangements not Entities (JANEs)

## (a) Definitions

FRS 9 defines this as:

> "A contractual arrangement under which the participants engage in joint activities that do not create an entity because it would not be carrying on a trade or business of its own. A contractual arrangement where all significant matters of operating and financial policy are predetermined does not create an entity because the policies are those of its participants, not of a separate entity".

An entity is defined as:

> "A body corporate, partnership, or unincorporated association carrying on a trade or business with or without a view to profit. The reference to carrying on a trade or business means a trade or business of its own and not just part of the trades or businesses of entities that have interests in it".

## (b) Application to Particular Industries

Commentators on FRS 9 have indicated that such arrangements may apply to specific industries such as oil, construction and engineering. An example could relate to a pipeline owned jointly by several oil companies where the throughout of oil is sold separately by each company.

## (c) Accounting – Individual and Consolidated Balance Sheet

FRS 9 requires that:

> "A participant in a structure with the appearance of a joint venture but used only as a means for each participant to carry on its own business should account directly for its part of the assets, liabilities and cash flows held within that structure".

### Illustration 2

Three Valleys Water plc, Accounting policies, 31 March 2000 (extracts).

**Partnership accounting**

The company has previously entered into a partnership arrangement. This partnership is accounted for in accordance with FRS 9 "Associates and Joint ventures" as a joint arrangement that is not an entity. The company's share of the assets, liabilities and cash flows in the joint arrangement have been included in these accounts. See note 25.

*Note 25 – Group partnership arrangement*

The company holds an investment in General Utilities Partnership, a partnership arrangement established with three other group companies, which gives each party equal control. The partnership provides technical services to the company. The company's share (65.6%) of the partnership's profit and loss account and balance sheet was incorporated into the accounts for the year ended 31 March 2000 as follows:

|  |  | £'000s |
|---|---|---|
| *Profit and loss account* | | |
| Depreciation | | (271) |
| Administration costs | | (409) |
| Other operating income | | 723 |
| Net interest payable | | (39) |
| Taxation | | – |
| Net profit | | 4 |
| *Balance sheet* | | |
| Fixed assets | cost | 1,258 |
| | depreciation | (523) |
| | net book value | 735 |
| Current assets: | work in progress | 858 |
| | debtors | 1,984 |
| | cash at hand and in bank | (57) |
| Current liabilities: | creditors – amounts falling due within one year | (2,147) |
| Reserves | | (28) |
| Net assets | | 1,345 |

General Utilities Partnership's principal office is located at 1 Three Valleys Way, Watford.

# 27.12 Investor not Preparing Consolidated Accounts

## (a) Requirements

Where an investor does not prepare consolidated accounts, FRS 9 requires it to present the relevant amounts for associates and joint ventures by providing information additional to its own accounts. This additional information may be presented in two forms:

- by preparing a separate set of financial statements, or
- by showing the relevant amounts together with the effects of including them.

## (b) When Applicable

The above situation is likely to apply to investors who have interests in associates or joint ventures, but no subsidiaries.

## (c) Exemption from Requirements

Exemption from the above requirements is available to:

- investing entities exempt from preparing consolidated accounts, for example parent companies heading up small or medium-sized groups;
- investing entities that would be exempt from preparing consolidated accounts if they had subsidiaries.

# 27.13    Associates and Joint Ventures – Further Disclosures

## (a) Method of Disclosure – Equity Method and Gross Equity Method

As indicated above, under accounting for associates and joint ventures respectively, certain disclosures must be made on the face of the financial statements. In addition, the disclosures referred to below should be given by way of note. The requirements of FRS 9 are extremely detailed—the headings below aim to provide a broad outline only.

Unless otherwise indicated, the disclosures below relate to all associates and joint ventures. Additional disclosures, referred to below, apply where specified 15% and 25% thresholds are exceeded.

## (b) General Information

For each associate and joint venture disclose:

- name;
- proportion of shares held;
- accounting periods/dates – if different from investing group;
- nature of business.

## (c) Other Disclosures

If applicable to the particular circumstances, the following should be given:

(1) information (whether or not provided in the notes to the accounts of the joint venture or associate) necessary for an understanding of the effect on the investment, for example share of contingent liabilities incurred jointly with other venturers or investors;

(2) extent of significant statutory, contractual or exchange control restrictions;

(3) debtor and creditor balances with associates and joint ventures analysed between loans and trading balances, combined where appropriate with FRS 8 disclosures;

(4) explanation of rebuttal of 20% significant interest presumption.

## (d) Additional Disclosures – Assessing the Threshold

Additional disclosures are required if specified 15% and 25% thresholds are exceeded—applied by comparing:

(1) the investor's share (for associates in aggregate *or* joint ventures in aggregate or individual associates or individual joint ventures, as appropriate) of any of the following:
  - gross assets;
  - gross liabilities;

- turnover;
- operating results (on 3-year average); with
(2) the corresponding amount for the investor group (excluding amounts for associates and joint ventures).

### (e) 15% Threshold Exceeded – Associates

If the aggregate of the investor's share in associates exceeds the 15% threshold regarding the investor group, disclosure is required of the aggregate of the investor's share in associates of:

- turnover (except where already included as memorandum item);
- fixed assets;
- current assets;
- liabilities due within one year;
- liabilities due after one year.

### (f) 15% Threshold Exceeded – Joint Ventures

If the aggregate of the investor's share in its joint ventures exceeds a 15% threshold regarding the investor group, disclosure is required of the aggregate of the investor's share in joint ventures of:

- fixed assets;
- current assets;
- liabilities due within one year;
- liabilities due after one year.

### (g) 25% Threshold Exceeded – Individual Associates and Joint Ventures

If the investor's share in an *individual* associate or joint venture exceeds a 25% threshold regarding the investor group, disclosure is required of:

- name of associate or joint venture;
- share of:
  - turnover,
  - profit before tax,
  - taxation,
  - profit after tax,
  - fixed assets,
  - current assets,
  - liabilities due within one year,
  - liabilities due after one year.

## (h) Further Disclosure – 15% and 25% Thresholds

Additional to the disclosures above, further analysis should be given where necessary to understand the nature of the total amounts disclosed.

## (i) Cash Flow Statement Disclosure

The main amendment to FRS 1 (revised) is that "dividends from joint ventures and associates" is to be an additional standard heading to follow immediately after "operating activities". Dividends from equity-accounted investments should no longer be included as part of operating cash flows.

# 27.14 International Financial Reporting Standards

## (a) IAS 28, Accounting for Investments in Associates

An associate is defined as:

> "An entity, including an unincorporated entity such as a partnership, over which the investor has significant influence and that is neither a subsidiary nor an interest in a joint venture".

The main basis of IAS 28 is the equity method defined as:

> "A method of accounting whereby the investment is initially recognized at cost and adjusted thereafter for the post-acquisition change in the investor's share of net assets of the investee. The profit or loss of the investor includes the investor's share of the profit or loss of the investee".

IAS 28 is similar to FRS 9 in terms of accounting, but there are differences of detail regarding presentation and disclosure.

## (b) IAS 31, Financial Reporting of Interests in Joint Ventures

Joint ventures as defined in IAS 31 involve contractual arrangements which establish joint control. This distinguishes them from investments in associates where the definition refers only to "significant influence".

Jointly-controlled entities are joint ventures that involve the establishment of a corporation, partnership or other entity, in which each venturer has an interest. The contractual arrangement between the venturers establishes joint control over the economic activity of the entity.

IAS 31 *recommends* the *proportionate consolidation method*, because it better reflects the substance and economic reality of a venturer's interest in a jointly-controlled entity (i.e. control over the venturer's share of the future economic benefits), although the equity method is also permitted.

Proportionate consolidation is a method of accounting whereby a venturer's share of each of the assets, liabilities, income and expenses of a jointly-controlled entity is combined line-by-line with similar items in the venturer's financial statements, or reported as separate line items in the venturer's financial statements.

# 28 Accounting for Overseas Operations

**This Chapter covers:**
* Individual company transactions
* Treatment of long-term monetary items
* Choice of translation method
* Operation of closing rate/net investment method
* Operation of temporal method
* Equity investments financed by foreign borrowings
* Foreign branches
* International Financial Reporting Standards

## 28.1 Introduction

This chapter follows the approach of SSAP 20 in dealing separately with two aspects of the subject:

(a) Overseas business transactions entered into by individual companies. This includes overseas borrowings and purchases from overseas suppliers. This aspect is dealt with in section 28.2.

(b) The foreign operations of a UK company conducted through foreign enterprises, whether they be subsidiaries, associated companies or branches. This aspect is dealt with in the remaining parts of the chapter, and revolves mainly around the preparation of consolidated financial statements.

## 28.2 Accounts of Individual Companies

### (a) Objective

A company may enter into transactions which are denominated in a foreign currency. For example, a UK company may borrow $100,000 repayable in ten years' time. At each balance sheet date it will be necessary to express this in sterling for inclusion in the UK balance sheet expressed in sterling.

It is important to remember what we are trying to achieve. SSAP 20 states that "the translation of foreign currency transactions ... should produce results which are generally compatible with the effects of rate changes on a company's cash flows and its equity and should ensure that the financial statements present a true and fair view of the results of management actions..."

## (b) Basic Rule

Assuming a UK company, the results of each transaction should normally be translated into £ sterling using the exchange rate in operation on the date on which the transaction occurred.

In certain circumstances, it may be acceptable to use an average rate for the period—this may be useful if there are a large number of transactions.

There are two important exceptions to this basic rule:

(1) where the transaction is to be settled at a contracted rate, the contracted rate should be used;
(2) where a trading transaction is covered by a related or matching forward contract, the rate of exchange specified in that contract may be used.

## (c) Non-monetary Assets

The term non-monetary assets include plant and machinery, land and buildings, equity investments and stock.

As soon as non-monetary assets have been translated into sterling (normally using the rate at the transaction date per (b) above) and recorded in the books, they should not be retranslated at a later date.

### Illustration 1

A UK company purchases plant and machinery for use in the United Kingdom from a Canadian company for $267,000. The exchange rate at the date of purchase was $1.8 = £1. So the company should record the fixed asset in its records at £148,333. The asset should not be translated again: subsequent changes in exchange rates will have no effect. The annual depreciation charge should be based on £148,333.

## (d) Monetary Assets and Liabilities

The term includes debtors, cash, creditors and loans payable. Two possible situations may arise:

(1) the transaction has been settled by the balance sheet date, e.g. the amount owing to an overseas supplier has been paid in full;
(2) the transaction is still outstanding at the balance sheet date.

In each case, exchange differences will arise. These will normally be included as part of the profit on ordinary activities for the year. The two examples immediately below illustrate the above points.

## Illustration 2

A UK company purchased goods from a French company in May 19X4 for Fr10,500 when the exchange rate was Fr11.6 = £1. The account was paid on 15 July 19X4 when the exchange rate was Fr11.9 = £1.

The supplier's account in the records of the UK company would appear as follows

A SUPPLIER

| 19X4 | £ | 19X4 | £ |
|---|---|---|---|
| 15 July Cash (10,500÷11.9) | 882 | May Purchases (10,500÷11.6) | 905 |
| 31 Dec P/L a/c | 23 | | |
| | 905 | | 905 |

## Illustration 3

A UK company purchased goods from a German supplier in November 19X4 for DM4,500 when the exchange rate was DM3.9 = £1. The account has not been settled by 31 December 19X4, the company's year end. At that date the exchange rate was DM3.8 = £1.

The supplier's account would appear as follows:

B SUPPLIER

| 19X4 | £ | 19X4 | £ |
|---|---|---|---|
| 31 December Balance c/d | | November Purchases | |
| (4,500÷3.8) | 1,184 | (4,500÷3.9) | 1,154 |
| | | 31 December P/L | 30 |
| | 1,184 | | 1,184 |

Note:

(1) In each case, the exchange gain or loss would form part of the profit (or loss) on ordinary activities before taxation. In the Companies Act 1985 formats they would normally be grouped within other operating income or expense, but there is no specific requirement to disclose separately.
(2) The exchange gain in A Supplier of £23 has already been reflected in cash flows (i.e. the amount paid was £882 as opposed to £905); The exchange loss in B Supplier is reasonably certain to be reflected in cash flows (it is only a matter of time before the bill is paid!).

## (e) Long-term Monetary Items

Exchange gains on short-term monetary items (considered in (d) above) are fairly straightforward to deal with as they are already (or soon will be) reflected in cash flows.

With long-term monetary assets, for example a loan repayable in several years' time in a foreign currency, there are additional considerations. It will be difficult (if not impossible!) to predict the exchange rate when the loan comes up for repayment. The basic approach of SSAP 20 is:

(1) outstanding loans should be translated into sterling at each balance sheet date using the year end exchange rate;
(2) exchange differences arising between successive balance sheet dates should normally be reported as part of the profit or loss on ordinary activities.

## Illustration 4

A UK company takes out a ten-year loan from an American bank in August 19X5 for US $800,000. The proceeds of the loan are converted to sterling and remitted to the UK when the exchange rate was 1.41 (so the proceeds amounted to £567,376).

At the company's year end at 31 December 19X5, the exchange rate was 1.42 and at 31 December 19X6 was 1.39.

The loan account in the books of the UK company would appear as follows:

### US LOAN ACCOUNT

| 19X5 | £ | 19X5 | £ |
|---|---|---|---|
| 31 December Balance c/d | | August Cash | 567,376 |
| (800,000÷1.42) | 563,380 | | |
| P/La/c | 3,996 | | |
| | 567,376 | | 567,376 |
| 19X6 | | 19X6 | |
| 31 December Balance c/d | | 1 January Balance b/d | 563,380 |
| (800,000÷1.39) | 575,540 | | |
| | | P/La/c | 12,160 |
| | 575,540 | | 575,540 |

The exchange gain in 19X5 of £3,996 would be included within other interest receivable and similar income, while the exchange loss of £12,160 would be included within other interest payable and similar charges.

In 19X5, the company's profit and loss account is credited with an unrealized gain of £3,996. This treatment is justified by SSAP 20, paras 10 and 11 as follows:

*Paragraph* 10
In order to give a true and fair view of results, exchange gains and losses on long-term monetary items should normally be reported as part of the profit or loss for the period in accordance with the accruals concept of accounting; treatment of these items on a simple cash movements basis would be inconsistent with that concept. Exchange gains on unsettled transactions can be determined at the balance sheet date no less objectively than exchange losses; deferring the gains whilst recognizing the losses would not only be illogical by denying in effect that any favourable movement in exchange rates had occurred, but would also inhibit fair measurement of the performance of the enterprise in the year. In particular, this symmetry of treatment recognizes that there will probably be some interaction between currency movements and interest rates and reflects more accurately in the profit and loss account the true results of currency involvement.

*Paragraph* 11
For the special reasons outlined above, both exchange gains and losses on long-term monetary items should be recognized in the profit and loss account. However, it is necessary to consider on the grounds of prudence whether the amount of the gain, or the amount by which exchange gains exceed past exchange losses on the same items, to be recognized in the profit and loss account, should be restricted in the exceptional cases where there are doubts as to the convertibility or marketability of the currency in question.

## (f) Equity Investments Financed by Foreign Borrowings

This special situation is dealt with in section 28.6.

## 28.3 Consolidation of Foreign Subsidiaries – an Introduction

### (a) Objectives

The objectives are set out in SSAP 20:

(1) Results should be produced which are compatible with the effects of exchange rates on a company's cash flows.
(2) The consolidated accounts should reflect the results and relationships which existed in the foreign currency statements (e.g. the relationship between profits earned and assets employed).

### (b) Method

There are two main methods available for translating the results of an overseas operation into sterling—the closing rate method, and the temporal method. The two methods are not alternatives.

In any given situation, the method to be used will depend on the relationship between the parent company and the overseas entity (assumed, for the present, to be a subsidiary). This may be illustrated diagrammatically:

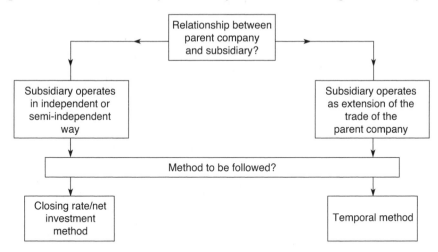

It is clear that SSAP 20 intends that the closing rate method will be appropriate in the vast majority of cases. This is confirmed by the English Institute's survey of published accounts of the leading UK companies.

### (c) Foreign Branches

Where a branch operates as a separate business with local finance, SSAP 20 states that the closing rate/net investment method should be used. If, however, the branch operates as an extension of the company's trade and its cash flows have a direct impact on those of the company, SSAP 20 requires the temporal method to be used.

The examples below relate to foreign subsidiaries but clearly the same principles should be applied to foreign branches. Foreign branches are considered further in section 28.7.

# 28.4   Closing Rate/Net Investment Method

## (a) When Appropriate

In broad terms, the method is appropriate whenever the subsidiary is independent or autonomous. Such situations may show the following characteristics.

(1) The parent company's investment is in the net worth of the foreign enterprise (as opposed to a direct investment in its assets and liabilities).
(2) The foreign enterprise will normally have both fixed assets and working capital, and these may be part-financed by local currency borrowings (as opposed to being entirely financed by the holding company).
(3) In its day-to-day operations, the foreign enterprise is not usually dependent on the reporting currency of the investing company (i.e. £ sterling).
(4) The parent company will expect dividends to be paid out of future profits, but its investment will remain until such future time as the foreign enterprise is liquidated, or the investment disposed of.

## (b) Basic Rules

| | |
|---|---|
| *Balance sheet* | All assets and liabilities translated at closing rate of exchange. |
| *Profit and loss account* | Two options permitted under SSAP 20 – either:<br>(1) all items at closing rate; or<br>(2) all items at average rate. |
| *Exchange differences* | Two types of translation differences may arise:<br>(1) exchange differences arising from the retranslation of the opening net investment at the closing rate;<br>(2) differences between P/L at average rate and P/L at closing rate (only applicable if P/L option (2) is adopted)<br><br>Both types of exchange differences should be recorded as reserve movements with no entry in the profit and loss account. |

## (c) Worked Example

On 2/1/19X0 Panther plc purchased a 70% holding of an overseas company called Clouseau SA. The investment cost £2,600 and at the date of acquisition, the reserves of Clouseau were Fr3,200.
   The relevant exchange rates were as follows:

| | |
|---|---|
| Date of acquisition | 7.0 Fr to £1 |
| 31.12.X2 | 5.6 Fr to £1 |
| Average for 19X3 | 5.1 Fr to El |
| At payment of interim dividend | 4.9 Fr to £1 |
| 31.12.X3 | 4.6 Fr to £1 |

The relevant final accounts are as follows:

**Balance sheet at 31.12.X3**

|  | Panther plc | Clouseau SA |
|---|---|---|
|  | £ | Fr |
| Tangible fixed assets – cost | 92,000 | 56,000 |
| – depreciation | (24,800) | (20,400) |
| Investment in Clouseau | 2,600 | – |
| Stock | 19,600 | 14,120 |
| Debtors | 14,130 | 15,270 |
|  | 103,530 | 64,990 |
| Cash at bank | 1,921 | 3,860 |
| Dividends receivable | 244 | – |
| Loans | (10,000) | (6,000) |
| Creditors | (10,430) | (13,040) |
| Taxation | (10,400) | (6,880) |
| Proposed dividends | (7,000) | (1,600) |
|  | 67,865 | 41,330 |
| Called-up share capital | 30,000 | 15,000 |
| Profit and loss account | 37,865 | 26,330 |
|  | 67,865 | 41,330 |

**Profit loss account for year end 31.12.X3**

|  | £ | Fr |
|---|---|---|
| Turnover | 80,000 | 37,890 |
| Cost of sales | (22,000) | (13,640) |
| Distribution costs | (16,500) | (2,090) |
| Administrative expenses | (14,600) | (7,200) |
| Dividends from Clouseau | 415 | – |
| Operating profit | 27,315 | 14,960 |
| Taxation | (10,400) | (6,880) |
| Profit on ordinary activities after tax | 16,915 | 8,080 |
| Exceptional items (non-operating) | 9,300 | – |
|  | 26,215 | 8,080 |
| Dividends – interim (paid) | (5,000) | (1,200) |
| – final (proposed) | (7,000) | (1,600) |
| Retained profit | 14,215 | 5,280 |
| P/L balance at 1.1.X3 | 23,650 | 21,050 |
| P/L balance at 31.12.X3 | 37,865 | 26,330 |

# (d) Workings

The recommended approach is to tackle the workings in the following sequence:

(1) Translation of subsidiary's balance sheet.
(2) Consolidated balance sheet workings.

(3) Consolidated balance sheet.
(4) Translation of subsidiary's profit and loss account.
(5) Calculation of total exchange difference.
(6) Analysis of total exchange difference.
(7) Consolidated profit and loss account workings.
(8) Consolidated profit and loss account.
(9) Statement of reserves.

Goodwill is assumed to have a useful life of 20 years.

## (e) Translation of Balance Sheet

| | Fr | Rate | £'000 |
|---|---|---|---|
| Fixed assets – cost | 56,000 | | 12,174 |
| – depreciation | (20,400) | | (4,434) |
| Stock | 14,120 | | 3,070 |
| Debtors | 15,270 | | 3,319 |
| Cash at bank | 3,860 | 4.6 | 839 |
| Loans | (6,000) | | (1,304) |
| Creditors | (13,040) | | (2,835) |
| Taxation | (6,880) | | (1,495) |
| Proposed dividends | (1,600) | | (348) |
| | 41,330 | | 8,986 |
| | | | |
| Ordinary share capital | 15,000 | | 2,143 |
| Pre-acquisition reserves | 3,200 | 7 | 457 |
| Post-acquisition reserves | 23,130 | Balancing figure | 6,386 |
| | 41,330 | | 8,986 |

### Explanatory notes

(1) All assets and liabilities are translated into £ sterling using the closing rate of exchange of 4.6.
(2) Shareholders' funds of £8,986 do not appear in the consolidated balance sheet as such – they are subject to consolidation adjustments in order to arrive at goodwill on consolidation, minority interest and consolidated profit and loss reserves.

In order to make the subsequent calculations easier, it is convenient (although not absolutely necessary) to divide into the three parts shown above. Since reserves at acquisition are stated as Fr3,200, the post-acquisition reserves of Fr23,130 are the carry forward of Fr26,330 less Fr3,200. Share capital and pre acquisition reserves are translated at 7 (these two figures are taken into account in calculating goodwill) and the figure of £6,386 is a balancing item.

## *(f) Consolidated Balance Sheet Workings*

**Analysis of equity**

|  | Total | Group share (70%) of pre-acquisition reserves | Group share (70%) of post-acquisition reserves | MI (30%) |
|---|---|---|---|---|
|  | £ | £ | £ | £ |
| Ordinary share capital | 2,143 | 1,500 |  | 643 |
| P/L reserves at acquisition | 457 | 320 |  | 137 |
| P/L reserves since acquisition | 6,386 |  | 4,470 | 1,916 |
|  | 8,986 | 1,820 |  |  |
| Cost of investment |  | 2,600 |  |  |
| Goodwill on consolidation |  | 780 |  |  |
| Reserves of Panther (including dividends received and receivable) |  |  | 37,865 |  |
| Cumulative amortization $3/20 \times £780$ |  | (117) | (117) |  |
| Consolidated balance sheet totals |  | 663 | 42,218 | 2,696 |
| Ml in proposed dividend (348–244) |  |  |  |  |

### CONSOLIDATED BALANCE SHEET

#### at 31 December 19X3

|  | £ | £ | £ |
|---|---|---|---|
| *Fixed assets* |  |  | 663 |
| Intangible assets |  |  | 74,940 |
| Tangible assets |  |  |  |
| *Current assets* |  | 22,670 |  |
| Stock |  | 17,449 |  |
| Debtors |  | 2,760 |  |
| Cash |  | 42,879 |  |
| *Less creditors: amounts falling due within one year* |  |  |  |
| Creditors | 13,265 |  |  |
| Taxation | 11,895 |  |  |
| Dividends payable: |  |  |  |
| Parent company shareholders | 7,000 |  |  |
| Minority shareholders | 104 |  |  |
|  |  | 32,264 |  |
| Net current assets |  |  | 10,615 |
| Total assets less current liabilities |  |  | 86,218 |
| Creditors amounts falling due after more than one year |  | (11,304) |  |
|  |  | 74,914 |  |

| | |
|---|---:|
| Called-up share capital | 30,000 |
| Profit and loss account | 42,218 |
| | 72,218 |
| Minority interest | 2,696 |
| | 74,914 |

## (g) Translation of Subsidiary's Profit and Loss Account

| | Fr | Rate | £ |
|---|---:|:---:|---:|
| Turnover | 37,890 | | 7,429 |
| Costs of sales | (13,640) | | (2,674) |
| Gross profit | 24,250 | | 4,755 |
| Distribution costs | (2,090) | 5.1 | (410) |
| Administration expenses | (7,200) | | (1,412) |
| Operating profit | 14,960 | | 2,933 |
| Tax | 6,880 | | 1,349 |
| | 8,080 | | 1,584 |
| Dividends – paid | (1,200) | 4.9 | (245) |
| – proposed | (1,600) | 4.6 | (348) |
| Retained profit | 5,280 | | 991 |

*Explanatory notes*

(1) All profit and loss items have been translated at an average rate for the period. (An acceptable alternative policy under SSAP 20 would have been to translate at closing rate.)
(2) Dividends paid are translated at the rate of exchange at the date of payments, while dividends proposed are translated at the closing rate. This should correspond with the rates used by the parent company in its own separate accounts.

## (h) Calculation of Total Exchange Difference

So far we have:

(1) Split the closing reserves of the subsidiary between pre-acquisition and post-acquisition (see working (e)).
(2) Translated various profit and loss items (working (g)).

Before we can calculate the total exchange difference on translation for the year, we need to know the equivalent split of opening reserves between pre-acquisition and post-acquisition. In practice, this information would be available from the previous year working papers. As this information is not available, it is necessary to carry out a rather artificial exercise of reconstructing the previous year's closing balance sheet.

Net assets at 31 December 19X2 may be calculated as a global total by adding together share capital and reserves (Fr15,000 + 21,050 = 36,050). Post-acquisition reserves (in francs) may again be calculated as a balancing figure.

| | Fr | Rate | £ |
|---|---:|:---:|---:|
| Sundry net assets | 36,050 | 5.6 | 6,438 |
| Ordinary share capital | 15,000 | | 2,143 |
| Pre-acquisition reserves | 3,200 | 7.0 | 457 |
| Post-acquisition reserves | 17,850 | Balancing figure | 3,838 |
| | 74,251 | | 6,438 |

*Explanatory notes*

(1) First of all, the opening balance sheet in francs should be reconstructed. Although the break-down of the net assets figure of Fr 36,050 is not known, this does not matter as all items included in this are translated at the same rate of exchange.

(2) The various items should be translated into £ sterling using the same procedures as in (e) above. The post-acquisition reserves of £3,838 are calculated as a balancing figure.

*Calculation of total exchange difference*

| | |
|---|---:|
| Post-acquisition reserves at 1.1.X3 (working (h)) | 3,838 |
| Post-acquisition reserves at 31.12.X3 (working (e)) | 6,386 |
| Increase | 2,548 |
| Retained profit (working (g)) | 991 |
| Exchange difference (gain) | 1,557 |

As the subsidiary is 70% owned, then 70% x £1,557, i.e. £1,089, will be shown as movement on group reserves (with no entry in the consolidated profit and loss account for the year).

## (i) Analysis of Total Exchange Difference

Where the profit and loss account of the subsidiary is translated at the average rate of exchange, SSAP 20 distinguishes between two elements of the exchange difference:

(1) exchange differences arising from retranslation of the opening net investment at the closing rate; and

(2) the difference between the profit and loss account translated at an average rate and at the closing rate.

The total exchange difference of £1,557 above may be analysed as follows:

| | *Fr* | *Rate* | *£* |
|---|---:|---:|---:|
| Equity interest at 1.1.X3 | 36,050 | 5.6 | 6,438 |
| Gain on retranslation at closing rate (bal figure) | – | – | 1.399 |
| Equity interest at 1.1.X3: | | | |
| Restated at closing exchange rate | 36,050 | 4.6 | 7,837 |
| Retained profit per p/l – workings | 5,280 | – | 991 |
| Exchange difference – p/l at average rate compared with closing rate | | | |
| 5280/4.6–991 | – | – | 158 |
| Equity interest at 31.12.X3 | 41,330 | 4.6 | 8,986 |

Total exchange difference = (1,399 + 158) = £1,557
Group share treated as movement on reserves during the year 70% × £1,557 = £1.089

## (j) Consolidated Profit and Loss Account Workings

For most items, it is simply a question of combining two sets of figures: those of the parent company, and the £ sterling figures for the subsidiary as calculated in (g) above.

The only other calculation required is that for minority interest. From working (g), Ml is calculated as follows:

30% × £1,584 = £475

*(k)*　　　　　　　CONSOLIDATED PROFIT AND LOSS ACCOUNT

for the year ended 31 December 19X3

| | £ | £ |
|---|---|---|
| Turnover | | 87,429 |
| Cost of sales | | 24,674 |
| Gross profit | | 62,755 |
| Distribution costs | 16,910 | |
| Administration expenses (14,600 + 1,412 + $780/_{20}$) | 16,051 | 32,961 |
| Operating profit | | 29,794 |
| Tax | | 11,749 |
| Profit on ordinary activities after tax | | 18,045 |
| Minority interest | | 475 |
| | | 17,570 |
| Non-operating exceptioned items | | 9,300 |
| | | 26,870 |
| Dividends – interim (paid) | 5,000 | |
| – final (proposed) | 7,000 | 12,000 |
| Retained profit | | 14,870 |

# (l) Statement of Reserves

This statement "links in" the retained profit in the P/L and the group share of the exchange difference with the reserves in the consolidated balance sheet.

| | £ |
|---|---|
| So far we have calculated: | |
| (i) Retained profit (from consolidated P/L); | 14,909 |
| (ii) Group share of exchange difference (workings (h) and (i)). | 1,089 |

We need to calculate the balance on consolidated P/L reserves at 1.1.X3 (this is the figure which appeared in last year's consolidated-balance sheet).

| | £ |
|---|---|
| This is calculated as follows: | |
| Panther reserves at 1.1.X3 | 23,650 |
| Panther's share of post-acquisition reserves at 1.1.X3 | |
| of Clouseau (working (h)): | |
| 70% × £3,838 | 2,687 |
| | 26,337 |
| *Less* cumulative amortization $^2/_{20}$ X 780 | 78 |
| | 26,259 |

The statement of reserves which would be disclosed in the published accounts would be:

| | £ |
|---|---|
| Profit and loss account at 1.1.X3 | 26,259 |
| Retained profit | 14,870 |
| Exchange differences | 1,089 |
| Profit and loss account at 31.12.X3 | 42,218 |

(Note that this last figure agrees with the consolidated balance sheet at 31 December 19X3.)

## 28.5  Temporal Method

### (a)  When Appropriate

The temporal method should be used in those relatively few cases where the foreign operations are carried out through foreign enterprises which operate as a direct extension of the trade of the investing company.

### (b)  Dominant Currency

The temporal method should be used where it is considered overall that the currency of the investing company (i.e. parent company) is the dominant currency in the economic environment in which the subsidiary operates.

This assessment will require the following to be taken into account:

- the extent to which the subsidiary's cash flows have a direct impact on the cash flows of the investing company;
- the extent to which the functioning of the subsidiary depends directly on the holding company;
- the currency in which the majority of trading transactions are denominated;
- the major currency to which the operation is exposed in its financing structure.

### (c)  Possible Situations

SSAP 20 gives the following as examples of situations where the temporal method may be appropriate:

(1) Where the foreign enterprise acts as a selling agency, receiving stocks of goods from the investing company and remitting the proceeds back to the company.
(2) Where the foreign enterprise produces a raw material or manufactures parts or sub-assemblies which are then shipped to the investing company for inclusion in its own product.
(3) Where the foreign enterprise is located overseas for tax, exchange control or similar reasons to act as a means of raising finance for other companies in the group.

### (d)  Basic Rules

(1) Balance sheet items

| Item | Examples | Exchange rate |
|------|----------|---------------|
| Monetary assets and liabilities | Debtors Cash Creditors Loans | Closing rate |
| Non-monetary assets | Stock | Rate at date of acquisition of stock (but closing rate is usually acceptable) |

| Item | Examples | Exchange rate |
|------|----------|---------------|
| | Fixed assets (cost less depreciation) | (1) Acquired before acquisition of subsidiary – rate at date of acquisition of subsidiary<br>(2) Acquired after acquisition of subsidiary – rate at date of purchase of fixed assets |

*(2) Profit and loss items*

| Item | Exchange rate |
|------|---------------|
| Sales<br>Expenses (excluding depreciation) | Average rate of exchange |
| Depreciation | Same rate as for fixed assets |
| Taxation | Closing rate (although some accountants consider that average rate should be used) |
| Dividends | Paid - rate at payment date<br>Proposed – closing rate |

*(3) Exchange differences*
These should be included in the profit and loss account and taken into account in arriving at profit on ordinary activities before taxation. They will normally be included under "other operating income or expense".

## 28.6    Equity Investments Financed by Foreign Borrowings

*(a) Background*

Exchange gains or losses on foreign currency borrowings would normally be reported as part of the company's or group's profit on ordinary activities.

However, where the purpose of such borrowings is to provide a hedge against the risks associated with foreign equity investments, an alternative may be available.

SSAP 20 deals with this in two parts:

- in the accounts of the investing company;
- in the group accounts.

*(b) Accounts of the Investing Company*

*(1) Situation*
Where an individual company has used borrowings in currencies other than its own, either:

(i) to finance foreign equity; or
(ii) where the purpose of such borrowings is to provide a hedge against the exchange risk associated with existing (i.e. previously acquired) equity investments;

then the company may be covered in economic terms against any movements in exchange rates.

## (2) Options

Provided the company can satisfy the conditions set out below, the company may denominate its foreign equity investments in the relevant foreign currency and translate the carrying amount at each balance sheet date at the closing rate of exchange.

Any resulting exchange differences *should* be taken direct to reserves. Against these exchange differences *should* then be offset exchange gains or losses on related borrowings.

## (3) Conditions

The three conditions to be satisfied are:

(i) In any accounting period, exchange gains or losses arising on the borrowings may be offset only to the extent of exchange differences arising on the equity investments.

(ii) The foreign currency borrowings (whose exchange gains or losses are used in the offset process) should not exceed, in the aggregate, the total amount of cash that the investments are expected to be able to generate, whether from profits or otherwise.

(iii) The accounting treatment adopted should be applied consistently from period to period.

## (4) Illustration 5

Suppose in the Panther example, the investment in Clouseau was part financed by loan of 12,600 francs repayable in twenty years' time. Assume this loan is part of Panther's total borrowings.

### (i) Ignoring SSAP 20 option

(a) The separate balance sheet of Panther will include:

| | | |
|---|---|---|
| Shares in group company | | £2,600 |
| Loan | $\left( \dfrac{\text{Fr}12{,}600}{4.6} \right)$ | £2,739 |

(£2,739 is part of larger total of £10,000.)

(b) The loss on translation of the loan during the year is calculated as:

| | £ |
|---|---|
| $\text{Fr} \dfrac{12{,}600}{5.6}$ | 2,250 |
| $\text{Fr} \dfrac{12{,}600}{4.6}$ | 2,739 |
| Translation loss, charged to profit and loss account | 489 |

**(ii) SSAP 20 option**

As an alternative, provided the above three conditions are satisfied, the company may take advantage of the option in SSAP 20 as follows:

(a) Shares in group company. Instead of showing this each year at an unchanged amount of £2,600, this equity investment may be denominated in francs, i.e. 18,200 francs (investment cost £2,600) when exchange rate was 7.0. This will then be retranslated each year at the closing rate of exchange:

Balance sheet 31.12.X2 $\dfrac{\text{Fr}\,18,200}{5.6}$ £3,250

Balance sheet 31.12.X3 $\dfrac{\text{Fr}\,18,200}{4.6}$ £3,957

(b) Loan in foreign currency borrowing:

Balance sheet 31.12.X2 $\dfrac{\text{Fr}\,12,600}{5.6}$ £2,250

Balance sheet 31.12.X3 $\dfrac{\text{Fr}\,12,600}{4.6}$ £2,739

(c) Exchange differences arising during the year:

| | £ |
|---|---|
| Exchange difference on investment (3,957–3,250) | 707 Cr |
| Exchange difference on loan (2,739–2,250) | 489 Dr |
| Net effect (credit) | 218 |

If the company takes advantage of the option, £218 should be credited direct to reserves (with no entry in the profit and loss account).

## (c) Group Accounts

### (1) Situation

Within a group, foreign borrowings may have been used to finance group investments in foreign enterprises (such as subsidiaries or associated companies) or to provide a hedge against the exchange risk associated with existing investments.

Any increase or decrease in the amount outstanding on the borrowings arising from exchange rate movements will probably be covered by corresponding changes in the carrying amount of the net assets underlying the net investments.

### (2) Option

In the consolidated accounts, provided the conditions below are satisfied:

 (i) exchange gains or losses on such currency borrowings (which would otherwise be passed through the consolidated profit and loss account) may be offset as reserve movements against;
(ii) exchange differences on retranslation of the net investments.

*(3) Conditions*

The conditions to be satisfied are:

(i) the relationship between the investing company and the foreign enterprises concerned should be such as to justify the use of the closing rate method for consolidation purposes;

(ii) "net investments in foreign enterprises" applies instead of "equity investments".

*(4) Illustration 6*

Using the data from the Panther example:

**(i) Ignoring SSAP 20 option**

- Loss on translation of loan of £489 is debited to profit and loss account.
- Group share of exchange differences (70% × £1,557 = £1,089) to reserves.

**(ii) SSAP 20 option**

The difference on translation of the foreign currency borrowings may be offset against the difference on retranslation of the opening net investment:

|  | £ |
|---|---|
| Gain on retranslation of opening net investment (see earlier workings) 70% × 1,399 | 979 |
| Loss on translation of foreign currency borrowings | 489 |
| Exchange gain after offset | 490 |
| Group share of exchange difference on P/L translation: 70% × £158 | 110 |
| So movement on reserves (credit) during the year is (490 + 110) i.e. | 600 |

# 28.7   Foreign Branches

## (a) Translation Method

The relationship between the branch and the head office will determine the translation method to be used. It is likely that most branches will conduct their business as an extension of the trade of the head office in which case the temporal method will be applicable.

This will not always be the case, however, and it is necessary to consider the definition of "foreign branch" provided by SSAP 20.

## (b) Definition

A foreign branch is either:

- a legally constituted enterprise located overseas, or
- a group of assets and liabilities which are accounted for in foreign currencies.

## (c) Special Situations

The extension of the definition above, to a "group of assets and liabilities" effectively means that certain branches (as defined) should be translated using the closing rate method.

The statement which accompanied the issue of SSAP 20 gave the following as examples of situations where a group of assets and liabilities should be accounted for using the closing rate/net investment method:

(i) a hotel in France financed by borrowings in French francs;
(ii) a ship or aircraft purchased in US dollars – with an associated loan in US dollars – which earns revenue and incurs expenses in US dollars;
(iii) a foreign currency insurance operation where the liabilities are substantially covered by the holding of foreign currency assets.

Both assets and liabilities will be translated at the exchange rate at the balance sheet date. Gains and losses on retranslation of opening "equity" will be taken direct to reserves.

## 28.8 Foreign Associated Companies

By definition an associated company is not "controlled" by the investor. Consequently, the closing rate/net investment method will usually be appropriate.

## 28.9 Disclosure in Financial Statements

### (a) Accounting Policies

The statement of accounting policies should disclose the translation method and the treatment of exchange differences.

### (b) Disclosure of Exchange Gains

The net amount of exchange gains or losses on foreign currency borrowing less deposits should be disclosed, showing separately:

(1) the amount offset in reserves as under SSAP 20, paras 51, 57 and 58 (i.e. the options referred to above); and
(2) the net amount charged or credited to the profit and loss account.

This is not required for exempt companies as defined by SSAP 20.

### (c) Movement on Reserves

Net movement on reserves arising from exchange differences should be disclosed.

## (d)  Unrealized Profits Included in Profit and Loss Account

If unrealized profits on long-term foreign loans are included in the profit and loss account, the Companies Act 1985 requires disclosure of:

- particulars of the departure (from the prudence concept);
- reasons for departure;
- effect of departure.

(See section 28.2(e) above.)

# 28.10  International Financial Reporting Standards/FRS 23

IAS 21/FRS 23, The effect of changes in foreign exchange rates.

The objective of IAS 21/FRS 23 is to prescribe how to include foreign currency transactions and foreign operations in the financial statements of an entity and how to translate financial statements into a presentation currency. In very broad terms, the standard is likely to achieve a similar effect to SSAP 20, although there are many differences of detail and terminology.

For UK GAAP, the implementation dates for FRS 23 are complex, and are linked to the dates relating to FRS 26, Financial instruments: measurement.

Fully listed companies, where the parent company accounts are *not* prepared in accordance with IFRS, will have to adopt FRS 26 [Financial instruments: measurement] for accounts periods commencing on or after 1 January 2005, and as a result will have to adopt FRS 23 for the same period.

For unlisted companies, FRS 23 is unlikely to be mandatory for accounts periods which begin before 1 January 2007.

### Accounting for foreign currency transactions

A foreign currency transaction is a transaction that is denominated or requires settlement in a foreign currency, including transactions arising when an entity:

- Buys or sells goods or services whose price is denominated in a foreign currency;
- Borrows or lends funds when the amounts payable or receivable are denominated in a foreign currency; or
- Otherwise acquires or disposes of assets, or incurs or settles liabilities, denominated in a foreign currency.

A foreign currency transaction shall be recorded, on initial recognition in the functional currency, by applying to the foreign currency amount the spot exchange rate between the functional currency and the foreign currency at the date of the transaction (FRS 23.21). This is more restrictive than the equivalent rules in SSAP 20 (see 28.2(b) above).

### Translation of a foreign operation

Subject to this, Paragraph 39 requires that the results and financial position of an entity shall be translated into a different presentational currency using the following procedures:

- Assets and liabilities for each balance sheet presented (i.e. including comparatives) shall be translated at the closing rate at the date of that balance sheet;
- Income and expenses for each income statement (i.e. including comparatives) shall be translated at exchange rates at the dates of the transactions; and
- All resulting exchange differences shall be recognized through the statement of total recognized gains and losses.

# Converging UK GAAP with IFRS – the Road Ahead

**This chapter covers:**
* Convergence experience to date
* What will have been achieved up to the end of 2005
  2006 and beyond

## 29.1   Convergence Experience to Date

Convergence is not a new development—it has been going on for several years. Several UK standards are either identical or close to IFRS equivalents. For example on provision accounting, FRS 12 and IAS 37 are identical. On deferred tax, the replacement of SSAP 15 with FRS 19 brought UK GAAP closer to IFRS, notwithstanding important differences remaining between FRS 19 and IAS 12. On impairment, FRS 11 and IAS 38 have many features in common.

ASB for many years has been working closely with IASB and national standard-setters worldwide.

During 2005, the ASB reviewed its approach towards converging UK GAAP with IFRS, and in June 2005 updated its work plan setting out an indicative timetable for issue of exposure drafts and standards. It also gave details of the process for replacing UK standards with International Standards (IASs/IFRSs) – the so-called "convergence programme". The intention in June 2005 was that the convergence process would be spread over a relatively long period of time, certainly beyond 2008 (the June 2005 update can be accessed from the FRC website).

More recent developments are referred to in 29.3 below.

## 29.2   Progress During 2005

Convergence developments during 2005 were as follows—the following are mandatory for accounts periods beginning on or after 1 January 2005 for the categories of companies indicated. Note that mandatory dates may varies as between listed and unlisted companies:

| Topic | FRS issued as part of UK GAAP | IFRS counterpart | Category of company for whom mandatory |
|---|---|---|---|
| Events after the balance sheet date | FRS 21 | IAS 10 | Listed and unlisted |
| Financial instruments – presentation | FRS 25 | IAS 32 | All listed and certain categories of unlisted |
| Financial instruments – disclosure | FRS 25 | IAS 32 | Listed |
| Financial instruments – measurement | FRS 26 | IAS 39 | All listed and certain categories of unlisted |
| Earnings per share | FRS 22 | IAS 33 | Companies whose shares are traded |
| Foreign currency (including hyperinflation) | FRS 23, 24 | IAS 21, 29 | All listed and certain categories of unlisted |
| Defined benefit pension arrangements | FRS 17 | IAS 19 | Listed and unlisted companies |
| Share-based payment | FRS 20 | IFRS 2 | Listed and unlisted |

## 29.3   ASB December 2005 Convergence Paper

On 21 December 2005, ASB published its most recent Convergence Paper (see FRC website, ASB Notice to Constituents). This paper indicated that ASB was reconsidering some of its earlier proposals, in particular its "Phased Approach" to converging UK GAAP with IFRS, as referred to in 29.1 above.

ASB is now considering a "Big Bang Approach" whereby any new standards issued would not be mandatory before a single date. This is currently estimated to be financial years beginning on or after 1 January 2009.

This issue will be amongst a number being debated during the early part of 2006.

## 29.4  And Finally

On a final note, this is not the end of the matter. IASB is currently taking an entirely fresh look at a number of key issues including performance reporting and revenue recognition. Even though it may be some years before these projects come to fruition, it is inevitable that they will result in a radical reshaping of how we today regard financial reporting. The accountancy profession—like it or not—faces enormous challenges in the years ahead.

# Implementation Dates for Unlisted Companies

Please note that different dates and transitional provisions apply to listed companies. These are not referred to in this Appendix.

## A1.1 Accounting Standards and UITF Abstracts: Mandatory

For accounts periods beginning on or after 1 January 2005, the following will be mandatory for *all* companies, including unlisted companies other than those who have adopted the FRSSE (effective January 2005):

FRS 21, Events after the balance sheet date;

FRS 25, Financial instruments: disclosure and presentation (the parts dealing with presentation only).

Note that *neither of the above may be adopted early*—this prohibition results from the changes to CA 85, referred to below.

UITF Abstract 38, Accounting for ESOP trusts, and UITF 17 (revised), Employee share schemes, are both mandatory for accounts periods ending on or after 22 June 2004.

UITF Abstract 40, Revenue recognition and service contracts, is mandatory for accounts periods ending on or after 22 June 2005.

The above Abstracts *may* be adopted early.

FRS 20, Share-based payment—accounts periods beginning on or after 1 January 2006.

## A1.2 Accounting Standards and UITF Abstracts: Optional*

FRS 22 can be adopted for accounts periods beginning on or after 1 January 2005.

*These standards are optional for unlisted companies only (they are mandatory for listed companies—FRS 26 contains complex transitional provisions).

FRS 26 *may* be adopted for accounts periods beginning on or after 1 January 2005, but if it is adopted, then FRS 25 (disclosure requirements), FRS 23 and FRS 24 *must be adopted at the same time.*

FRSs 25, 23 and 24 cannot be adopted *unless* FRS 26 is adopted.

# A1.3 Company Law Changes

Changes to the Companies Act 1985;

| Title of Regulation | Specific Aspect | Implementation Date |
|---|---|---|
| Companies Act 1985 (International Accounting Standards and Other Accounting Amendments) Regulations 2004 [SI 2947] | Prohibition on accrual of proposed equity dividends<br><br>Reporting substance IAS option Fair value disclosures | FYs commencing on/or after 1 January 2005 (but not sooner) |
| Companies (Audit, Investigations and Community Enterprise) Act 2004 | Directors' report statement reinformation to auditors | FYs commencing on or after 1 April 2005 |
| Companies Act 1985 (Operating and Financial Review and Directors' Report, etc.) Regulations 2005 [SI 1011] | Business review (within directors' report)<br><br>OFR (quoted companies)* | FYs commencing on or after 1 April 2005 |

* Statutory OFR requirement due to be repealed by Regulations coming into force in January 2006.

# UK GAAP Status Report as at 31 January 2006

**App 2**

## A2.1 Statements of Standard Accounting Practice

| Number | Title | Status/Developments |
|--------|-------|---------------------|
| SSAP 4 | The accounting treatment of government grants | |
| SSAP 5 | Accounting for value added tax | |
| SSAP 9 | Stocks and long-term contracts | FRED 28 – Inventories; Construction and service contracts |
| SSAP 13 | Accounting for research and development | FRED 37 – Intangible assets |
| SSAP 17 | Accounting for post balance sheet events | Superseded by FRS 21, Events after the balance sheet date |
| SSAP 19 | Accounting for investment properties | |
| SSAP 20 | Foreign currency translation | FRS 23 – The effects of foreign exchange rates |
| SSAP 21 | Accounting for leases and hire purchase contracts – amended in relation to treatment of tax-free grants | |
| SSAP 24 | Accounting for pension costs | Superseded by FRS 17 – Retirement benefits |
| SSAP 25 | Segmental reporting | |

## A2.2   Financial Reporting Standards

| Number | Title | Status/Developments |
|---|---|---|
| FRS 1 | Cash flow statements | |
| FRS 2 | Accounting for subsidiary undertakings | Amended December 2004 as a result of legal changes in SI 2947<br><br>FRED 36 |
| FRS 3 | Reporting financial performance | FRED 32 – Disposal of noncurrent assets and presentation of discontinued operations |
| FRS 4 | Capital instruments | Partly superseded by FRS 25, Financial instruments: disclosure and presentation |
| FRS 5 | Reporting the substance of transactions | Application Note G on Revenue recognition<br><br>UITF Abstract 40 |
| FRS 6 | Acquisitions and mergers | FRED 36 – Business combinations |
| FRS 7 | Fair values in acquisition accounting | FRED 36 – Business combinations |
| FRS 8 | Related party disclosures | FRED 25 – Related party disclosures |
| FRS 9 | Associates and joint ventures | |
| FRS 10 | Goodwill and intangible assets | FRED 36 – Business combinations |
| FRS 11 | Impairment of fixed assets and goodwill | FRED 38 – Impairment of assets |
| FRS 12 | Provisions and contingencies | FRED 39 – Amendments to FRS 12 |
| FRS 13 | Derivatives and other financial instruments | FRED 33: Financial instruments: disclosures<br>FRS 25 issued December 2004 |
| FRS 14 | Earnings per share | FRS 22 issued December 2004 |
| FRS 15 | Tangible fixed assets | FRED 29 – Property, plant and equipment; Borrowing costs |

*Continued*

| Number | Title | Status/Developments |
|--------|-------|---------------------|
| FRS 16 | Current tax | |
| FRS 17 | Retirement benefits | Abstract 35 – Death-in service and incapacity benefits<br>FRED 39, Amendments to FRS 17 |
| | | Mandatory date for full implementation is periods commencing on or after 1 January 2005. |
| FRS 18 | Accounting policies | |
| FRS 19 | Deferred tax | |
| FRS 20 | Share-based payment | |
| FRS 21 | Events after the balance sheet date | Supersedes SSAP 17, Accounting for post balance sheet events. |
| FRS 22 | Earnings per share | Supersedes FRS 14 |
| FRS 23 | The effects of changes in foreign exchange rates | Supersedes FRS 20 |
| FRS 24 | Financial reporting in hyperinflationary economies | Supersedes UITF Abstract 9 |
| FRS 25 | Financial instruments: Disclosure and presentation | Supersedes most parts of FRS 4 |
| FRS 26 | Financial instruments: Measurement | Supersedes UITF Abstract 11 |
| FRS 27 | Life Assurance | |
| FRS 28 | Corresponding amounts | Effectively replaces equivalent requirements previously contained in CA 85. |
| FRS 29 | Financial instruments: disclosure | Extends disclosure requirements in FRS 25 |
| FRSSE | Financial Reporting Standard for Smaller Entities (effective June 2002) | Superseded by FRSSE (effective January 2005) |
| Other | Statement of Principles for Financial Reporting (SOP) | A cornerstone of UK GAAP although it does not have the mandatory status of an FRS. |

## A2.3    Financial Reporting Exposure Drafts

| Number | Title | Status/Developments |
|--------|-------|---------------------|
| FRED 25 | Related party disclosures | |
| FRED 28 | Inventories<br><br>Construction and service contracts | |
| FRED 29 | Property plant and equipment<br><br>Borrowing costs | |
| FRED 32 | Disposal of non-current assets and presentation of discontinued operations | |
| FRED 36 | Business combinations | |
| FRED 37 | Intangible assets | |
| FRED 38 | Impairment of assets | |
| FRED 39 | Amendments to FRS 12 and FRS 17 | |

## A2.4    Abstracts Issued by UITF

| Number | Title | Status/Developments |
|--------|-------|---------------------|
| Abstract 4 | Presentation of long-term debtors in current assets | |
| Abstract 5 | Transfers from current assets to fixed assets | |
| Abstract 6 | Accounting for post-retirement benefits other than pensions | Superseded by FRS 17 |
| Abstract 9 | Accounting for operations in hyperinflationary economies | Superseded by FRS 24 |
| Abstract 11 | Accounting for issuer call options | Superseded by FRS 26 |
| Abstract 15 (revised) | Disclosure of substantial acquisitions | |

*Continued*

| Number | Title | Status/Developments |
|---|---|---|
| Abstract 17 (revised) | Employee share schemes | Revised December 2003<br><br>Superseded by FRS 20 |
| Abstract 19 | Tax on gains and losses on foreign currency borrowings that hedge an investment in a foreign enterprise | Amended by FRS 23 |
| Abstract 21 | Accounting issues arising from the proposed introduction of the euro | Amended by FRS 23 |
| Abstract 22 | The acquisition of a Lloyd's business | |
| Abstract 23 | Application of transitional rules in FRS 15 | |
| Abstract 24 | Accounting for start-up costs | |
| Abstract 25 | National Insurance contributions on share option gains | |
| Abstract 26 | Barter transactions for advertising | |
| Abstract 27 | Revisions to estimated useful economic life of goodwill and intangible assets | |
| Abstract 28 | Operating lease incentives | |
| Abstract 29 | Website development costs | |
| Abstract 30 | Date of award to employees of shares or right to shares | Superseded by FRS 20 |
| Abstract 31 | Exchanges of businesses or other non-monetary assets for an interest in a subsidiary, joint venture or associate | |
| Abstract 32 | Employee benefit trusts and other intermediate payment arrangements | |
| Abstract 33 | Obligations in capital instruments | Superseded by FRS 25 |

| Number | Title | Status/Developments |
|--------|-------|---------------------|
| Abstract 34 | Pre-contract costs | |
| Abstract 35 | Death-in service and incapacity benefits | |
| Abstract 36 | Contracts for sales of capacity | |
| Abstract 37 | Purchases and sales of own shares | Superseded by FRS 25 |
| Abstract 38 | Accounting for ESOP trusts | |
| Abstract 39 | Members' shares in co-operative entities and similar instruments | |
| Abstract 40 | Revenue recognition and service contracts | |

# A2.5    Statements of Recommended Practice (SORPs)

| Title and Year of Issue/Revision | Issuing Body | Recent Developments |
|----------------------------------|--------------|---------------------|
| Authorized Unit Trust Schemes and Authorized Open-ended Investment Companies | The Investment Management Association | Issued November 2003 replacing two previous SORPs |
| Banking Fissues:<br><br>Segmental Reporting (1993) Contingent liabilities and commitments (1996) Derivatives (2001) Securities (1990) | British Bankers' Association | |
| Accounting and Reporting by Charities | Charity Commission for England and Wales | Issued March 2005<br><br>Applies to accounting years commencing on or after 1 April 2005 |
| Accounting for Further and Higher Education | Universities UK | Issued October 2003 |

*Continued*

| Title and Year of Issue/Revision | Issuing Body | Recent Developments |
| --- | --- | --- |
| Accounting for Insurance | Association of British | Revised November 2003 |
| Business | Insurers | |
| Financial Statements of Investment Trust Companies | Association of Investment Trust Companies | Revised January 2003 |
| Accounting issues in the Asset Finance and Leasing Industry (2000) | Finance and Leasing Association | |
| Limited Liability Partnerships (2002) | The Consultative Committee of Accountancy Bodies (CCAB) | Exposure draft issued 30 September 2005 |
| Code of Practice on Local Authority Accounting in the United Kingdom 2004 | The Chartered Institute of Public Finance and Accountancy | Issued July 2005 |
| Accounting for Oil and Gas Exploration, Development, Production and Decommissioning Activities (2001) | Oil Industry Accounting Committee | |
| Financial reports of Pension Schemes (revised 2002) | Pensions Research Accountants Group (PRAG) | Revised November 2002, Updated May 2005 |
| Accounting by Registered Social Landlords (updated 2002) | National Housing Federation | |

# Extant IASs and IFRSs: Status Report as at 31 January 2006

## A3.1 International Accounting Standards (IASs)

| Number | Title | Status/Developments |
|---|---|---|
| 1 | Presentation of financial statements | |
| 2 | Inventories | |
| 7 | Cash flow statements | |
| 8 | Net profit or loss for the period, fundamental errors and changes in accounting policies | |
| 10 | Events after the balance sheet date | |
| 11 | Construction contracts | |
| 12 | Income taxes | |
| 14 | Segment reporting | |
| 16 | Property, plant and equipment | |
| 17 | Leases | |
| 18 | Revenue | |
| 19 | Employee benefits | Amended December 2004<br><br>Exposure draft of proposed amendments (issued June 2005) |
| 20 | Accounting for government grants and disclosure of government assistance | |
| 21 | The effect of changes in foreign exchange rates | |

*Continued*

| Number | Title | Status/Developments |
|---|---|---|
| 23 | Borrowing costs | |
| 24 | Related party disclosures | |
| 26 | Accounting and reporting by retirement benefit plans | |
| 27 | Consolidated financial statements and accounting for investments in subsidiaries | Exposure draft of proposed amendments (issued June 2005) |
| 28 | Accounting for investments in associates | |
| 29 | Financial reporting in hyperinflationary economies | |
| 30 | Disclosures in the accounts of banks and similar financial institutions | Superseded by IFRS 7 (issued August 2005) |
| 31 | Financial reporting of interests in joint ventures | |
| 32 | Financial instruments: Disclosure and presentation | Amended by IFRS 7 (issued August 2005) |
| 33 | Earnings per share | |
| 34 | Interim financial reporting | |
| 36 | Impairment of assets | |
| 37 | Provisions, contingent liabilities and contingent assets | Exposure draft of proposed amendments (issued June 2005) |
| 38 | Intangible assets | |
| 39 | Financial instruments: Recognition and measurement | Amended for the following: <br><br> Fair value hedge accounting for a portfolio hedge of interest rate risk (March 2004); <br><br> Cash flow hedge accounting of forecast intragroup transactions (April 2005); |

| Number | Title | Status/Developments |
|--------|-------|---------------------|
|  |  | The Fair Value Option (June 2005); Financial guarantee contracts (August 2005); Proposed amendment on transition and initial recognition of financial assets and financial liabilities (July 2004) |
| 40 | Investment property |  |
| 41 | Agriculture |  |

## A3.2   International Financial Reporting Standards

| Number | Title | Status/Developments |
|--------|-------|---------------------|
| N/A | Preface to International Financial Reporting Standards | Foreword to accounting standards |
| IFRS 1 | First-time adoption of IFRSs |  |
| IFRS 2 | Share-based payment |  |
| IFRS 3 | Business combinations | Exposure draft of proposed amendments (issued June 2005) |
| IFRS 4 | Insurance contracts |  |
| IFRS 5 | Non-current assets held for sale and discontinued operations |  |
| IFRS 6 | Exploration for and evaluation of mineral resources |  |
| IFRS 7 | Financial instruments: disclosures | Issued August 2005 |

# App 4 · Useful Website Addresses

| | |
|---|---|
| www.icaew.co.uk | Institute of Chartered Accountants in England & Wales |
| www.cimaglobal.com | Chartered Institute of Management Accountants |
| www.icas.org.uk | Institute of Chartered Accountants of Scotland |
| www.accaglobal.com | Association of Chartered Certified of Accountants |
| www.frc.org.uk | Financial Reporting Council (*including ASB, FRRP, APB*) |
| www.iasb.org | International Accounting Standards Board |
| www.dti.gov.uk/cld | DTI – Company Law and Investigations |
| www.opsi.gov.uk | Office of Public Sector Information |
| www.fsa.gov.uk | The Financial Services Authority |
| www.companieshouse.gov.uk | Companies House |
| www.opra.gov.uk | Occupational Pensions Regulatory Authority |
| www.charity-commission.gov.uk | Charity Commission |
| www.actuaries.gov.uk | Actuarial profession |

# Index